Laughing
MATTERS

Laughing MATTERS

Humor and American Politics in the Media Age

EDITED BY
JODY C BAUMGARTNER AND
JONATHAN S. MORRIS

Routledge
Taylor & Francis Group

New York   London

Routledge
Taylor & Francis Group
270 Madison Avenue
New York, NY 10016

Routledge
Taylor & Francis Group
2 Park Square
Milton Park, Abingdon
Oxon OX14 4RN

© 2008 by Taylor & Francis Group, LLC
Routledge is an imprint of Taylor & Francis Group, an Informa business

International Standard Book Number-13: 978-0-415-95748-9 (Softcover) 978-0-415-95747-2 (Hardcover)

Library of Congress Cataloging-in-Publication Data

Laughing matters : humor and American politics in the media age / edited by Jody C. Baumgartner and Jonathan S. Morris.
   p. cm.
   ISBN-13: 978-0-415-95747-2 (hbk : alk. paper)
   ISBN-13: 978-0-415-95748-9 (pbk : alk. paper)
   ISBN-13: 978-0-203-94229-1 (ebook : alk. paper)
   1. United States--Politics and government--1989- 2. United States--Politics and government--1945-1989. 3. United States--Politics and government--1989---Humor. 4. United States--Politics and government--1945-1989--Humor. 5. American wit and humor--History and criticism. 6. Mass media--Political aspects--United States. 7. Political culture--United States. 8. Public opinion--United States. I. Morris, Jonathan S. II. Baumgartner, Jody C., 1958-

E839.5.L385 2007
973.928--dc22   2007015948

Visit the Taylor & Francis Web site at
http://www.taylorandfrancis.com

and the Routledge Web site at
http://www.routledge.com

For Kathryn Bernice Morris,
and the player(s) to be named later

Contents

III.   Ready for Prime Time? Televised Political Humor

IV.   Does It Really Matter? The Effects of Late Night Televised Humor

Contents   ix

Tables, Boxes, and Figures

Preface
The "Truthiness" of American Politics

Jody C Baumgartner and Jonathan S. Morris

Political satire was dead. The "age of irony" had officially met its demise.[1] The failure of Americans to take things seriously had been realized, and we were moving into a "new and chastened time."[2] Young adults, always the most appreciative of parody and irreverent mockery, wondered aloud, "maybe a coddled generation that bathed itself in sarcasm will (finally) get serious…maybe we'll stop acting so jaded."[3] America had encountered a "seismic shift,"[4] and "a crushing defeat" had been dealt to "irony, cynicism, and hipness."[5]

The terrorist attacks of September 11, 2001 had shaken the American public to its core. There was nothing to laugh about. Roger Rosenblatt of *Time* magazine even appeared to blame satirists for America's pre-9/11 naiveté, arguing that "the ironists, seeing through everything, made it difficult for anyone to see anything. The consequence of thinking that nothing is real—apart from prancing around in an air of vain stupidity—is that one will not know the difference between a joke and a menace."[6]

Satirists and comedians temporarily dropped out of sight. When they reemerged in the months following the attacks, they treaded very lightly. Late night talk show hosts such as David Letterman and Jay Leno dropped their lighthearted approach to politics in favor of a more somber mood, and even the classically irreverent *Saturday Night Live* (*SNL*) decided to suspend its parodies of President Bush.[7]

Of course, political humor was not gone for good. In the months following September 11, comics began to slowly tread back into familiar waters. In late September, *SNL* returned to the airwaves, and New York mayor Rudolph Giuliani made a guest appearance on the program to publicly proclaim the importance that *SNL* continue broadcasting.[8]

"Can we be funny?" questioned *SNL* producer Lorne Michaels.
"Why start now?" retorted Giuliani.

Post-9/11 political humor was quite benign. The most common target was Osama Bin Laden and the terrorist themselves. The satire-
laced publication *The Onion*, for example, ran with stories such as,
"Hijackers Surprised to Find Selves in Hell: 'We Expected Eternal
Paradise for This' Say Suicide Bombers" and "God Angrily Clarifies
'Don't Kill' Rule."[9] *SNL* ran a skit that chronicled Bin Laden's dialogue with the hijackers on 9/11. The parody was a fictitious scenario
in which the suicide bombers phoned Bin Laden from the airplanes
and desperately tried to talk him into a new plan that didn't involve
them killing themselves.

A late September episode of *Mad TV* featured a skit of President
Bush (played by Will Sasso) attempting to sneak out of the White
House to go to Afghanistan and fight the Taliban himself. When
caught by then National Security Advisor Condoleezza Rice, a frustrated Bush explains that he needs to "kick a little a--." Eventually,
the president joins up with pro wrestler Triple H to parachute into
Afghanistan and personally hunt the terrorist. After dispatching the
enemy in hand-to-hand combat, the Bush character triumphantly
declares himself "President of the United States of Pain!" Also, in
an unintended twist of irony, the skit ends with Triple H suggesting, "I'll tell you what, what's the name of that guy in Iraq that your
old man couldn't take care of? . . . Why don't we go show up your old
man, [and] head over to Iraq and take care of him?" To which Bush
responds, "That's a fantastic idea!"

Political humor that pointed almost exclusively at the enemy
could only last for so long. As time passed, the political divisions
in America that were temporarily wiped away in the aftermath of
9/11 began to reemerge. The same Democrats and Republicans that
embraced one another in the fall of 2001 began to settle back into
the standard rhetorical jousting on issues such as post-9/11 civil lib-
erties, tax cuts, and the possibility of invading Iraq. As the cloud of
"politics as usual" began to loom over Washington again, political
satirists were once again free to ridicule those in power.

Although humor may take temporary hiatus from time to time,
it has always been—and will continue to be—part of the political
landscape. In fact, similar versions of the same political jokes can
be found dating back to ancient Greece. In the postcolonial era in

America, the partisan press often relied on satire to smear the opposition. Decades later, the penny press ushered in the era of yellow journalism in which political humor was used to entertain and sell newspapers.[10] Literary figures have also been quick to poke fun at the absurdities of the political system and those who run it. For example, Mark Twain has been credited with several humorous quips about politics, such as his observation that "First God created idiots, that was for practice. Then he made school boards."

In the past half century several stand-up comics like Dick Gregory and George Carlin gained prominence with their edgy sociopolitical humor. Garry Trudeau continues to take on controversial issues of the day in his *Doonesbury* comic strip. On television, sketch comedy on *Saturday Night Live* has poked fun at politicians since the 1970s, and cartoons such as *South Park* and *The Simpsons* are laden with political satire. Even late night talk shows such as *The Late Show with David Letterman* and *The Tonight Show with Jay Leno* are making light of current political events with increased frequency. On the Internet, thousands of Web logs (blogs) are bursting with humorous observations, and sites such as JibJab.com and Theonion.com have gained notoriety for their satire as well. Political humor is also prevalent on the big screen. Michael Moore's brand of humor-laced social commentary won him an Oscar for *Bowling for Columbine*, and filmmakers Trey Parker and Matt Stone poked fun at a wide range of political issues in their marionette-based farce, *Team America: World Police.*

In recent years, political satirists have gained a great deal of visibility and influence. Preceding the 2004 presidential election, *Newsweek* featured Jon Stewart on the cover and touted him as one of the most powerful media figures in the election. That same year Stewart and the writers of *The Daily Show* published a parody of an American government textbook titled *America (The Book): A Citizen's Guide to Democracy Inaction*,[11] which landed on the *New York Times* bestseller list. In 2005, comic Steven Colbert, host of *The Colbert Report* (a spin-off of *The Daily Show*), was honored by the American Dialect Society for creating the word of the year, "truthiness." Colbert noted on his inaugural program that

> I will speak to you in plain, simple English. And that brings us to tonight's word: *truthiness*. Now I'm sure some of the word police, the wordinistas over at Webster's are gonna say, "Hey, that's not a word." Well, anyone who knows me knows I'm no fan of dictionaries or reference books. I

don't trust books. They're all fact, no heart. And that's exactly what's
pulling our country apart today. [Be]cause face it, folks; we are a divided
nation.... [D]ivided between those who think with their head, and those
who *know* with their heart.

Like Stewart, Colbert's popularity has soared. In 2006 he was the
featured speaker at the annual dinner of the Washington Press
Corps. He addressed the audience, which included the president of
the United States, in satirical neoconservative persona. Colbert said
about the president

> I stand by this man because he stands for things. Not only for things, he
> stands on things. Things like aircraft carriers and rubble and recently
> flooded city squares. And that sends a strong message: that no matter
> what happens to America, she will always rebound—with the most pow-
> erfully staged photo ops in the world.

Americans love to laugh about politics, and political humor is taken
more seriously than ever before. Modern American political humor is
not only poignant, but it is also influential. The most recent example
of this influence could be seen during the 2004 presidential election,
when more than a quarter (26 percent) of all Americans reported that
they sometimes *learned* about the presidential candidates from comedy programs such as *Saturday Night Live* and *The Daily Show*. For
adults under the age of 30, this percentage jumps to over 50 percent.

For this reason, we have collected the essays in this volume for the
purpose of examining the role of political humor in context of the
modern media environment in America. We have assembled a wide
range of authors from the fields of political science and communication to discuss this phenomenon. The book is organized according to
two general topics: (1) how the modern media present political humor,
and (2) the various ways in which political humor influences politics.
The book will rely on original research, both quantitative and qualitative, to paint a picture of the role of humor in American politics.

The first section, "Foundations: Humor and Politics," lays the theoretical significance of humor in politics. In Chapter 1, Rachel Caufield suggests that understanding differences in political humor can
broaden our understanding of how humor influences politics. In her
discussion, she pays special attention to differences between political
satire and "conventional" political humor, and explores how methods used by humorists and the targets of the humor might shape how
the audience is affected.

Geoffrey Baym, in Chapter 2, argues that the distinctions between news and entertainment, fact and fiction, the serious and the funny have never been as clear-cut as they may seem, and especially fail to describe the world we now live in. The chapter tracks the emergence of humor as an increasingly prevalent method for understanding politics. He concludes his analysis with a detailed discussion of the significance of Stephen Colbert's aforementioned controversial address at the Washington Press Corps dinner. In Chapter 3, Josh Compton provides an exhaustive survey of the research on the effects of humor on political attitudes and behavior. While research into this subject has been thought to be sparse and disparate, Compton shows that this situation is changing. The chapter also suggests, based on the state of existing research, which aspects of humor are ripe for future investigation.

Section II, "Political Humor in the World Beyond Television," takes a selective look at non-televised political humor. Because so much of our information and culture comes from television, it is perhaps natural to include, as we do, so much scholarship on televised political humor. However, we should not forget that humor, like all communication, can be found in a variety of media sources.

One such source of humor is the political cartoon, which has a long and rich history in American politics. In Chapter 4, Alleen and Don Nilsen, perhaps the most noted students of political cartoons, provide a glimpse into the world of political cartooning. One of the points they make in their survey is that while there has always been an unspoken "line of decency" in terms of sexuality, religion, and vulgarity, in political cartoons, recently developed taboos and censorship of political cartoons have forced cartoonists to become more careful of ethnic, gender, ageist, and disabled targets.

In Chapter 5, Geoffrey Sheagley, Paula O'Laughlin, and Timothy Lindberg compare the political content of the humorous newspaper *The Onion* and a more mainstream newspaper. They find that *The Onion*, like other political humor, presents a negative image of the political world that may threaten political disengagement on the part of its readership. In Chapter 6, Eric Shouse and Todd Fraley offer a compelling analysis of several recent comedic motion pictures that have touched on political themes. They argue that some of the most well-known movies, *Bulworth, Bob Roberts, Wag the Dog,* and *Head of State*, perpetuate a myriad of negative stereotypes of American politics and government that typically have been cited as reasons why today's young adults tend to stay disengaged from the process. Interestingly, Shouse and Fraley find a more positive message about politics from a recent cult-classic success, *Napoleon Dynamite*.

The following two chapters both deal with political humor on the Internet. In Chapter 7, Monica Postelnicu and Lynda Lee Kaid examine the use of humor in political advertising on the Web during the 2004 campaign. As an affordable channel for political advertising, citizens and independent groups distributed their own "advertisements" about candidates. Postelnicu and Kaid suggest that in an environment that has little or no regulation to temper advertising, the Web became the "Wild Wild West" of political advertising during the 2004 campaign. The final chapter of this section (Chapter 8) examines the effects of a clip from the popular Internet humor site, JibJab.com, on youth. Jody Baumgartner finds that exposure to the clip made viewers more cynical about political institutions, even when controlling for partisanship and other demographic variables. However, the comedy of JibJab.com significantly raised support for the actual comedic target of the clip, George W. Bush. Furthermore, Baumgartner found that JibJab.com made watchers feel better about their own ability to understand the world of politics, primarily because they feel they "get" the jokes.

In the third section of the book, "Ready for Prime Time? Televised Political Humor," the attention turns to televised political humor. While most of the chapters in this section are descriptive, each adds to our understanding of the landscape of televised political humor. The importance of this is hard to overstate because television is how most people experience the world of politics. In Chapter 9, David Niven, S. Robert Lichter, and Daniel Amundson explore popular conceptions of Bill Clinton through the lens of late night humor, with special attention to the amount of attention he received, the topics for which he was mocked, and the portrayal of his political associates. The authors find that the Clinton administration was an easy target for late night talk show hosts, but they also delve into the nature of the jokes and illustrate how some of the subtle nuances may not have been as damaging to Clinton's popularity as first thought.

Josh Compton takes on the subject of how political debates were treated on late night television in Chapter 10. His textual analysis of hundreds of jokes about the 2004 presidential and vice presidential debates told by Jay Leno, David Letterman, and Conan O'Brien from September through November 2004 explores viewers' perceptions of these jokes. In Chapter 11, Peter Francia ambitiously explores different political eras of television comedy, beginning with a fairly comprehensive overview of status quo television of the 1950s and mid-1960s through the 1990s. He then illustrates that the so-called "culture war" has manifested itself in the situation comedy viewing habits of Bush and Kerry voters.

In Chapter 12, Nicholas Guehlstorf, Lars Hallstrom, and Jonathan Morris provide an analysis of one of the longest-running prime-time television programs in American history, *The Simpsons*. Drawing on references from sixteen years of episodes, the chapter illustrates how the cartoon has portrayed the mass public, political elites, and organized interests, suggesting that while *The Simpsons* exploits political stereotypes for quick and cheap laughs, the writers employ meaningful satire about American politics. They also demonstrate that the show's criticism of the uninformed, irrational, and disengaged public is harsher and more frequent than that of political elites.

In Chapter 13, Ben Voth looks into the hilarious and controversial portrayals of presidential candidates Al Gore and George W. Bush in the 2000 election on *Saturday Night Live*. Voth argues that the popularity of Darrell Hammond's parody of Al Gore may have had enough of an influence on the public's perception of Gore to sway the close race. Voth also argues that the portrayals of candidates John Kerry and George W. Bush on *SNL* did not play nearly as instrumental of a role in 2004. He explores in detail why this was the case, and the prospects for presidential parodies on *SNL* in the future.

In the final chapter (Chapter 14) of this section, Dannagal Goldthwaite Young explores how *The Daily Show* has emerged as a response to, and remedy for, the shortcomings of contemporary journalism. Incorporating public statements made by host Jon Stewart and interviews with *Daily Show* producers, she argues that Stewart's conceptualization of what news ought to be is precisely what *The Daily Show* is. She concludes with an examination of the show's content through the lens of Lance Bennett's *The Politics of Illusion*, illustrating how *The Daily Show* addresses and remedies problematic aspects of news such as indexing and content biases.

Section IV of the book, "Does it Really Matter? The Effects of Late Night Televised Humor," tackles the issue of why this all matters. Each chapter is devoted to an examination of the attitudinal and behavioral effects of political humor. Is political humor benign? Or, does it have adverse effects on how people view the political world and whether and how they participate? In other words, what effects, if any, does political humor have on real politics? In Chapter 15, Paul Brewer and Xiaoxia Cao challenge the view that late night and comedy television shows are key sources of political information for Americans in general and young people in particular. Using survey data from 1989 to 2004, it looks at how Americans have used these shows, what they have learned about particular political topics from them, and which political figures they saw appearing on them.

In Chapter 16, Brandon Rottinghaus, Kenton Bird, Travis Ridout, and Rebecca Self illustrate that *Daily Show* viewers are better educated about politics, more liberal, and more politically involved. They explore these findings further with focus group research, revealing that students use political humor in ways that may not be intended by the humorist. In Chapter 17, Patricia Moy takes a revisionist view of the role of late night comedy and "new news" in contemporary American politics. Specifically, she argues that late night comedy viewing and other "nontraditional" forms of political news increase learning among particular segments of the electorate and that such media use is associated with forms of political behavior deemed necessary for a healthy democracy.

Jonathan Morris and Jody Baumgartner keep the focus on *The Daily Show* in Chapter 18. Their discussion illustrates the notion that Stewart and his colleagues primarily satirize the news media in their coverage of politics and social issues. While politicians and political institutions receive a good deal of criticism on *The Daily Show*, the news media take even more. Drawing from survey data and an experimental analysis, they then show that exposure to the program negatively influences respondents' trust in the media.

In the concluding chapter (Chapter 19), Doris Graber pulls the threads of this volume together. Drawing on her vast experience in media studies and political psychology, Graber outlines how the contributing authors in this volume have furthered the general understanding of humor's role in the world of politics. She concludes that laughing does matter when it comes to politics in America, but that we have just begun to scratch the surface of this vast topic in academic research.

Notes

1. Roger Rosenblatt, "The Age of Irony Comes to an End," *Time*, September 13, 2001.

2. Ibid.
3. Camille Dodero, "Gen (X+Y) + WTC = ?," *The Boston Phoenix,* September 20–27, 2001.
4. Richard Leiby, "But Seriously, Folks...; Pundits Say Irony Is Now Out. Don't Laugh," *The Washington Post,* September 27, 2001, C1.
5. James Pinkerton, "Tuesday's Act Was Not About Nothing." *Newsday,* September 17, 2001.
6. Rosenblatt, "The Age of Irony Comes to an End."
7. Julie Patel, "Laughing Through Our Tears," *Chicago Sun-Times,* September 30, 2001.
8. Ibid.
9. "Onion View of Sept. 11," *Atlanta Journal-Constitution,* September 29, 2001; Patel, "Laughing Through Our Tears."
10. Darrell M. West, *The Rise and Fall of the Media Establishment* (Boston: Bedford/St. Martin's, 2001).
11. Jon Stewart, Ben Karlin, and David Javerbaum, *America (The Book): A Citizen's Guide to Democracy Inaction* (New York: Warner Books, 2004).

Acknowledgments

We would like to take this opportunity to thank a number of people who have been instrumental to this project. First, and perhaps obviously, each of the various contributors has contributed something intellectually stimulating—and in some cases, humorous—and has been a joy and a privilege to work with. Our graduate assistants, Michael Shaw and Kara Craig, were also very helpful in gathering materials, editing and proofing, and a number of other valuable tasks. Also, to our wives, Lei Baumgartner and Erica Morris, we are most thankful. While this book has been a pleasure to put together, it has taken a good deal of time and energy. We sincerely appreciate Lei and Erica's patience throughout the process.

I

Foundations:
Humor and Politics

1

The Influence of "Infoenterpropagainment"

Exploring the Power of Political Satire as a Distinct Form of Political Humor

Rachel Paine Caufield

Over the past few decades, scholars in a wide variety of disciplines have noted a distinct change in the social landscape—the increasing tendency to combine "hard" information and entertainment. In 1984, Neil Postman argued that we were in danger of "amusing ourselves to death," and that the fusion of information and entertainment, led by television, would diminish public dialogue and foster widespread indifference.[1] Although scholars have sometimes had difficulty agreeing on what defines so-called "soft news," there is agreement on a few fundamental characteristics. Soft news tends to be personality driven, focuses on sensationalism and drama rather than facts, and conveys less public affairs information to its audience than hard news.[2] Nonetheless, soft news programs significantly alter public perceptions of candidates and political events.[3]

Existing scholarship has examined the soft news phenomenon by differentiating between various formats.[4] Thus, daytime talk shows (*Oprah, The View*), evening news magazines (*20/20, 60 Minutes*), late night comedy programs (*The Late Show with David Letterman, The Tonight Show with Jay Leno, The Daily Show with Jon Stewart*), radio call-in shows (*The Rush Limbaugh Show*), and morning news shows (*The Today Show, Good Morning America*) are treated as distinct manifestations of the same fundamental phenomenon.[5] While drawing distinctions based on the format of the program is often helpful, we will be well served by an effort to differentiate based on content as well.

3

For obvious reasons, I limit attention to those programs within the "political humor" genre. Obviously, some soft news like late night talk shows or *The Daily Show* is included, but today's political humor also includes a number of programs or formats that are generally ignored in studies of soft news and instead relegated to the arena of pure entertainment. Television programs like *The Simpsons, South Park, Chappelle's Show, Family Guy,* and *Futurama,* movies such as *Team America: World Police, Thank You for Smoking,* and *Silver City,* and online cartoons produced by JibJab and Mark Fiore are almost never included in studies of soft news. Yet they regularly contain political humor and use satirical methods to convey overtly political messages to their audience. In a 2004 interview with *Entertainment Weekly,* Jon Stewart (host of the popular *The Daily Show*) uses the apt phrase "info-enter-propa-gainment" to describe this new genre of popular culture.[6]

To understand the full impact of political humor, we must first start our inquiry by disabusing ourselves of the notion that all televised political humor is the same. Although all are humorous, air at night, and contain interview segments with well-known celebrities in politics and entertainment, *The Daily Show* and *The Colbert Report* are not necessarily the equivalent to *The Late Show* or *The Tonight Show.* What differentiates them from other late night comedy programs is their use of satire to convey a coherent political message. Based on their content, we can expect that they will have far more in common with other satiric outlets than they do with shows that happen to air in the late evening.

Satire is not often considered an important form of political dialogue, but it serves many distinct and important roles in a democratic society: it encourages critical debate, sheds light on perceived wrongs within society and government, points out hypocrisy, and makes political criticism accessible to the average citizen. Satire is not unique in its aim, which is to expose wrongdoing and hypocrisies. Popular commentators in both print and broadcast media have a platform to express their critiques. Satire, however, is unique in its approach. By subtly exposing the audience to the critique, creating laughter, and using a combination of wit, humor, and playfulness to engage the audience, satire is *artful* political critique. In this way, satire is unlike other forms of political commentary. It is, however, an equally *important* forum for political commentary.[7]

To say, as A. O. Scott does in his review of *Team America: World Police*, that "we are living in a golden age of political satire" is an important observation.[8] Trey Parker and Matt Stone, the creators of *South Park* and the force behind *Team America*, have been quite successful with their politically charged social commentary masquerading as overly simplistic animation. Matt Groening, the creator of TV's *The Simpsons*, has certainly had an opportunity to inform viewers young and old of his political critiques week in and week out for over fifteen years. Most recently, the rise of Jon Stewart's *The Daily Show* as a popular source of political information for young voters certainly attracted the attention of the 2004 presidential candidates, eight of whom appeared on the program. JibJab Media, creators of a parody called *This Land!* (JibJab.com), reached millions of Internet users during the 2004 presidential election.[9] In short, satire is alive and well in modern American society.

Despite the fact that political satire is flourishing in virtually every medium of current American life and has achieved remarkable popular success, scholars who study satire seem to pay it little attention.[10] Similarly, political scientists have put a great deal of time and energy into studying the effects of popular culture, soft news, and political humor on voting behavior, but few have singled out satire as a distinct phenomenon. Conventional wisdom often relegates satire to its heydays in ancient Greece and Rome and seventeenth-century England and Ireland. But today's political satire is not your great-great-great-great grandparents' satire. This is not the age of Aristophanes, nor of Pope, nor of Swift, nor even of Twain. It is, rather, the age of the Internet, mass media, and punk rock. These mediums have fundamentally altered the messages, meanings, and methods used by the satirist. So what effect is satire having in modern American society?

The remainder of this chapter focuses on modern political satire and the ways it differs from other forms of political humor in the methods popular satirical outlets use, and the effect on the audience.

Satire: A Unique Pursuit

Satire has a long and varied history throughout human society. In early societies, a satirist was characterized as a type of magician, "one to be regarded with awe, with reverence and with fear."[11] Satirists were thought to possess a gift to ward off evil by harnessing the magical powers of words: "the satire might be hurled at wicked individuals by name or at evil influences generally."[12] Even in ancient Greek and Roman societies, Robert Elliott argues that satirists were seen as suspicious individuals who held pseudo-magical powers (Plato proposed legal penalties for "magical incantations," which included satire).[13] The relationship between satirist and society is largely defined by this suspicion. Elliott writes

> The magician has always and everywhere been the focus of strong and conflicting feelings on the part of his society. Insofar as he uses his great powers to enhance the well-being of society—defending it from its enemies, coercing the powers of nature into favorable performance, enriching the inner life of society through ritualistic ceremony, etc., he is honored and revered.... For the powers of the magician are only in a very limited sense amenable to social control; in them is potentiality for benefit, but also for danger, both social and personal. The magician is at once prop and threat to society and to each individual. Consequently, the relation of the magician to society is always colored by the ambivalent emotional attitudes generated by this knowledge. Clearly the situation of the satirist-magician is very similar. His satire may be incorporated into ritual...and thus contribute materially to the social cohesiveness which it is one of the functions of ritual to bring about.
>
> Or it may be employed in straightforward and warlike defense of his tribe against threat from without.... But in other, and possibly more characteristic roles, the satirist becomes the object of fear and hate; as testimony we have many legends where the fear is expressed either directly or symbolically, and we have the evidence of ancient law.... The Roman Twelve Tables invoke the death penalty for defamatory and libelous verse (which was thought to be magically efficacious); and the Irish laws are full of specific injunctions against satire. These latter, however, distinguish between lawful and unlawful satire and provide rewards for "good" satire and punishments for "bad." Here are codified, in legal formulas, the ambivalent attitudes of a society toward its satirists.[14]

The role of the satirist changed, however. No longer was satire associated with magical power, but instead, it was looked upon as an aesthetic pursuit—a literary art form. Even with the introduction of the classical literary satire that has maintained the attention of literary scholars for centuries, "satire has never enjoyed a very high reputation with literary critics," and "the satirist has skated on the thin edge of censorship and legal retribution."[15]

Today's satirists serve a decidedly different social role, but satire as a form of political speech is as potent as ever. At heart, the role of the satirist remains the same—to attack a society for its "evils."

How, then, does satire differ from other forms of political critique or political humor?

To answer this question, one must first develop a definition of satire. This formulation has been notoriously difficult. Robert Elliott, among the most dedicated observers of satire, concluded in a 1962 essay that the "staggering diversity of forms, tones, and materials" precluded any single definition. This conclusion was seconded by Leonard Feinberg, in his 1968 article "Satire: The Inadequacy of Recent Definitions."[16] Instead, Elliott recommended an approach that would use familiar shared traits among works already designated as satire to arrive at a rubric that would allow the classification of future work. Using Elliott's recommendation, George Test has arrived at a set of shared traits that best captures the "spirit and art" of modern satire, in all its various forms. He argues

> satire, whether literary or media-induced, rests on a substratum of ritual and folk behavior that continues to be present.... Restricting the study of satire to its literary manifestations has in effect cut off satire from its roots. Literary forms have not been able to confine or define satire, nor can satire be restricted by or to any other medium in which it occurs...no classification by genre or kind has ever succeeded in fully integrating these diverse forms [of satire] into a system.[17]

Test's four characteristics, which can be thought of as necessary but not sufficient, include aggression, play, laughter, and judgment. Although other forms of political critique or political humor may contain one or more of these characteristics (or, possibly, all of them), satire always contains all of them in some combination.[18] Each is considered in turn.

Aggression, or attack, is the most common trait of satire. The very intent of the satirist is critical here. Satire is specifically created as a means to attack perceived wrongs or ills within society. For this reason, it should come as no surprise that satirists have been described as "biting, snarling, railing, and carping, reviled as dogs, vipers, and other serpent-like creatures, beasts (of prey, of course), and (all-purpose) monsters."[19] The satirist, by creating satire, is attacking the people, institutions, and processes that populate the social system they inhabit. By using satire to diminish or discredit an individual, an idea, an argument, an institution, or any other target, the satirist is assuming a position of superiority and the satire itself is intended as a form of aggression to expose the problems. Aggression is at the very core of satire.

But satire is not just aggression—it is aggression combined with judgment. Satire must have a target. As a form of artistic expression, satire is, in itself, neutral.[20] When the artistic expression is focused on attacking a target, it necessarily must judge that target. This judgment is central to the spirit of satire—the critique must be intentional and focused. Test writes that "whether the target is vice or folly, absurdity or enemies of the state, the satirist is concerned with passing judgment."[21] Alvin Kernan explains

> Although there is always at least a suggestion of some kind of humane ideal in satire—it may in the blackest type of satire exist only as the unnamed opposite of the idiocy and villainy portrayed—this ideal is never heavily stressed, for in the satirist's vision of the world decency is forever in a precarious position near the edge of extinction and the world is about to pass into eternal darkness. Consequently, every effort is made to emphasize the destroying ugliness and power of vice.[22]

Thus, satire must judge some aspect of society in a way that lends itself to correction. It has been argued that all satirists are, to a greater or lesser degree, optimists, seeking to fix society's broken pieces. To do this, the satirist exposes and critiques something in a way that offers the audience a way to judge the society in which they live.

Aggression and judgment, however, can come in many forms. Every day, commentators and political figures attack people, ideas, arguments, institutions, or processes. One could turn on any number of television shows on a given night and see aggression and judgment (for example, try *The Bill O'Reilly Show, Hannity and Colmes, Hardball, The Rush Limbaugh Show,* or Air America radio). Political parties, interest groups, and candidates offer their combination of aggression and judgment in campaign commercials, public statements, and interview appearances. What differentiates satire, of course, is that the aggression and judgment are combined with play and elicit laughter from the audience.

Play is a central element to satire, as it provides the artful interaction between the satirist and her audience. Satire is clever, witty, and engaging. That play and aggression appear, on the face of it, to be incompatible does not diminish the importance of both to satire. By constructing a type of "game" with the audience, the satirist is able to pull the audience into the aggressive judgment that she is offering. The play of satire may take many forms, from actual game images, to wordplays, to the symbolic use of toys or childlike features to evoke playfulness, to clever and witty dialogue between characters.[23]

This intentional playfulness makes the attack something that generates laughter among the audience. This is what differentiates satire from other forms of pure attack. This laughter makes the attack more accessible to the audience, thus opening them to judgment that they may otherwise be unwilling to accept. Satirists have long accepted that

> laughter has been an agent of change for the better in those who have shared the laughter. The laughter of ridicule or the truth coated with laughter shames the fool into changing his ways. Such a concept is at the heart of the belief in satire's ability to reform those who have fallen into vice or folly…the laughter evoked by satire is rarely simple, sometimes strained, occasionally strange, capable of cutting both ways.[24]

In addition to these characteristics, however, I would add one additional trait of satire that I believe combines all of the above characteristics in a unique way—satire demands knowledge by the audience. Because of its playfulness, a consumer of satire must bring some level of knowledge to bear on his or her experience or risk being left out of the joke. In order to engage in the play set up by the satirist, the audience member must have some existing level of knowledge if he or she is to engage. To illustrate the importance of this pre-existing knowledge, consider Al Franken's *Lies and the Lying Liars Who Tell Them*. It has been argued that Al Franken is one of today's preeminent satirists. After all, his work would constitute a judgmental work of aggression designed to evoke laughter, and pieces of the book certainly demonstrate aspects of playfulness in the use of "naughty" phrases, over-the-top wordplays, logical inconsistencies, and game-like themes (take, for example, his deceptive visit to Bob Jones University with a research assistant posing as his prospective student "son"). So, is the book "satirical"?

My answer would be no. The reason is simple. It does not assume any prior knowledge on the part of the reader. This diminishes its capability to fully engage the reader in "play." Good satire demands an informed audience to engage in the experience of the satire and arrive at the conclusions on their own. An ill-informed consumer of the satire is left out of the joke. Consider the oft-used example of the person who, after reading *Gulliver's Travels*, went to find Lilliput on the map. In short, *Lies and the Lying Liars Who Tell Them* is too literal to be satire. It does not allow the reader to engage in the endeavor and draw out the judgments offered on his or her own terms.

This distinction is important because it points to an important point in today's political satire—satire is not the same as political humor. Although the two are often confused, satire is a unique pursuit.

The Distinguishing Features of Satire

To say that satire is a unique form of political humor is not as self-evident as it may appear. Consider, for example, the fact that the satirical *The Daily Show* is so often lumped in with *The Late Show* and *The Tonight Show* in analyses of how political humor influences young voters.[25] When David Letterman makes a joke about George W. Bush or John Kerry, it can be aggressive and can contain implicit or explicit judgments about the personality or political platform of the candidate (usually the former). It may also be funny. But it is not satirical. In contrast, when *Saturday Night Live* parodies political debates, it requires that the viewer know something about the candidates to be fully effective (about their speech patterns or behavior in debates or policy positions). Without that prior knowledge, the skit is simply not as funny or as meaningful to the viewer.

Furthermore, satire is, by its very nature, offensive. Satire is intended to do more than make people laugh. It is also meant to critique the people who are laughing. As satirist Paul Krassner (editor of *The Realist*, a 1960s alternative magazine based in New York) wrote, "the ultimate target of satire should be its own audience."[26] Most political humor is aimed to entertain the audience by poking fun at outsiders—political candidates, government officials, or public figures. In contrast, satire's target is broader—it is meant to attack political institutions, society's foibles, or public vices.[27] Put simply, conventional political humor is often geared at making the audience laugh at others, while satire is designed to make the audience laugh at itself as well as others, therefore allowing the audience to realize a larger set of systemic faults. *The Colbert Report* (which follows *The Daily Show* on Comedy Central) is more than a random collection of funny jokes designed to make the audience laugh. Rather, it offers a coherent and consistent attack on political pundits generally and critiques the cult of personality that develops around today's more vocal political commentators.

The methods used by the satirist also differ from those used by the conventional comedian. One standard satirical method, anthropomorphism, has become common. By using animals to convey human characteristics, the satirist can simplify the message and make extreme statements from an outsider's perspective.[28] Today's satirists often employ animation to the same effect. We all know people who vaguely resemble Homer Simpson in his naive simplicity (or stupidity) or *American Dad*'s Stan Smith in his misplaced patriotism and masculinity. These animated characters can serve as "the dunce" or "the jester" who may represent the worst characteristics of human behavior or speak truth to power without the same repercussions that a human would encounter. In short, they are caricatures who can push boundaries in ways that human actors cannot because animated characters are removed enough from our reality to be true "outsiders."

In addition, satire often relies on utopian and dystopian conditions to point out perceived wrongs, a technique often used by *South Park* creators Trey Parker and Matt Stone. Consider an episode of *South Park* in which the teacher, Mr. Garrison, brings in "Mr. Slave" (who wears a black leather vest, boots, and a hat) as his "teacher's assistant" after learning that he could become rich by suing the school for discrimination if they punish him for being gay. After Garrison engages in blatantly graphic sexual behavior with Mr. Slave in front of a classroom of fourth graders, the kids complain to their parents who decry that the kids are exhibiting unacceptable intolerance. Eventually, the kids are sent to "tolerance camp," where they are put behind barbed wire fences and forced to fingerpaint images of tolerance while being yelled at by a stern camp leader. Meanwhile, Mr. Garrison wins an award for being "Courageous Teacher of the Year."[29] By turning the ideal of tolerance into a dystopia of forced acceptance of over the top offensive behavior, Parker and Stone make their point clear.

In short, satire is unlike the conventional humor that is generally the subject of scholarly inquiry in both substance and method. As such, it deserves more focused attention as a unique form of political critique and political humor.

Audience Reaction

In today's political environment, satire is thriving. *The Simpsons* (which is looking to become television's longest-running cartoon with 20 consecutive seasons in 2009), *South Park*, and *Family Guy*— all animated shows that include political, social, and religious satire on a regular basis—have all been named to a list of the top fifty TV cartoons of all time (in fact, they were all in the top five, with *The Simpsons* at number one, *South Park* at number three, and *Family Guy* at number five).[30] Comedy Central's *The Daily Show with Jon Stewart*, a scathing satire of the American news media,[31] won two Emmy Awards in 2004. *Saturday Night Live* continues to top the list among older viewers who are looking for irreverent coverage of political campaigns. In addition, Jon Stewart's *America (The Book): A Citizen's Guide to Democracy Inaction*, a satire of American government textbooks, outsold every other book in 2005 with 1.9 million copies in print and has reportedly generated a new wave of proposals for similar books from conservatives who want to write satire about "comedians on the left."[32]

There is no doubt that satire was alive and well during the 2004 presidential election. And, there is no doubt that these satirical shows were targeted primarily at young audiences. More than any time in recent history, young voters now have a multitude of sources to look to when seeking political information and perspectives. Polls indicate that they are increasingly taking cues from these sources. So how does audience reaction to satire differ from reaction to other forms of political humor?

Research on the influence of so-called "soft news" is instructive in thinking about audience reaction to the various forms of political humor or satire. While hard news is driven by news first and entertainment second, soft news emphasizes entertainment as its primary goal and political information as an afterthought.[33] How do soft news programs influence the political knowledge of viewers or listeners?

There is ongoing debate about the impact of the new media on American voters. There has been widespread hand-wringing about the declining attention to so-called "hard news."[34] But there are also notable claims that this new emergence of soft news has positive consequences by tuning in those who would otherwise remain ignorant of political affairs. Christine Ridout argues that political talk shows enhance democracy precisely because they bypass the traditional news emphasis on process and strategy and instead allow a political dialogue about issues of interest to the voting public. She even goes so far as to say that talk shows allowed Clinton to alter the course of his campaign in 1992 by addressing substantive questions that were not being asked by the news organizations.[35] Matthew Baum has furthered this argument by claiming that entertainment-based talk shows help enhance political knowledge among those voters who would otherwise not pay attention to news.[36] By reaching voters via entertainment, political information is conveyed to voters who otherwise would be completely uninformed, therefore enhancing the democratic process.

Beyond soft news, what influence do other forms of popular culture, specifically television and film, have on the electorate? There is little research examining the influence of film and television with political content. Among existing research, Miller and Reeves found that television characters had an impact in helping children define sex roles.[37] Meyer examined the influence of the 1970s TV show *All in the Family* and found that the program reinforced the political views of adult watchers, but had little if any impact on children.[38] Stanley Feldman and Lee Sigelman's 1985 study of the TV movie *The Day After* (1983), a fictitious account of a nuclear attack on the United States, found that the movie had no impact on political beliefs of viewers, although the discussions in the media that followed the movie did have the effect of influencing viewers' beliefs about nuclear war.[39] Michael Delli Carpini and Bruce Williams showed that messages about toxic waste in entertainment television influenced opinions about the issue as much as news coverage did.[40] More recently, David Barker's study of listeners of *The Rush Limbaugh Show* found that simply listening to the program increased voters' propensity to vote for Republicans in House, Senate, and presidential elections, independent of political ideology.[41]

Although past research provides some basis upon which to assess the influence of satire on its audience, it is incomplete for several reasons. First, existing literature tends to emphasize the format or medium rather than the content of the program. Although *The Daily Show* could be categorized as a talk show or even a soft news program, *The Simpsons* could not. Similarly, although *South Park* would be characterized as a popular TV program, the animated song parodies of JibJab.com would not. Second, most voters are exposed to satire without even knowing it. Watching *The Simpsons* or *South Park*, *Thank You for Smoking*, or *Wag the Dog* is typically not considered a "political" experience, although the messages conveyed are political in content. In addition, some voters regularly expose themselves to multiple forms of satire on a regular basis (often without recognizing it as satire). This would not happen with, say, talk shows or even a television movie about a nuclear attack. Therefore, simply acquiring information about voters' exposure to satire is a difficult task. Third, the audience for satire is generally self-selected. Satire, in its effort to expose the faults of society, is likely to attract those who are already cynical about societal or political conditions, who then gravitate toward these satirical outlets precisely because they confirm their political views. Last, given my condition that satire should require political knowledge in order to "be in on the joke," it is entirely possible that someone could regularly be exposed to satire and simply not get the social critique because ho or she does not understand. Millions tune in to watch *The Simpsons*, but it is entirely possible that many viewers do not pick up the more subtle satirical points made by Groening and the show writers.

What is the importance of satire in today's political environment? Consider that approximately one in five Americans report that they regularly get campaign news from comedy shows like Comedy Central's *The Daily Show* or NBC's *Saturday Night Live*. For Americans under thirty years of age, these shows are mentioned as sources for election news almost as often as daily newspapers or evening network news programs.[42] In a poll conducted in December 2003 and January 2004 by the Pew Internet & American Life Project, 21 percent of eighteen- to twenty-nine-year-olds report regularly getting campaign news from late night comedy shows, a 12 percent increase from 2000 (the percentage is particularly high for young men, 27 percent of whom report getting information from comedy programs, compared to 14 percent of young women). In addition, the programs provided these viewers new information, not simply repetition of information they already had—27 percent of all 18- to 29-year-old respondents say they learned things about the candidates and campaigns from comedy TV. The survey's summary of findings reports that "people who regularly learn about the election from entertainment programs whether young or not are poorly informed about campaign developments." Only 15 percent of eighteen- to twenty-nine-year-olds could identify which (Democratic primary) candidate was a general in the army or which had been majority leader of the House. Sixty-four percent of young voters reported that they "are not even somewhat interested in news about the Democratic primary campaigns."[43]

There are important distinctions to be made, however, between late night television talk shows. Not all "entertainment" shows are the same. Viewers of *The Daily Show* are more informed than viewers of other late night comedy shows, and more informed than those who watch network or cable news. In September 2004, the National Annenberg Election Survey released a report stating that young viewers of *The*

Daily Show "score higher on campaign knowledge than young people who do not watch the show, even when education, following politics, party identification, gender, viewing network news, reading the newspaper, watching cable news and getting campaign information on-line are taken into account."[44]

The survey, based on a six-question quiz, also reports that scores for viewers of Stewart's *Daily Show* were higher than scores from those who read a newspaper or watched network news four days a week. This creates an interesting puzzle. If young voters are apathetic, uninterested in politics, and ill-informed, how is it that (1) *The Daily Show* has maintained such a high level of popularity among these same voters, and (2) those who do watch the show are actually more knowledgeable than their peers who use more traditional sources like newspapers and network news? The answer is probably two-fold: first, viewers self-select, and those who have the knowledge to "be in on the joke" opt to watch *The Daily Show*; and second, the satirical elements of the show demand that viewers be more engaged in the experience of learning about politics.

The Daily Show has received widespread attention as of late. But other forms of political satire also appear to be reaching new voters. Jonathan Brown, in London's *The Independent*, writes that "U.S. political pundits have identified a new breed of '*South Park* Republicans': twenty-something males who favour rampant libertarianism over liberal sensitivities."[45] In fact, Brian Anderson is so enamored with the new "*South Park* Conservatives" that he has used them as an icon of the growing ideological strength of the Republican Party in the world of entertainment.[46] Paul Cantor begins his analysis of the political themes that appear in *The Simpsons* with the following anecdote culled from a *Roll Call* report of the incident.

> When Senator Charles Schumer (D-N.Y.) visited a high school in upstate New York in May 1999, he received an unexpected civics lesson from an unexpected source. Speaking on the timely subject of school violence, Senator Schumer praised the Brady Bill, which he helped sponsor, for its role in preventing crime. Rising to question the effectiveness of this effort at gun control, a student named Kevin Davis cited an example no doubt familiar to his classmates but unknown to the senator from New York: "It reminds me of a *Simpsons* episode. Homer wanted to get a gun but he had been in jail twice and in a mental institution. They label him as 'potentially dangerous.' So Homer asks what that means and the gun dealer says: 'It just means you need an extra week before you can get the gun.'"[47]

Cantor then offers the following by way of introducing his topic.

> Without going into the pros and cons of gun control legislation, one
> can recognize in this incident how the Fox Network's cartoon series *The
> Simpsons* shapes the way Americans think, particularly the younger gen-
> eration.... *The Simpsons* may seem like mindless entertainment to many,
> but in fact, it offers some of the most sophisticated comedy and satire ever
> to appear on American television. Over the years, the show has taken on
> many serious issues: nuclear power safety, environmentalism, immigra-
> tion, gay rights, women in the military, and so on. Paradoxically, it is the
> farcical nature of the show that allows it to be serious in ways that many
> other television shows are not.[48]

Furthermore, there have been (limited) calls to use more satire as
a way to engage students as they learn about American history and
politics. James Norton has advocated the use of *The Onion* (the emi-
nent online satirical newspaper) and Modern Humorist's *My First
Presidentiary* in his only partially tongue-in-cheek "Modern-Day
History Lessons."[49] In the essay, he argues that

> Ideally, history education asks two questions. The first question is, "what
> are the facts?"...the second question is more interesting. "How did we
> discover these facts in the first place?" Attached to it are the support-
> ing question of, "could there be other facts we're overlooking?" and "is it
> possible that these facts don't actually represent the era we're supposedly
> studying in the first place?" If history is going to remain relevant as a
> discipline, kids must be taught to be skeptical. There must be room for
> counter-history, even when it's not patriotic and causes students to ques-
> tion the way the American political system works—and has worked—for
> decades. In other words: We need to get kids asking and answering the
> second question.[50]

That satire can not only prompt political understanding but also
generate critical thinking is something that deserves more attention,
particularly in the study of new voters.

What can we conclude from all this? First, we need to recognize
the importance of content as we continue to study the influence of
entertainment and politics. Satirical content is unique in the world
of political humor and should be treated as such. It is not enough to
simply use the format of various media to make conclusions about
their importance in the modern political environment. Instead, we
need to take a closer look at the methods used and the messages conveyed. Second, it is a mistake to underestimate the power of "entertainment" as a genre. We need to expand our definition of political
humor to include material that has traditionally been left out of our
analysis. Political humor comes in any number of forms, some of
which may masquerade as simple entertainment. It is a mistake to

ignore these forms if we truly want to understand the impact of humor on political attitudes. In short, we need to expand our definitions of political humor and we need to have a more nuanced approach that allows us to explore the distinctions within this new genre of "info-enter-propa-gainment."

Notes

1. Neil Postman, *Amusing Ourselves to Death* (New York: Penguin Press, 2005).
2. See, for example, Jody Baumgartner and Jonathan S. Morris, "The Daily Show Effect: Candidate Evaluations, Efficacy, and American Youth," *American Politics Research* 34 (2006): 341; Matthew A. Baum, "Soft News and Political Knowledge: Evidence or Absence or Absence of Evidence?," *Political Communication* 20 (2003): 173; Thomas E. Patterson, *Out of Order* (New York: Vintage Books, 2000); Kathleen Hall Jamieson and Paul Waldman, *The Press Effect: Politicians, Journalists, and the Stories That Shape the Political World* (Oxford, UK: Oxford University Press, 2003).
3. Baumgartner and Morris, "The Daily Show Effect"; Matthew A. Baum, "Talking the Vote: Why Presidential Candidates Hit the Talk Show Circuit," *American Journal of Political Science* 49 (2005): 213–234; Jamieson and Waldman, *The Press Effect*; Patterson, *Out of Order*.
4. See, for example, Baum, "Soft News and Political Knowledge," 119–125.
5. Ibid.
6. Gregory Kirschling, "Friend & Faux," *Entertainment Weekly* (September 17, 2004), http://www.ew.com/ew/article/0,,695301,00.html.
7. I preface the remainder of this paper with an apology. Murray Davis quotes E. B. White, who said that "Humor can be dissected, as a frog can, but the thing dies in the process and the innards are discouraging to any but the pure scientific mind." Such is the case with satire. The beauty of satire as a form of political commentary comes in its ability to make us laugh, opening ourselves to a message that otherwise may not resonate with us. Sadly, this academic paper that considers satire as a form of political commentary will probably not make you laugh. See Murray S. Davis, *What's So Funny?: The Comic Conception of Culture and Society* (Chicago: University of Chicago, 1993), 2.
8. A. O. Scott, "Moral Guidance from Class Clowns," *New York Times*, October 15, 2004, E1.
9. J. Patrick Coolican, "Read, Rinse, Repeat: Bipartisan Jab Is an Internet Sensation," *Houston Chronicle* (July 21, 2004), 01.

10. The vast majority of scholarship devoted to satire comes from literary scholars. It is likely that this field has been limited in recent years by the fact that satire is no longer an exclusively literary pursuit. In fact, no modern literary satire—beyond Jon Stewart's *America (The Book)*, which I would argue is not literary satire in the traditional sense—has achieved widespread popular or critical success.

11. Robert C. Elliott, "The Satirist and Society," in *Modern Satire*, ed. Alvin B. Kernan (New York: Harcourt, Brace, & World, 1962), 148.

12. Ibid.

13. Ibid., 151.

14. Ibid.

15. Ibid., 147, 152.

16. George A. Test, *Satire: Spirit and Art* (Tampa: University of South Florida Press, 1991), 7; see also Robert C. Elliott "The Definition of Satire: A Note on Method," *Yearbook on Comparative and General Literature* 11 (1962): 19; Leonard Feinberg, "Satire: The Inadequacy of Recent Definitions," *Genre* 1 (1968): 31–37.

17. Test, *Satire*, 9–10.

18. Ibid., 15.

19. Ibid.

20. Ibid., 27.

21. Ibid., 28.

22. Alvin B. Kernan, "A Theory of Satire," in *Modern Satire*, ed. Alvin B. Kernan (New York: Harcourt, Brace & World, 1962), 168.

23. Test, *Satire*, 19–21.

24. Ibid., 24–26.

25. See, for example, Baumgartner and Morris, "The Daily Show Effect"; and Baum, "Soft News and Political Knowledge."

26. Paul Krassner, *Confessions of a Raving, Unconfined Nut: Misadventures in the Counter-Culture* (New York: Simon & Schuster, 1993), 144.

27. Jeffrey P. Jones, *Entertaining Politics: New Political Television and Civic Culture* (Lanham, MA: Rowman & Littlefield, 2005), 10.

28. Ellen D. Leyburn, "Animal Stories," in *Satire: Modern Essays in Criticism*, ed. Ronald Paulson (Englewood Cliffs, NJ: Prentice Hall, 1971), 217–32.

29. See Brian C. Anderson, *South Park Conservatives: The Revolt Against Liberal Media Bias* (Washington, DC: Regnery, 2005), 78–80.

30. Jonathan Brown, "From Homer to Scooby Doo: Our Love Affair with the Cartoon," *Independent*, February 28, 2005, 12–13.

31. Although many consider *The Daily Show* a satire about political personalities, issues, and current events, it was conceived as a critique on the news media and continues to target the media. This misunderstanding

may, in fact, make *The Daily Show* more effective in that the target of the critique is incidental to the information that it provides to young voters. This question is taken up later in the paper.

32. Bob Minzesheimer, "After 'America,' A Liberal Dose of Political Satire," *USA Today*, January 27, 2005, 5D.

33. Patterson, *Out of Order*; Barry A. Hollander, "The New News and the 1992 Presidential Campaign: Perceived Versus Actual Political Knowledge," *Journalism and Mass Communication Quarterly* 72 (1995): 786.

34. See, for example, Patterson, *Out of Order*; Hollander "The New News and the 1992 Presidential Campaign"; and Matthew R. Kerbel, *Remote and Controlled: Media Politics in a Cynical Age* (Boulder, CO: Westview Press, 1999).

35. Christine F. Ridout, "News Coverage and Talk Shows in the 1992 Presidential Campaign," *PS: Political Science and Politics* 26 (1993): 715; see also Patterson, *Out of Order*.

36. Baum, "Soft News and Political Knowledge."

37. Mark M. Miller and Byron Reeves, "Dramatic TV Content and Children's Sex-Role Stereotypes," *Journal of Broadcasting* 20 (1976): 36.

38. Timothy Meyer, "Impact of 'All in the Family' on Children," *Journal of Broadcasting* 20 (1976): 23.

39. Stanley Feldman and Lee Sigelman, "The Political Impact of Prime-Time Television: 'The Day After,'" *The Journal of Politics* 47 (1985): 556.

40. Michael X. Delli Carpini and Bruce A.Williams, "Constructing Public Opinion: The Uses of Fictional and Non-fictional Television in Conversations about the Environment," in *The Psychology of Political Communication*, ed. Ann N. Crigler (Ann Arbor: University of Michigan Press, 1996), 160–166.

41. This research is particularly interesting for the topic of this paper because it has very similar features. The audience initially tunes in only for entertainment value or because a peer or family member is a regular listener (or watcher). But, even small amounts of exposure do seem to have an effect. David C. Barker, "Rushed Decisions: Political Talk Radio and Vote Choice 1994–1996," *The Journal of Politics* 61 (1999): 527.

42. "Cable and Internet Loom Large in Fragmented Political News Universe: Perceptions of Partisan Bias Seen as Growing, Especially by Democrats," *The Pew Research Center for the People & the Press*, January 11, 2004. http://people-press.org/reports/pdf/200.pdf.

43. Ibid.

44. National Annenberg Election Survey, "Daily Show Viewers Knowledgeable About Presidential Campaign," September 21, 2004. http://www.annenbergpublicpolicycenter.org/naes/2004_03_late-night-knowledge-2_9-21_pr.pdf.

45. Brown, "From Homer to Scooby Doo."
46. Anderson, *South Park Conservatives.*
47. Paul A. Cantor, "The Simpsons: Atomistic Politics and the Nuclear Family," *Political Theory* 27 (1999): 734.
48. Ibid., 747.
49. James Norton has worked with the Al Franken show since 2004 and prior to that at the *Christian Science Monitor.* He is also the founder and editor of Flak Magazine (http://www.flakmag.com).
50. James Norton, "Modern-Day History Lessons," April 21, 2001. http://flakmag.com/jim/resume/sampled3.html.

2

Serious Comedy
Expanding the Boundaries of Political Discourse

Geoffrey Baym

> I stand by this man, because he stands for things. Not only *for* things, he
> stands *on* things. Things like aircraft carriers, and rubble, and recently
> flooded city squares. And that sends a strong message that no matter
> what happens to America, she will always rebound ... with the most pow-
> erfully staged photo ops in the world.
>
> Comedian Stephen Colbert on President George W. Bush[1]

I begin this chapter by quoting from the 2006 White House Correspondents Association dinner, that strange annual black-tie affair in
which an odd assortment of power brokers, reporters, and celebrities
gather with the president for a night of good-natured ridicule. This
year, the keynote speaker was fake newsman and pundit Stephen
Colbert, who, standing only two seats away from Bush, unleashed
a biting monologue on the president, accusing him, among other
things, of responding to national tragedy with spectacle instead of
substance, with publicity in place of policy. By all accounts, the president does not care much for criticism and those who disagree with
him almost never get a seat at the same table. Yet here, in an unlikely
venue and coming from a most unlikely source, was a serious challenge, a stinging critique clad in the guise of good humor.

Simultaneously funny and fierce, this was serious stuff—*serious
comedy* perhaps—and as such it raises a set of important questions
that we must consider if we hope to come to terms with the nature of
contemporary political discourse. *Serious comedy* is a contradiction
in terms. *Serious* implies weight and gravity, and a "serious matter"
necessitates sober consideration. By contrast, *comedy* entails laughter

and levity, intoxication and delight. Indeed, Webster's dictionary defines the two as antonyms; the very definition of "being serious" is "not joking." Colbert's performance for the president, however, offers compelling evidence that Webster's, at least on this issue, could use revision. If *serious* and *comedy* were once assumed to be oppositional terms, it is clear that the two are less distinct than they were once thought to be. Programs such as *The Colbert Report* and Jon Stewart's *The Daily Show* suggest that the serious and the silly are blending, interweaving in powerful ways and challenging a host of assumptions about how we can, and should, talk about politics.

The commonsense distinction between the serious and the comedic speaks to a host of related oppositions, each problematic in its own right. It invokes the familiar assumption that *news* and *entertainment* are (or should be) different things, that one rightly is the domain of *public affairs*, the other the realm of *popular culture*. Michael Delli Carpini and Bruce Williams have challenged this assumption, arguing that it is difficult, and perhaps impossible, to define clear borders between news and entertainment or public affairs and popular culture.[2] Similarly, the theorist Michel Foucault once questioned the difference between *politics* and *literature*,[3] a division that itself rests on distinctions between *argument* and *art*. Foucault argued that these sets of oppositions, however familiar and taken for granted, are in fact arbitrary, existing not in nature but in social convention. He suggested that such distinctions are always tenuous and temporary, continuously shifting agreements about how one legitimately can talk about, think about, and act within the world.

It seems clear that these binaries—serious/comedy, news/entertainment, public affairs/popular culture, politics/literature, and argument/art—no longer serve to adequately describe or delimit political discourse on television today. In this chapter, I explore the historical opposition between the serious and the comedic and its contemporary collapse. I suggest that the divide between the two can be understood as a legacy of *modernity*, a framework of social organization that shapes our assumptions, but has grown increasingly unstable. A number of technological, economic, and cultural transformations have resulted in an age of *discursive integration*— the fundamental blurring of conceptual categories and media discourses that has created both the conditions *and the need* for the emergence of comedy as a site of political conversation.[4] Finally, I offer a rhetorical reading of Stephen Colbert's performance at the

White House dinner that reveals some of the ways in which the serious and the silly, the artistic and the political, have blended in contemporary culture.

Modernity

In their recent review of the changing nature of political communication, Jay Blumler and Michael Gurevitch argue that we have entered an "era of indeterminancy" in which politics has become "porous" and political communication has turned "far more complex and fluid than before."[5] In an age when Jon Stewart has become an important news broadcaster and Stephen Colbert can criticize the president to his face on live television and through streaming video on the Internet, the boundaries that once structured what Blumler and Gurevitch call the "political communication field" have largely dissolved. The notion of a *field* is important here. Like a baseball diamond or football field, it suggests a terrain demarcated by clear borders, a space governed by rules that dictate what kinds of activities may be conducted there and what kinds of behaviors will be seen as "out of bounds." Among the rules that once structured the political communication field are those that divided the serious from the funny and the political from the entertaining.

The central premise of this discussion is that those borders between comedy and news, politics and popular culture, and even argument and amusement are historical traces, residual leftovers from the *project of modernity*. Theoretical definitions of "modernity" differ widely. Here I use the term not to refer to a clearly definable historical period (although the sociologist Anthony Giddens locates its emergence in seventeenth-century Europe), but more importantly to a set of conceptual categories—a framework for making sense of the world—and, to quote from Giddens, corresponding "modes of social life or organization."[6] That is to say, modernity can be understood both as a set of ideas about how society should be organized *and* as the particular social institutions and practices that developed as a result. To call modernity a *project*, as many theorists have, is to recognize that these conceptual categories and organizational structures were, at their core, normative, that is, ideals of how society and its practices could best be realized.

Building on the work of Max Weber, Jürgen Habermas argues that modernity is the project of *social rationalization*, the dividing of social and cultural activity into autonomous spheres, each entrusted with advancing a particular aspect of the human condition.[7] In particular, Habermas defines three spheres, which he roughly labels as science, morality, and art. The first is the domain of the *cognitive-instrumental*, or the rational search for empirical truth. The second is what he calls the realm of the *moral-practical*, or what I will refer to as the *political-normative*. In this arena, questions of social justice and the public good are to be determined. Finally, the third is the sphere of the *aesthetic-expressive*: the pursuit of the beautiful, the poetic, and the pleasurable.

The project of modernity was one of segmentation or sociocultural differentiation. In this framework, systems of governance, resource allocation, and conversations about social value and the collective good are located in the political-normative sphere. By contrast, cultural practice, in its "high" form of literature, theater, and art, as well as its more popular manifestations of movies, music, and television, is properly located within the aesthetic-expressive sphere. Each sphere thus is assumed to *contain*, without overlap, particular types of cultural activities and concerns. In turn, each sphere gives rise to clearly demarcated sets of institutions and professional organizations and practices. Particular kinds of work are to be done by certain kinds of people in clearly demarcated spaces. The business of politics, for example, is not to be mistaken for art.

Neither is the language of art to be confused with the language of politics. To put the point differently, modernity gives rise to a differentiated set of discourses. In answering his own question, Foucault suggests that "literature" and "politics" could best be understood as different kinds of *discursive formations*.[8] For Foucault, the term *discourse* refers to the use of language within specific domains of cultural practice. Foucault argues that a discursive formation is more than just a way of speaking about a particular aspect of the world. A discursive system of knowledge is one that draws the conceptual boundaries around its given domain, simultaneously making that domain knowable and constraining the ways in which it can be understood. He suggests that discursive formations define the objects of which they speak: not their "internal constitution," but the ways in which they can be recognized and discussed. A discursive formation authorizes particular speakers, conferring what the philosophers of knowledge call "epistemic warrant" (the presumption that what one says is true), to certain kinds of people and not others. Finally, a discursive formation endorses particular modes of representation, constraining the strategies and styles of language (here language refers to the verbal and the symbolic), as well as accepted media forms, genres, and techniques. When understood as contrasting discourses, art and politics—or comedy and news—authorize different kinds of speakers who speak in incompatible ways about fundamentally different things.

In this discursively differentiated framework of modernity, politics was assumed to be the province of journalism, which itself was seen as residing within the political-normative sphere. Modernity gave rise to the familiar notion of the press as the Fourth Estate, or a light of public inquiry that could hold a democratic leadership accountable for its actions and perhaps speak truth to power. In the mid-twentieth century (what Daniel Hallin has called "late-modernity"), this ideal of public service provided an organizing principle for the professionalization of journalism. Here the ideal journalist became a credentialed expert who utilized the pseudoscientific methods of objective inquiry to uncover the reality of the political domain.[9] In the discourse of professional journalism, politics was seen as the institutional process of reasoned debate and decision making. In turn, journalism was assumed to be an essential resource for citizen engagement in politics, providing the factual information necessary for the rational-critical dialogue of democracy.

For network television, which quickly became the central location of political discourse after the widespread adoption of TV in the 1950s, news and public affairs programming were seen as directly contrasting with the aesthetic-expressive content that filled the rest of the television landscape. During the heyday of CBS News, for example, news president Richard Salant worried that audiences might confuse the two and argued that "because it all comes out sequentially on the same point of the dial and on the same tube," news must be clearly differentiated from entertainment programming. His official book of standards forbade CBS news producers from using any production techniques common to entertainment, hoping to make it clear to the audience that "our *field* is journalism, not show business."[10] As Delli Carpini and Williams note, this demarcation of news and politics from entertainment and pop culture was propped up by a host of other institutional conventions.[11] These included the internal division within network television between news and entertainment production units. The two were also held to different expectations of profitability. Considered a public service, news was not expected to turn a profit, while entertainment paid its bills. Further, programming schedules were routinized, with news and public affairs confined to particular and predictable times (say, early evenings and Sunday mornings), except for the rare instances when they were allowed to "break in" to "regularly scheduled programming."

In practice, these conventions—conceptual, institutional, and discursive—constrained the nature of televised political discourse. Of course, anyone could talk politics, but to be considered legitimate, political discourse had to conform to a set of narrow expectations that limited who was authorized to speak, how they could speak, and what they were allowed to talk about. For many, it became common sense that politics should be neatly distinguishable from the aesthetic, the former rational argument, the latter expressive and affective; that news, and not entertainment, should be where we learn about the political; and that news itself should be serious and dispassionate. Political information, argument, and commentary emanating from alternative locations and unauthorized speakers, such as the stand-up comedian who challenged political authority from the shadows of the nightclub, more often than not was obscured or overlooked, considered irrelevant to the national political conversation.

Beyond Modernity

Sociocultural conditions have changed radically, however, because a quarter of all people in the United States watched network news every night and Walter Cronkite could so confidently insist that "that's the way it is." Although I hesitate to embrace the whole of postmodern theory, it is undeniable that the conceptual boundaries of modernity have grown porous, engendering a historical moment of equal parts uncertainty and possibility, a time in which the rules governing the field of political discourse have become fundamentally open to experimentation.

We can define three interrelated sets of transformations—technological, economic, and cultural—that have led to remarkable change.[12] Rapid technological development has radically altered the media environment. The dominance of broadcast network television has been fractured by twenty-four-hour cable, which itself has become complicated by digital, on-demand, and Web-based content. As the Internet continues to expand, the number of media sources has increased infinitely, while the number of people paying attention to any one of them has shrunk correspondingly. In economic terms, technological multiplication and audience fragmentation have been countered by conglomeration—the consolidation of ownership and the integration of formerly independent media companies. Now housed under the same corporate umbrella, once-distinct media outlets are encouraged to share resources, personnel, and agendas in the name of economic efficiency. At the same time, in the effort to chase shrinking audiences, contemporary media conglomerates have abandoned earlier institutional arrangements such as the wall between news and entertainment, and increasingly seek to reinvent programming to appeal to narrowly defined demographic groups.

Finally, these changes are imbricated with the wider turn toward multiculturalism, the unavoidable reality that Western culture today is increasingly heterogeneous. In a landscape marked by diversity, earlier cultural standards have become relativized, no longer points of accepted truth, but sites of disagreement and contestation. We have become increasingly distrustful of authority and skeptical of claims to objectivity. Rationality itself has become decentered, seen by many as a competing belief system, not a privileged path to truth. Here the thinking of Mikhail Bakhtin is remarkably insightful. Bakhtin argued that as a society becomes less homogeneous, it is subject to a process of "verbal-ideological decentering," which is the multiplication of languages, voices, and perspectives—what he called "socio-linguistic points of view." In a heterogeneous culture in which multiple languages and discourses are constantly bumping up against each other, the result, he said, inevitably is *hybridization*, the blending of discursive styles and standards, voices, and points of view.[13]

Although Bakhtin was describing literature, his argument equally fits televised political discourse today. Hybridization can be an intentional stylistic device, designed to intrigue or challenge an audience, but on a deeper level it represents a more fundamental perforation of boundaries among social spheres and discursive formations. John Corner and Dick Pels make a similar argument, suggesting both politics and media are being subject to a "process of de-differentiation" and the "mutual interpenetration of formerly distinct 'field-logics' or 'system codes.'"[14] Elsewhere, I have called this phenomenon *discursive integration*: "a way of speaking about, understanding, and acting within the world defined by the permeability of form and the fluidity of content."[15] As the borders between the political-normative and the aesthetic-expressive spheres have become difficult to locate, media forms of news and entertainment—of politics and art—have at the same time proliferated and become less distinguishable, with each borrowing from and influencing the others in continuously shifting ways.

From Politics to Infotainment

Perhaps one of the primary effects of discursive integration has been the dissolution of an earlier model of professional journalism.[16] A journalism fashioned as a democratic resource largely has been replaced by a commodified form of infotainment. News and public affairs programming have become shaped by a commercial logic, less a public service than a market-driven commodity packaged for sale. No longer the profession of accurately describing reality, most television news has been reconceptualized as the business of telling good stories, another variety of "reality-based programming." Previous institutional arrangements that privileged newsmakers have largely collapsed. It is now expected to be both a profit center friendly to the interests of its advertisers, and a synergistic resource integrated with the rest of the parent corporation's entertainment holdings. Its producers readily utilize the techniques of entertainment once considered out of bounds for the field of journalism. Broadcast journalists have become television personalities, valued more for their good looks and emotive screen appeal than their reportorial skills. The newscast itself is built around compelling visuals and emotionally engaging storylines—an attempt less to inform than to try to entice the audience to watch through the next commercial break.

If past professional journalism saw politics as the institutional process of rational argument in the service of the public good, today, politics is largely understood through two other discursive frames. In one, it has become sport, with campaigns and elections approached not in terms of policies and proposals, but of competitors and strategy—who's playing, who's winning, and how they are trying to get ahead.[17] Political discussion shows likewise have devolved into bizarre sporting contests: yelling matches between partisan players who try more to shout down the other side than construct a compelling argument.

Here, politics is less a dialogue about the collective good than a spectator sport in which contestants vie for a prize while the audience can only jeer or cheer. In the other predominant discursive frame, politics is represented as theater.[18] Governance is seen as drama and spectacle, while politicians are said to be role-playing on the public stage. Here news employs the conventions of screenwriting, building stories around protagonists and antagonists—compelling characters developed in telephoto clarity—who move through the dramatic cycle from crisis to resolution and back again. The citizenry again is transformed into the audience as politics becomes just another story on the TV screen.

For their part, politicians have become remarkably adept at playing to the conventions of television news. Political journalism has fused with the logic of entertainment, and so too has politics become inseparable from show business. Corner and Pels suggest that an integrated "media culture" has engendered the aestheticization of politics, the blending of governance with popular culture. At least on television, distinctions between political practice and "symbol-making and aesthetic design" have collapsed.[19] With the media paying far more attention to politicians' ways "of speaking, acting, looking, displaying, and handling things" than to their policy preferences, personal style has become the coin of the political realm.[20] In turn, the lines between the message and its delivery, between argument and ritual, reason and sentiment have become deeply obscured. Politicians actively encourage affective identification or emotional affiliation from their constituents, as much as they argue for their rational support. Thus the aestheticization of politics interweaves the objective and the rational with the subjective and the emotional, elevating the latter, if not altogether abandoning the former.

Corner and Pels argue that in a time of decreasing citizen engagement, this "restyling" of politics has the potential to democratize political practice, legitimizing emotional and affective forms of decision making. At the same time, however, political discourse equally has fused with the discourse of marketing. Constructing a brand identity based on image and style, professional political communicators attempt to control the public conversation with a continual stream of carefully crafted sound bites and photo ops. Candid dialogue and reasoned argument have been replaced by self-promoting spectacle and spin designed to convert news into free advertising. In this regard the corporate commodified media are too willing to play along, eager for easy and compelling content and equally averse to the time- and resource-intensive labor that critical journalism demands. So too have the mainstream news media become generally unwilling, or unable, to confront the status quo and pierce the bubble of spectacle and spin. Loathe to offend the parent company and its advertisers or to lose access to the halls of power, too many national journalists have abdicated their critical function, now actors in the theater of politics they have helped to construct.[21] In practice, the boundaries between press and politics have become obscured with neither side providing a discourse that is especially useful for the democratic process.

From Art to Politics

As we can track the aestheticization of the political-normative sphere, we can also think of the politicization of the aesthetic-expressive sphere. To put it differently, if press and politics have come to resemble show business, so too have politics and news become staples of show business. Prime-time drama and Hollywood films are now saturated with plotlines drawn from the political domain. During campaign season, politicians have become regular guests on the network late night talk shows. And of course, one can find various discursively integrated versions of political news and public affairs discussion on HBO and Comedy Central, where comedians such as Bill Maher, Jon Stewart, and Stephen Colbert blend humor and politics on a nightly basis. Jeffrey Jones has dubbed such programs "New Political Television," suggesting that they have arisen in part as a countermeasure to the "fakery in public life."[22] The argument here is that the collapse of the boundaries between discursive spheres has created both the conditions and the need for the emergence of serious comedy as an increasingly legitimate and salient location for political discourse.

To consider some of the ways in which discourses of politics and comedy now interact, we can return to Stephen Colbert and his performance at the White House Correspondents Association dinner, which itself is a hybrid affair, merging humor, celebrity, press, and politics. This year the president appeared alongside his own doppelganger, and the two entertained an audience that included strategist Karl Rove, former ambassador Joe Wilson and wife Valerie Plame, rapper Ludacris, and the Washington DC press corps. Of course, the keynote address was provided by Colbert, a point that supports some of the central contentions of this essay. Colbert, or at least the character he has perfected, is an example of discursive border crossing, a blend of the political-normative and the aesthetic-expressive. In differing combinations each night, Colbert borrows from and reassembles a number of discursive styles and traditions, melding the content of news and public affairs, the form of cable television's partisan punditry, and the style of edgy nightclub comedy. Neither a journalist nor political expert, he plays both on television, and in *that* role—the pretend pundit—he was invited to speak before the president and the national press. Taking the stage in what was supposed to be an annual ritual of frivolity, Colbert instead unleashed a powerful stream of satire—sarcasm, irony, and double entendre that sounded like praise but in actuality was blistering criticism. His performance thus illustrates the degree to which both popular culture and public affairs have fused and the serious and the silly have become intertwined.

At first blush, Colbert may have seemed to be a perfect match for the Correspondents Dinner, a night when otherwise serious people bracket their professional responsibilities and public concerns. The ideal of the dinner is for the supposed antagonists of press and politics to momentarily bury the hatchet and "kid each other and have good fun together."[23] Thus the expected fare at the Correspondents Dinner is the kind of humor Colbert offered in his opening remark.

> Wow, what an honor.... To sit here, at the same table, with my hero, George W. Bush. To be this close to the man. I feel like I'm dreaming. Somebody pinch me.... You know, I'm a pretty sound sleeper, that may not be enough. Somebody shoot me in the face.

His reference, of course, was to Vice President Dick Cheney's hunting accident, the kind of personal issue in which late night comedians delight. Such humor can be considered benign: it may not be supportive of the administration nor necessarily appreciated, but by focusing on the trivial it avoids any significant contact with the domain of governance.[24] Such satirical humor functions more to showcase the performer's wit than to critique or challenge policy. This kind of comedy, to borrow from Griffin's typology of satire, can be considered a *rhetoric of play*, an aesthetic performance whose purpose is to entertain an audience. Satire-as-play can be seen as an ornamental use of language, one that dazzles the ear and engages the emotions in the pursuit of pleasure. Like the notion of play itself, such humor is assumed to be confined to an arena, like the dinner, that is "marked off from business or serious purpose, reserved for self-delighting activity that has no concern for morality or for any real-world consequence save the applause of the spectators."[25]

At the same time, though, political comedy also can be a *play of ideas*, a juxtaposition of incompatible positions (the scholar of political humor Charles Schutz called it the "collision of alternative logics")[26] in which contrasting ideas "jostle against each other in a open and free-wheeling contest."[27] In that vein, Colbert touches on Iraq.

> I believe that the government that governs best is the government that governs least. And by that standard, we have set up a fabulous government in Iraq.

Colbert here juxtaposes conventional conservative wisdom with a brief, yet thought-provoking critique of presidential policy. In moments such as these, satire becomes what Griffin has called a *rhetoric of inquiry*, an exploration of ideas and arguments, and perhaps, he suggests, a search for truth.[28]

One can see such a strategy of inquiry at work in Colbert's opening "praise" for the president.

> We're not so different, he and I. We both "get it." Guys like us, we're not some brainiacs on the nerd patrol, we're not members of the "factanista." We go straight from the gut. Right, sir? That's where the truth lies, right down here in the gut.

Colbert here uses humor not just to poke fun at the president for his alleged lack of intelligence (the primary comic take on Bush), but to raise the fundamentally serious question of truth in a postmodern world. Colbert, of course, insists that he doesn't give his audience truth, but "truthiness," a concept he explained on his debut program.

> Now I'm sure some of the word police—the "wordanistas" over at Webster's are gonna say, hey that's not a word. Well, anybody who knows me knows I'm no fan of dictionaries or references books. They're elitist. Constantly telling us what is or isn't true, or what did or didn't happen. Who's Britannica to tell me the Panama Canal was finished in 1914? If I want to say it happened in 1941, that's my right. I don't trust books. They're all fact and no heart. And that's exactly what's pulling our country apart today. And let's face it America, we are a divided nation...divided between those who *think* with their heads, and those who *know* with their heart.[29]

Repeating much of this bit at the Correspondents Dinner, Colbert uses satire-as-inquiry to grapple with one of the primary philosophical problematics in an age of discursive integration. In an era of collapse between the political and the aesthetic, the objective and the subjective, and the rational and the affective, political discourse becomes a site of contestation over the nature of knowledge and the parameters of epistemological authority. Colbert's satire constructs a set of oppositions between fact and heart, thinking and knowing, truth and truthiness, and in turn calls on the audience to move beyond the laugh to his underlying critique that knowledge without fact can at best be truthiness—a pale imitation of truth.

Colbert himself is an imitation, and as such his humor further functions as serious critique. Through parody, Colbert engages in what Griffin labels satire-as-provocation, a "critique of false understanding" and an attempt to "expose or demolish a foolish certainty."[30] Parody can be understood as a polemical imitation that exposes the flaws in its "pretext"—that which it imitates. For Colbert, of course, the pretext is the blustering partisan pundit (think Fox's Bill O'Reilly, whom he insists is his mentor—"papa bear" he calls him). Proudly insisting that he is "immune to logic," Colbert becomes the epitome of the foolishly certain. He echoes the point at the dinner.

> Every night on my show I speak straight from the gut, ok? I give people the truth, unfiltered by rational argument. I call it the "No Fact Zone".... Fox News, I hold a copyright on that term.

His "No Fact Zone" is a direct challenge to O'Reilly's "No Spin Zone." But of course, even as he delights in his own absurdity, Colbert never seems to quite mean what he says. That too is a powerful critique, suggesting that those who would be so certain may not mean what they say either, that they too may be playing a role in today's political theater.

Ultimately, when understood as a rhetoric of provocation, Colbert's humor is a challenge to the news media that have abdicated much of their democratic function in favor of theatrical spectacle. Directly addressing the press corps who had invited him to speak, Colbert confronted their passivity, their unwillingness following September 11 to investigate the serious issues of the times. In a voice thick with irony, he worries that the press might be awakening from its noncritical slumber.

> What happened to you guys?.... Over the last five years, you people were
> so good. Over tax cuts, WMD intelligence, the effect of global warming,
> we Americans didn't want to know...and you had the courtesy not to try
> to find out. Those were good times...as far as we knew.

Griffin suggests that satire-as-provocation intends to be unsettling,
to challenge the complacency of the audience and to confront the
"human tendency to avert our eyes from whatever is disagreeable
to contemplate."[31] In an age when an entertainment-based news
media would rather contemplate *American Idol*, Colbert's criticism
was indeed unsettling. The mainstream press didn't know how to
deal with it. Even the *New York Times* avoided reporting on Colbert's
performance for several days, and an op-ed piece in the *Washington
Post* dismissed it as "so not funny."[32] For many, Colbert's provocation
was out-of-bounds, perhaps too serious for a crowd that expected the
benignly silly.

Conclusion

This raises a final question: *was* Stephen Colbert out-of-bounds at
the Correspondents Dinner? Or perhaps more importantly, *could*
he have been? By definition, one can only be "out-of-bounds" on a
field demarcated by clear boundaries. A central contention of this
essay, however, has been that in an age of discursive integration,
the boundaries that are supposed to frame political discourse have
become harder and harder to discern. The Correspondents Dinner is
supposed to be a space in which political and journalistic seriousness
is bracketed in favor of comedy and entertainment; a night when
the political-normative is suspended while the aesthetic-expressive is celebrated. But that assumes the participants in the dinner
are actually serious elsewhere. Many scholars of politics and media
have become well aware that journalism has fused with entertainment and the political has become inseparable from the aesthetic.
The dinner is by no means the only arena in which journalists and
politicians perform on the public stage rather than discuss the collective good.

By contrast, Stephen Colbert, an actor from the aesthetic-expressive sphere whose profession is entertainment, offered a performance
that was laced with political-normative content. Jon Stewart, for one,
was confused by the reaction. On *The Daily Show*, he suggested that

Colbert must have assumed he was being hired to perform the same politically oriented act he does every night on his comedy show. Postmodern theory contends that borders of all sorts—among them time, space, and any range of cultural practices—largely have dissolved. Thus Colbert and Stewart would seem to be the quintessential postmodernists: comedians who paradoxically offer some of the most serious political critique on television. Postmodern theory, though, also suggests that facts are cultural constructs and truth is always relative. I want to conclude, therefore, by suggesting that the kind of serious comedy represented by Stewart and Colbert can better be understood as a fusion of postmodern style and modernist intentions.

Stylistically, serious comedy is a boundary-transcending discursive blend that melds entertainment with news, the aesthetic with the political, and the emotional with the rational. It is a collage of once-disparate forms and techniques that results in an unpredictable and continuously shifting ensemble of politics, information, and humor. At the same time, however, serious comedy is motivated by a particularly modernist sensibility: a faith in fact and accountability, in truth and not truthiness. It advocates rational-critical discourse and citizen engagement in politics. Serious comedy thus *uses* humor and postmodern stylistics to critique a political culture of sound bite and sentiment—of "powerfully staged photo ops"—and to demand a professional journalism of inquiry. Thoroughly blending previously incompatible discourses of argument and art, serious comedy is at once political and pleasurable; it is humor committed to the serious work of democracy.

Notes

1. All quotes are from the 2006 White House Correspondents Association dinner. C-SPAN, "Colbert Roasts President Bush," http://video.google.com/videoplay?docid=-869183917758574879.

2. Michael X. Delli Carpini and Bruce A. Williams, "Let Us Infotain You: Politics in the New Media Environment," in *Mediated Politics: Communication in the Future of Democracy*, eds. W. L. Bennett and R. M. Entman (New York: Cambridge University Press, 2001), 160–181.

3. Michel Foucault, *The Archaeology of Knowledge* (New York: Pantheon Books, 1972).

4. Geoffrey Baym, "The Daily Show: Discursive Integration and the Reinvention of Critical Journalism," *Political Communication* 22 (2005): 259–276.

5. Jay G. Blumler and Michael Gurevitch, "Rethinking the Study of Political Communication," in *Mass Media and Society*, 4th ed., eds. J. Curran and M. Gurevitch (New York: Oxford University Press, 2005), 104–121.
6. Quoted in Nigel Dodd, *Social Theory and Modernity* (Malden, MA: Blackwell, 1999), 1.
7. Jürgen Habermas, "Modernity—An Incomplete Project," in *The Anti-Aesthetic: Essays on Postmodern Culture*, ed. H. Foster (Seattle: Bay Press, 1983), 3–15.
8. Foucault, *Archaeology of Knowledge*.
9. Daniel C. Hallin, "Commercialism and Professionalism in the American News Media," in *Mass Media and Society*, 3rd ed., eds. J. Curran and M. Gurevitch (New York: Oxford University Press, 2000), 218–237.
10. Richard J. Schaefer, "The Development of the CBS News Guidelines during the Salant Years," *Journal of Broadcasting and Electronic Media* 42 (1998), 1–20.
11. Delli Carpini and Williams, "Let Us Infotain You," 165.
12. See Baym, "The Daily Show"; Delli Carpini and Williams, "Let Us Infotain You."
13. Mikhail M. Bakhtin, *The Dialogic Imagination* (Austin: University of Texas Press, 1981).
14. John Corner and Dick Pels, "Introduction: The Restyling of Politics," in *Media and the Restyling of Politics*, eds. J. Corner and D. Pels (Thousand Oaks, CA: Sage, 2003), 1–18.
15. Baym, "The Daily Show," 262.
16. See Hallin, "Commercialism and Professionalism in the American News Media."
17. Thomas E. Patterson, *Out of Order* (New York: Knopf, 1993).
18. Geoffrey Baym, "Strategies of Illumination: U.S. Network News, Watergate, and the Clinton Affair," *Rhetoric & Public Affairs* 6 (2003): 633–656.
19. Corner and Pels, "The Restyling of Politics."
20. Dick Pels, "Aesthetic Representation and Political Style: Re-balancing Identity and Difference in Media Democracy," in *Media and the Restyling of Politics*, eds. J. Corner and D. Pels (Thousand Oaks, CA: Sage, 2003), 45.
21. See Robert W. McChesney, *Rich Media, Poor Democracy: Communication Politics in Dubious Times* (New York: The New Press, 1999).
22. Jeffrey P. Jones, *Entertaining Politics: New Political Television and Civic Culture* (New York: Rowman & Littlefield, 2005).
23. David L. Paletz, "Political Humor and Authority: From Support to Subversion," *International Political Science Review* 11 (1990): 486.

24. Ibid.
25. Dustin Griffin, *Satire: A Critical Reintroduction* (Lexington: The University Press of Kentucky, 1994), 84.
26. Charles E. Schutz, *Political Humor: From Aristophanes to Sam Ervin* (Cranbury, NJ: Associated University Presses, 1977), 29.
27. Griffin, *Satire*, 87.
28. Ibid.
29. Colbert Report, October 17, 2005.
30. Griffin, *Satire*, 52.
31. Ibid., 63.
32. Richard Cohen, "So Not Funny," *Washington Post*, May 4, 2006, A25.

3

More Than Laughing?
Survey of Political Humor
Effects Research

Josh Compton

A general consensus is that humor does matter, with some scholars calling it "a most essential element in a democracy"[1] and "one of the most basic and effective ways of responding [to politics]."[2] Yet despite its importance, scholarly scrutiny of humor is limited—a dearth recognized by political players and academics. Robert Orben, former head of President Ford's speechwriting staff, noted: "It seems to me that we've only scratched the surface in our study of the effective use of humor."[3] Communication theorist Owen Lynch offered a similar conclusion: "[C]uriously the communication field has only skimmed the surface of the world of humor."[4]

Whether we have skimmed or scratched, there is little doubt that there's much more to learn about humor, and particularly, what happens when it goes political. Rhetorical and critical scholarship has, in many areas, given us rich, nuanced views of political humor. Less common are empirical investigations of effects, which are the focus of this essay.

The first section of this chapter examines effects research on two popular forms of political humor, editorial cartoons and late night comedy television programming. The second half of the chapter explores other venues for political humor, including entertainment television, print media, Internet, film, and campaign events. Throughout, I highlight the ways that humor effects research can continue to clarify when, in politics, laughing matters.

Political Cartoons

Cartoons are a unique persuasive medium,[5] visually impacting
and often humorous.[6] According to William Koetzle and Thomas
Brunell, "the defining characteristic of the editorial cartoon is its
use of humor to make a political point."[7] Audrey Handelman noted
that editorial cartoonists "are a special breed in the mass media;
they make no claims on objectivity."[8] With this journalistic freedom,
political cartoonists go after public figures with vigor, subjecting
them to "exaggeration, ridicule, and sarcasm."[9]

Many have described political cartoons as powerful forces in affecting attitudes and beliefs. Cartoons have been called "one of the most
powerful weapons in the journalistic armoury,"[10] "a vital component
of political discourse,"[11] and "a cornerstone of American democracy."[12] David Ammons, John King, and Jerry Yeric argued that with
cartoons, images of politicians are "lodged [in the mind] perhaps
more forcefully...than by the myriad news stories and editorials."[13]

A couple of historical examples are typically often offered as proof
of the power of political cartoons, specifically, Thomas Nast's cartoons
attacking the Tweed gang and Herbert Block's caricatures of Richard
Nixon.[14] The Tweed case elicited the now famous quotation by William Marcy Tweed, "I don't care what they print about me, most of
my constituents can't read anyway.... But them damn pictures!"[15]
As for Nixon, Pulitzer Prize–winning cartoonist Patrick Oliphant
asserted: "It is no stretch to claim that the political cartoon had a distinct influence on the termination of the Nixon presidency."[16] Most
historians believe that these cartoonists had some influence over the
chain of events that followed publication of their cartoons.[17]

An impressive body of rhetorical and critical work has examined
political cartoons, revealing rich, nuanced meanings. Yet empirical
support for political cartoon effects is limited. Matthew Morrison's
observation in 1969, "There has been a paucity of quantitative research
on the effects of editorial cartoons,"[18] continues to ring true.

Fortunately, a few empirical effects studies have highlighted the
unique and at times confounding reactions viewers have toward this
potentially powerful, and often humorous, political force. LeRoy
Carl's study highlighted an inconsistency between what cartoonists
intend and what readers perceive. Random samples of citizens in
two towns and a university city revealed that small-town residents
were in disagreement 70 percent of the time with what the cartoonist

intended. The university-city sample, which included more professional and academic readers, scored only slightly better, as 63 percent did not correctly perceive the cartoonists' intended messages. Several times, readers' interpretations were not only a little off, but were in direct opposition to what was intended by the cartoonist. The findings came as a surprise to many, including editorial cartoonists. On hearing the results, one cartoonist apologized, while another expressed embarrassment that he was not able to more clearly articulate his point.[19]

Political cartoons seldom appear in isolation, so Del Brinkman wondered how cartoons fared when paired with editorials. His experimental study found that cartoons accompanied by editorials were more persuasive than either alone, but that a cartoon was less persuasive than an editorial. The most effective was a cartoon that made the same argument as the accompanying editorial.[20]

Caricatures, or humorous visual representations, play prominent roles in many political cartoons. Mary Wheeler and Stephen Reed used a particularly creative method for studying them. Participants in the study were given cut-out, caricatured faces of Richard Nixon. The researchers had participants sort the faces into those they found positive and those they found negative. The researchers discovered that faces sorted in the negative category were from a time period that reflected low approval of the president, while the positive faces were from a period of high presidential approval.[21] While we are limited in the extension of this study into political cartoon effects research (disembodied heads are not the norm in editorial cartoons!), this experiment clarifies the power of caricatures to elicit affective evaluations.

Perhaps scarce political cartoon effects research reflects general neglect of political cartoons.[22] Matthew Diamond noted that cartoons "often get short shrift in the academy."[23] Then again, existing empirical effects research, combined with the complex nature of cartoons demonstrated by rhetorical and critical analyses, may reflect challenges to assessing effects—"the insurmountable barriers to controlling how readers will use a text's irony."[24] Or, it might be that many agree with the assessment by Haydon Manning and Robert Phiddian that "thinking [of the effects of political cartoons] will remain in the realms of speculation until someone is courageous (or foolish) enough to embark on extensive quantitative research on the effects of cartooning."[25] Continued empirical effects research will continue to clarify the unique and powerful effects of political cartoons.

Late Night Television Comedy

Late night television comedy is increasingly political, drawing the attention of communications scholars and political scientists. Like political cartoons, political players and journalists think that late night television comedy matters. Mandy Grunwald, former media advisor to Bill Clinton, noted: "If [comics] are making jokes about you, you have a serious political problem."[26] Jeff Simon, writing for *Buffalo News*, called late night comedy the place "where the real climate of opinion is now being forged."[27] But it appears late night comics don't give themselves much credit for affecting viewers. When asked about studies showing young viewers reportedly learning from his show, Jon Stewart of Comedy Central's *The Daily Show* replied, "I just don't think that's possible."[28]

Many young viewers think it matters. According to The Pew Research Center for the People and the Press, 61 percent of young people reported regularly or sometimes learning campaign information from comedy television, meaning late night talk shows and/or comedy shows like *The Daily Show* and *Saturday Night Live (SNL)*.[29] "My best resource [for presidential election news in 2000] has been *Saturday Night Live*," offered Chaz Duncan, a high school sophomore.[30] Young people are turning to late night comedy for political information, supplementing what they learn from traditional news.[31] But are viewers really learning anything? And are there any other effects of this late night laughter?

Some of our insight into late night comedy effects comes from studies that looked at broader genres, sometimes called new media, nontraditional news media, or soft news. This moniker usually includes late night comedy, but also includes other shows like daytime talk and entertainment news. Research exploring this genre has examined influences on candidate image,[32] political knowledge (some argue it helps,[33] others argue it may not help that much[34]), campaign interest,[35] and levels of support for U.S. policies.[36] Other research has looked specifically at late night comedy as a genre. Analyzing data from the 2004 Political Communications Study of the Pew Research Center for the People and the Press, Barry Hollander found that the younger viewers who watch late night comedy programs for political information are more likely to *recognize* than *recall* political information.[37] Finally, other research has focused on specific types of late night comedy, including talk shows, variety shows, and "fake news." These specific types of late night comedy are surveyed next.

Darrell West and John Orman labeled late night hosts "the high priests of political comedy that can make or break a politician."[38] Of course, political joking on late night talk shows did not begin with Jay Leno, David Letterman, and Conan O'Brien. Their predecessors, including Johnny Carson, "middle America's contemporary Will Rogers," broached political issues years earlier.[39] President George H. W. Bush, speaking after Carson's death in 2005, noted, "His wit and insight made Americans laugh and think, and had a profound influence on American life and entertainment."[40] Scholars have increasingly turned to late night talk shows to assess their effects, peaking with the 2000 presidential campaign.

Content analyses reveal a negative tone of monologue jokes—focusing on image over issues.[41] A recent textual analysis of late night jokes about Vice President Cheney's heart problems highlighted a case where personality was not the only target of image attacks. Even health is grounds for ridicule.[42] But beyond knowing what monologue jokes are targeting, we also have a better idea of what they seem to be doing. Dannagal Goldthwaite Young found that those with lower political knowledge were most influenced by late night comedy viewing.[43] In another study, Young assessed whether late night comedy made candidate traits more salient. While her analysis did not reveal a direct influence of late night viewing on salient character traits, Young found evidence that late night comedy viewers with lower political knowledge were most likely to reflect the negative character traits ridiculed in monologue jokes in their evaluations of these candidates.[44]

Late night comedy may be affecting more than evaluations of candidates. Patricia Moy, Michael Xenos, and Verena Hess assessed whether viewing "infotainment" programming was associated with political behaviors. The researchers found a positive association between late night comedy viewing (*The Tonight Show with Jay Leno, The Late Show with David Letterman*) and political involvement and political discussions. Viewers who were more politically sophisticated were even more likely to vote and talk to others about politics.[45] Assessing effects of communication forms, including late night comedy, Michael Pfau, Brian Houston, and Shane Semmler found that late night talk shows such as *The Tonight Show* and *The Late Show* exerted a positive influence on political expertise and attitude toward the process during the 2004 presidential campaign.[46]

Collectively, these studies reveal late night talk shows as a potentially powerful force in politics, but not necessarily in ways we might have expected. There is not much evidence for direct effects on assessments of candidates, but the comedy may have some influence on how viewers evaluate them. Moreover, it may also have an effect on their engagement in and attitude toward politics.

Other research has focused on late night comedy shows, including *Saturday Night Live* and *The Daily Show*. *Saturday Night Live* has a history of political mockery. Historical and rhetorical analyses argue that this mockery matters. Consider President Ford. Gerald Gardner concluded that *SNL*'s mockery of Ford (even his own children laughed at the clumsy caricature of their father)[47] squashed his chances in 1976.[48] Drawing on Burke's comic frame, Chris Smith and Ben Voth examined how *SNL*'s political parodies served as political argument, noting how comedic treatments of Bush and Gore in 2000 "evolved into a legitimate disseminator of information for the political and public sphere."[49] Empirical effects research on *Saturday Night Live* is rare, but some evidence suggests that shows like *SNL* had a negative influence on political knowledge and participation during the 2004 campaign.[50]

While *The Daily Show* fits into the genre of late night political comedy, many observers consider it a unique player in the field. A *Newsweek* profile noted, "Unlike late-night talk shows that traffic in Hollywood interviews and stupid pet tricks, *The Daily Show* is a fearless social satire."[51] Geoffrey Baym explained that *The Daily Show* "undoubtedly is comedy—often entertaining and at times absurd—but it is also an informative examination of politics and media practices, as well as a forum for the discussion of substantive public affairs."[52] Its viewers are also unique. "*Daily Show* viewers have higher campaign knowledge than national news viewers and newspaper readers," noted Dannagal Goldthwaite Young.[53] Young emphasized that the data assessed correlation between *Daily Show* viewership and knowledge, not causation, and that it is probably a matter of both: people with more political knowledge watch *The Daily Show*, and they learn some things while watching.[54]

We have some empirical evidence of *The Daily Show*'s attitudinal effects on viewers. Jody Baumgartner and Jonathan S. Morris found that viewing *The Daily Show*'s ridicule of 2004 presidential candidates George W. Bush and John Kerry derogated both candidates' images and led viewers to feel more cynical about government and the news media. However, viewers were more likely to report higher levels of internal efficacy, or the confidence to successfully deal with politics.[55]

Political appearances on these shows have also received scholarly attention. These appearances have not always been popular. Mandy Grunwald, Clinton's former media advisor, recalled Clinton's appearances on talk shows in 1992: "The notion a presidential candidate would go on any of these shows was denigrated, laughable. People really made fun of us."[56] Now candidates appear on programs to banter with genial hosts, or even show off a talent, like when Bill Clinton played saxophone on *The Arsenio Hall Show*. Some candidates even *become* candidates there (e.g., Arnold Schwarzenegger on *The Tonight Show* and John Edwards on *The Daily Show*).

Why the change? Probably because it works. Matt Baum found that interviews with candidates feature fewer partisan cues than conventional news, portray candidates in a decisively positive light, and slight issues. He also revealed that appearances on daytime talk shows matter to politically unaware viewers. These viewers were more likely to have higher opinions of candidates and vote for them, even if it meant crossing party lines.[57] Paul Brewer and Xiaoxia Cao revealed a positive relationship between seeing candidates on late night or political comedy shows and political knowledge, suggesting that candidate appearances may help promote the democratic process.[58] Using data from the 2000 National Annenberg Election Survey, Patricia Moy, Michael Xenos, and Verena Hess revealed that George W. Bush's appearance on *The Late Show* seems to have led viewers to rely more on character in their overall evaluations of him.[59]

From conventional late night talk shows to variety shows to "fake news," there is evidence that humor matters. After reviewing political humor effects research in political cartoons and late night comedy, we can now turn to some future directions for effects research. We will start with the two forms already surveyed, cartoons and late night television comedy, before turning to other venues of political humor.

Directions for Political Humor Effects Research

Political Cartoons

There are several directions to pursue with political cartoon effects research. Scholars can continue to assess cartoons' overall effects on attitudes toward those being caricatured, but can also increase the scope to other types of effects, like those pursued by late night comedy effects researchers. Might political cartoons also have effects on cynicism, faith in the media, political involvement, political knowledge, and so on?

As Edward Lordan observes in his review of political cartoons, it is difficult to determine the effects of cartoons in isolation.[60] One study looked at cartoons along with editorials[61]; future experimental research should continue to explore context in this manner. For example, what occurs when multiple cartoons appear on the same page but with counter-attitudinal interpretations? Would multiple cartoons be more influential than a single editorial? Political cartoon researchers can also further consider the political knowledge of readers in assessing effects, as late night comedy researchers have done.[62] Edward Lordan observed that "the editorial cartoon requires a relatively sophisticated audience to be successful."[63] Effects researchers should find out how much political knowledge matters with effects of political cartoons.

Comic strips have received even less empirical analysis than editorial cartoons. Scholars have noted that political comic strips, such as Garry Trudeau's *Doonesbury*, are different from political cartoons.[64] "*Doonesbury* is perhaps a truer indicator of our culture than any other comic strip," argued Christopher Lamb.[65] Perhaps comic strips like *Doonesbury* do more than reflect, but also affect their readers in ways effects research could reveal.

Late Night Television Comedy

While it is the focus of increasing scholarship, late night comedy has not been exhausted as an object of study. Monologue jokes have received analyses, as have candidate appearances. However, the skits and clips on talk shows have not received much specific attention. Consider a recurring feature on *The Late Show*, "Great Moments in Presidential Speeches." During this segment, Letterman plays clips of eloquent past presidential speeches, and then ends with a clip of President Bush bungling a phrase. "In many ways on Letterman," said Robert Thompson, director of Syracuse University's Center for the Study of Popular Television, "the president is telling the joke about himself."[66] Likewise, Conan O'Brien has a recurring skit that uses politicians' faces on a large-screen TV, but with actors' mouths mimicking their voices in conversations with the host. Marshall Sella called these "[t]he most subtle—that is, most exquisitely biased—caricatures."[67] Empirical research should see if these unique types of political humor have influences that differ from conventional monologue jokes or actual appearances.

New late night comedy shows also warrant attention, including *The Colbert Report*, a spin-off of Comedy Central's *The Daily Show*. Called "jujitsu satire" by one television critic,[68] *The Colbert Report* parodies political talk shows like Bill O'Reilly's *The O'Reilly Factor*, featuring a satirical combination of monologue, recurring skits, guest interviews, and often, appearances by politicians. Some politicians believe they benefit from appearing on the show. "When people who are 25 who have never voted for you think you are funny because you did the show, that's instant validity," said Rep. Jack Kingston (R-GA).[69] Others are not so quick with praise. Rep. Barney Frank (D-MA), who was unhappy about his own experience with the show, thinks it "degrades politics. It's not a good way to engage young people."[70] Others simply are not sure. Interviewed about her experience, Rep. Donna Christensen (D-VI) remarked, "Most of the time, you're trying to project your very best image, and this could leave you vulnerable. Now that you're asking me, I'm kind of wondering why I did agree to it so quickly."[71]

We have evidence that not all late night comedy functions in the same way.[72] What differences would we find between candidate appearances on traditional late night talk shows, such as *The Tonight Show*, and "fake" news interview shows such as *The Colbert Report*? Candidate appearance effects research would benefit from distinguishing the "good" from the "bad." For example, many television critics and political pundits considered John Kerry's first appearance on *The Tonight Show* (an appearance that had him bantering with Triumph the Insult Comic Dog, a sock puppet) a disaster.[73] Similar assessments were made of an appearance by George W. Bush on

The Late Show in 2000.[74] Effects research can offer clarity as to when appearances work for candidate image, when they do not, and why.

Researchers should also further assess what occurs when late night comedy clips are shown during conventional news broadcasts. *Saturday Night Live* skits commonly popped up on traditional news outlets during Campaign 2000,[75] and ABC's Sunday morning political talk show, *This Week*, featured a series of segments from humor-based comedy programs titled "Funny Pages." An experiment conducted by Dolf Zillman and his colleagues raises interesting implications for comedic content featured on conventional news programs. In their experiment, when newscasts ended with humorous content, viewers were less worried about the preceding serious news stories and found the issues less severe. The researchers used a humorous clip of Jay Leno, David Letterman, and *SNL* actors making fun of politicians as their experimental material for the humorous content, showing yet another potential effect of late night comedy political humor.[76]

Entertainment Television

There is growing scholarly interest in entertainment television. Robert Lichter, Linda Lichter, and Daniel Amundson analyzed how government officials were portrayed on entertainment television (including comedy shows like *The Simpsons* and *Spin City*) and found a predominance of negative portrayals.[77] Michael Pfau, Patricia Moy, and Erin Szabo found some positive relationships with situation comedy viewing and attitudes toward some aspects of government,[78] and other research examined how prime-time television viewing can affect trust in government.[79] Lance Holbert and his colleagues have empirically investigated entertainment television viewing effects on myriad political issues: environmental attitudes and behaviors,[80] portrayals of the president,[81] women's rights,[82] and capital punishment and gun rights.[83] Holbert also created a nine-part typology for continued study of the distinct genres of entertainment television. Three parts of his typology include programming that often features, explicitly or implicitly, political humor: traditional satire (e.g., *The Daily Show*), situation comedy satire (e.g., *The Simpsons*), and entertainment talk show interviews with politicians (e.g., Leno and Letterman). Holbert notes that there is a growing body of empirical research in some of these areas, but not all, including situation comedies.[84]

Indeed, a later chapter in this volume by Peter L. Francia examines the evolution of political-based situational comedies. As Francia argues, situation comedies can matter in a political context, and often reflect the current state of American political and popular culture. Even animated situational comedies can have meaning. In this regard, *The Simpsons* is particularly promising.[85] Bruce Williams and Michael Delli Carpini offered: "We may well conclude that the political relevance of a cartoon character like Lisa Simpson is as important as the professional norms of Dan Rather, Tom Brokaw, or Peter Jennings."[86] John Alberti argued that this show "represents some of the most daring cultural and political satire in television history."[87] Animated political humor may underscore the complexity of some political and social problems,[88] and by leaving many conclusions open-ended, the show "actively solicits political engagement."[89] Empirical research could further complement our understanding of the effects of television programming like *The Simpsons*.[90] Later in this book, Nicholas P. Guehlstorf, Lars K. Hallstrom, and Jonathan S. Morris highlight the rich array of various forms of humor prevalent in *The Simpsons*. In their estimation, not only is *The Simpsons* critical of politicians in its humor—it is also quick to highlight the political flaws and hypocrisies of the American mass public.

Other Print Media

Cartoons and comics are not the only places we find political humor in newspapers. Editorials and columnists often use humor to discuss political issues. Here, we have some effects research from which to build. James Powell's experimental research found political satire was not very effective in changing the attitudes of highly involved subjects, but was effective in bolstering attitudes against subsequent attempts at counter-persuasion.[91] We may find order effects of humorous newspaper columns, meaning that *when* an editorial is read has impacts on effects.

Then there are humorous newspapers and other publications that periodically feature political humor, from *Entertainment Weekly* (e.g., pitting rapper Lil' Kim against North Korean Dictator Kim Jong Il)[92] to the more highbrowed *New Yorker* (e.g., a commentary regarding the success and appeal of conservative "red-neck" humor).[93] Perhaps *The Onion* is the best-known contemporary satirical newspaper in this country. This newspaper and its online version have garnered the attention and laughs of readers with what the *American Journalism Review* called "its often hilarious, pitch-perfect parody of newswriting conventions."[94] In her review of one of *The Onion*'s ancestors, the humor magazine *Ballyhoo* launched in 1931, Margaret McFadden concluded: "The case of *Ballyhoo* suggests the tremendous power of humor to debunk or reinforce cultural norms and ideologies and therefore to have profound cultural and political effects."[95] Empirical effects research of humorous periodicals could offer empirical support to claims like these.

Humorous political books are popular, but empirical assessments of their effects are rare. A Pew Internet & American Life Project report indicated that 16 percent of adult Americans read a political book during the 2004 presidential campaign. The report noted that Comedy Central's Jon Stewart had a best-selling book during this time, *America (The Book): A Citizen's Guide to Democracy Inaction*, which satirized civics textbooks.[96] Timothy Weiskel observed: "Capturing and publishing collected 'Bushisms' has become a modest industry in its own right."[97] Discovering what effects these books have, if any, on political attitudes, values, and behaviors would be a welcome addition to the literature on political humor effects.

Film

Humorous political film is another rich field for effects researchers. John Nelson argued that "attention to popular films can help us learn how genre conventions communicate politics."[98] But it has received scant attention. William Elliott and William Schenck-Hamlin noted that film, in general, has been reduced to "a second class medium for communication research."[99] Their own experimental research found some effects of watching a political film, *All the President's Men*.[100] Contemporary political comedy films include 2006's *American Dreamz*, which presented an *American Idol* spoof involving the president as a guest judge, and 2004's *Team America: World Police*, a puppet action film that skewered action movies and political issues. Besides comedies, other film genres feature at least some political humor.

Consider Michael Moore's 2004 documentary, *Fahrenheit 9/11*. According to a Pew Internet & American Life Project report, 31 percent of adult Americans watched a political documentary film about the 2004 election. Michael Cornfield, senior research consultant, noted that this was unique: "Rarely do voters in the digital age spend a long time paying close attention to a single message about an upcoming election."[101] While *Fahrenheit 9/11* is not a comedy, it did feature prominent comedic elements. G. Thomas Goodnight said it "packed a whallop of satire."[102] We also have some empirical evidence of the effect of this film on viewers. Lance Holbert and Glenn Hansen's experimental study revealed that *Fahrenheit 9/11* influenced viewers' affective ambivalence toward President Bush, finding evidence of an interaction among watching the film, political party, and need for closure.[103] This is but one area of potential future scholarship relating to film effects.

The Internet

Another area that warrants more scrutiny from empirical assessments of effects is political humor on the Internet. We find similarities to the type of political comedy we find on "fake news" programs such as *The Daily Show* and *The Colbert Report*, as well as *Saturday Night Live*'s "Weekend Update." As Brad Reagan put it, "Dummied-up 'official' reports are the stock in trade of numerous humor sites, whether phony news stories, mock memos or parodies of commercials."[104] Kirsten Foot and Steven Schneider's overview of election-oriented Web sites during the 2000 presidential election campaigns included a section they labeled "carnival," offering a smorgasbord of political humor Web content that warrants further study and analysis.[105] Effects of this type of political comedy are, for the most part, unknown, although there is some speculation regarding its impact. Karl Frish, Howard Dean's multimedia communications director in 2004, noted that the volume of Dean-scream parodies following his infamous yell after the Iowa primary "certainly quickened the death" of his campaign.[106] D. Travers Scott proposed that academics turn their attention to these political e-mail *virals*, or messages that are designed to pass to others.[107]

Speeches, Campaign Advertisements, and Other Political Events

Before turning to the use of humor in political speeches, we will consider another type of "speech" that features political humor:

political comedy routines. While comedians with late night television shows have been studied, other comics have received little
attention.[108] Stand-up comics (e.g., Mark Russell, Janeane Garofalo,
Dennis Miller, and Al Franken), political comedy troupes (e.g., San
Francisco Mime Troupe), and political impersonators (e.g., Andy
Borowitz's John Kerry and Steve Bridges' George W. Bush) give live
performances that are often broadcast on television. Critics seem to
think these "politicomics"[109] have effects on their audiences. Reviewing one of Bill Maher's shows for *Toronto Star*, Richard Ouzounian
notes that the "[i]nitially shocked crowd [was] won over by edge and
wit."[110] Comics hope they have effects, too. Paul D'Angelo suggests
that "if I can make people laugh and at the same time educate them,
that's a real challenge, and it validates both views."[111] We have some
empirical evidence for the impact of humor routines from James
Powell's study of how Art Buchwald's speeches affected attitudes.
He found that the comical treatment of an issue "inoculated" some
viewers against subsequent serious treatments of the issues.[112] But
much more is to be studied in terms of how stand-up comedy affects
its audiences. Whoopi Goldberg's fundraiser speech for John Kerry's
campaign during the summer of 2004 was controversial after her
use of sexual puns to mock President Bush.[113] It cost her a Slim-Fast
endorsement deal[114]—but does humor like this have other effects?

Of course, politicians use humor in their own speeches and campaign events as well. Gerald Ford was the first president to hire a
professional comedy writer solely to write one-liners, jokes, and
anecdotes,[115] but he certainly wasn't the first or last politician to try
humor. Gerald Gardner argued that political humor has influence,
including salvaging an image when used well (e.g., Reagan, Kennedy,
Johnson), and derogating an image when used poorly (e.g., Carter,
Ford) or not used enough (e.g., Mondale, Nixon).[116] Empirical effects
research can further assess this power, both as a persuasive function and as an influence on image. Charles Gruner's early experiment found that satire was ineffective in changing attitudes, and
furthermore, derogated the image of the speaker.[117] His follow-up
study supported the original finding that satire was not very effective in changing attitudes, but he did not find derogation of the
speaker's image.[118] Later, he reasoned that the key issue is whether
the humor is considered appropriate.[119] Other research has found the
use of humor to decrease image.[120] In short, political humor does not
always work as planned. As Don Nilsen noted, "like other powerful

weapons, [humor] can backfire."[121] Continued effects research can clarify when and why it works, and what it means when it doesn't.

Other political events provide forums for humor. David Paletz called the annual Gridiron dinner "one of Washington D.C.'s strangest events."[122] At this event, politicians mingle with journalists, humorously approaching serious topics of the day. As Linton Weeks noted, although journalists are not supposed to report on what goes on there, "information does leak out."[123] The White House Correspondents Association dinner is also known as a humorous event. At the 2006 event, Comedy Central's Stephen Colbert delivered a keynote speech that received rants and raves. It became one of the most viewed clips on the Internet and rose to the top of iTunes charts.[124] It also got a lot of play on blogs.[125] Additionally, President Bush gave a speech that parodied himself by speaking simultaneously next to an impersonator. This skit was generally well-received and was also replayed extensively in the mainstream media. While the live audience for these events is relatively small, clips of humorous moments are often replayed during news broadcasts or shared via streaming clips on the Internet. These clips can serve as unique experimental materials for political humor effects researchers.

Humor used in campaign advertising also warrants further study by effects researchers. L. Patrick Devlin's survey of presidential campaign commercials during the 2000 election revealed a number of humorous television advertisements for third-party candidates. Using a reactive focus group composed of undergraduate college students, Devlin found that the humorous ads were most popular with her students.[126] We even find political humor in presidential candidates' videocassettes, known as "meet the candidate videos." Bill Bradley included a joke he told in a campaign speech, and Al Gore included a segment of his appearance on *The Late Show with David Letterman*.[127]

The broad categories surveyed here miss many other forms of political humor, including political bumper stickers,[128] lapel buttons,[129] political graffiti,[130] word-of-mouth political jokes,[131] and humorous political stories.[132] Any of these, and many more, could be intriguing areas of study for effects researchers delving even further into political humor.

Conclusion

This survey of effects research highlights a high proportion of television studies. This may be attributed to the characteristics of television and political humor. Political humor as a genre is usually negative. Theoretical musings about political humor[133] and content analyses[134] alike reveal that attacks on character and image are common. It is perhaps little surprise that so much political humor effects research turns to television as the medium of choice. Television's visual nature makes character issues salient,[135] and television allows viewers to literally peer into the otherwise private lives of politicians.[136] Further, this is where most people get most of their political information.[137] If political humor is most likely to target character, television would be the best place to do so. But as this review highlighted, television is not the only place to find political humor, and researchers should continue to explore the effects of political humor in all of its venues.

While the latter part of this chapter focused on venues for political humor, continuing effects research should also look at different types of political humor. It is not all the "badoom-boom formula favored by late-night comedians."[138] Some political humor is harsh and biting, while other humor is warm and lighthearted.[139] It can support or subvert authority.[140] Hans Speier notes how political humor can be used as both a weapon and as a defense.[141] Different senses of humor also warrant further scrutiny regarding political humor effects. Glenn Wilson's review of psychological humor reaction research finds distinct differences in how conservatives and liberals respond to different types of humor.[142] Researchers have offered helpful taxonomies to guide such research, including David Paletz's categories of targets, focus, social acceptability, and presentation,[143] and John Meyer's analysis of the four basic functions of humor.[144] For example, Michael Nitz and his colleagues used Paletz's work to guide their content analysis of late night humor.[145] Political humor effects research can also be guided by taxonomies such as these.

Some observers are clearly concerned about the potential effects of political humor. Noting that young people reportedly get political news from late night comedy shows, Timothy Weiskel warned: "We could perhaps all laugh if the results were not so tragic and devastating in the world at large."[146] Continuing empirical research will help as we appraise effects of political humor. When we find ways humor hurts the political process, we can find ways to fix it. When we find ways that it is helping, we can all laugh a little easier.

Notes

1. Gerald Gardner, *The Mocking of the President: A History of Campaign Humor from Ike to Ronnie* (Detroit: Wayne State University Press, 1988); Michael Nitz, Alyson Cypher, Tom Reichert, and James E. Mueller, "Candidates as Comedy: Political Presidential Humor on Late-Night Television Shows," in *The Millenium Election: Communication in the 2000 Campaign*, eds. Lynda Lee Kaid, John C. Tedesco, Dianne G. Bystrom, and Mitchell S. McKinney (Lanham: Rowman & Littlefield, 2003), 165–175.
2. Don L. F. Nilsen, "The Social Functions of Political Humor," *Journal of Popular Culture* 24 (1990): 35–47.
3. Gage William Chapel, "Humor in the White House: And [sic] Interview with Presidential Speechwriter Robert Orben," *Communication Quarterly* 26 (1978): 44–49.
4. Owen H. Lynch, "Humorous Communication: Finding a Place for Humor in Communication Research," *Communication Theory* 12 (2002): 423–445.
5. Martin J. Medhurst and Michael A. Desousa, "Political Cartoons as Rhetorical Form: A Taxonomy of Graphic Discourse," *Communication Monographs* 48 (1981): 197–236.
6. Of course, not all political cartoons use humor. Matthew Diamond notes this important reminder: "To be sure, humor and satire, comedy and irony are all frequent elements of political cartoons, but they are not necessary ones." Matthew Diamond, "No Laughing Matter: Post-September 11 Political Cartoons in Arab/Muslim Newspapers," *Political Communication* 19 (2002): 251–272.
7. William Koetzle and Thomas L. Brunell, "Lip-Reading, Draft-Dodging, and Perot-noia," *Press/Politics* 1 (1996): 94–115.
8. Audrey Handelman, "Political Cartoonists as They Saw Themselves During the 1950s," *Journalism Quarterly* 61 (1984): 137–141.
9. Joan L. Conners, "Hussein as Enemy: The Persian Gulf War in Political Cartoons," *Press/Politics* 3 (1998): 96–114.
10. Steve Plumb, "Politicians as Superheroes: The Subversion of Political Authority Using a Pop Cultural Icon in the Cartoons of Steve Bell," *Media, Culture & Society* 26 (2004): 432–439.
11. Harry Katz, "An Historic Look at Political Cartoons," *Nieman Reports* 58 (2004): 44–46.
12. Ibid.
13. David N. Ammons, John C. King, and Jerry L. Yeric, "Unapproved Imagemakers: Political Cartoonists' Topic Selection, Objectives and Perceived Restrictions," *Newspaper Research Journal* 9 (1988): 79–90.

14. Edward J. Lordan, *Politics, Ink: How America's Cartoonists Skewer Politicians, from King George III to George Dubya* (Lanham: Rowman & Littlefield, 2006).
15. Abel Mattos, "Utilizing the Political Cartoon in the Classroom," *History Teacher* 5 (1972): 20–27.
16. Patrick Oliphant, "Why Political Cartoons Are Losing Their Influence," *Nieman Reports* (2004): 25–27.
17. Lordan, *Politics, Ink*.
18. Matthew C. Morrison, "The Role of the Political Cartoonist in Image Making," *Central States Speech Journal* 20 (1969): 252–260.
19. LeRoy Carl, "Editorial Cartoons Fail to Reach Many Viewers," *Journalism Quarterly* 45 (1968): 533–535.
20. Del Brinkman, "Do Editorial Cartoons and Editorials Change Opinions?" *Journalism Quarterly* 45 (1968): 724–726.
21. Mary E. Wheeler and Stephen K. Reed, "Response to Before and After Watergate Caricatures," *Journalism Quarterly* 52 (1975): 134–136.
22. W. A. Coupe, "Observations on a Theory of Political Caricature," *Comparative Studies in Society and History* 11 (1969): 79–95.
23. Diamond, "No Laughing Matter," 252.
24. Kathryn M. Olson and Clark D. Olson, "Beyond Strategy: A Reader-Centered Analysis of Irony's Dual Persuasive Uses," *Quarterly Journal of Speech* 90 (2004): 24–52.
25. Haydon Manning and Robert Phiddian, "In Defence of the Political Cartoonists' Licence to Mock," *Australian Review of Public Affairs* 5 (2004): 25–42.
26. Howard Kurtz, "Amid the Yuks About Clinton, Serious Information," *Gazette*, January 30, 1999.
27. Jeff Simon, "Check Late-Night Hot Air to Gauge Which Way Wind Blows," *Buffalo News*, November 5, 2000.
28. Marc Peyser and Sarah Childress, "Red, White & Funny," *Newsweek*, December 29, 2004, 70–77.
29. "Cable and Internet Loom Large in Fragmented Political News Universe," *The Pew Research Center for the People and the Press*, January 11, 2004. http://people-press.org/reports/pdf/200.pdf.
30. Maureen Downey and Joe Earle, "Bush, Gore Not Rocking the Vote with Young Americans," *Atlanta Journal and Constitution*, November 5, 2000.
31. Dannagal G. Young and Russell M. Tisinger, "Dispelling Late Night Myths: News Consumption Among Late-Night Comedy Viewers and the Predictors of Exposure to Various Late-Night Shows," *Press/Politics* 11 (2006): 113–134.

32. Michael Pfau and William P. Eveland Jr., "Influence of Traditional and Non-Traditional News Media in the 1992 Election Campaign," *Western Journal of Communication* 60 (1996): 214–232; Michael Pfau, Jaeho Cho, and Kristen Chong, "Impact of Communication Forms in Presidential Campaigns: Influences on Candidate Perceptions and Democratic Process," *Press/Politics* 6 (2001): 88–105.
33. Matthew A. Baum, "Soft News and Political Knowledge: Evidence of Absence or Absence of Evidence?" *Political Communication* 20 (2003): 173–190; Steve H. Chaffee, Xinshu Zhao, and Glenn Leshner, "Political Knowledge and the Campaign Media of 1992," *Communication Research* 21 (1994): 305–324.
34. Markus Prior, "Any Good News in Soft News? The Impact of Soft News Preference on Political Knowledge," *Political Communication* 20 (2003): 149–171; Barry Hollander, "The New News and the 1992 Presidential Campaign: Perceived vs. Actual Political Knowledge," *Journalism & Mass Communication Quarterly* 72 (1995): 786–798.
35. Jack M. McLeod, Zhongshi Guo, Katie Daily, et al., "The Impact of Traditional and Nontraditional Media Forms in the 1992 Presidential Election," *Journalism & Mass Communication Quarterly* 73 (1996): 401–416.
36. Matthew Baum, "Circling the Wagons: Soft News and Isolationalism in American Public Opinion," *International Studies Quarterly* 48 (2004): 313–38; Matthew Baum, "Sex, Lies, and War: How Soft News Brings Foreign Policy to the Inattentive Public," *The American Political Science Review* 96 (2002): 91–109.
37. Barry Hollander, "Late-Night Learning: Do Entertainment Programs Increase Political Campaign Knowledge for Young Viewers?" *Journal of Broadcasting & Electronic Media* 49 (2005): 402–415.
38. Darrell M. West and John Orman, *Celebrity Politics* (Upper Saddle River: Prentice Hall, 2003).
39. Gardner, *The Mocking of the President*, 77.
40. Roderick Nordell, "Carson's Legend," *Christian Science Monitor*, January 25, 2005.
41. David Niven, S. Robert Lichter, and Daniel Amundson, "The Political Content of Late Night Comedy," *Press/Politics* 8 (2003): 118–133; Dannagal Goldthwaite Young, "Late-Night Comedy in Election 2000: Its Influence on Candidate Trait Ratings and the Moderating Effects of Political Knowledge and Partisanship," *Journal of Broadcasting & Electronic Media* 48 (2004): 1–22; "Daily Show Viewers Knowledgeable About Presidential Campaign, National Annenberg Election Survey Shows," *Annenberg Public Policy Center*, September 21, 2004.
42. Josh Compton, "Serious as a Heart Attack: Health-Related Content of Late-Night Comedy Television," *Health Communication* 19, no. 2 (2006): 143–151.

43. Young, "Late-Night Comedy in Election 2000."
44. Dannagal Goldthwaite Young, "Late-Night Comedy and the Salience of the Candidates' Caricatured Traits in the 2000 Election," *Mass Communication & Society* 9 (2006): 339–366.
45. Patricia Moy, Michael A. Xenos, and Verena K. Hess, "Communication and Citizenship: Mapping the Political Effects of 'Infotainment,'" *Mass Communication & Society* 8 (2005): 111–131.
46. Michael Pfau, J. Brian Houston, and Shane M. Semmler, "Presidential Election Campaigns and American Democracy: The Relationship Between Communication Use and Normative Outcomes," *American Behavioral Scientist* 49 (2005): 48–62.
47. Gardner, *The Mocking of the President*, 72.
48. Ibid, 75.
49. Chris Smith and Ben Voth, "The Role of Humor in Political Argument: How 'Strategery' and 'Lockboxes' Changed a Political Campaign," *Argumentation and Advocacy* 39 (2002): 110–129.
50. Pfau, Houston, and Semmler, "Presidential Election Campaigns and American Democracy."
51. Peyser and Childress, "Red, White & Funny."
52. Geoffrey Baym, "The Daily Show: Discursive Integration and the Reinvention of Political Journalism," *Political Communication* 22 (2005): 259–276.
53. National Annenberg Election Survey, "Daily Show Viewers Knowledgeable About Presidential Campaign," September 21, 2004. http://www.annenbergpublicpolicycenter.org/naes/2004_03_late-night-knowledge-2_9-21_pr.pdf.
54. Ibid.
55. Jody Baumgartner and Jonathan S. Morris, "The Daily Show Effect: Candidate Evaluations, Efficacy, and American Youth," *American Politics Research* 34 (2006): 341–367.
56. Kurtz, "Amid the Yuks About Clinton, Serious Information."
57. Matthew A. Baum, "Talking the Vote: Why Presidential Candidates Hit the Talk Show Circuit," *American Journal of Politics* 49 (2005): 213–234.
58. Paul R. Brewer and Xiaoxia Cao, "Candidate Appearances on Soft News Shows and Public Knowledge About Primary Campaigns," *Journal of Broadcasting & Electronic Media* 50 (2006): 18–35.
59. Patricia Moy, Michael A. Xenos, and Verena K. Hess, "Priming Effects of Late-Night Comedy," *International Journal of Public Opinion Research* 18 (2005): 198–210.
60. Lordan, *Politics, Ink.*
61. Brinkman, "Do Editorial Cartoons and Editorials Change Opinions?"
62. Young, "Late-Night Comedy in Election 2000."
63. Lordan, *Politics, Ink.*

64. Denise M. Bostdorff, "Making Light of James Watt: A Burkean Approach to the Form and Attitude of Political Cartoons," *Quarterly Journal of Speech* 73 (1987): 43–59.

65. Christopher Lamb, "Changing with the Times: The World According to 'Doonesbury,'" *Journal of Popular Culture* 23 (1990): 113–129.

66. Robert Laurence, "President as Political Punch Line," *Copley News Service*, May 4, 2006.

67. Marshall Sella, "The Stiff Guy vs. The Dumb Guy," *New York Times Magazine*, September 24, 2000.

68. Alessandra Stanley, "Bringing Out the Absurdity of the News," *New York Times*, October 25, 2005.

69. Susan Milligan, "TV Show Puts Lawmakers on Comedic Hot Seat," *Boston Globe*, March 27, 2006.

70. Ibid.

71. Matea Gold, "The Truly Serious Appear on 'The Colbert Report,'" *Los Angeles Times*, March 27, 2006.

72. Moy, Xenos, and Hess, "Communication and Citizenship."

73. Joshua Green, "Funny Business," *Atlantic Monthly*, May 2004.

74. "Bush to Appear Again on Letterman," *New York Times*, October 3, 2000.

75. Smith and Voth, "The Role of Humor in Political Argument."

76. Dolf Zillmann, Rhonda Gibson, Virginia L. Ordman, and Charles F. Aust, "Effects of Upbeat Stories in Broadcast News," *Journal of Broadcasting & Electronic Media* 38 (1994): 65–78.

77. S. Robert Lichter, Linda S. Lichter, and Daniel Amundson, "Government Goes Down the Tube: Images of Government in TV Entertainment, 1955–1998," *Press/Politics* 5 (2000): 96–103.

78. Michael Pfau, Patricia Moy, and Erin A. Szabo, "Influence of Prime-Time Television Programming on Perceptions of the Federal Government," *Mass Communication & Society* 4 (2001): 437–454.

79. Patricia Moy and Michael Pfau, *With Malice Toward All? The Media and Public Confidence in Democratic Institutions* (Westport, CT: Praeger, 2000).

80. R. Lance Holbert, Nojin Kwak, and Dhavan V. Shah, "Environment Concern, Patterns of Television Viewing, and Pro-Environmental Behaviors: Integrating Models of Media Consumption and Effects," *Journal of Broadcasting & Electronic Media* 47 (2003): 177–196.

81. R. Lance Holbert, Owen Pillion, David A. Tschida, et al., "*The West Wing* as Endorsement of the American Presidency: Expanding the Domains of Priming in Political Communication," *Journal of Communication* 53 (2003): 427–443; R. Lance Holbert, David A. Tschida,

Maria Dixon, et al., "*The West Wing* and Depictions of the American Presidency: Expanding the Domains of Framing in Political Communication," *Communication Quarterly* 53 (2005): 505–522.

82. R. Lance Holbert, Dhavan V. Shah, and Nojin Kwak, "Political Implications of Prime-Time Drama and Sitcom Use: Genres of Representation and Opinions Concerning Women's Rights," *Journal of Communication* 53 (2003): 45–60.

83. R. Lance Holbert, Dhavan V. Shah, and Nojin Kwak, "Fear, Authority, and Justice: The Influence of TV News, Police Reality, and Crime Drama Viewing on Endorsements of Capital Punishment and Gun Ownership," *Journalism & Mass Communication Quarterly* 81 (2004): 343–363.

84. R. Lance Holbert, "A Typology for the Study of Entertainment Television and Politics," *American Behavioral Scientist* 49 (2005): 436–453.

85. Paul A. Cantor, "The Simpsons: Atomistic Politics and the Nuclear Family," *Political Theory* 27 (1999): 734–749.

86. Bruce A. Williams and Michael X. Delli Carpini, "Heeeeeeeeeeeere's Democracy!" *Chronicle of Higher Education*, April 19, 2002.

87. John Alberti, "Introduction," in *Leaving Springfield: The Simpsons and the Possibility of Oppositional Culture*, ed. John Alberti (Detroit: Wayne State University Press, 2004), xi–xxxii.

88. Kevin J. H. Dettmar, "Countercultural Literacy: Learning Irony with The Simpsons," in *Leaving Springfield: The Simpsons and the Possibility of Oppositional Culture*, ed. John Alberti (Detroit: Wayne State University Press, 2004), 85–106.

89. Vincent Brook, "Myth or Consequences: Ideological Fault Lines in The Simpsons," in *Leaving Springfield: The Simpsons and the Possibility of Oppositional Culture*, ed. John Alberti (Detroit: Wayne State University Press, 2004), 172–196.

90. Holbert, "A Typology for the Study of Entertainment Television and Politics."

91. James Larry Powell, "The Effects of Ego Involvement on Responses to Editorial Satire," *Central States Speech Journal* 26 (1975): 34–38.

92. Vanessa Juarez, "Lil' Kim vs. Kim Jong Il," *Entertainment Weekly*, July 21, 2006.

93. Tad Friend, "Blue-Collar Gold," *New Yorker*, July 10 & 17, 2006.

94. Kathtyn S. Wenner, "Peeling *The Onion*," *American Journalism Review* 24 (2002): 48–53.

95. Margaret McFadden, "'WARNING—Do Not Risk Federal Arrest by Looking Glum!'": Ballyhoo Magazine and the Cultural Politics of Early 1930s Humor," *The Journal of American Culture*, 26 (2003): 124–133.

96. "'Fahrenheit 9-11' Had Broad Political Reach," *Pew Internet & American Life Project*, January 24, 2005. http://www.pewinternet.org/pdfs/PIP_Politicaldocus.pdf.

97. Timothy Weiskel, "From Sidekick to Sideshow—Celebrity, Entertainment, and the Politics of Distraction: Why Americans are 'Sleepwalking Toward the End of the Earth,'" *American Behavioral Scientist* 49 (2005): 393–409.

98. John S. Nelson, "Horror Films Face Political Evils in Everyday Life," *Political Communication* 22 (2005): 381–386.

99. William R. Elliott and William J. Schenck-Hamlin, "Film, Politics, and the Press: The Influence of 'All the President's Men,'" *Journalism Quarterly* 56 (1979): 546–553.

100. Ibid.

101. "'Fahrenheit 9-11' Had Broad Political Reach."

102. G. Thomas Goodnight, "*The Passion of the Christ* Meets *Fahrenheit 9/11*: A Study in Celebrity Advocacy," *American Behavioral Scientist* 49 (2005): 410–435.

103. R. Lance Holbert and Glenn J. Hansen, "Fahrenheit 9-11, Need for Closure and the Priming of Affective Ambivalence: An Assessment of Intra-Affective Structures by Party Identification," *Human Communication Research* 32 (2006): 109–129.

104. Brad Reagan, "This Just In: Fake News Is Big Laughs," *Wall Street Journal*, July 15, 2002.

105. Kirsten A. Foot and Steven M. Schneider, "Online Action in Campaign 2000: An Exploratory Analysis of the U.S. Political Web Sphere," *Journal of Broadcasting & Electronic Media* 46 (2002): 222–244.

106. Bret Schulte, "There's Something Funny Going On," *U.S. News & World Report*, September 6, 2004.

107. D. Travers Scott, "Protest Email as Alternative Media in the 2004 U.S. Presidential Campaign," *Westminster Papers in Communication and Culture* 2 (2005): 51–71.

108. Bernard Grofman examines the political satire of stand-up comic David Frye. Bernard Grofman, "Richard Nixon as Pinocchio, Richard II, and Santa Claus: The Use of Allusion in Political Satire," *Journal of Politics* 51 (1989): 165–173.

109. Geoff Edgers, "Politics? Or Comedy?," *Boston Globe*, July 25, 2004.

110. Richard Ouzounian, "Maher Takes No Prisoners," *Toronto Star*, May 7, 2003.

111. Dean Johnson, "Comic Meets Terror with Humor," *Boston Herald*, January 18, 2002.

112. James Larry Powell, "Satirical Persuasion and Topic Salience," *Southern Speech Communication Journal* 42 (1977): 151–162.

113. Michael Cornfield, "'The Daily Show' Revolution," *Campaigns & Elections*, September 2005.
114. Edgers, "Politics? Or Comedy?"
115. Gardner, *The Mocking of the President*.
116. Ibid.
117. Charles R. Gruner, "An Experimental Study of Satire as Persuasion," *Speech Monographs* 32 (1965): 149–153.
118. Charles R. Gruner, "A Further Experimental Study of Satire as Persuasion," *Speech Monographs* 33 (1966): 184–185.
119. Charles R. Gruner, "Effect of Humor on Speaker Ethos and Audience Information Gain," *Journal of Communication* 17 (1967): 228–233.
120. Pat M. Taylor, "An Experimental Study of Humor and Ethos," *The Southern Speech Communication Journal* 39 (1974): 359–366.
121. Nilsen, "The Social Functions of Political Humor," 45.
122. David L. Paletz, "Political Humor and Authority: From Support to Subversion," *International Political Science Review* 11 (1990): 483–93.
123. Linton Weeks, "The Gridiron's Betters, Skewered With a Butter Knife," *Washington Post*, March 12, 2006.
124. Tom Feran, "True Jesters Are Power Brokers," *Plain Dealer*, May 26, 2006.
125. Troy McCullough, "Traditional Media Miss the Mark on Colbert Speech," *Baltimore Sun*, May 7, 2006.
126. L. Patrick Devlin, "Contrasts in Presidential Campaign Commercials of 2000," *American Behavioral Scientist* 44 (2001): 2338–2369.
127. John Parmelee, "Presidential Primary Videocassettes: How Candidates in the 2000 U.S. Presidential Primary Elections Framed Their Early Campaigns," *Political Communication* 19 (2002): 317–331.
128. Gardner, *The Mocking of the President*, 13.
129. Arthur P. Dudden, "The Record of Political Humor," *American Quarterly* 37 (1985): 50–70.
130. Emma Otta, "Graffiti in the 1990s: A Study of Inscriptions on Restroom Walls," *The Journal of Social Psychology* 133 (1993): 589–590.
131. Alan Dundes, "Six Inches from the Presidency: The Gary Hart Jokes as Public Opinion," *Western Folklore* 48 (1989): 43–51.
132. Dean L. Yarwood, "Humorous Stories and the Identification of Social Norms: The Senate Club," *Administration & Society* 35 (2003): 9–28.
133. Charles E. Schultz, *Political Humor: From Aristophanes to Sam Ervin* (London: Associated University Press, 1977).
134. Niven, Lichter, and Amundson, "The Political Content of Late Night Comedy"; Young, "Late-Night Comedy in Election 2000."
135. Michael Pfau and Jong G. Kang, "The Impact of Relational Messages on Candidate Influence in Televised Political Debates," *Communication Studies* 42 (1991): 114–128.

136. Joshua Meyrowitz, *No Sense of Place: The Impact of Electronic Media on Social Behavior* (New York: Oxford University Press, 1985).
137. Moy, Xenos, and Hess, "Communication and Citizenship."
138. Alexander Rose, "When Politics is a Laughing Matter," *Policy Review* 110 (2001/2002): 62.
139. Gardner, *The Mocking of the President*, 231.
140. Paletz, "Political Humor and Authority."
141. Hans Speier, "Wit and Politics: An Essay on Laughter and Power," *American Journal of Sociology* 103 (1998): 1352–1401.
142. Glenn D. Wilson, "Ideology and Humor Preferences," *International Political Science Review* 11 (1990): 461–472.
143. Paletz, "Political Humor and Authority."
144. John C. Meyer, "Humor as a Double-Edged Sword: Four Functions of Humor in Communication," *Communication Theory* 10 (2000): 310–331.
145. Nitz, Cypher, Reichert, and Mueller, "Candidates as Comedy."
146. Weiskel, "From Sidekick to Sideshow," 402.

II

Political Humor in the World Beyond Television

4

Political Cartoons
Zeitgeists and the Creation and Recycling of Satirical Symbols

Alleen Pace Nilsen and Don L. F. Nilsen

When looked at cumulatively, either in a contemporary or a histori-cal situation, cartoons provide a *zeitgeist*,[1] an enjoyable and revealing portrayal of the ever-changing "spirit of the times." And while some political cartoons highlight life's ironies, most of them develop from their creators' belief that they may have some influence on public thinking. This belief is probably not unfounded. As a visual medium, political cartoons do have political power. For example, we still use the designs that Thomas Nast (1840–1902), who is acknowledged as the father of American political cartooning, created for the Repub-lican Party's elephant logo. In the 1870s, Nast's cartoons about Boss Tweed and the Tammany Hall corruption in New York City so infu-riated Tweed that he ordered, "Stop them damn pictures! I don't care so much what papers write about me. My constituents can't read. But damn it, they can see the pictures!" Tweed is said to have offered Nast a half million dollars to "study art in Europe." Ironically, Nast chose to stay in the United States, while Tweed fled to Europe only to be arrested and brought back for trial when a Spanish official recog-nized him from one of Nast's drawings.

What Tweed implied about pictures being more damaging to his career than words is probably true. This point has been illustrated by recent incidents relating to the war in Iraq. The Pentagon initially refused to let photographers take pictures of flag-draped coffins but were forced to give up on the policy after cartoonists began drawing pictures of the coffins. One of the earliest by Walt Handelsman (*News-day*) won the 2003 Scripps-Howard Award for showing soldiers carrying coffins past a podium labeled "W." Only the top of Bush's head is visible but his message is in large print: "MAJOR COMBAT OPERA-TIONS IN IRAQ ARE OVER." A year later, Handelsman illustrated the caption "They'll be Greeted with Flowers" through a picture of border-to-border coffins topped with funeral bouquets. In 2004, Paul Conrad (*Los Angeles Times*) drew a single casket but replaced the stars on the flag with tally marks. Steve Sack (*Minneapolis Star-Tribune*) showed a blindfolded Uncle Sam standing respectfully with his hat off in front of eleven coffins, while James McCloskey (*Daily News Leader,* Staunton, Virginia) drew eight coffins on a tarmac with a plane in the background under the caption "Partial Troop Withdrawal."

In this chapter we review the basic elements of successful political cartoons, and discuss how they capture a *zeitgeist*. Like the symbols that political cartoonists employ, the examples we use will be familiar to most, if not all.

The Craft of Political Cartooning

Cartoonists' ability to draw pictures gives them an advantage over writers and stand-up comedians because of the power they have to balance their work between using commonly accepted and recognized visual symbols and creating new and original ones. But because the motifs, the little reoccurring elements, in cartoons have to be instantly recognizable, cartoonists cannot be totally original. They are forced by the nature of their craft to recycle well-known symbols as well as to adapt visual and verbal icons to create and communicate their unique points of view. Among their "frozen" symbols are such things as snakes to represent evil, skulls to represent death, Adam and Eve to comment on gender issues, bombs and firecrackers to warn of imminent danger, the three monkeys to hint at purposeful ignorance, a Trojan horse to warn against trickery, and pointing fingers or arrows to send blame elsewhere. These symbols are the stock characters that authors take off the shelf to fill the backgrounds of their stories. The most common visual symbols have been used so often that viewers take them for granted as "cartoon talk."

Viewers and cartoonists have both become so accustomed to standard icons that if changes are made the viewers' attention will be focused on trying to figure out what is behind the change. Viewers expect everything that is a backdrop for the joke to be presented in

traditional terms, which is why white-collar workers are usually portrayed as men in suits, farmers as men in overalls, and blue-collar
workers as wearing hard hats and tool belts. For example, in one of
Steve Benson's (*Arizona Republic*) cartoons in which he was complaining about the preponderance of malpractice suits, he drew an
operating room in which the patient on the table is old, the nurses
are all women, and the doctors are all men. Two men, also around
the operating table, have signs affixed to their surgical gowns. One
says "Patient's Attorney," while the other says "Surgeon's Attorney."

For the success of the cartoon, Benson wanted viewers' eyes to skim
over the entire setting and then light on the two attorneys. If Benson
had followed real-life practices and made one of the attorneys or one of
the doctors a woman or one of the nurses a man or the patient a child,
and so forth, viewers would have been confused about the joke.

This same need for speedy comprehension also limits the number of
words that cartoonists can use, which is why they are on the lookout for
catchy phrases and slogans that they can put to good use through adaptation and recycling. For example, in 1978 Harry Truman's "The buck
stops here" was recycled by Kevin McVey (*The Record*) for a cartoon
about Jimmy Carter. He showed Truman's sign being taken away and
replaced with "What's left of the buck stops here." In 2004, Jim Morin
(*Miami Herald*) recycled the slogan to show George W. Bush sitting at
his desk behind a slogan, "The Buck Stops *Anywhere* But *Here!*"

In short, familiarity in symbols and words facilitates quick comprehension of political humor. Political cartoons are so compact,
and the attention given them is so brief, that a cartoonist who strays
too far from the familiar risks not making the point.

Common Symbols: Old and New

For purposes of comparison, we went looking for a universally recognized symbol to illustrate how cartoonists go about creating "variations on a theme." Presented in Box 4.1 are descriptions of thirteen
portrayals of the Statue of Liberty, sometimes called Lady Liberty,
which we found reproduced in three historical collections of political cartoons: *Attack of the Political Cartoonists: Insights & Assaults
from Today's Editorial Pages*,[2] *Drawn and Quartered: The History of
American Political Cartoons*,[3] and *Drawn to Extremes: The Use and
Abuse of Editorial Cartoons*.[4]

Box 4.1. Selected Historical Depictions
of Lady Liberty in Political Cartoons

1882: Thomas Nast covered the statue with signs and billboards to protest big business and the trusts controlling such commodities as lumber, sugar, and tin.

1939: Under the caption "Back Home" (apparently a criticism of isolationist attitudes), Vaughn Shoemaker showed an American citizen punching the statue in the eye.

1947: Daniel Fitzpatrick drew Lady Liberty and Uncle Sam sitting on a park bench talking. The cutline reads "Everyone is a little subversive, but thee and me, and sometimes I think even thee..."

1949: Herbert Block drew a man frantically carrying a bucket of water up a ladder. He is labeled "Hysteria" and is rushing up to throw it on Lady Liberty's torch.

1950: In Charles Warner's drawing related to integration problems in the southern United States, a discouraged Statue of Liberty is parodying the song "Georgia on My Mind."

1960: Duncan Macpherson shows Lady Liberty frowning deeply with the construction cracks showing in her face. Fidel Castro and Nikita Khrushchev are sitting on her crown as if at a picnic with Castro pointing a camera at Khrushchev and saying "Smile."

1971: Daniel Aguila (El Dani), who published a 240-page collection of Statue of Liberty cartoons, is represented here by a "Lib And Let Live!" cartoon in which Lady Liberty is shown holding aloft a large pair of scissors that she has just used to turn her robes into a minidress.

1980: Doug Marlette, under the caption "Drawing Blood," shows Lady Liberty sweeping dirt under a rug designed as a flag.

1984: Signe Wilkinson shows her carrying a clipboard with "Sweeps of Aliens OK'd." She is going through a sewing factory (where four people are hiding under a table) and shouting, "OK, You huddled masses. I know you're in here!"

1987: In an unpublished, but now included in *Drawn to Extremes*, cartoon, Doug Marlette portrayed Howard Stern imitating the "Expose Yourself to Art" poster from Portland, Oregon, that sold 500,000 copies and made Bud Clark, who posed for it to benefit a local arts group, so famous that in 1984 he was elected Portland's mayor. Controversial talk show host Howard Stern had announced he would run against New York's incumbent governor Mario Cuomo, and was shown from the back wearing a trench coat and gartered socks. Lady Liberty is saying, "It looks like a challenge to Cuomo's Leadership—only smaller!"

2001: Mike Lukovich drew only her face shot with a tear coming out of one eye. Both eyes reflect the plane running into the second of the Twin Towers.

2003: Milt Priggee drew an angry Statue of Liberty who has had her torch taken away from her by a police officer who is explaining on the telephone, "Yeah. She's from France, wearing robes, and spouting immigration morality...with an ignition source!"

2003: Don Landgren, Jr., drew an impatient Ms. Liberty looking at her watch and saying "Geez, two years and still no capture of Osama... or Saddam...or Al Qaida...or WMD...or the Taliban, or Justice, or...." A side note reads "In a city accustomed to the New York Minute."

Symbols do not have to be old to be effective. The only requirement is that they be mainstream and easily recognizable. Cartoons depicting the 2004 Abu Ghraib prison scandal demonstrated this, as well as the power that political cartoons have. Cartoons about the scandal seemed to stretch viewer's emotions between shame and the guilty feelings of amusement that accompany black humor. Photographs of prison abuse, which many soldiers took and sent home through e-mail, were so emotionally wrenching that many Americans regretfully agreed with the sentiments expressed in a cartoon drawn by Mike Keefe of the *Denver Post*. He showed an Al-Qaeda operative coming to Uncle Sam and asking "to buy the reprint rights for our recruitment poster!"

The three most startling pictures included a pile of nude prisoners, a photo of Private Lynndie England holding an Iraqi prisoner on a dog leash, and a photo of a hooded prisoner silhouetted in a ragged black blanket while standing on a box with outstretched arms hooked to electric wires. In their photo forms, the three pictures were equally gut-wrenching, but judging from a sampling of thirty-nine cartoons about the scandal reprinted in *The Best Political Cartoons of the Year*,[5] cartoonists seemed drawn to the power of the hooded, silhouetted figure. The image is so dramatic that it is hard to imagine even someone as skilled as Alfred Hitchcock creating a more jarring scene. Fifteen of the cartoons in the book featured this hooded figure, while only five focused on Private England and her leash. Others focused on giving new meanings to such phrases as "the chain of command" and "a few bad apples" or on people outside of the scandal. Daryl Cagle's cartoon on Slate.com is an example, where two children are saying, "Hey! Let's play Army." "Ok. You get naked. I'll get the bullwhip and electrodes."

But the hooded figure dominated. Cagle's book opens with Steve Breen's (*San Diego Union-Tribune*) full-page drawing of the saddened face of Uncle Sam, who has been given a black eye in the shape of the figure. John Sherffius drew a serious portrait of Donald Rumsfeld's face with the lenses of his glasses reflecting on one side a flag-draped coffin and on the other side the hooded figure; the caption read "Rumsfailed." Mike Thompson (*Detroit Free Press*) placed the image next to one of a hooded Ku Klux Klan member under the caption "Sadistic Violation of Human Rights Is So Un-American!" Printed in the lower right-hand corner as an afterthought was "Really?" Michael Ramirez (*Los Angeles Times*) labeled the figure "U.S. Credibility" and drew Uncle Sam's clothing peeking out from under the blanket. He also put some emphasis on the electric wires to hint at imminent electrocution. Bob Englehart (*Hartford Courant*) showed a badly beaten-up and bloody-nosed Uncle Sam saying, "American soldiers at Abu Ghraib Prison did this to me."

Dennis Draughon (*Scranton Times*) placed the hooded figure looming behind the naked girl in the famous photo of children running from a napalm bombing in Vietnam. Steve Greenberg (*Ventura County Star*) showed stars on an American flag gradually evolving into the five-pointed figure reminiscent of Michelangelo's pentagram drawing. His caption asked, "What Happened to the Values We Project to the World?" David Catrow (*Springfield News-Sun*) laid the figure on an upside-down compass beside the heading "The Moral Compass."

We include these examples of recycling to illustrate how an icon—either a new one like the Abu Ghraib figure or a long-standing one like the Statue of Liberty—inspires variations on a theme. While the two sets of cartoons circle around common icons, each cartoon is unique. The Statue of Liberty cartoons are more varied simply because they are spread over 120 years and therefore reflect the concerns of different time periods. They highlighted issues including the rise of big business, isolationism, and World War II, hysteria about Communism and the power of the Soviet Union, challenges connected to integration, the women's movement, corruption in Washington, controversial immigration policies, the rise of talk radio, and finally, terrorism.

Children's Symbols

Because people now have more choices with regard to what they read, watch, and listen to, it is harder to find allusions or symbols that everyone will recognize. For this reason many cartoonists have turned to folktales and children's literature to find common and familiar references. For example, early in the 1989 presidential race, several cartoonists dismissed the Democratic challengers of Michael Dukakis (Bruce Babbit, Joseph Biden, Richard Gephardt, Al Gore, Gary Hart, Jesse Jackson, and Paul Simon) as "The Seven Dwarves." In January of 1990, Jeff MacNelly (*Chicago Tribune*) drew a wonderful portrait of Manuel Noriega as the trickster, Br'er Rabbit, happily sitting in the briar patch, which was labeled "U. S. Legal System." In 2004 Jack Chapman (*Desoto Times Today*) used the Uncle Remus "Tar Baby" story to show Uncle Sam getting stuck to a figure labeled "Iraq." The cutline reads "The Lesson of the 'TAR BABY' or Should That Be 'OIL BABY'?"

In August of 2004, Steve Benson (*Arizona Republic*) showed President Bush being hit on the head with an acorn and yelling "The Sky is Falling!" The nearby Karl Rove explains, "Actually, Mr. President, It's your polls that are falling." Also in 2004, Steve Greenberg (*Ventura County Star*) used "Pandora's Bottle" as a comparison to the ancient myth of Pandora's Box. President Bush has just pulled a "Saddam Hussein" cork from a champagne bottle and amid the fire and smoke bursting from the bottle are ghosts, skeletons, bats, and devils' pitchforks.

Pinocchio's nose is such a good symbol to use in accusing someone of lying that cartoonists have drawn Boris Yeltsin with an elongated nose for saying that he would not bomb civilians in Chechnya; the Ayatollah Komeini for saying, "Our nuclear program is for peaceful purposes only"; Bill Clinton for saying he did "not have sex with that woman"; and George W. Bush for his statements about weapons of mass destruction in Iraq.

Virtually everyone in the United States knows something about *The Wizard of Oz* and so could laugh at a cartoon showing Bob Dole waking up after his miserable run for the presidency: "Bob, Bob Dole, Are you all right? You're back in Kansas, it was just a bad dream!" They could also empathize with a 2004 Randy Bish (*Tribune Review*) drawing of France as the "NO COURAGE" Cowardly Lion, The UN as the "NO BRAIN" Scarecrow, and Iraq with Saddam Hussein's head as the "NO HEART" Tin Woodman. Also in 2004, David Horsey (*Seattle Post Intelligencer*) portrayed Vice President Cheney as "The WICKED WITCH of the WEST WING" sending out such talk radio "monkeys" as Rush Limbaugh, Sean Hannity, and Ann

Coulter to "Fly! Fly!" and destroy Richard Clarke for saying, "The Bush Administration was obsessed with Iraq and Ignored the Threat from Al Qaeda."

Alice in Wonderland is the all-time supplier of cartoon allusions. During the Watergate scandal, cartoonists showed incredulous Americans "believing as many as six impossible things before breakfast." The hookah-smoking caterpillar is regularly consulted with such questions as "What was in your pipe when you made this decision?" while "Going down the rabbit hole" is used as a metaphor for things as varied as hunting for Osama Bin Laden and schools trying to meet the requirements of the "No Child Left Behind" Act. After the 2004 death of Yasser Arafat, a four-panel drawing by Michael Ramirez (*Los Angeles Times*) showed the disappearing Cheshire Cat with the face and head covering of Arafat. His big grin was labeled "Terrorism," and in the last panel was all that was left. The cutline came directly from Lewis Carroll: "And this time it vanished quite slowly, beginning with the end of the tail, and ending with the grin, which remained some time after the rest of it had gone."

In 1999, adults who had learned to read from such Dr. Seuss books as *The Cat in the Hat* and *Green Eggs and Ham* were surprised when The New Press published a collection edited by Richard H. Minear, *Dr. Seuss Goes to War: The World War II Editorial Cartoons of Theodor Seuss Geisel*. Geisel, who took the pen name of Dr. Seuss, was a commercial illustrator who had written and illustrated three marginally successful children's books when he took the job of editorial cartoonist for *PM*, a leftist New York newspaper. This was long before he was contracted to do the easy-to-read books that made him famous, but readers can nevertheless recognize many of the characters and images that would later find their way into his children's books. The tall, horizontally striped hat worn by Seuss's famous Cat in the Hat started out on a bedraggled Uncle Sam. The piles of turtles in his *Yertle the Turtle* were first drawn for a hortative "V for Victory" cartoon, while the smug elephant he drew holding up a "Non-Violent Non-Cooperation" sign in a "Gateway to India" cartoon became the quiet hero of *Horton Hatches the Egg*.

Seuss, who died in 1991, would probably have been amused to see his work come full circle and return to editorial cartoons as it did in 1994 when Gary Varvel (*Indianapolis News*) drew "The Gingrich who stole Christmas." This criticism of Republican Speaker of the House Newt Gingrich was a play on the title of Seuss's *The Grinch Who*

Stole Christmas. Varvel showed Gingrich saying "No Compromise" and tiptoeing away with the Christmas tree in his pack labeled "The Great Society." Stolen gifts were labeled "Political Power," "Social Spending," and "Health Care."

In 2000, just before Attorney General Janet Reno ordered a SWAT team to snatch six-year-old Elian Gonzalez from the Miami home of relatives and return him to Cuba, Mike Peters (*Dayton Daily News*) drew Reno wearing one of the Cat in the Hat's striped and half-cocked hats while declaring, "I will not grab Elian at the door, I will not grab him on the floor, I will not grab him in the yard, I will not grab him with a guard."

Presidential Zeitgeists

Another way to illustrate the work of cartoonists is to look at the zeitgeists that have developed around particular U.S. presidents. For example, during Lyndon Johnson's presidency the country was so conflicted over the war in Vietnam that all of Johnson's actions were viewed through their relationship to Vietnam. The best cartoon to show this is David Levine's uncaptioned drawing of Johnson for the *New York Times Magazine*. It showed Johnson at the 1966 press briefing where he surprised the world by pulling up his shirt to show reporters the scar from his recent gallbladder operation. In his caricature, Levine changed the scar into the shape of Vietnam, an action that Steven Heller, the art director of the *New York Times*, described as "pinpointing a benign physical feature and metamorphosing it into a fatal character flaw."[6]

The longevity of the association between Johnson and Vietnam was illustrated in 2003 when Draper Hill drew a cartoon for the *Oakland Press* in which LBJ, dressed in Texas cowboy attire, is talking to his fellow Texan "W," also in cowboy attire. They are both waist-deep in a swamp. "Vietnam 1965–1968" is printed in the water rippling around LBJ, while the water around "W" reads "IRAQ-ETC. 2001–2004." LBJ is saying, "Let me be direct, Sonny—Haven't you kids learned anything in the last 36 years?"

When Ronald Reagan was president between 1981 and 1989, Hess and Northrop observe that he "told history as Hollywood might reconfigure it, referring to the Soviet Union as *The Evil Empire*, a proposed space-based defense system as *Star Wars*, and

rebel soldiers in Nicaragua as *Freedom Fighters*."[7] The showman-
ship, which he transferred from his Hollywood career as an actor
and president of the Screen Actors Guild, made him a favorite with
cartoonists as well as with the general public. In a 1984 cartoon by
Paul Szep (*Boston Globe*), a little old lady is pushing through the
Secret Service guards to gush at Reagan, "I've seen your movies and
TV shows...but I just love the way you play an American President best!" When Reagan died in 2004, Jerry Barnett (*Indianapolis
Star*) drew God—or maybe it was St. Peter—asking Reagan if he
had "Ever played an angel?" Doug Marlette (*Tallahassee Democrat*)
showed Reagan at the Pearly Gates saying, "St. Peter, Tear down
this wall!"; while Jimmy Margulies (*The Record*, Hackensack, New
Jersey) recalled one of Reagan's most famous slogans by having
Reagan appear from a cloud and push Nancy forward with a "Support Stem Cell Research" placard. Reagan is saying, "Nancy, Go
out there and win one for the Gipper!"

Reagan, like Franklin Roosevelt, was so popular that many cartoonists avoided criticizing him, and when there was opposition
most of it was either good-natured or forgiving. For example, in
1986, Mike Keefe (*Denver Post*) won the National Headliner Award
when he drew a reporter asking President Reagan, "What do we do,
Mr. President, if the Russians keep testing weapons?" The president
responds, "We will continue testing." The reporter asks, "What if the
Russians stop testing nuclear weapons?" The president responds, "We
will continue testing." The reporter asks, "In other words we're going
to continue testing?" The president responds, "Well, that depends on
the Russians."

When during an argument over privacy rights, Paul Conrad,
who is known for his hard-hitting approach, drew Reagan holding
up a beaker of urine for drug testing with the message, "Uncle Sam
Wants Yours!", the *Los Angeles Times* received more protest letters
than for any other cartoon or article published during the Reagan
administration.[8]

Theodore Roosevelt (1901–1909) spoke in the same kind of pictur-
esque terms as did Reagan. Cartoonists could immediately translate
the names he bestowed on his "Rough Riders" and on the journalists
he called "muckrakers" into their cartoons. It was also easy for them to
illustrate such colorful statements as "My hat's in the ring" and "Speak
softly and carry a big stick," both of which are regularly recycled. For
example, in 1978 when John Trevor (*Albuquerque Journal*) protested

President Carter's Panama Canal Treaty, he showed Jimmy Carter happily carving Roosevelt's big stick into a loving cup named "Canal Treaty." Nearly twenty years later Jim Berry (NEA) drew a picture of Bill Clinton standing with a twig in his hand and saying to a representative of China, "Let me share a thought with you. We don't feel you are doing very well, when it comes to human rights." The cutline read "China Policy: Speak softly and carry a stick."

It is totally in keeping with Teddy Roosevelt's personality that the English language took the term "teddy bear" from a cartoon that Clifford Berryman drew for the *Washington Star*. It showed Roosevelt on one of his famous hunting trips refusing to shoot a bear cub that was clinging to a tree. Shortly afterward in 1902 a Brooklyn candy store owner started selling the first "teddy" bears.

Jeff MacNelly's (*Chicago Tribune*) 1997 cartoon entitled "That Legacy Thing" is a history lesson. It shows Abraham Lincoln's legacy of "With malice toward none and charity toward all," Teddy Roosevelt's "Speak softly and carry a big stick," Franklin Delano Roosevelt's "We have nothing to fear but fear itself," Jack Kennedy's "Ask not what your country can do for you, but ask what you can do for your country," Ronald Reagan's "Mr. Gorbachev, tear down that wall," and, finally, Bill Clinton's "Never met her." The same year, Jeff Stahler (*Cincinnati Post*) did a similar cartoon but had Bill Clinton saying, "Show me the money." Jim Palmer's (*Dallas News*) 1978 "Great Slogans in History" ended with Jimmy Carter's framed message being "Keep off the grass."[9]

Summary

As these examples show, cartoons provide a record of not only the events and concerns of a time period, but also of the "spirit" of the times. The late folklorist Alan Dundes of the University of California, Berkeley, used to say, "Nothing tells more about a culture than what makes the people laugh." Even when icons have been adapted to make different points, they teach history lessons because viewers are motivated to understand the original lest they miss the new joke. For example, the first successful American political cartoon is usually considered to be Benjamin Franklin's 1754 drawing of a snake cut into thirteen parts, each given the initials of one of the original thirteen colonies. The cutline "JOIN or DIE" helped colonists make up their minds about seeking independence from England. In a recent cartoon reprinted in Chris Lamb's *Drawn to Extremes*,[10] Doug Marlette shows Franklin bringing his cartoon to an editor who is saying, "Sorry, Ben…. Nice cartoon, but King George may be offended." Marlette was using the cartoon to illustrate the ongoing argument that cartoonists have with newspaper editors who want their cartoons to be funny and insightful, but not "offensive."

The point is that because cartoonists have only seven to ten seconds to grab the attention of a viewer, they are obligated to dip into what Carl Jung has called "the collective unconscious" so that at least some of their images will be immediately familiar to viewers. When cartoonists go fishing in the deep stream of images that flows through each of our minds they may pull up visual icons as old as the Trojan Horse or as new as the photos from the 2004 Abu Ghraib prison. Verbal allusions can range from biblical scriptures and historical slogans to reminders of both old and new folk literature or the latest gaffes made by politicians and other newsmakers.

Although fewer newspapers now have their own cartoonists, political cartooning will remain a vibrant field. This is because political cartoons fit so well into today's penchant for instant information combined with instant amusement. Hundreds of cartoonists have their own Web sites, while the *New Yorker* has organized the *Cartoon Bank,* an online collection of tens of thousands of cartoons, which can be searched through a variety of cross-indexes and purchased for use in advertisements, books, direct mail, magazines, newsletters, presentations, product development, and Web pages. The collection extends beyond those originally published in the *New Yorker.* Also, as seen below in the "Notes" section, writing and publishing books about cartoons is popular. Late night television comedians sometimes choose to show especially interesting cartoons and so do the editors of Sunday newspapers and serious news magazines. For example, *Newsweek* does this on its "Perspectives" page, while *Time* does it on its "Punchlines" page.

While even the most tragic and serious happenings will find their way into cartoons, the cartoonists are not making fun of the tragedies themselves, but of the behavior of humans dealing with serious matters. Political cartoonists are cynical optimists hoping through their edgy insights to do what satirists have always done, which is to use new combinations of old symbols to lead readers to question both attitudes and actions.

Notes

1. From the German *zeit*, meaning "time," and geist, meaning "ghost" or "spirit."

2. J. P. Trostle, ed., *Attack of the Political Cartoonists: Insights and Assaults from Today's Editorial Pages* (Madison, WI: Dork Storm Press, 2004).

3. Stephen Hess and Sandy Northrop, *Drawn and Quartered: The History of American Political Cartoons* (Montgomery, AL: Elliott and Clark, 1996).

4. Chris Lamb, *Drawn to Extremes: The Use and Abuse of Editorial Cartoons* (New York: Columbia University Press, 2004).

5. Daryl Cagle and Brian Fairrington, eds., *The Best Political Cartoons of the Year, 2005 Edition* (New York: Que Publishing, 2005).

6. Hess and Northrop, *Drawn and Quartered*, 117.

7. Ibid., 130.

8. Lamb, *Drawn to Extremes*, 119.

9. Charles Brooks, ed., *Best Editorial Cartoons of the Year* (Gretna, LA: Pelican, 1978), 48.

10. Lamb, *Drawn to Extremes*, 152.

5

New Humor, Old School Style
A Content Analysis of the Political Cues Offered by The Onion on the 2000 and 2004 Elections

Geoffrey Sheagley, Paula L. O'Loughlin,
and Timothy Lindberg

And the thing about my jokes is, they don't hurt anybody. You can take 'em or leave 'em—you can say they're funny or they're terrible or they're good, or whatever, but you can just pass 'em by. But with Congress, every time they make a joke, it's a law! And every time they make a law, it's a joke![1]

Reports of a shadowy figure in the woods and heavy breathing heard in the night, coupled with a recent series of grisly murders, have generated rumors that U.S. Vice-President Dick Cheney has returned to terrorize the counselors at Camp Crystal Lake, sources reported Friday.... "Cheney is an unstoppable killing machine," CNN's Anderson Cooper said via telephone. "He has been burned, stabbed, slashed, hacked, bludgeoned, and shot, only to get back up and continue his rampage."[2]

Finding humorous elements to American politics has never been difficult. Traditionally, however, humor was absent from the way the public learned about politics—the news. Finding out what was happening in the world involved reading humorless newspaper articles or watching a dignified Edward R. Murrow or someone similar deliver a summary of the day's events in a serious tone. The clear message was that the news was serious business and politics was not a laughing matter.

In recent years, however, as the nature of the media voices in the political information environment has changed, the rules have changed. The barriers between traditional news coverage and entertainment have eroded, leading to "a convergence (or at least blurring) of the types of media...and media genres."[3] News/entertainment media hybrids such as Jon Stewart's *The Daily Show* and Web sites like JibJab.com, which offer political news embedded in humor, are increasingly important in conveying political information to the public. While such media are growing in market share for the population as whole, they appear to have achieved their most significant popularity and usage among young people.[4]

The traditional low political engagement of young people, coupled with their high attention to news/humor hybrids, makes the cues these hybrids offer regarding politics normatively significant. Interestingly, up until now, political scientists have only looked at the electronic forms of these hybrids. If we want to have a full picture of the political cues these news/humor hybrids provide, then we need to consider print examples of these hybrids as well.

This chapter examines the nature of the political cues offered by *The Onion*, one of the oldest, best-known, and widely read print news/humor hybrids. *The Onion* has been around longer than Jon Stewart's *Daily Show* and the explosion of political humor on the Web. Since its founding in 1988, *The Onion* has had a large and ever-expanding readership.[5]

Today it is available free in many major metropolitan areas in the United States, with a total print circulation of approximately 600,000 papers and millions of visitors per month to its Web site.[6] While there are other, older print news/humor hybrids, such as *Mad* magazine, none has been so successful. Importantly, *The Onion*'s youthful readership profile also matches the demographic most likely to use electronic news/humor programming for its news sources.[7] In short, for purposes of comparison, *The Onion* is perhaps the ideal print news/humor hybrid.

Three questions seem particularly important. First, does *The Onion* cover politics similarly to so-called "old school" traditional news print media? Second, if *The Onion* covers politics differently, how does it vary? For example, does *The Onion* provide the same information regarding a political issue, but frame the material differently? Third, given the youthful market demographics of *The Onion*'s readers, does it present positive or negative cues regarding the political process?

Satiric Hybrids

R. Lance Holbert classifies political entertainment television into nine distinct categories, or types of information sources.[8] Most relevant for the purposes of this research is Holbert's category of traditional satire. Mockery is central to traditional satire. As such, satiric hybrids on television often place greater emphasis on the negative elements of politics than traditional television news.[9] According to Holbert, when political entertainment television takes the form of traditional satire, the transmission of political information does not occur in the same way it does with traditional news. Satires grounded in what Holbert refers to as "fake news" are expected to convey political information in the form of humor. To decode the information the audience must know enough about the material being presented to understand its humorous nature, and be sufficiently motivated to deconstruct the satire.[10]

Clearly, as a satire, *The Onion* should engage in clever mocking of politics as well as other subjects. However, for *The Onion* to function as a political information cue-giver similar to traditional news, its coverage of political material needs to have three elements. First, because when reading *The Onion* the audience expects humor, cues have to be embedded in humor. Second, the information should be sufficiently grounded in political reality that the audience can recognize the satire and will be motivated to decode it. Third, the satiric hybrid's cues should be accessible for deconstruction. This accessibility might take the form of using the names of real political figures or placing the story into a commonly understood frame.

Together, the research on framing, agenda setting, and satiric hybrids suggests that *The Onion* should be similar to traditional news media and yet also markedly different. The lead issues, or those that appear above the proverbial fold, should focus on the main political story of the moment. Thus, during a presidential election campaign, like traditional news sources, the most common subject of a satiric hybrid such as *The Onion*'s coverage should be the campaign. Because satire only works if people understand what is being lampooned and are motivated to deconstruct it, *The Onion*'s story's subject, frame, or main characters could be expected to parallel what leads in traditional news outlets.

Yet the way a satiric news/humor hybrid like *The Onion* presents this information to its audience likely will differ in two ways from traditional print news. The content of the frames should vary from what traditional news media provides. Unlike traditional news where the focus is on diffusion of information, the satiric hybrid's goal is to entertain through satire. Thus, satiric hybrids' cues regarding politics will only resonate with the public if they are humorous. Jokes and mockery of political figures that are not funny and fall flat will not convey political cues. Because of the nature of satire, *The Onion*'s frames are also likely to be somewhat negative regarding politics.[11]

Successful satire also requires that the audience have enough prior knowledge of a subject to understand the difference between the satire and the truth about a subject. One way such prior knowledge can easily be conveyed is through the use of a frame narrative.[12] Thus, a satiric hybrid like *The Onion* should use frame narratives more than individualized frames. During an election year, for example, while we might expect the individual episodic horse race frame to dominate traditional print media, it should be less common in satiric hybrids like *The Onion*. Instead, frame narratives that draw on shared negative understandings of political candidates, the two-party system, and so on should dominate coverage in satiric news/humor hybrids like *The Onion*.

We expect satiric print news/humor hybrids to frame politics during an election year through the use of frame narratives (as opposed to traditional news' thematic or individualized episodic frames such as a horse race). These frame narratives should bear some resemblance to real world events so that they can be deconstructed and mocked. We expect the print news/entertainment hybrids' coverage during an election year to provide cues to readers that promote negative characteristics of politics. Again, however, for the satiric messages to resonate, they need to be funny.

Methods

We assess these expectations regarding *The Onion* through a content analysis of its coverage of the 2000 and 2004 presidential elections. We chose to focus on the climatic final weeks of these two presidential election years, from September through the week following the election, in the hope that they would yield the largest number of politically related stories. The Minneapolis-St. Paul *Star Tribune*'s Sunday coverage over the course of the same two time periods was also content analyzed. The *Star Tribune* was chosen for our comparative benchmark because it was an accessible example of nonelite print media. Because *The Onion* is a weekly periodical, only the Sunday edition of the *Star Tribune* was included in our analysis. Twenty issues of *The Onion* were reviewed over the two years with a review of 60 unique articles. Over the same time period, 258 stories from the *Star Tribune* appeared and were also analyzed.

For both sources, two indicators of their coverage were examined. All of what we classified as "headline stories" were analyzed. Because we conducted our content analysis using *The Onion*'s online archives, we defined a "headline" article as the uppermost story on the left side of the page.[13] For the *Star Tribune*, a headline story is defined as an article appearing on page 1A. In addition, all stories that were not headline stories, but were related to politics, were reviewed.[14] All articles were coded for their positive and negative cues about the branches of government as well as the type of political frame they presented: individual, narrative, or both. There were six possible categories of individual frames: horse race (polling and/or fund-raising numbers), issue (positions or outside influences on the race), personal (characteristics of the candidates), local coverage, foreign policy, and other. Stories with frame narratives were categorized into twenty-six possible categories or narratives. Some examples of frame narratives are: two-party system is limiting, corruption, and "politics is stupid."[15] The creation of frame narratives was somewhat organic; as articles were read new narratives emerged and were added to our original list. Additionally, articles that contained both frame narratives and individual frames were coded as such.[16]

The content coding of both *The Onion* and the *Star Tribune* was done by two trained researchers. All conflicts between the coders were resolved by a third trained researcher. Intercoder reliability was strong.[17]

Findings

Our first expectation was evaluated by analyzing both the headline stories and the politically related coverage. The subject for the vast majority of *The Onion*'s headline articles during the 2000 and 2004 fall campaigns was politics. Table 5.1 shows *The Onion*'s and the *Star Tribune*'s headline coverage from 2000 and 2004.

TABLE 5.1.   *The Onion's* and *Star Tribune's* **Headline Coverage**

Headline Type	2000		2004	
	The Onion	Star Tribune	The Onion	Star Tribune
Political: Campaign	40%	33%	73%	32%
Political: War	—	—	9%	2%
Political: Foreign policy	10%	—	9%	—
Political: Other	30%	18%	9%	9%
Nonpolitical	20%	49%	—	57%
N	10	39	11	37

While the specific topics ranged widely, coverage of politics clearly dominated *The Onion's* headline stories. Examples of this range include these article excerpts.

> With his lead in presidential polls narrowing to just four points over Republican challenger George W. Bush, an already anxious Al Gore wondered aloud Monday whether the latest *Doonesbury* is about him.... The controversial strip, which ran in hundreds of newspapers across the U.S., depicts an unnamed political figure engaged in a top-secret strategy session with a group of shadowy advisors. At first glance, the character, which Trudeau will neither confirm nor deny represents Gore, appears to be seeking out advice of a substantive, political nature...however, it becomes apparent that he is actually consulting his advisors on matters of fashion.[18]

> Freshly unearthed public documents, ranging from newspapers to cabinet-meeting minutes, seem to indicate large gaps in George W. Bush's service as president, a spokesman for the watchdog group Citizens for an Informed Society announced Monday.[19]

While dealing with different subjects, both articles are remarkably similar to the coverage the traditional media might provide, each addressing politics. Of the twenty-one total headline stories analyzed across both years, only one was nonpolitical. Interestingly, looking at the raw percentages, it appears the *Star Tribune's* headline stories focus less on politics than *The Onion's* do. However, this is an artifact of the circumstance that each issue of the *Star Tribune* has multiple headline stories (and thus more nonpolitical headline articles). Each issue of *The Onion* contains only one headline story.[20] In short, although *The Onion* has fewer headline stories overall, its coverage clearly parallels traditional print media.

As another way to ask the same question, we analyzed the total proportion of stories on politics in each paper. Looking at both years for each paper together, a significant difference appears. For the two years, over 50 percent (standard deviation of 9 percent) of the *Star Tribune*'s Sunday coverage concerned politics, compared to roughly 22 percent (SD = 11 percent) for *The Onion*. This difference is statistically significant (p <.001). Thus, when we expand beyond headline stories, *The Onion*'s overall, and proportional, coverage of politics is less than the *Star Tribune*'s.

It is also apparent that *The Onion*'s overall coverage of politics increased from 2000 to 2004. The proportion of political articles to the total number of stories in an issue of *The Onion* during the 2000 campaign was 18 percent (SD = 12 percent). In 2004 this number increased to 25 percent (SD = 8 percent). A comparison of means via analysis of variance shows this increase in *The Onion*'s political coverage from 2000 to 2004 to be borderline statistically significant ($f = 3.120$; $p = .093$). Looking at some of the stories in 2004 suggests the reason for this increase lies in the resonant material the prior experience of election 2000 offered. For example, the following story satirizes the commonly understood narrative that Nader's involvement cost Gore electoral votes and thus the presidency.

> Supporters of presidential candidate Ralph Nader blamed his defeat Tuesday on George W. Bush and John Kerry, claiming that the two candidates "ate up" his share of the electoral votes. "This election was stolen out from under Mr. Nader by Bush and Kerry, who diverted his votes to the right and the left," Nader campaign manager Theresa Amato said. "It's an outrage. If Nader were the only candidate, he would be president right now." In his concession speech, Nader characterized Bush and Kerry as spoilers.[21]

Still, these findings offer only mixed support for our first expectation. While *The Onion*'s headline stories were overwhelmingly political, looking at the overall proportion of its articles devoted to politics, it was much less than that of a traditional newspaper. Yet, over the course of the two campaign seasons, more than a quarter of the articles in the paper were devoted to politics.

Much stronger evidence appears that the frames used in political coverage differ from traditional media sources. Narrative frames were identified as the primary frame used for approximately two-thirds of all *The Onion*'s political stories in both 2000 and 2004. The remainder fit one of the individual frames.[22] In contrast, only 32 percent of *Star Tribune* articles were coded as frame narratives in 2000, while 39 percent of stories were coded as narratives in 2004. This difference is

TABLE 5.2.   Frame Narratives in *The Onion*

Frame Narrative	2000	2004	n
Red state vs. Blue state	0	2	2
Nation at war/terrorism	3	6	9
Politics is dirty	0	4	4
Politics is only about the money	3	1	4
Two-party system is limiting	0	1	1
Making fun of the media	4	0	4
Politics is stupid	6	4	10
Economy	1	1	2
Religious Right	1	0	1
Liberal Left	0	1	1
Corruption	1	2	3
Foreign policy	2	0	2
President Bush is stupid	1	1	2
Iraq War debacle	0	1	1
Battle over abortion	0	1	1
Vice President Cheney is scary	0	2	2
N	22	27	49

statistically significant ($p < .05$). Table 5.2 lists all the frame narratives present in *The Onion* during 2000 and 2004. The table also lists the number of stories appearing with each narrative and further breaks down the findings by year.

In total, there are seventeen unique frame narratives present in *The Onion*'s coverage. The five frame narratives that appear most common across both years are: "politics is stupid" (n = 10), "nation at war/terrorism" (n = 9), "politics is dirty" (n = 4), "politics is only about the money" (n = 4), and "making fun of the media" (n = 4). Interestingly, four of these most common frame narratives would also be likely to appear in conventional news.

"Politics is stupid" is the general idea that politics is a waste of time and boring, and thus there is no reason to engage in it. The following story from 2000 provides a good example of this narrative, regarding elections in particular.

> During their weekly canasta game Monday, area octogenarians Beatrice Evans and Ida Hollings discussed the relative merits of the candidates for Webster County Clerk. "I like the fact that Wayne Speno wants to lower passport fees," Evans said. "On the other hand, he wants to keep the vital-statistics office open only until 4 p.m. weekdays, which isn't late enough."

> Hollings said she plans to vote for Speno opponent Mary Lodge. "[Lodge] did a fine job as assistant county clerk these past six years," Hollings said, "and I really feel like she's ready."[23]

The issues and qualifications of those who run for political office are trivialized. Another example from 2004 follows the same story outline.

> Football fan Ben Pellett first became aware of the upcoming presidential election Tuesday, thanks to a tangential reference to it made in the Sept. 28 issue of *Sports Illustrated*. "One of the columnists said that picking who'll dominate the NFC North would be 'tougher than predicting the winner on Nov. 2,'" Pellett said. "At first I had no idea what that meant, but then I realized it's been a while since we voted for president. I asked my roommate, and sure enough, there's an election this year." Pellett added that he thinks both the Vikings and the Republicans have what it takes to go all the way.[24]

Again, the idea is that politics is boring and meaningless—that here, picking a president is less substantive and less interesting than football standings. By emphasizing the meaninglessness and irrelevance of elections, both stories mock the premise that politics matters.

"Nation at war/terrorism" speaks to the United States's fear of terrorist attack and the need for the public to be vigilant regarding such threats. A good example of this frame narrative appears in 2000.

> "I do *not* have time for this," said Hanani, seated at a Burger King in Concourse C, a plastic-explosives-filled duffel bag at his feet. "My *jihad* against the West was supposed to be carried out shortly after takeoff at 8:35 this morning. It is now 2:50 p.m. How much longer must I sit around this airport like an idiot before God's will is done?[25]

This narrative links to a very real aspect of the serious political environment and the danger the United States faces. At the same time, however, by focusing on the whininess of a potential terrorist, it mocks the significance and danger of such a threat. In retrospect, of course, this article is even more ironic given the tragic events of 9/11. A 2004 article draws on the same narrative.

> Fears of possible terrorist attacks have led organizers of the Sept. 27–30 al-Qaeda International Convention to take unprecedented security measures, sources reported Monday.... "It's a sad day when an overzealous madman with a bomb strapped to himself can threaten our divinely inspired wave of destruction," Jassem said, idly polishing a rifle. "How in the world did we get to this point?"[26]

Here comments and fears that are eerily familiar as actual U.S. policy makers' post-9/11 rhetoric ironically comes from the country's arch enemy.

"Politics is dirty" is the premise that politics is unsavory and those who engage in it are unscrupulous. Thus in 2004, *The Onion* offers the following story.

> With the knowledge that the minority vote will be crucial in the upcoming presidential election, Republican Party officials are urging blacks, Hispanics, and other minorities to make their presence felt at the polls on Wednesday, Nov. 3.... GOP committees in Ohio, Iowa, Wisconsin, Minnesota, Pennsylvania, Oregon, and Florida have spent more than $3 million on pamphlets, posters, stickers, and T-shirts bearing such slogans as "Put America First—Vote On The Third!" and "November 3rd Is *Your* Time To Be Heard".... Republican Party leaders expressed pride in what they characterized as a true alternative to other programs that encourage voting, such as Rock The Vote.[27]

Of course, Election Day 2004 was a different day. By using the rhetoric of "Get Out The Vote" efforts, the story suggests political party leaders are corrupt and interested in suppressing participation in the democratic process. The story also hearkens back to the real allegations that Republican Party leaders actually tried to minimize minority groups' votes.

"Politics is only about the money" suggests that public policy decisions and people interested in social change are both driven by monetary reasons. People who seek political office are motivated by the financial benefits such positions offer. A 2000 article draws on the common theme in popular discourse of questioning presidential candidate George W. Bush's intelligence. In the process, however, the article also suggests his motives for public service are self-serving.

> Republican presidential candidate George W. Bush was aghast to learn Monday that the position of U.S. president, the highest office in the land and most powerful in the free world, pays just $200,000 a year.
>
> "That's it?" asked Bush, struggling to comprehend the figure reported to him by aides. "A measley couple hundred grand a year? Not per month, even? Because I've already spent more than $60 million to get this job. I'll have to be president for 300 years just to break even."[28]

This same theme shows up in a 2004 article that mocks people interested in social change and the viability of such change. The only people capable of making a difference in the world as individuals are those with resources.

Cynics often say that one man can't make a difference in a huge and complicated world. But this week in New York a few tremendously rich and powerful men have given those naysayers reason to reconsider their views.... "One must not doubt the ability of a few dedicated wealthy people to alter the course of history," the billionaire said. "Indeed, it's the only thing that ever has."[29]

In different ways, both these articles emphasize the perceived self-serving nature of people who appear to be driven by public purposes and point to the impact of money on political outcomes. "Making fun of the media" satirizes conventional media for failing to cover substantive political events and for its overemphasis on dramatic stories with limited political significance.

CNN officials announced Tuesday that the cable network is "making good progress" in its ongoing effort to release the vast backlog of news accumulated during Elián González's headline-dominating seven-month odyssey in the U.S.

Among the backlogged stories to air during recent CNN "News You Didn't Hear" coverage: the formation of the new Eastern European nation of Molbania last December...and the June 4 congressional vote to grant federal legislators a 400 percent pay hike.[30]

Does *The Onion*'s coverage of politics offer cues that citizens should be disenchanted with politics? As noted above, three of the most frequently used frame narratives were present in both years we analyzed, offering negative messages about politics and/or a main actor in the political arena, such as the media. Other less frequently used frame narratives, such as the idea that the two-party system is limiting, offer the same antipolitics message.[31] A good example of this appears in *The Onion*'s coverage of the 2000 election and the two-party system.

AUSTIN, TX, OR NASHVILLE, TN—In one of the narrowest presidential votes in U.S. history, either George W. Bush or Al Gore was elected the 43rd president of the United States Tuesday, proclaiming the win "a victory for the American people and the dawn of a bold new era in this great nation."

Bush or Gore attributed his victory to his commitment to the issues that matter to ordinary, hardworking Americans. Throughout the campaign, the Republican or Democrat spoke out in favor of improving educational standards, protecting the environment, reducing crime, strengthening the military, cutting taxes, and reforming Social Security. He also took a strong pro-middle-class stand, praising America's working families as "the backbone of this great nation."[32]

While accurately reflecting the uncertainty of the election, the idea of no difference between the major candidates also shines through in this article.

A number of stories also portrayed either the executive and/or congressional branches of government negatively. Six articles framing public servants in the executive branch as incompetent appear in *The Onion* during the periods under examination. Congress also comes under *The Onion*'s satiric knife. For example, the following article outlines the incompetence of Congress.

> After three hours of congressional debate, it was decided that the investigative panel would consist of Sen. Trent Lott (R-MS), because he's a real leader; Sen. Jack Reed (D-RI), because he's small and good at sneaking into tight spots; and Rep. Steve Largent (R-OK), because, as a former NFL player, he's the most athletic member of Congress.
>
> [they urged] Congress to increase federal funding for the expedition, which will require a length of rope, extra flashlight batteries, three bottles of grape soda, and a jackknife. As of Tuesday, the trio had collected from Congress $4.74 million and a slingshot.[33]

The implications are twofold: that Congress deals with meaningless issues, and that while doing so, they spend large amounts of money. While the total number of negative institutional articles was less than one-fifth of *The Onion*'s political coverage across both years, it is important to remember this is explicitly negative coverage. There are no countervailing positive articles regarding either.

In total, sixteen articles framed with one of these antipolitical themes appeared in *The Onion* during the fall of 2000. Across both years, narratives that suggest a negative conception of politics framed over two-thirds of *The Onion*'s stories.

Implications

There is at least some evidence supporting each of our hypotheses. Like traditional print news media, *The Onion* also offers substantial coverage of politics during electoral campaigns. There is also strong support for the idea that *The Onion* utilizes frame narratives to a greater extent than a traditional news source. Further, while *The Onion*'s articles draw on a wide range of frame narratives, the bulk fit into a category that may serve to disengage citizens from politics. These findings present some normatively interesting implications.

While politics by no means takes up all of *The Onion*'s space, it does play a large role in its content. Therefore, we imagine that it does function as an agenda setter for some of its readership.

Yet the fear that hybrids such as *The Onion* will appeal especially to the politically ignorant seems unfounded. Both satire as a device and the use of a frame narrative require a certain baseline level of prior political knowledge. Without such knowledge, political satire and frame narratives are likely to be largely ineffective. Since frame narratives dominate *The Onion*'s coverage, those without a foundation of political knowledge will neither understand its jokes nor fully absorb its political cues. This is not to say that political satire such as *The Onion* presents does not have the capacity to influence members of the public. In fact, for the same reasons political novices may be unable to fully recognize satiric hybrid cues (a requirement for traditional satire and frame narratives to work), the population more vulnerable to humor-based print hybrids may be the politically knowledgeable. Of course, such expert political knowledge may also serve to insulate them from traditional framing effects.

The large proportion of potentially disengaging cues presented in *The Onion*'s coverage of the two elections is a greater concern especially given the demographic group that dominates the readership of humor-based hybrid news/entertainment print media. Young people are already less likely to be interested in politics and have the least positive views regarding the political process. Reading cues that reinforce these attitudes would seem unlikely to increase their civic engagement.

Clearly, several questions merit further research. One is a closer analysis of how the credibility of print news/entertainment hybrids affects how people evaluate them as a source. Most importantly, it is imperative to evaluate whether the cues offered by hybrid print media such as *The Onion* actually influence people's opinions about politics. Particularly interesting would be to examine whether hybrids' negative cues regarding politics prime negative evaluations among those with low levels of political knowledge or merely reinforce the attitudes of the already politically alienated public.

Notes

1. This quotation was retrieved from http://www.brainyquote.com/quotes/authors/w/will_rogers.html.

2. "Cheney Returns To Camp Crystal Lake," *The Onion*, September 15, 2004. http://www.theonion.com/content/node/30709.

3. Michael X. Delli Carpini and Bruce A. Williams, "Let Us Infotain You: Politics in the New Media Age," in *Mediated Politics*, eds. W. Lance Bennett and Robert M. Entman (New York: Cambridge University Press, 2001), 160–181.

4. For example, according to a recent Pew Center survey cited by Geoffrey Baym (2005), "21 percent of people ages 18–29 say they regularly learn about the news and politics from comedy shows such as *Saturday Night Live*, and 13 percent report learning from late-night talk shows such as NBC's *Tonight Show with Jay Leno*." Geoffrey Baym, "The Daily Show: Discursive Integration and the Reinvention of Political Journalism," *Political Communication* 22 (2005): 259–276, 260.

5. See CNN's coverage of *The Onion*, " The Onion: Funny Site Is No Joke," August 29, 2003. http://edition.cnn.com/2003/TECH/ptech/08/28/bus2.feat.onion.site/index.html.

6. For more information, see *The Onion* Media Kit 2007. http://mediakit.theonion.com/print_main.html.

7. Most readers have at least some college education, and in most areas, over 50 percent of readers have at least a college degree. Further, the majority of readers are under the age of thirty-five. For more information, see http://mediakit.theonion.com/print_main.html.

8. These nine types are: entertainment talk show interviews with politicians, soft news, entertainment television events, fictional political dramas, political docudramas, reality-based programming/documentaries, traditional satire, satiric situational comedies, and lifeworld content. R. Lance Holbert, "A Typology for the Study of Entertainment Television and Politics," *American Behavioral Scientist* 49 (2005): 436–453.

9. Geoffrey Baym, "The Daily Show and the Redefinition of Political Journalism" (presented at the annual meeting of the 3rd Annual Pre-Conference on Political Communication, American Political Science Association, Chicago, 2004).

10. Holbert, "A Typology for the Study of Entertainment Television and Politics."

11. Baym, "The Daily Show and the Redefinition of Political Journalism."

12. Framing is the power of the media to create the lens, or context, through which issues are analyzed. See Shanto Iyengar, *Is Anyone Responsible? How Television Frames Political Issues* (Chicago: University of Chicago Press, 1991). A frame narrative is a frame that is rooted in already held beliefs about a topic or an issue. See Robert M. Entman, "Framing U.S. Coverage of International News: Contrasts in the Narratives of the KAL and Iran Air Incidents," *Journal of Communication* 41 (1991): 6–27.

13. The headline story is also easily identified because it is listed above all the others and the title is displayed using large bold text.

14. "Political" stories were any stories that raised issues of political behavior or national political institutions.

15. Complete list of frame narratives: President vs. Congress, interest group vs. interest group, Red state vs. Blue state, nation at war, politics is dirty, politics is only about money, inside the beltway vs. outside the beltway, government bureaucracy, two-party system is limiting, making fun of major media, civic engagement is good, politics is stupid, young people vs. old people, economy, religious right, liberal left, terrorism, corruption, political apathy, foreign policy, President Bush is dumb, Iraq war debacle, and Vice-President Cheney is scary.

16. In 2000 there were three stories that coders concluded had both narrative and individual frames. In 2004 there were five such stories.

17. For *The Onion* analysis, intercoder reliability was very strong for headline stories (Scott's Pi, .92 in 2000 and 2004). Intercoder reliability was not as strong when coding individual vs. narrative stories (Scott's Pi, .63 in 2000 and .62 in 2004). Similar scores also appear for the coding of frame narrative stories. While on the surface these scores may seem low, they are not surprising given the number of possible frame narratives. Intercoder reliability was very strong: Scott's Pi of at least .90 for individual stories, branches of government, and the *Star Tribune*.

18. "Gore Wondering If Latest Doonesbury Is About Him," *The Onion*, September 27, 2004. http://www.theonion.com/content/node/28218.

19. "Documents Reveal Gaps In Bush's Service As President," *The Onion*, September 29, 2004. http://www.theonion.com/content/node/30725.

20. For instance, while campaign coverage accounts for only 32 percent of the *Star Tribune*'s headline coverage in 2004, this still equates to twelve stories. This amount is one more story than all of *The Onion*'s 2004 headline stories.

21. "Nader Supporters Blame Electoral Defeat On Bush, Kerry," *The Onion*, November 3, 2004. http://www.theonion.com/content/node/32964.

22. Combining both years, the individual frames present in *The Onion* are: horse race (6 percent), candidate issue stance (22 percent), impact of issues on the race (6 percent), negative personal (50 percent), horse race and issue stance (6 percent), and negative personal and issue stance (10 percent).

23. "Senior Citizens Discuss Merits Of County-Clerk Candidates," *The Onion*, September 13, 2000. http://www.theonion.com/content/node/31574.

24. "Upcoming Election Deduced From Sports Illustrated Content," *The Onion*, September 29, 2004. http://www.theonion.com/content/node/32942.
25. "Terrorist Extremely Annoyed By Delayed Flight," *The Onion*, September 13, 2000. http://www.theonion.com/content/node/28295.
26. "Organizers Fear Terrorist Attacks On Upcoming Al-Qaeda Convention," *The Onion*, September 22, 2004. http://www.theonion.com/content/node/30716.
27. "Republicans Urge Minorities To Get Out And Vote On Nov. 3," *The Onion*, October 27, 2004. http://www.theonion.com/content/node/30760.
28. "Bush Horrified To Learn Presidential Salary," *The Onion*, October 18, 2000. http://www.theonion.com/content/node/28192.
29. "Small Group Of Dedicated Rich People Change The World," *The Onion*, September 1, 2004. http://www.theonion.com/content/node/30699.
30. "CNN Still Releasing News Piled Up During Elián González Saga," *The Onion*, October 18, 2000. http://www.theonion.com/content/node/28200.
31. Antipolitics includes the following narratives: dirtiness of politics, politics is all about the money, two-party system is limiting, making fun of the media, politics is stupid, corruption, President Bush is stupid, and Vice President Cheney is scary.
32. "Bush Or Gore: 'A New Era Dawns,'" *The Onion*, November 8, 2000. http://www.theonion.com/content/node/28068.
33. http://www.theonion.com/content/node/28212.

6

Vote for Pedro
Film Comedy, Youth, and Electoral Politics

Eric Shouse and Todd Fraley

A popular explanation for why so few young Americans exercise their right to vote is circular. It suggests, "Many young people do not follow politics; therefore, they do not vote. Because relatively small percentages of young people vote, parties and politicians frequently neglect them."[1] While this account is reasonable, it does not explain why so few young people follow politics in the first place. Too often we are told young people do not pay attention to politics because they are politically apathetic. Supposedly young people find politics boring and do not pay attention to political conversations because they would rather be entertained.[2] This explanation neglects the way youth have been "framed" by political discourse. It *blames the victims* for not tuning into a conversation in which they are either ignored or stereotyped as "unmotivated, navel-gazing slackers intent on making do without the slightest interest in a larger social and political world."[3] Given the messages they receive about themselves, young people would have to be self-destructive to tune in to the majority mainstream political news.

Because they have so often been belittled by the political discourse of older Americans, getting young adults interested in politics is not always easy. One way to get more youth to participate in the political process might be through popular culture. Giroux explains popular culture's importance, "Kids no longer view schools as the primary source of education, and rightfully so. Media texts—videos, films, music, television, radio, computers—and the new public spheres they inhabit have far more influence on shaping the memories, language, values, and identities of young people."[4] Having a conversation in a college classroom about films—or any form of popular culture our students appreciate—is important because popular culture is where young people come to know who they are and what they care about. In that spirit, this chapter will discuss film comedies about elections.

While many people associate comedy with outlandish and even "subversive" behavior, political comedy is not inherently radical. On the contrary, more often than not political humor reinforces the status quo.[5] It reminds us of our shared norms and values by ridiculing those who fail to live up to established standards of behavior. Film comedies about politics often rely upon stereotypes because "they help to establish instantly recognizable character types [and because] stereotype-based jokes also constitute a source of humor."[6]

This chapter will begin by describing four contemporary film comedies about electoral politics: *Bulworth, Bob Roberts, Wag the Dog,* and *Head of State.* After we describe these films, we will explain how they reinforce negative stereotypes that discourage young people from participating in the political process. Then we will describe how *Napoleon Dynamite* challenges the stereotype that teenagers are naturally stupid, dangerous, and disengaged from politics and explain why we feel it provides an accessible model of civic engagement for young people.

Shooting the Bull: Warren Beatty's *Bulworth*

Bulworth (20th Century Fox, 1998) is the story of California Democratic senator Jay Billington Bulworth, a career politician who can no longer balance his 1960s civil rights altruism with the corruption and greed of political life in the 1990s. Bulworth is so distraught about becoming a political monster that he hires a contract killer to take his life. Once the arrangements have been made, Bulworth sets out on a forty-eight-hour push for reelection. Mentally and physically exhausted from the demands of his job and the pressure to maintain a clean-cut public image amidst a sea of scandal and self-service, Bulworth arrives in Los Angeles expecting a contract killer to put him out of his misery. However, when his plane touches down a C-SPAN camera crew is there to greet him. They will be following the senator for the next forty-eight hours (so much for a clean hit).

Bulworth's first stop is an African American church in South Central L.A. The senator takes a prepared speech from one of his handlers and reads two lines of empty rhetoric about how our nation "is standing on the doorstep of a new millennium." He quickly becomes bored and opens the floor for questions. A woman in the audience wants to know, "Are you sayin' the Democratic Party don't care about the African American community?" In the midst of a nervous breakdown, Bulworth responds

> Isn't that obvious? You got half your kids out of work and the other half are in jail. Do you see any Democrat doing anything about it? Certainly not me! So what're you gonna do, vote Republican? Come on! Come on, you're not gonna vote Republican! Let's call a spade a spade! I mean, come on! You can have a Billion Man March! If you don't put down that malt liquor and chicken wings, and get behind someone other than a running back who stabs his wife, you're never gonna get rid of somebody like me!

As he lets the stereotypes fly, Bulworth is rushed out of the church by his staff, but not before agreeing to hire three young African American women to serve as volunteers on his campaign.

Next, Bulworth and his entourage make it to Beverly Hills for his meeting with members of the film and entertainment industry. When asked if he believes people in the entertainment business need help from the government in setting limits on sex and violence, Bulworth suggests the problem is not sex or violence: the problem is that most of their films are not good. Bulworth continues, "But my guys are not stupid. They always put the big Jews on my schedule. You're mostly Jews, right? [Bulworth looks down at the script of his prepared speech.] I bet they put something bad about Farrakhan in here for you!"

Bulworth is rushed from the lavish home in Beverly Hills and finds himself back in his limo with two aides, a C-SPAN cameraman, and his new volunteers. The ghetto girls quickly give him a lesson in slang. These terms lay the groundwork for Bulworth's new identity. You see, despite being a seasoned veteran of Congress, Jay Billington Bulworth cannot effectively and legitimately express his opinions about important social issues. Thus, he must transform himself into "M. C. Bulworth," a sixty-year-old rapping senator who speaks truth to power.

Bulworth's transformation continues as he visits an urban afterhours club where patrons are allowed to pass through a guarded chain-link fence only after discarding their weapons. As they enter, Bulworth's female volunteers pull chains and knives from their undergarments. Here, Bulworth meets L. D. (the local drug king-pin) who offers the senator privileged insight into the lifestyles of young African Americans. According to L. D., he is helping the twelve-year-olds slinging dope for him by "giving them entry-level positions into the only growth sector occupation that's truly open to them...the substance supply industry." He tells Bulworth that politicians like him do not care about poor black kids: "That's what you tell me every time that y'all vote to cut them school programs; every time y'all vote to cut them funds to the job programs." And in one of the more poignant moments of the film, L. D. suggests the exploitation of young people by urban drug dealers is no worse than the exploitation of young soldiers by wealthy politicians: "I'm a busi-nessman, and as a businessman, you gotta limit your liabilities. And that's what these shorties offer me: limited liabilities; because of their limited vulnerability to legal sanctions, man. It's the same...thing in politics, Dog. You find an edge, you gotta exploit [it].... That's why y'all sent...teenagers to Iraq."

Energized by what he has learned, Bulworth heads to his next engagement at the Beverly Wilshire Hotel. Once there, "M. C. Bulworth" puts away his carefully prepared speech and begins an obscenity-laced rant about the corruption of government and its consequences for the common citizen. When questioned about his use of obscenities, Bulworth responds

> Obscenity? The rich is getting richer and richer and richer while the mid-dle class is getting more poor / Making billions and billions and billions of bucks / well my friend if you weren't already rich at the start well that situation just sucks /....
>
> We got factories closing down / Where the hell did all the good jobs go? Well, I'll tell you where they went / My contributors make more prof-its makin, makin, makin, Hirin' kids in Mexico / Oh a brother can work in fast food / If he can't invent computer games / But what we used to call America / That's going down the drains/ How's a young man gonna meet his financial responsibilities workin' at mother----in' Burger King?

The rest of the film follows this same format. We follow Bulworth through the dark and dangerous streets of South Central (are there really no streetlights in Compton?) as he meets his constituents and learns of their struggles, all the while dropping F-bombs. Bulworth comes to believe the "real obscenity" is not foul language; rather, it is what has happened to poor people in this country, especially African Americans.

The Freewheeling Conservative: *Bob Roberts*

Bob Roberts (Paramount, Miramax, 1992) is the story of a Yale graduate and self-made millionaire who transforms himself into a "conservative rebel" politician. Frustrated by liberals who refuse to take personal responsibility for their problems, Roberts travels the country singing folk music and rallying support from Americans who believe in making money, being rich, and not needlessly supporting the disenfranchised. His folk ballads anger the liberal establishment, especially those in the music industry. On the other hand, his constituents/fans see him as a kind, thoughtful man of the people. As far as they are concerned, Bob Roberts is the leader of a new generation. In his tune, "Complain and Complain," Roberts tells his constituents

> Some people will have / Some simply will not / But they'll complain and complain and complain and complain and complain / Some people will work / Some never will / But they'll complain and complain and complain and complain and complain / Like this: / It's society's fault I don't have a job / It's society's fault I'm a slob / I'm a drunk, I don't have a brain / Give me a pamphlet while I complain / Hey pal you're living in the land of the free / No-one's gonna hand you opportunity.

Bob Roberts is shot in the pseudo-documentary or "mockumentary" style. Through this device we learn the anti-hippie message of Roberts's music and his campaign stem from his childhood. Young Bob was raised on a commune by overindulgent parents, yet has come to reject their liberal worldview as thoroughly as his 1960s-style parents rejected the conservative worldview of their parents. In one ballad, Roberts sings, "Grandma felt guilty 'bout being so rich and it bothered her until the day she died. But I will take my inheritance and invest it with pride, yes invest it with pride." Where previous folk singers suggested "this land [America] was made for you and me," Roberts sings, "This land was made for *me*." In his mind, consumer capitalism and God are equally divine.

The Roberts campaign devises a strategy to unseat liberal incumbent senator Brickley Paiste through a series of dirty tricks. Unfortunately for Roberts, there are lingering questions about his own campaign regarding possible involvement in the Iran-Contra scandal. While local TV news outlets fawn over Bob Roberts's wonderful and multifaceted personality, they fail to investigate these serious allegations. However, *Troubled Times* (an independent alternative publication) finally manages to force the story about the Roberts campaign's involvement in the Iran-Contra scandal into the mainstream media, and it looks like Roberts may crack under the pressure.

With questions unanswered and protestors demonstrating at his concerts, a distraction is required. As if it was planned, Roberts is shot while leaving an event. He suffers serious injuries leaving him wheelchair bound. Images of Bob Roberts immediately begin to grace the cover of every major newsmagazine in the United States. His supporters stand vigil outside his hospital room waiting for the latest word, and the campaign is quietly cleared of any wrongdoing by the media-savvy members of Congress.

In a strange twist of fate, "Bugs" Raplin, the reporter for *Troubled Times* who sparked the investigation, is identified as the shooter. Roberts's loyal followers immediately head to the precinct where the reporter is being held. They hope to lynch him before he has a chance for a trial. They are unsuccessful, which is fortunate, as we learn the accused suffers from a physical condition that would have made it impossible for him to fire a handgun. When he is released, "Bugs" reveals to a documentary filmmaker that Roberts faked the shooting. Unfortunately, the truth matters not. Roberts emerges from the shooting as a national hero and is elected senator. His album is released and it tops the charts. With the documentary cameras still rolling, the folk-singing politician taps his foot to the beat as he sings a song praising the greatness of our nation, a nation he has obviously duped.

Media Bites Man: *Wag the Dog*

Wag the Dog (New Line Cinema, 1997) is a story about the complex relationship between politicians, public relations liaisons, and the mainstream media. Two weeks before a presidential election, the White House Press Office receives word an underage girl has accused the president of inappropriate sexual conduct. Enter the world's greatest PR man, Conrad Bream, or "Mr. Fix-It." He asks for $20,000 and a plane ticket to Los Angeles, and then he assures the president's people he will take care of everything. Before heading off to L.A., Mr. Fix-It hands out assignments to the president's communication staff intending to divert the attention of the press with contrived news stories. He tells the president's staff to deny the existence of the new secret B3 Bomber (lie #1); to deny the trip to Seattle has anything to do with Muslim fundamentalists in Albania (lie #2); and to delay the president's return trip from China until a more extravagant set of lies can be concocted—a major diversion with another round of lies to be named later.

Traveling with a senior White House communications official, Mr. Fix-It devises a plan to create the appearance of a war with Albania. Why Albania? Why *not* Albania? Americans know very little about Albania. For that matter, according to the film, Americans know very little about anything outside the border of our television screens. In order to pull off his plan, Mr. Fix-It enlists the aid of Hollywood producer Stanley Motss. Motss sips on a veggie shake as he begins spinning a tale about how Albanian terrorists have a "suitcase bomb" somewhere on the Canadian border.

In addition to the narrative about Albanian terrorists, Motss gives the American people what they really need in wartime: patriotic songs, corporate product tie-ins, and a bevy of "Support the Troops" symbols. *Wag the Dog* explains how public relations people can sell the American citizen anything: yellow ribbons, a president, and even a war provided the packaging is dramatic and compelling. According to Mr. Fix-It, the American public bought the first Persian Gulf War and the only thing most people remember about it is a single image of one bomb falling down a chimney. Mr. Fix-It implies that the image was a ten-inch model made out of Legos blown up on a Hollywood film set.

This time Mr. Fix-It wants to fake an entire war. He asks the producer to sell the American public a "pageant." The producer agrees and shortly thereafter an unknown actress carries a bag of Tostitos across a Hollywood soundstage. Later, through the miracle of digital editing, the Tostitos become a cat, the soundstage becomes a bombed-out village, and the actress becomes a refugee who was raped by Albanian terrorists. On the set, the floor director instructs the makeup person, "go easy, she's just been raped by terrorists." Unfortunately for Mr. Fix-It and the producer, there are a few hiccups with their production: Albania is denying there is a conflict, nobody can get in touch with the president who is still stuck in China, and his opponent has just gone on national TV and told the American public the conflict in Albania is over. Mr. Fix-It responds, "That's it. The war is over...I saw it on TV."

Despite the war being prematurely ended by the president's rival, the producer refuses to yield to the facts. Nobody tells him how to tell a story. He responds to the reality of the Albanian situation by creating Act 2: The Captured Hero. The producer leaks a photograph to the press in which Sergeant Schuman ("Ol' Shoe") appears to have been taken hostage by Albanian terrorists. However, Ol' Shoe, being the brave soul he is, has sent a message in Morse code by tearing dashes and dots into his military-issue sweater. We are told the sweater reads, "Courage Mom—Courage Mom—Courage Mom." Within days, old shoes hang from every tall tree and telephone wire in the country as U.S. citizens rally behind a fabricated American war hero. The producer hires musicians to write a song about the event, and a newly created "historic" blues ballad entitled "Ol' Shoe" climbs the charts.

Enter the CIA. They know this is a fraud, and they inform Mr. Fix-It and the producer that they will not be allowed to continue. However, when the CIA tries to intimidate Mr. Fix-It, he turns the tables. He convinces them that if there is no war in Albania (or somewhere) everyone will realize the CIA has become useless and they will call for the organization to be disbanded. The next thing we know, the president is climbing in the polls. The election is only a few days away and a potential presidential sex scandal has left the media radar. The news media is far more concerned about fabricated reports that indicate Ol' Shoe has been rescued and is coming home from Albania. This series of events ensures the president's reelection. There is only one more problem. In their haste to find a soldier with a name that sounds like shoe—to match the song and marketing campaign—one of the producer's liaisons inadvertently chose a soldier who was in "Special Projects," not "Special Forces." It turns out Ol' Shoe has been locked away in military prison for raping a nun. Luckily for Mr. Fix-It and the producer, the nun rapist dies in an accident before anyone uncovers the potential PR disaster. Ol' Shoe receives a war hero's welcome when he returns to U.S. soil in a flag-draped coffin.

Mr. Fix-It thanks the producer for a job well done. However, the producer decides he cannot sit by and let his talent go unappreciated. He sold pageantry to the American people and made them believe it was a war; he made a total fraud look real. He feels his efforts must not go unnoticed. Why is there no Oscar for producing? The producer desperately wants to tell the American people the truth. Of course, if he does, men in dark suits and indoor shades are standing by. It is their job to kill when necessary to protect Americans from the truth.

Fear of a Black President: *Head of State*

Head of State (DreamWorks, 2003) is the story of Washington, DC
alderman Mays Gilliam. As Gilliam explains, he is not from the DC
we see on TV or on bus tours of the Capital. He is from a DC "where
you get shot while getting shot." It is also the DC where people buy
stolen meat from a man selling it by the package outside a gas station.
Gilliam cares about these people. As his story begins, the caring and
compassionate public servant promises to drive his constituents to
work if the city buses stop running. Sadly, Gilliam's dedication to his
people is the cause of his downfall. As a result of saving an elderly
woman and her cat from a condemned building (her house), Gilliam
loses his girlfriend, his car, his bike, and even his job, all in the same
day. He cares too much, and because he does not play politics "correctly," Gilliam is condemned for being a "troublemaker."

Meanwhile, in the other Washington, DC, the presidential election
is just a few weeks away. As crazy as it sounds, the Democratic candidates for president and vice president are both simultaneously killed in
a plane crash. Gilliam learns about the tragedy on his car radio when an
announcer interrupts a Jay-Z song for all of six seconds to pass along the
news. Shortly thereafter, in a dark office somewhere in the heart of DC,
political party leaders decide the best way to respond to the disaster is
to choose a candidate who cannot win the election, but who will position them for success in 2008. They need a minority candidate to take
advantage of the shift in demographics that America will soon experience. Gilliam fits the bill because he is young, he is black, and he is so
passionate about making a difference he will never be elected.

After accepting his party's nomination for president of the United
States, Gilliam is provided with a campaign tour bus, security
agents, a speechwriter, and a "super-whore" (a stunning blonde who
will make sure there are no sex scandals by keeping everything "in
house"). At his first campaign function, Gilliam meets very briefly
with the Teamsters (a group of fat Italian men) and then proceeds to
get the party started (like only a black man can) by getting a group
of rich white people to join him in the electric slide. The barrage of
racial stereotypes mercifully ends when an elderly white woman tells
Gilliam his party "was off the hizzle fo shizzle."

During his campaign tour, Gilliam travels to middle America to
deliver his stock campaign speech. He tells the people of Wisconsin that
they are the backbone of the country. Milk makes the body strong, and

Wisconsin makes the nation strong. But when Gilliam gets to Chicago his brother Marty (played by Bernie Mac) shows up and tells him to put away the script. What does a Chicago bail bondsman know about successful politics? Probably nothing, but like every other movie we reviewed, this political comedy needs a black man to represent "the other America" in order to make the "truth" come out. Taking the cue from his brother, Gilliam stops spewing the boring party line and regains his passion for service. He goes off script and discusses "what ain't right about America." Low wages, poor schools, bad health care, greed, and corruption top his list. And, of course, the crowd responds.

Gilliam "keeps it real" by trading in Brooks Brothers suits for Adidas sweats and Kangol hats. His poll numbers rise as his new style resonates with the people. Believing he can win, Mays tries to line up a debate with his opponent, Vice President Lewis, who was not aware his previous opponent had died. This supports the theme that politicians are simply idiots in suits who repeat the same catchy phrases over and over. Although Mays is convinced he can win, his people unceremoniously explain to him he was handpicked to lose. Instead of quitting, Mays names his brother (the bail bondsman) as his running mate. Together, they campaign even harder, helped along by the insightful advice of a young black woman working as a gas station attendant. Who needs a think tank like the Economic Policy Institute when you have access to the pretty girl at the Gas-n-Go?

Mays finally manages to force Lewis into a debate by taunting him with a series of "yo momma" jokes. With the theme to Monday Night Football playing in the background and people upset *Martin* has been preempted, the presidential debate begins. VP Lewis emits empty campaign promises but garners applause for his popular line, "God bless America and no place else." Mays answers the critics who charge he is an amateur and unqualified for the office of the presidency by arguing he is a real American—he's been broke, he's been high, and he's been robbed—and he believes political leaders should help people who need help. The public embraces his "honesty," and the country elects its first African American president.

Political Stereotypes and Political Comedy

Bulworth, Bob Roberts, Wag the Dog, and *Head of State* all reinforce the following negative stereotypes about the political process: (1) politicians are corrupt and/or stupid, (2) in politics, anyone who would speak the truth is immediately silenced by sinister forces, and (3) the average citizen lacks the intelligence to see beyond the media spectacle and understand the political process. The first stereotype, that all politicians are corrupt and/or stupid, can prevent rational political dialogue. As Mark Sachleben and Kevan Yenerall proposed

> One of the major concerns when using film to teach politics and provoke discussion and debate is to get students and citizens to get beyond—or at least temporarily throw aside—the cynical, oft-repeated mantra that all office-holders and candidates are vision-less, shameless, plotting scam artists devoted to winning at any cost, public interest be damned.[7]

Senator Bulworth feels so bad about the way the political system has *corrupted* his values he wants to die. Bob Roberts fakes paralysis to divert attention from his *corruption* to improve his chances of being elected. In *Wag the Dog*, the president sexually assaults a young girl and then authorizes the staging of a fake a war to *cover up* his wrongdoing. In *Head of State* the vice president of the United States does not follow current events, but he expects to be elected because he is Sharon Stone's cousin. He is the quintessential *dumb politician*, an idiot in an expensive suit. While Mays Gilliam begins the movie as a likable and caring alderman, by the end of the film he has become just as dumb as his opponent. In a nationally televised debate he tosses out the childish retort, "I know you are, but what am I?" All in all, none of these films presents a politician who deserves the support of the American public.

Bulworth, Bob Roberts, Wag the Dog, and *Head of State* are not only critical of politicians, they are critical of the entire political system. The second major stereotype in these films is that our nation is not really ruled by elected officials. The politicians are presented as merely window dressing for sinister forces that actually pull the strings of power. In *Bulworth* it is the special interests groups. They operate behind the scenes and have all the real political power. In *Bob Roberts*, Roberts is in on a conspiracy involving his campaign manager, the CIA, the banking industry, drug smugglers, and others. In *Wag the Dog*, the spin doctors produce the "truth." And, when one of them threatens to let the proverbial cat out of the bag, he is reminded of the "powers that be." Finally, in *Head of State*, several jokes play on the perceived likelihood that if a truth-telling black man were to run for president, white America would conspire to have him assassinated.

However, as potentially damaging to democracy as the conspiracy theories in these films are (why vote for the rare honest politician if he or she will be silenced or killed?), the biggest problem with *Bulworth*, *Bob Roberts*, *Wag the Dog*, and *Head of State* is the way they stereotype the average citizen. The premise of *Bulworth* is that voters have continued to elect the same corrupt politician for thirty years. In *Head of State*, Mays Gilliam becomes "presidential material" by putting on a FUBU suit. *Bob Roberts* runs a crooked campaign, but because American voters believe everything the mainstream media tell us, he is elected senator. In *Wag the Dog*, everything the average citizen knows about politicians and the government is a lie constructed by public relations people. Thus, *Bob Roberts* and *Wag the Dog* suggest it is pointless to try to learn more about politics because all we can know is what the media tell us. Moreover, what the media tell us are lies. In this view, the voting citizen will always be too ignorant to make a rational choice.

These four movies rely on the use of stereotypes to create comedy. Unfortunately, while these stereotypes are sometimes good for a laugh they are likely to provoke the following sorts of questions: Why vote when every politician is either corrupt or painfully stupid? Why vote when the people we elect are not really in charge of the government? And why vote when our fellow citizens are so dumb or ignorant they will cancel out any intelligent choice on our part? We do not find these questions especially interesting. In fact, when it comes to trying to get young people who are already cynical about politics interested in political dialogue, watching films that reinforce cynicism is probably downright counterproductive. We would like to suggest an alternative, *Napoleon Dynamite*.

Napoleon Dynamite Is Not an Explosive Device

Napoleon Dynamite (Fox Searchlight, 2004) is the story of high school angst, friendship, and triumph in the face of adversity. The title character, Napoleon, sports a red afro, cotton cargo sweat pants, a T-shirt with the image of Pegasus on the front, and a pair of navy blue moon boots. His voice is one part deep and two parts whiny, and he lives with his grandmother, his thirty-two-year-old brother, and Tina the Llama. In his spare time, Napoleon plays tetherball alone and hunts wolverines in Alaska with a twelve-gauge shotgun. Napoleon has mastered the bow staff and nunchaku, and has been asked to join several of the "butt-load of gangs" claiming turf in Preston, Idaho. He can also identify defects in fresh cow milk. Yet, for some reason, Napoleon is not the most popular kid in school.

Napoleon's best friend is Pedro Sanchez, a Mexican American cowboy who is new to Preston High School. Pedro shares Napoleon's interest in cows and dairy farming, and like Napoleon he is a proud member of the Future Farmers of America (FFA). A confident young man who possesses skills with the ladies, Pedro also has a few flaws. He always seems to be sick and wears a woman's wig to cover his impulsively shaved head. Pedro is also so noncommunicative that Preston High's principal is not sure he speaks English.

Pedro and Napoleon become fast friends, but their friendship looks like it may be put in jeopardy by Deb, an entrepreneurial girl-next-door type who favors stirrup pants and a ponytail on the side of her head. She is earning money for college by selling handmade key chains and glamour shots. Napoleon approaches her in the cafeteria and says, "I see you're drinking 1%. Is that 'cause you think you're fat? 'Cause you're not. You could be drinking whole if you wanted to." Despite Napoleon's sweet moves, Deb goes to the dance with Pedro.

The other major romance in *Napoleon Dynamite* revolves around Napoleon's brother Kip, a frail, unemployed thirty-two-year-old who is training to become a cage fighter, and his online girlfriend LaFawnduh, a full-figured black woman from Detroit. At first LaFawnduh frustrates Kip because she refuses to send him a "full body shot," but sparks fly when the two meet in person. Although Kip and Napoleon have their differences, it is apparent they genuinely care for each other. At one point in the film, Kip straps on his inline skates and asks Napoleon for a tow. Napoleon mounts his ten-speed and pulls his older brother into town where the two enroll in an introductory karate class.

While Napoleon has obvious affection for his older brother, he has no love for his Uncle Rico. Rico lives in a camper van in a field somewhere in Idaho. When Napoleon's grandmother injures herself in a dune buggy accident, Rico agrees to stay with Napoleon and Kip while she recovers. Rico's wife has left him because he is stuck in 1982. Throughout the film, he relives his glory years as a backup high school quarterback. When he is not videotaping himself throwing a football, he peddles knockoff Tupperware in the hopes of buying a time-travel machine. Rico wants desperately to return to 1982 so he can throw the winning touchdown in the state championship game and change the course of his life. Unfortunately, when he starts peddling a breast-enhancing formula to girls at Napoleon's high school, Uncle Rico ruins Napoleon's life.

Ultimately, Pedro decides to run for class president with the help of Napoleon. Pedro's opposition is Summer Wheatly, a pretty and popular cheerleader. She tells her classmates that if she wins, "It will be summer all year in Preston." Summer also promises to secure new cheerleading uniforms if she is elected and ends her campaign speech by cajoling her classmates, "Besides, who wants to eat Chimi-ney Changas all year, next year?"

Although clearly nervous, Pedro counters Summer's campaign speech by following Napoleon's advice and "listening to his heart." Pedro simply says

> Hello. I don't have much to say. But I think it would be good to have some holy Santos brought to the high school to guard the hallway and to bring us good luck. El Santo Nino de Atocha is a good one. My Aunt Cocha has seen him. And we have a great FFA schedule lined up, and I'd like to see more of that. If you vote for me, all of your wildest dreams will come true. Thank you.

In a sense, Pedro was already delivering on one of his campaign promises. Holy Santos (in the form of his older cousins) had been protecting meeker students from Preston High's bullies. As Napoleon explained to one student who was being bullied, "Pedro offers you his protection." After his speech, Pedro runs offstage to a smattering of applause, and Napoleon (who has been practicing his dance moves thanks to a "D-Quon Dance Video" purchased at the thrift store) takes the stage. Napoleon busts out with every "sweet move" in D-Quon's choreography catalog and the student body erupts with a standing ovation. They elect Pedro class president. *Napoleon Dynamite* is a movie about a how one event can make the world a better place. After Napoleon selflessly risks humiliation to support his friend, he no longer has to play tetherball alone.

Why the Kids "Vote For Pedro"

Napoleon Dynamite is a film rooted in Mormon culture and set in rural Idaho. Because the producers were Mormon, the characters in the film do not swear, drink, take drugs, or have sex. There is not even a gratuitous girls' locker room scene. None of the central characters are physically attractive. And on top of that, the film lacks a plot. *Napoleon Dynamite* is basically just a random series of events strung together. So why did this movie become a cult hit with teens and young adults and become one of the most profitable independent films of all time? Part of the answer is obvious: *Napoleon Dynamite* is just plain funny. But there is another reason as well. For young people, Napoleon Dynamite is a "culture-bearing" story.[8]

Culture-bearing narratives have a major impact on a culture not because of their high quality, but because they speak to people who desire change.[9] For example, "*Uncle Tom's Cabin* was no literary masterpiece but it was a culture-bearing book. It came at a time when the entire culture was about to reject slavery. People seized upon it as a portrayal of their own new values and it became an overwhelming success."[10] Like *Uncle Tom's Cabin*, *Napoleon Dynamite* came along at a time when a certain segment of the American population was ready for a cultural transformation. Teens, who were righteously upset at the way they and their friends had been "framed" as potentially dangerous and violent after the Columbine tragedy, seized upon *Napoleon Dynamite* because it recast the high school outsider as a hero.

Historically, the outsider (nerd) has been seen as a member of the high school community who is not only harmless and endearing, but also as someone who eventually triumphs over the insider (bully). The role of the nerd had been firmly established in popular culture as a moral character. After Columbine, however, the outsider was transformed by politicians and the media into *someone to be feared*. The outsider/nerd was presented as more dangerous than even the bully. Napoleon Dynamite, a moon-boot-wearing, red-afro-sporting, mountain-bike-crashing, colossal doofus, single-handedly deconstructed the myth of the killer nerd.[11]

Throughout the film, Napoleon says outrageous things that are completely ignored by others. Napoleon tells Deb she should get her things out of his school locker because "I can't fit my nun chucks in there anymore." And he tells Pedro, "There's like a butt-load of gangs at this school. This one gang kept wanting me to join because I'm pretty good with a bow staff." As any good school psychologist might point out, the American Psychological Association lists "gang membership or strong desire to be in a gang" and "fascination with weapons" as youth violence warning signs. Other warning signs

include "frequent physical fighting" (Napoleon gets in physical alter-
cations with both his brother and his Uncle Rico) and "having been
a victim of bullying" (Napoleon is repeatedly bullied by jock types
throughout the film).[12] In short, the film strongly implies Napoleon
may be the "killer nerd" the media has warned us about in the post-
Columbine era. Worse than that, everyone around him seems to be
ignoring the warning signs. And, yet, Napoleon does not burn down
his school or turn his wolverine-hunting twelve-gauge on his classmates as the post-Columbine popular press might have predicted.
The movie was a success with young people because it reaffirmed
something they already knew to be true: they had less to fear from
bike-riding geeks like Napoleon than steak-throwing bullies like
Napoleon's Uncle Rico.

One reason *Napoleon Dynamite* is politically important is because
it speaks to a voiceless minority—the majority of people under eighteen who will never start a fire or pick up a gun regardless of how
often they play *Grand Theft Auto*. It tells them if they work hard at
things they enjoy, such as dancing for hours to a "D-Quon Dance
Video," taking glamour shots, or building a cake, then they can
find happiness. *Napoleon Dynamite* encourages young people to be
themselves and to be accepting of others. In a world fascinated with
consumer culture, Napoleon's crew had the cards stacked against
them. They achieved happiness by remaining true to themselves and
finding value in things others discarded (including one another).

Conclusion: The Politics of Small Things

As a movie about the electoral process, *Napoleon Dynamite* is superior to the other films we discussed. Those films stereotype politicians
as corrupt and/or stupid, suggest sinister forces would silence the
truth, and portray the average citizen as not bright enough to make
rational political decisions. While Pedro may not be the brightest
candidate, he and Napoleon are able to overcome a corrupt system.
The high school principal, who is clearly racist, never told Pedro he
would need to put on a skit after his campaign speech. Determined
to support his friend, Napoleon quickly improvises a skit by displaying his "D-Quon dance-video-skills" in front of the entire student
body. Napoleon and Pedro's triumph in the face of adversity conveys the message that sinister forces do not always win the day. The

third stereotype, that the average voter is blinded by the political spectacle, is challenged as well. The student body at Preston High is able to see through Summer Wheatly's self-serving and race-baiting campaign. Pedro may not be the perfect choice, but he is the best choice, and voting for him makes a difference. The idea that voting for an imperfect candidate can make the world a better place is an important idea young people need to hear. Unfortunately, it is sorely missing in most film comedies about elections. *Napoleon Dynamite* teaches us that politics starts when ordinary people have conversations about the things that are important in their lives.

The politics of small things—constituted as individuals interact with one another—gives rise to a situational reality that is a significant political force: "When people freely meet and talk to each other as equals, reveal their differences, display their distinctions, and develop a capacity to act together, they create power."[13] *Napoleon Dynamite* created this power as Preston High students participated in local politics and helped to shape new identities for themselves and others. The tall, awkward, geeky kid became a dancing machine. The quiet, sickly Mexican kid became class president. Because of the behind-the-scenes work of Napoleon as well as some members of Pedro's family, victims became empowered voters. Jeffrey Goldfarb argues this process of defining one's reality redistributes and re-creates democratic power. Simply by speaking to one another and developing projects in common, everyday people create a politics that matters.[14] While this politics of small things was at the heart of *Napoleon Dynamite*, it was noticeably absent in the other films we reviewed. *Bulworth, Bob Roberts, Wag the Dog,* and *Head of State* make the corruption, greed, and misuse of political power appear insurmountable; *Napoleon Dynamite* demonstrates how participatory politics can create change. Napoleon, Pedro, and Deb talk to one another as themselves, in their own terms, and develop a capacity to act in concert. For Goldfarb, this is the beginning of constituting a democratic alternative.[15]

Ultimately, mass media offers potential as a mechanism for creating "common interests and instill[ing] a sense of community without overtly promoting political engagement."[16] This is one reason popular culture matters politically, because as Henry Jenkins puts it, "it doesn't seem to be about politics at all."[17] For a generation leery of politics and politicians this is significant. *Napoleon Dynamite* is not a political film, yet a short time ago it was virtually impossible to walk across a college campus without seeing a slew of "Vote for Pedro" T-shirts. Individuals who scapegoat young people likely saw this as an apolitical statement from an apolitical generation unable to distinguish fantasy from reality. On the contrary, we think "Vote for Pedro" T-shirts *are* politically important. They are a strong marker of identification with the film *Napoleon Dynamite*, a film that represents a model of how young people can engage one another, create a meaningful civic culture, and enact political change.

Notes

1. George C. Edwards III, "Series Preface," in Martin P. Wattenberg, *Is Voting for Young People?* (New York: Pearson Longman, 2007) ix–x.
2. Martin P. Wattenberg, *Is Voting for Young People?* (New York: Pearson Longman, 2007).
3. Henry A. Giroux, "Where Have All the Public Intellectuals Gone? Radical Politics, Pedagogy, and Disposable Youth," *JAC Online* 17.2 (1997). http://jac.gsu.edu/jac/17.2/Articles/3.htm.
4. Giroux, "Where Have All the Public Intellectuals Gone?"
5. Jeffery P. Jones, *Entertaining Politics: New Political Television and Civic Culture* (Lanham, MD: Rowman & Littlefield, 2005).
6. Ji Hoon Park, Nadine G. Gabbadon, and Ariel R. Chernin, "Naturalizing Racial Differences Through Comedy: Asian, Black, and White Views on Racial Stereotypes in Rush Hour 2," *Journal of Communication* 56 (2006): 157–177.
7. Mark Sachleben and Kevan M. Yenerall, *Seeing the Bigger Picture: Understanding Politics Through Film & Television* (New York: Peter Lang, 2004), 169–170.
8. Robert M. Pirsig, *Zen and the Art of Motorcycle Maintenance* (New York: Bantam Books, 1984), 376.
9. Ibid.
10. Ibid.
11. The authors wish to thank Kevin Collins for his insight that Napoleon Dynamite helped to reestablish the cultural role of the outsider/nerd after Columbine. Personal communication, December 13, 2006.
12. "Warning Signs of Youth Violence," *APA Help Center*. http://www.apahelpcenter.org/featuredtopics/feature.php?id=38.
13. Jeffrey C. Goldfarb, *The Politics of Small Things* (Chicago: University of Chicago Press, 2006).
14. Ibid., 5.
15. Ibid., 8.

16. Josh Pasek et al., "America's Youth and Community Engagement: How Use of Mass Media is Related to Civic Activity and Political Awareness in 14- to 22-Year Olds," *Communication Research* 33.2 (2006): 115–135.

17. Henry Jenkins, *Convergence Culture: Where Old and New Media Collide* (New York: New York University Press, 2006) 239.

7

Air Amusement versus Web Wit
Comparing the Use of Humor in 2004 Political Advertising on Television and the Internet

Monica Postelnicu and Lynda Lee Kaid

Political advertising in the 2004 presidential campaign was not "business as usual." Not only did the spending for presidential advertising reach unprecedented levels (over $600 million), but the sources, the channels, and the formats for political advertising were dramatically different from prior presidential campaign cycles.[1] These new approaches were partly the result of changes in the campaign finance regulations passed by Congress in 2002 and partly the consequence of expanded use of the Internet. Together, these innovations led to an explosion of political humor. In this chapter, we discuss these new media and campaign environment factors and their humorous outcomes in political ads on television and on the Web.

Expanded Voices and Channels in 2004

Because of long-term concerns about loopholes in campaign finance regulations, concerns about the use of "soft money" raised outside the legal constraints of the Federal Election Campaign Act, and growing concerns about the proliferation of negative advertising, in 2002 Congress passed the Bipartisan Campaign Reform Act (BCRA).[2] One of the ironies of BCRA has been its exemplification of Congress's ability to create new problems in the well-intentioned attempt to correct old problems. Thus, the new law, while tightening soft money expenditures by political parties, led to the proliferation of political advertising expenditures by unregulated independent political groups,[3] who coincidentally spent huge majorities of their advertising funds on negative advertising.[4] As a result spending on advertising for the 2004 campaign almost tripled the 2000 campaign.

Increased spending by independent groups did not represent the only new voices in the 2004 campaign. The growth of the World Wide Web and its open availability to individuals and groups at very low cost also spawned new political voices on a new channel. For the first time, ordinary citizens could join in the discourse of political campaigns by using the Web to express their own views. Many individuals did this, not only through chat rooms and blogs, but also by creating their own political advertisements on the Web.

Consequently, the 2004 environment led to more money and more voices, but another factor also helped create a climate that led to increased humor in advertising messages. In interpreting BCRA, the Federal Election Commission (FEC) basically took a "hands off" approach to the Internet. The FEC did not apply campaign finance, accounting, expenditure, disclosure, or sponsor identification regulations to most Internet messages, leaving individuals and groups free to say or do almost anything in their political advertising in almost any format with almost any type of visual or audio device.[5] Freedom of expression, coupled with the Internet's inexpensive character, low entry-barrier, and also inexpensive and relatively simple video editing technology, has transformed the political monologue into a dialogue with many participants.

With only weak libel laws as a deterrent, the Internet became a truly "anything goes" medium, a sort of "wild wild west" communication channel. It seems almost inevitable that such an environment would encourage political humor in many forms.

Humor in Political Advertising

It is important to remember, however, that political advertising prior to 2004 had not been without humor. Communication scholars from Aristotle to the present have agreed with political consultants that the use of humor can be an effective tool in political advertising.[6]

Karla Hunter analyzed a sample of 379 humorous ads between 1952 and 1996 taken from the Political Commercial Archive at the University of Oklahoma. These ads came from candidates and issues at all levels, from the presidency down to lower-level races. She found that 68 percent of the humorous ads were negative ads that used a high amount of fear appeals and were more likely to focus on candidate image than on campaign or policy issues.[7] Likewise, in their analysis of presidential spots from 1952 through 1996, L. L. Kaid and Anne Johnston found that in negative ads that attack the image or personal qualities of an opponent, humor is one of the most frequently used strategies or devices for making the attack.[8]

Although humor has been used in positive spots, it is considered especially effective as a device in negative advertising.[9] Research has suggested several reasons why humor may be effective in negative advertising. For instance, audiences are attracted to the entertainment value provided by humorous ads, eliciting feelings of cheerfulness and happiness in viewers.[10] Humorous advertising is also generally effective in drawing the attention of the viewer and thus may be able to distract the viewer from the true purpose of the attacker, making attack ads seem less vicious and even helping to prevent backlash effects from negative advertising.[11] Others have argued that political humor can be an effective strategy by focusing attention on the idiosyncrasies of the opponent target and by providing images that make information processing easier for the voter.[12]

In 2004 the use of humor in political ads was particularly in evidence on the Web where campaign strategists stressed the viral nature of the Web, encouraging supporters to distribute humorous messages to their friends and colleagues.[13] At least 32 million Internet users said they engaged in such viral messaging in 2004, exchanging jokes and humorous materials with others.[14] This expanded use of humor and the freedom of individuals, as well as groups to get their messages out, raised questions about comparisons between the use of humor in traditional television advertising versus Web advertising.

Comparing Humorous Ads on Television and the Web

In order to compare the use of humor on television and the Web in 2004, we applied content analysis techniques to samples of the ads from each medium. A total of 280 television ads and 273 Web ads referring to the 2004 U.S. presidential election were collected during the campaign period. The television spots were produced by the candidates, their political parties, and independent groups. With the exception of one spot,[15] no commercials produced by private citizens

ran on television. In contrast, the majority of the Web ads were produced by citizens (216 ads, or about 80 percent of the Web advertising).
The online spots analyzed by this study refer exclusively to advertising
messages distributed through the producer's own Web site(s), which
means our sample does not include banner ads placed predominantly
on third-party Web sites.

The television ads were analyzed by seven coders who achieved an
intercoder reliability of .895 using Holsti's formula, while the Web
ads were examined by two coders whose level of agreement was .899.
The coding instrument used for the analysis of the sampled ads was
developed based on previous research on political advertising (such
as VideoStyle) and looked at the sponsorship of the ads and their
verbal content.[16] Each ad was examined for the presence or absence
of humor, focus (issue or image), tone (positive or negative), issue
agenda (such as the economy, the war in Iraq, education, etc.), the
presentation of candidates (positive, neutral, negative), and their
image attributes promoted by the ads, among other variables.

Characteristics of Humorous TV and Web Ads

One of the most striking differences between television and Web ads
was the difference in their lengths. The average length of television
ads was 31.35 seconds, while the Web ads were significantly longer
and averaged 66.06 seconds, twice the length of television commercials (t (170) = −2.69; p = .01).

Sponsorship

Of the total number of political ads in our sample, 46 of the TV ads
(16 percent) and 133 (48 percent) of the Web ads were categorized
as humorous ads. Overall, a Web ad was three times as likely to be
humorous as a TV ad, indicating a statistically significant difference
between TV and Web ads (χ^2 = 65.83; df = 1; $p \leq$ .001).

However, the majority of the humorous Web ads were produced
by citizens, not by candidates or the independent groups. The citizen producers created 112 ads out of a total of 133 humorous ads on
the Web, while the candidates preferred the traditional medium of
television over the new online medium to distribute most of their

TABLE 7.1. Comparison of Sponsors for Humorous TV and Web Ads in 2004

	TV Ads (n = 46)	Web Ads (n = 133)
Bush	12 (71%)	5 (29%)
Pro-Bush groups	13 (100%)	0
Kerry	10 (67%)	5 (33%)
Pro-Kerry groups	11 (50%)	11 (50%)
Citizens	0	112 (100%)

$\chi^2 = 114.25; df = 4; p \le .001.$

ads, including those with humor. As Table 7.1 shows, the ratio of humorous ads on television compared with the Web was two to one in favor of television ads.

The most notorious citizen-created humorous ad was "This Land" produced by a private family-owned entertainment company called JibJab. The ad is a two-minute cartoon animation that showed George W. Bush and John F. Kerry dancing and singing together while exchanging musical epithets such as "sissie," "liberal wienie," and "right-wing nut job." Despite this highly unusual political rhetoric, the media's attention and the Web traffic to the page hosting this animation were overwhelming, reaching an audience estimated between 50 and 65 million people.[17] The JibJab Web site received 10.4 million unique visitors in July 2004 alone, after parts of the clip were aired on several television newscasts. During the same month, the two presidential candidates' Web sites were accessed by only 1.5 million visitors each and reached their largest audience in October 2004 when GeorgeWBush.com attracted 3.2 million visitors, and JohnKerry.com 3.7 million visitors (ComScore 2004).[18] Even taken together during their busiest month, the candidates' Web sites received much less traffic than JibJab.com.

After JibJab's resounding success, a multitude of political actors— candidates and their parties, advocacy groups, and individuals alike— began using online advertising to make their voices heard. Animations by political cartoonist Mark Fiore, who resigned his job at the *San Jose Mercury News* after being asked by the management to make his clips less critical of Bush, attracted about 12,000 visitors a day the month before the election.[19] Fiore estimated that each animation was seen by 230,000 people.[20] Advertising created by an individual under the name of Kerrycore.com, which parodied the Democrats, received 20,000 unique visits per day in August. CrushKerry.com and TooStupid-ToBePresident.com, also created by private citizens, received 75,000 and 56,000 unique visitors per week on average, respectively.[21] Based on the number of Web sites that linked directly to these advertisers, the most popular independently produced ads were the following (in descending order): JibJab, Mark Fiore, Bush in 30 Seconds, Swift-boat Veterans, Music For America, White House West, Crush Kerry, Operation Truth, Billionaires for Bush, Too Stupid To Be President, Eric Blumrich, Kerry and Edwards in Love, and Dumb and Dubya.[22] The overwhelming majority of these ads were political parodies of the two candidates, their parties, and their associates. A press release from Nielson/NetRatings labeled political parody Web sites as the fastest growing type of site on the Internet during the month of October 2004, just a few weeks before the election.[23]

The two presidential candidates tried their hand at parody as well. Both George Bush and John Kerry created humorous Web-only ads, which creatively combined video elements with cartoon animation and game features. Bush's campaign Web site featured "The Flip-Flop Olympics," a Flash game that asked voters to recall Kerry's conflict-ing positions on a variety of issues such as education, tax cuts, and the Iraq war. The humorous elements in the game included a cartoon car-icature of Kerry and "judges" Hillary Clinton, Edward Kennedy, and Howard Dean, as well as carnival music playing in the background.

Content

The examination of the content of the spots in terms of tone, empha-sis on issues versus candidate image, and type of appeal revealed dif-ferences in how the humor was used on each medium.

Television political commercials, humorous or not, have been dominated by discussion of issues rather than image since the very first U.S. presidential campaign used them in 1952.[24] The humor-ous television ads created in 2004 continued this trend. As Table 7.2 shows, 65 percent of the television ads in this sample were issue centered, while the remaining 35 percent were image focused. In contrast, Web advertising gave image discussion a central role in a statistically significant way ($\chi^2 = 18.59$; df = 1; $p \leq .001$). About seven in ten Web ads focused on the discussion of candidate's image, while

TABLE 7.2. Comparison of Content for Humorous TV and Web Ads in 2004

	TV Ads (n = 46)	Web Ads (n = 133)
Negative ad	44 (96%)	131 (98%)
Ad emphasis*		
Issues	30 (65%)	39 (29%)
Image	15 (35%)	94 (71%)
Appeals		
Logical*	45 (98%)	36 (73%)
Emotional	34 (75%)	98 (74%)
Ethos*	22 (48%)	13 (10%)

* Indicates the difference between TV and Web is significant at p ≤ .01.

only about three in ten Web ads discussed issues. This finding is particularly important connected with the fact that Web advertising was predominantly negative. Based on the figures in Table 7.2, we conclude that humor on television was used to poke fun at the opponent's issue stances, while on the Web humor was targeted at the opponent's image attributes.

Humorous ads on the Web were more likely to be parodies. About 96 percent of the humorous Web ads contained some parody, but only 17 percent of the humorous TV ads used this type of humor ($\chi^2 = 49.20$; df = 1; $p ≤ .001$). Humorous elements in television ads border on irony, satire, and ridicule rather than on parody. A Bush ad called "Yakuza" is representative of the humor present in television ads, implying that Kerry's plan to win the war on terror is appropriate for fighting the Japanese Yakuza—not "real" terrorist organizations like Al-Qaeda. The ad shows a photo of Kerry next to a cartoon of a member of the Japanese mafia (called Yakuza); the announcer's tone is scornful about Kerry's position on protecting the United States against terrorism, but overall the ad provides the viewer with serious, straightforward criticism about Kerry's security plan. It is typical for political television commercials to use humorous elements while keeping the general message relatively serious due to candidates' fear of not being taken seriously if the ads are too funny.[25]

However, fears of not being taken seriously were not so obvious in the 2004 online political advertising. Both candidates and their supporting groups took advantage of the new medium to trash their opponent's character. For instance, the Republican National Committee (RNC) created an ad called "A Very Kerry Weekend" to attack Kerry simply for being wealthy. The viewer hears the sound of ocean waves and sees caricatured photos of Kerry performing leisure and expensive activities such as sailing, biking, and surfing in the sea resort of Nantucket. The ad invites viewers to vote on where Kerry might spend his next vacation. Another RNC clip called "John Kerry, International Man of Mystery" ridicules Kerry on his plans to bring more allies into Iraq. An announcer imitating movie character Austin Powers's voice says "Allow myself to introduce...myself," while the viewer sees altered images of John Kerry and a collage of media sound bites intertwined with computer graphics reminiscent of the Austin Powers movies. Throughout the clip, an Austin Powers-type voiceover makes fun of Kerry's comments.

Kerry replied with spots such as a clip entitled "Faces of Frustration," which ridiculed Bush's uncomfortable facial expressions during the first presidential debate. The Democratic National Committee joined the war of political parodies with a clip called "Republican Survivor," which portrays Bush as the winner of a contest against several prominent Republicans in the style of the television reality show *Survivor*. Another clip, called "Click to Kick Bush Out," contained a cartoon of Bush and sound bites of the president talking about various issues. Every time Bush spoke, a donkey kicked him into the air. Apart from these humorous image attacks, the Kerry camp used parody to attack the president on issue stands as well with a computer animation titled "Pump." This clip transformed the White House into a big gas pump to illustrate the connection between Bush and members of his administration like Dick Cheney and Condoleezza Rice to big oil companies.

The use of humor in negative advertising is a tactic frequently used by candidates. Many television attack ads from presidential races between 1960 and 1988 rely on humor to disparage the opponent.[26] Humor is a popular attack strategy because it helps to soften the blow and minimizes the risk of voter backlash against the attacker, as long as the ridicule is not directed at someone held by viewers in high esteem.[27] Humorous appeals increase attention and reduce the irritation often created by exposure to advertising, negative or not.[28]

On the Web, humor is used to reduce backlash but also to transform the ad into a witty criticism that facilitates its integration into the online popular culture. Humor is a strong incentive for people to pass the clip along to their acquaintances. One political consultant suggests that

> Part of the goal here is to get people to send this on inside of their own networks, the recipients can, as we've said, be force multipliers for the message. In research that has been done by the George Washington University and others, we found consistently that the things that people forward to their friends, generally are funny things. And so I do think that obviously the nature of the medium impacts the message and I think we'll see things that are built for this medium more likely.[29]

There are some rare instances when humor was used to promote a candidate positively, such as a clip in which the Bush twins urge viewers to vote for and support their dad. The ad was featured both on Bush's campaign Web site and Rock The Vote's Web site, and showed clips from Bush's campaign trail. The president is presented in informal situations such as making jokes, petting his dog, or stammering during a commercial shoot session. This endorsement of President Bush by his own daughters is illustrative of the relatively permissive environment of online advertising. Such an ad could never have aired on television without severe (negative) consequences for the president. But the Bush camp felt that the Internet is a medium that allows for this high degree of informality, which would be atypical and inappropriate as content for mainstream media (such as television advertising).

Clearly, the Bush campaign perceived the Internet as a medium with different, more relaxed standards than television. Additionally, the audience for this ad differed from the audience of television advertising, which aims at older, sometimes undecided voters.[30] Unlike television advertising, this online clip used Bush's daughters to target young voters. Using humor is not an unusual strategy for this audience segment, eighteen- to thirty-year-old voters, whose media consumption tends to revolve around infotainment and alternative sources of information such as *The Daily Show* rather than mainstream media.

Issue Agenda of Humorous Ads

The humorous television and Web ads have a relatively similar issue agenda, except on three issues. The top five most discussed issues in

TABLE 7.3.   Presentation of Issues for Humorous TV and Web Ads in 2004

	TV Ads (n = 46)	Web Ads (n = 133)
Economy	15 (33%)	54 (41%)
Iraq/military spending*	11 (24%)	56 (42%)
Terrorism	9 (20%)	22 (17%)
Government corruption*	2 (4%)	25 (19%)
Gun control*	7 (15%)	2 (2%)
Education	4 (9%)	23 (17%)
Environment	5 (11%)	33 (24%)
Health care	4 (9%)	11 (8%)
Moral values	1 (2%)	7 (5%)

Indicates the difference between TV and Web is significant at p ≤ .01.

the television spots were the economy, the war in Iraq, terrorism, crime, and the environment. The war in Iraq was given a significantly higher importance in the Web ads, which mentioned this issue in 42 percent of cases, compared with only 24 percent of the television ads. Almost all the humorous ads discussing this issue were produced by private citizens who ridiculed Bush's motives to invade Iraq, his failure to find weapons of mass destruction, or his overhasty declaration of victory onboard a U.S. navy carrier.

Government corruption was also a popular issue online, mentioned in 19 percent of the Web humorous ads, while it was barely mentioned on television (only 4 percent of the ads). In return, television ads emphasized gun control significantly more than Web ads. Table 7.3 presents a complete list of all issues mentioned in the ads on each medium.

Conclusion

The present study was designed to identify trends in the use of humor in political Web advertising compared with the traditional political television ads. The Web opens up new opportunities for citizens to make their voices heard. Unconstrained by traditional formats and able to take advantage of less structured lengths than television advertising offers, Web ads allowed citizens to express their frustrations with government and with leaders. This study revealed that the political advertising discourse online created by private citizens in 2004 often took the form of parody ads produced mostly in a Flash format because it allows the use of animation, which enhances humor. Citizens were more likely to use parody than the two presidential candidates, although the candidates also used this type of humor more frequently on the Web than on television.

The present inquiry also confirms previous research showing that humorous elements are used most frequently in negative political ads as a way to challenge the opponent's character and/or issue stance while avoiding the audience backlash. In 2004, the lack of regulation to moderate Web advertising resulted in virulent character attacks against the two candidates. The Institute for Politics, Democracy, and the Internet has warned that "along with reinvigorated civic participation there exists a darker and angrier side of the political Internet.... Some independently produced Web videos... used heavily edited photographs or film from campaign events or news stories, juxtapositioning sometimes graphic and emotional images with news headlines, voting records and political statements. Others were animated, a format that some video producers feel increases the humor of their work and makes their scathing commentary all the more lethal."[31]

Apart from humor, a relatively high number of online messages contained falsities, indecency, vulgar content, and technological abuse. Citizens and candidates seem to have shared the belief that nothing can be too extreme on the Internet. Perhaps the popularity of violent and negative clips produced by citizens may have even encouraged the Bush and Kerry campaigns to create Web advertising at lower standards than their usual television messages. As Web advertising becomes as indispensable a form of communication as televised advertising, Web sites, and blogs, the question is whether the Internet discourse will tend to smooth out and go mainstream, or whether it will conserve the sharp, negative, and parodic nature observed in 2004.

Notes

1. L. Kaid, "Videostyle in the 2004 Political Advertising," in *The 2004 Presidential Campaign: A Communication Perspective*, ed. R. E. Denton, Jr. (Lanham, MD: Rowman & Littlefield, 2005), 283–299; L. L. Kaid, "Political Web Wars: The Use of the Internet for Political Advertising,"

in *The Internet Election: Perspectives on the Role of the Web in Campaign 2004*, eds. J.C. Tedesco and A. P. Williams (Rowman & Littlefield, 2006).

2. Bipartisan Campaign Reform Act of 2002 (BCRA), 116 Stat. 81.

3. These independent groups have often been referred to as "527" groups, after the number of the Internal Revenue Service Code that regulates their tax-exempt status. In reality, the 527s are only one of the types of independent groups that joined in the advertising fun in 2005. Other such groups included traditional political action committees of organizations such as the AFL-CIO labor unions, the National Rifle Association, and many others.

4. L. L. Kaid and D.V. Dimitrova, "The Television Advertising Battleground in the 2004 Presidential Election," *Journalism Studies* 6 (2005): 165–175.

5. In May 2006 new FEC interpretations of the Bipartisan Campaign Reform Act of 2002 redefined "political communications" to include limited paid Internet political activity, including paid political ads on Web sites the purchaser does not control.

6. R. Janko, *Aristotle on Comedy: Towards a Reconstruction of Poetics II* (Berkeley: University of California Press, 1984); P. Wendel, "Making Political TV Spots That Work in an Age of Media Clutter," *Campaigns & Elections* 19 (1998): 18–22.

7. Karla Hunter, "(Not So) Divine Comedy: A Content Analysis of Humorous Political Ads," (unpublished PhD diss., University of Oklahoma, 2000).

8. L. L. Kaid and Anne Johnston, "Negative versus Positive Television Advertising in U.S. Presidential Campaigns, 1960–1988," *Journal of Communication* 41 (1991): 53–64; L. L. Kaid and Anne Johnston, *Videostyle in Presidential Campaigns: Style and Content of Televised Political Advertising* (Westport, CT: Praeger/Greenwood, 2001).

9. J. Rowley, "Humorous and High Concept Advertising," in *Political Campaign Communication: Inside and Out*, eds. L. Powell and J. Cowart (Boston: Allyn & Bacon, 2003), 118.

10. R. A. Coulter, G. Zaltman, and K. S. Coulter, "Interpreting Consumer Perceptions Of Advertising: An Application of the Zaltman Metaphor Elicitation Technique," *Journal of Advertising* 30 (2001), 1–21; S. Shavitt, P. Lowrey, and J. Haefner, "Public Attitudes Toward Advertising: More Favorable Than You Might Think," *Journal of Advertising Research* 38 (1998), 7–22; M. Geuens and P. De Pelsmacker, "Feelings Evoked By Warm, Erotic, Humorous or Non-emotional Print Advertisements for Alcoholic Beverages," *Academy of Marketing Science Review* 19 (1998): 1–32.

11. T. J. Madden and M. G. Weinberger, "The Effects of Humor on Attention in Magazine Advertising," *Journal of Advertising* 11 (1982): 8–14; Hunter, "(Not So) Divine Comedy"; M. Pfau, R. Parrott, and B. Lindquist, "An Expectancy Theory Explanation of the Effectiveness of Political Attack Television Spots: A Case Study," *Journal of Applied Communication Research* 20 (August 1992): 235–253.

12. T. Hollihan, *Uncivil Wars: Political Campaigns in a Media Age* (Boston: Bedford/St. Martin's, 2001); D. Paletz, *The Media in American Politics* (New York: Longman, 1999).

13. Kaid, "Political Web Wars"; Rand Ragusa, "Using Humor in Online Attack Ads," *Campaigns & Elections* 25 (August 2004), 32–33.

14. L. Rainie, M. Cornfield, and J. Horrigan, *The Internet and Campaign 2004* (Washington, DC: PEW Internet & American Life Project, March 6, 2005).

15. This one spot won a political advertising contest initiated by MoveOn in 2003. The contest challenged voters to create a thirty-second TV ad that "tells the truth about George Bush." About 1,500 entries were received, 150 of them were posted on a Web site called "Bush in 30 Seconds," and the winning ad ran on television. Most of the citizen ads in our sample came from the ads produced by citizens for the MoveOn contest and posted on their Web site. This may explain in part why the ads were all so negative; the charge to contestants presumed that the ad would be critical of Bush.

16. L. L. Kaid and J. Davidson, "Elements of Videostyle: Candidate Presentation through Television Advertising," in *New Perspectives on Political Advertising*, eds. L. L. Kaid, D. Nimmo, and K. R. Sanders (Carbondale: Southern Illinois University Press, 1986), 184–209.

17. "Under the Radar and Over the Top: Online Political Videos in the 2004 Election," *Institute for Politics, Democracy & the Internet (IPDI)*, October 20, 2004. http://www.ipdi.org/UploadedFiles/under_the_radar_and_over_the_top.pdf.

18. "25 Million Americans Visited Politics Sites in the Final Month of the Presidential Race," *ComScore*, November 15, 2004. http://www.comscore.com/press/release.asp?press=517.

19. L. Witt, "Online Political Clips Get Nasty," *Wired News*, October 25, 2004. http://www.wired.com/news/politics/0,1283,65439,00.html.

20. IPDI, "Under the Radar and Over the Top."

21. Ibid.

22. Ibid, 15.

23. Ibid.

24. R. A. Joslyn, "The Content of Political Spot Ads," *Journalism Quarterly* 57 (1980), 92–98; Kaid and Johnston, *Videostyle in Presidential Campaigns*; T. Patterson and R. McClure, *The Unseeing Eye* (New

York: Putnam, 1976); L. Shyles, "Defining the Issues of a Presidential Election from Televised Political Spot Advertisements," *Journal of Broadcasting* 27 (1983): 333–343.

25. Hunter, "(Not So) Divine Comedy."
26. Kaid and Johnston, *Videostyle in Presidential Campaigns.*
27. K. Larson and N. Barbee, "A Systematic Examination of Humor in Negative Political Ads: Is Laughter the Best Medicine for Curing the Ills of Backlash?" (paper presented at the Sooner Communication Conference, Norman, OK, March 1994); D. Zillman, "Disparagement Humor," in *Handbook of Humor Research*, vol. 1, eds. P. E. McGhee and J. H. Goldsteing (New York: Springer-Verlag, 1983), 85–107.
28. K. S. Johnson-Cartee and G. A. Copeland, *Manipulation of the American Voter: Political Campaign Commercials* (Westport, CT: Praeger, 1997).
29. Online News Hour, "Cyber Ads," *PBS transcript*, February 20, 2004. http://www.pbs.org/newshour/bb/media/jan-june04/cyberads _02-20.html.
30. D. West, *Air Wars: Television Advertising in Election Campaigns, 1952–2004*, 4th ed. (Washington, DC: CQ Press, 2005).
31. IPDI, "Under the Radar and Over the Top," 5.

8

American Youth and the Effects of Online Political Humor

Jody C Baumgartner

The past decade has seen an increased focus by scholars and political observers on political humor. Various studies, for example, have examined such shows as *The Late Show with David Letterman, The Tonight Show with Jay Leno, The Daily Show, Saturday Night Live*, and others.[1] Less studied has been the veritable explosion of Web sites carrying humorous political content. A Google search for the term "political humor" in early 2006 yielded roughly 46 million results; Yahoo returned 23 million sites. One can now find any variety of political cartoons, jokes, satire, editorial cartoons, political comedy, political comics, and more on the Internet. What effect do these sites have, beyond making us laugh?

In this chapter I discuss the results of an online experiment designed to test the effects of a humorous animated clip from JibJab. com on the political attitudes of eighteen- to twenty-four-year-old youth. The results of the experiment were mixed. I found that exposure to a two and a half minute clip parodying President George W. Bush raised respondents' evaluations of him as well as levels of internal efficacy. However, respondents who viewed the clip had more negative evaluations of other political institutions, even when controlling for partisanship and other demographic variables.

The focus on youth, here defined as those eighteen- to twenty-four years of age, is justified for several reasons. First, although youth historically participate at lower levels than their older counterparts, there is abundant evidence that the youth of today are more disengaged than those from previous eras. While it is true that youth turned out to vote at historically high levels in 2004, their turnout rate is still the lowest of all age groups.[2] Youth also appear, according to some research, to be more cynical about and disengaged from politics as well.[3]

Moreover, many youth are getting their political information from nontraditional sources (e.g., network Internet, cable news, and entertainment-based programming).[4] For example, over half (54 percent) reported they got at least some news about the 2004 presidential campaign from comedy programs like *The Daily Show* and *Saturday Night Live* (as opposed to 15 percent of those over the age of forty-five).[5] In other words, youth are increasingly less likely to follow traditional hard news on a regular basis and, conversely, are more likely than older Americans to get at least some of their news from alternate sources, including the Internet. If online political humor has a negative effect on youth perceptions of political institutions and political leaders, there is a danger that youth might become even more alienated from politics and less likely to participate.

Internet Humor and JibJab.com

As might be expected with so many Web sites offering politically humorous content, there are now several portals that track and link to other sites featuring political humor.[6] Many of these sites are well established and quite popular. For example, *The Onion*, a popular satire site, has been online since 1996, and according to one estimate has 2 million hits per week.[7] Any number of Web sites feature satire, pictures, video clips (from television and elsewhere), and animated videos.

What of the content of online political humor? It is rather varied, but much is anti-Bush. This mirrors the anti-presidential bias of televised and other forms of political humor.[8] On any given day, a cursory examination of search results for "political humor" or the front page of About.com's "Political Humor" page reveals a significant number of Bush parodies, spoofs, jokes, cartoons, and so on. According to one study, about two-thirds of the Internet videos during the 2004 campaign were anti-Bush, while only one-third were anti-Kerry.[9] Of course other political figures are targeted as well (e.g., Hillary Clinton, Dick Cheney) in addition to various political scandals and so on. In short, Internet political humor casts a wide net.

One of the developments in Internet humor during the 2004 campaign was the increased availability and popularity of high-quality humorous videos. Produced specifically for the Internet, many were quite popular. Estimates suggest that the videos of Eric Blum-rich (bushflash.com), David Counts (toostupidtobepresident.com), John Wooden (whitehouse.org), Mark Fiore (markfiore.com), and others were viewed by upward of several hundred thousand people throughout the campaign. Some were popular enough to have mer-ited the attention of mainstream news organizations.[10]

In this context, the site JibJab.com took the political world by storm. Founded in 1999 by Gregg and Evan Spiridellis, JibJab Media's clients have included USA Network, Disney, Cartoon Network, Sony, and Kraft.[11] Their initial foray into the world of political humor came in 2003, with the release of a short, animated Flash movie titled "Ahhnold for Governor." Subsequently shown at the Sundance Film Festival, the clip was intended to promote their commercial activi-ties.[12] In summer 2004 the company released a two-minute political satire titled "This Land."

The animated Flash movie, adopted from Woody Guthrie's folk classic "This Land is Your Land," took aim at George W. Bush and John Kerry and became an instant sensation. On July 9, the Spiridellis sent an e-mail announcing the release of the clip to roughly 200,000 people. Word of the clip spread like wildfire, with people sending the link to the clip via e-mail to their friends, family, and coworkers. Within three days the brothers received 30,000 e-mails, some from as far away as Jordan, Brazil, and Cameroon. Viewership of the clip tripled virtually every day following its release, and the site's serv-ers repeatedly crashed as a result. By the end of the first week after its release, viewership reached one million people per day, and the brothers were forced to move the hosting of the clip to AtomFilms, a site that specializes in showing short films over the Internet.[13]

On July 26, the clip aired, and the Spiridellis brothers appeared, on *The Tonight Show with Jay Leno*.[14] By the end of the month, portions of the clip had been shown on Fox News, CNBC, CBS's *Early Show*, *NBC Nightly News*, and elsewhere. By the end of July "This Land" had been seen by 10.4 million viewers. This was, by contrast, three times the amount of combined viewers that the Bush and Kerry sites had during the entire month.[15] By the first week in August, the term "JibJab" ranked ninth on the "Lycos 50" list of most popular searches. A Google search at about the same time turned up some 87,000 Web pages that mentioned JibJab.[16] "This Land" has, according to the brothers, been seen on "every continent, including Antarctica. NASA even [asked] permission to send a copy to the International Space Station."[17] The Library of Congress requested a copy of "This Land" to put in its archives. During the course of their appearance on *The Tonight Show*, Jay Leno asked the brothers to create another clip. On October 7, their second election short, "It's Good To Be In D.C.," premiered. This clip, sung to the tune of "Dixie," was not as critically acclaimed as the first. However, by election day the two clips had been viewed better than 80 million times.

Part of the near universal appeal of the two election shorts was the fact that the brothers seemed to be equal opportunity humorists. Both candidates were targeted equally by the clips. The following excerpt from "This Land," an exchange between Bush and Kerry, illustrates.

> *Bush:* You're a liberal sissy.
> *Kerry:* You're a right wing nut job.
> *Bush:* You're a pinko commie.
> *Kerry:* You're dumb as a doorknob.

Likewise, most of the other clips the brothers produced seem to have little if any partisan bias.

In January of 2005 JibJab released a new clip titled "Second Term." As the title suggests, the clip dealt with Bush's victory in the 2004 election and what his plans were for the next four years. It opens with Bush taking the oath of office, then features the president singing about his victory while various Democrats lament their loss. Bush then begins to describe (in song) some of his plans for the next four years, including stabilization of Iraq, amending the Constitution to ban gay marriage, and more tax cuts. Jacques Chirac and the United Nations General Assembly express their disbelief that Bush won reelection, and the president is shown extending a "friendly offer [to all, for] barbeque and beers in Crawford" in order to mend the "fences broken by pre-emption." The clip ends with this same conciliatory note, with the president suggesting that everyone put aside their differences and work together.[18] Box 8.1 presents the text from the two and a half minute clip, which was the experimental stimulus used for this research.

Box 8.1. Transcript: JibJab's "Second Term"

(Introduction: Bush shown at the inauguration)
Voice: Do you swear to preserve, protect, and defend the constitution?
Bush: You betcha!
Bush: Yes, I'm comin' back to serve a second term, this time I won the national elec-she-un!

Bush: Oh, thanks to you O-hi-a, and dear brother Jebedia, we get four more years to rule in Washington!

Democrats: Good God he's comin' back to serve a second term,

Kerry, Edwards: We were hoping in '04 we'd get a turn,

Democrats: But we lost the vicious battle,

Bush: Now they're stuck without a paddle!

Clinton: Who will save us from con-ser-va-tiz-eum?

Bush: I will stabilize Iraq in my second term, and I will amend the con-sti-tu-sheun,

Bush: Then I'll eliminate all the taxes,

Wall St. Bankers: That are breakin' all our back-siz,

Bush: And push for more pri-vat-i-za-she-un!

UN General Assembly: We cannot believe he won a second term,

French Pres. Chirac: He destroyed the trans-Atlantic alli-unce!

Bush: Heck, I'll extend a friendly offer, barbeque and beers in Crawford!

Bush: Mending fences broken by pre-emp-she-un!

Religious Leaders: We want peace on earth throughout his second term,

American Soldiers: We want Iraqis to have free elec-she-uns,

Bush: There's a beef here, let's dispatch it, and bury that ol' hatchet, yes, we've been through stormy weather, now it's time to work together!

Bush: Gather round the ol' chuck wagon, it's a grand time we'll be havin', in the four years we have left in Wash-ing-ton!

Bush: Yee-Haw!

From *"Second Term," JibJab Media (www.jibjab.com).*

Political Humor and Its Effects

The general research question guiding this project was, What effect does online humor have on how youth perceive political institutions and public officials? Existing theory suggests that political humor should have *some* effect on the political attitudes of youth, in part because young people are particularly susceptible to persuasion.[19] Research in the fields of advertising and psychology demonstrates that humorous messages are memorable, and have the potential to be persuasive under certain conditions.[20] In addition, some political science and political communications suggests that humor has the potential to affect political attitudes.[21]

For this analysis I employed a posttest only control group design in an online survey.[22] The design consists of an experimental group and a control group, each of which is independently randomly selected. The experimental group viewed an online video clip prior to taking the survey, and their responses were then compared to those of the control group, which did not view the clip.

The experiment was conducted in the first two weeks of October 2005. Participation was solicited via e-mail. I received two lists, each of them independent random samples, of 2,500 e-mail addresses of undergraduate students from East Carolina University (ECU). The invitation e-mail included a link to one of two Web sites, based on which group the respondent was assigned to. One Web site directed respondents directly to the survey. The other asked subjects to first watch "Second Term" and then proceed to the survey.

I sent the e-mails over a period of five days, in daily waves of 1,000. Follow-up e-mails were sent roughly ten days after the first e-mail. The response rate for both groups combined was just over 20 percent (21.3 percent), which yielded 1,063 usable surveys. A total of 133 cases were excluded from the analysis because they were over twenty-four years of age; an additional 51 cases were excluded from the experimental group because they reported not viewing the clip prior to taking the survey.[23] Analysis of the sample confirmed that it was sufficiently representative of the ECU student population. A manipulation check of the experimental group showed that better than half of those who saw the clip (60.3 percent) enjoyed it, while only 15.8 percent did not.

To test for the effects of online humor on internal and external efficacy, I included several standard questions in the survey about how much respondents trusted government, public officials, the media, and the electoral system. Three of these questions have been included in the American National Election Studies for many years. Two measure internal efficacy: "People like me don't have any say about what the government does" and "Sometimes politics and government seem so complicated that a person like me can't really understand what's going on." A third, "I don't think public officials care much what people like me think," measures external efficacy.[24] In addition, I included another question that asked respondents to rate the performance of the media in covering politics and one that asked respondents to gauge whether Republicans and Democrats could put aside their differences and do what is best for the country. In all cases, responses were measured on a five-point scale that ranged from "strongly agree" to "strongly disagree," with a neutral choice of "neither agree nor disagree."

Finally, I measured respondents' evaluations of President George W. Bush—the subject of the animated video clip—in terms of competence, leadership, honesty, trust, and overall approval. Measurement of these traits took the form of asking respondents, "Does the word *competent* describe George W. Bush extremely well, quite well, not too well, or not well at all?"

In addition to using an experimental design, I statistically controlled for the usual array of demographic characteristics, including party identification, age, race, and gender. I also included control questions that measured respondents' media habits, political knowledge, and interest. Political knowledge was a cumulative measure of correct answers to four separate public affairs questions, while political interest was measured with the question, "How closely would you say you followed news about last year's presidential campaign and election?"

Since comedic frames generally accentuate the negative, we could expect that exposure to political humor would have a negative effect on evaluations of political institutions and public officials. This speaks to the idea that political humor might lower external efficacy, or the "beliefs about whether elected officials are sufficiently responsive to their constituents."[25] Prior research also suggests that internal efficacy, or the "beliefs about one's own competence to understand, and to participate effectively in, politics,"[26] tends to increase based on exposure to political humor.[27] This may be because comedy tends to simplify complex reality, giving viewers the sense that they "get" politics as the result.

Research on televised humor suggests that since comedic frames draw on negative caricatures,[28] exposure to political humor has a negative effect on the evaluations of individual political leaders when they are the target of jokes told by others. For example, exposure to *The Daily Show* lowered subjects' evaluations of John Kerry and George W. Bush in 2004.[29] This, however, is the case only when these leaders are being lampooned by others. I would expect that negative effects on Bush evaluations would be seen in the analysis of the control group. However, the JibJab clip functions as an example of self-effacing humor, features "Bush" in a first-person role. In this case, therefore, I expect that exposure to the clip will have a *positive* effect. Nonempirical studies suggest that presidents and others can increase their likability by poking fun at themselves. For example, Nancy Reagan discovered this at the 1982 White House Correspondents Association dinner when she sang "Secondhand Clothes," lampooning her taste in designer clothing.

Results

The first set of results I present are from an analysis of the control group, as a stand-alone survey. The survey asked respondents how often they visited online political humor Web sites (e.g., JibJab.com or *The Onion*). Responses to this question ranged from "never" to "hardly ever," "sometimes," and "regularly." The responses to this question were then cross-tabulated with the various dependent variables. Table 8.1 presents the results that attained statistical significance (based on chi-square tests).

The first two rows of Table 8.1 are measures of internal political efficacy. "People like me have no say" measured agreement with the statement, "People like me don't have any say about what government does." The second row, "Politics and government are too complicated," measured agreement with the statement, "Sometime politics and government seem so complicated that a person like me

TABLE 8.1.   Cross-Tabulation of Online Political Humor Viewing with Efficacy

	View Online Humor	
	Never or Hardly Ever (%)	Sometimes or Regularly (%)
"People like me have no say"		
Agree	39.6	25.0
Neither agree nor disagree	9.0	12.5
Disagree	50.4	62.5
"Politics and government are too complicated"		
Agree	48.3	34.2
Neither agree nor disagree	10.7	9.2
Disagree	41.0	56.7
Media displays		
No bias	17.8	9.2
Slight bias	49.8	54.2
A strong bias	32.5	36.7

can't really understand what's going on." In both cases, agreement points to lower levels of internal efficacy, while disagreement suggests higher internal efficacy. In both cases we see substantial gaps in the response categories between those who view online political humor sometimes or regularly and those who do so hardly ever or never. This lends support to the idea that online political humor increases levels of internal efficacy.

The third row of the table presents another measure of external efficacy, this one dealing with perceived levels of media bias. In this case the survey prompted, "Generally, it seems to me as if the media displays," and respondents were given five choices that ranged from "a strong liberal bias" to "a strong conservative bias," with a neutral category of "little or no bias." Here we can see that those who view Web humor were more likely to see the media as biased. This result is in line with my expectations that online political humor lowers trust in political institutions.

By themselves, of course, these cross-tabulations do not provide sufficient proof for any of the hypotheses in this chapter. There is the possibility that those who seek out online humor are already less trusting of political institutions or have a greater sense of self-efficacy. Thus the question of causality arises. Moreover, no other variables are controlled for. They are, however, controlled for in the experimental analysis.

For the experimental results, the variable of interest is whether the respondent viewed the online clip. I ran an ordered probit analysis on the various dependent variables, holding the other independent variables constant. Ordered probit is a statistical technique used when the dependent variable has ordinal values (e.g., low, medium, high). Unfortunately, the coefficients generated by ordered probit cannot be interpreted in as straightforward a manner as those in regression analysis. Therefore, I generated predicted probabilities from each of the ordered probit models. Predicted probabilities are produced by first setting all of the independent variables at their mean, thus producing an "average" case. After running the procedure, we can then make statements about the probability that a given category of the dependent variable would be selected by the "average" respondent. Tables 8.2 and 8.3 present the results from the ordered probit and predicted probabilities analyses (for the sake of space, nonsignificant results are not presented).[30]

TABLE 8.2. Viewing JibJab's "Second Term": Experimental Results

Variable	Officials Care	Bipartisan	Media Performance	Bush Cares
JibJab	−.17 (.08)†	−.10 (.08)*	−.15 (.08)†	.14 (.11)*
Knowledge	.06 (.03)†	−.04 (.03)	−.10 (.03)‡	−.03 (.04)
Republican	.32 (.04)‡	.07 (.04)†	−.12 (.04)‡	.95 (.06)‡
Male	−.02 (.08)	−.11 (.08)*	−.09 (.09)	−.06 (.12)
Age	−.02 (.04)	.01 (.04)	−.05 (.04)	−.01 (.06)
Race	−.09 (.08)	.05 (.07)	−.06 (.08)	−.26 (.12)†
Cut 1	−.43	−1.04	−1.48	2.78
Cut 2	.82	−.09	−.37	—
Cut 3	1.16	.29	.74	—
Cut 4	2.43	1.39	—	—
Log likelihood	−963.26	−1211.35	−1105.57	−365.03
Chi-square (7)	33.54	11.36	97.73	68.2
N	809	809	809	809

"Knowledge" was an index compiled from the responses to four questions, with possible scores ranging from 0 to 4. "Republican" was coded 1 = strong Democrat to 5 = strong Republican. "Male" was coded 0 = female, 1 = male. Age was coded 1 = under 18 years of age to 8 = 24 years old. "Year in College" was coded 1 = have not completed first year to 5 = senior. "Race" was coded 1 = Caucasian, 2 = African American, and 3 = Other (Asian, Hispanic, American Indian, and other). All estimates are ordered probit coefficients, with standard deviation errors in parentheses.

*p < .10; †p < .05; ‡p < .01 (one-tailed).

In general, the effects of the animated clip were mixed. First, neither of the internal efficacy measures was significantly affected. This seems to disconfirm my hypothesis that viewing the animated clip would increase respondents' feelings of internal efficacy, although we did see significant results in that regard in Table 8.1.

The clip did have the expected effect on all three measures of external efficacy. In all three cases, those who viewed the clip reported more negative attitudes toward political institutions. Those in the experimental group were 6 percent more likely to agree with the statement, "I don't think public officials care much what people like me think," and slightly more than 6 percent less likely to disagree. They was a slightly smaller (4 percent) differential in the probability of agreement and disagreement with the statement, "I believe that the Democrats and Republicans in Washington can put aside their differences to do what is best for America." We see a similar

TABLE 8.3. Viewing JibJab's "Second Term": Predicted Probabilities

	Control Group (%)	Experimental Group (%)
"I don't think public officials care"		
Agree	44.4	50.9
Neither agree nor disagree	13.5	13.3
Disagree	42.1	35.8
"Democrats and Republicans can put differences aside"		
Agree	41.7	37.8
Neither agree nor disagree	15.1	15.0
Disagree	43.3	47.2
Rate performance of media		
Poor to fair	69.4	74.4
Good to very good	30.6	25.6
"Really cares"		
Describes Bush well (agree)	33.1	38.6
N = 809		

(5 percent) difference in the probability of respondents' rating of the media in covering politics.

The effects of the clip on various measures of how respondents' evaluate George W. Bush were, with one exception, insignificant. The exception was agreement with the statement, "Does the phrase 'really cares about people like me' describe George W. Bush extremely well, quite well, not too well, or not well at all?" We see in Table 8.2 that experimental group respondents were 5.5 percent more likely to agree with the statement, meaning that the clip changed evaluations of Bush in the direction of that which was hypothesized.

Discussion

My findings present a mixed picture with respect to the effects of political humor on political attitudes. First, the stimulus had a positive effect on at least one measure of evaluations of President Bush. This was because unlike most political humor, the clip basically functioned as an example of the president poking fun at himself. This is a new finding, suggesting the need to specify the type of humor that is being tested.

On the other hand, exposure to the animated clip from JibJab.com lowered subjects' trust in the media and political institutions. Messages that highlight the (seeming) absurdities of the political world seem to breed or reinforce cynicism about government and politics. Overexposure to comedic frames during formative years could then, potentially, have implications for political participation.

Are there behavioral consequences to the attitudinal effects that result from exposure to online political humor? All other things being equal, we might expect decreased external efficacy to depress political participation; "A mountain of empirical evidence links political efficacy to electoral involvement."[31] Low levels of external efficacy may dampen participation among an already cynical youth audience by increasing their sense of alienation from the political process.[32]

However, it may not be the case that viewing the online clip lowers participation. In fact, analysis of the control group suggests that viewership of online political humor may have positive effects on internal efficacy. Research on televised political humor supports this idea as well. This probably relates to the fact that political humor tends to simplify political reality, making it easier for viewers to understand. Moreover, the fact that the complexities of politics are presented in terms of the absurdity and incompetence of political elites probably leads viewers to affix blame on those who run the system. All other things being equal, this could contribute to greater participation, because citizens who understand politics are more likely to participate than those who do not.

In fact, relying again only on descriptive statistics, we can see that online humor viewership had a significant and positive effect on two measures of political participation in 2004. Table 8.4 shows that those who viewed online political humor sometimes or regularly were more likely to have followed the 2004 campaign and voted in 2004 than those who did so never or hardly ever.

There are several limitations to this study, most of which deal with the generalizability of the sample. First, the experiment was carried out on students from only one university (ECU). The university is located in a relatively conservative, rural area, and the partisan makeup of the sample was weighted more heavily Republican (44 percent Republicans, 33 percent Democrats, 22 percent Independents or don't know). This hardly makes this a representative sample of university students. Moreover, the research question concerns itself with the effect of Web humor on *all* youth.

TABLE 8.4. Cross-Tabulation of Online Political Humor Viewing with Participation

	View Online Humor	
	Never or Hardly Ever (%)	Sometimes or Regularly (%)
Followed 2004 election campaign		
Closely or very closely	82.7	95.0
Not closely or not at all	17.3	5.0
Voted in 2004 election?		
No	41.5	32.8
Yes	58.5	67.2

In addition, the research question itself is open to questions of relevance. Why bother studying the effects of online political humor, when so few people go to political humor Web sites? Only 13 percent of the sample (from both groups) reported going to political humor Web sites either sometimes or regularly, while 87 percent claimed they did so hardly ever or never. In fact, only the politically interested do so as a rule. However, as noted earlier, the JibJab clip ("This Land") from the summer of 2004 became, for all practical purposes, mainstream. These visits must have included the politically uninterested or less interested, especially considering that youth seem to be drawn to alternative sources of political information.[33]

In fact, we can have some confidence in the results of this analysis. First, the results presented in Table 8.2 were from an experiment, which means that the effects can be attributed to the experimental stimulus: the online clip. Moreover, because subjects viewed the clip and took the survey online and on their own computers (or other computers they were accustomed to using), the experiment itself was high in mundane realism.[34] The observed effects on the sample were unlikely to have been produced by any aspect of the experimental environment.

Second, the sample may be less *un*representative than other non-probability samples. This is because youth who are not enrolled in university are online. By some estimates over 80 percent of eighteen- to twenty-four-year olds have access to the Internet. Although a digital divide still exists with respect to Internet access, it is less pronounced among youth.[35] So, while only college students at a single university were sampled, it remains true that the vast majority of youth are in fact online. The point is that while the results of this analysis may not be generalizable to all youth, we should not dismiss the results too quickly.

Some research suggests that soft news, or programming that blends information with entertainment, might be good for citizenship. For example, Matt Baum's research suggests that it informs an otherwise less attentive public about foreign policy by capturing their attention.[36] However, it appears as if all variants of soft news are not created equal. Further research is needed into the relationship between political humor and trust, political efficacy, and political participation.

Notes

1. See, for example, previous and present work by the contributors to this volume.
2. Jose Antonio Vargas, "Vote or Die? Well, They Did Vote," *Washington Post*, November 9, 2004, C1; Stephen Watson, "Younger Voters Came Out at High Rate, But Percentage of Total Didn't Change," *Buffalo News*, November 9, 2004, B6.
3. For a review of the research on some of the aspects of the civic disengagement of youth, see Michael X. Delli Carpini, "Gen.com: Youth, Civic Engagement, and New Information Environment," *Political Communication* 17 (2000): 341–349; and William A. Galston, "Political Knowledge, Political Engagement, and Civic Education," *Annual Review of Political Science* 4 (2001): 217–234 (223–225); Stephen E. Bennett, "Why Young Americans Hate Politics, and What We Should Do about It," *PS: Political Science and Politics* 30 (1997): 47–53; The Institute of Politics, "Attitudes Toward Politics and Public Service: A National Survey of College Undergraduates," *Harvard University*, April 11–20, 2000. http://www.iop.harvard.edu/pdfs/survey/2000.pdf.
4. "News Audiences Increasingly Politicized: Online News Audiences Larger, More Diverse," *The Pew Research Center for the People and the Press*, June 8, 2004. http://people-press.org/reports/display.php3?ReportID=215; Richard Davis and Diana Owen, *New Media and American Politics* (New York: Oxford University, 1998).
5. "Cable and Internet Loom Large in Fragmented Political News Universe: Perceptions of Partisan Bias Seen as Growing, Especially by Democrats," *The Pew Research Center for the People and the Press*, January 11, 2004. http://people-press.org/reports/display.php3?ReportID=200.

6. See, for example, "Political Humor Today: News, Cartoons, Jokes, Videos & Satire," which is updated daily. http://politicalhumor.about.com/.
7. Laura Ridge, "The Politics of Satire: A Look at American Satire from the Stamp Act to The Simpsons," *HPR Online*, January 25, 2003, http://www.hpronline.org/news/2003/01/25/BooksAndArts/The-Politics.Of.Satire-357280.shtml. Grant Widmer, "Website Mocks Traditional Media: *The Onion* Delivers Newsworthy Satire," *Daily Reveille*, November 18, 2002. http://media.www.lsureveille.com/media/storage/paper868/news/2002/11/18/Entertainment/Web-Site.Mocks.Traditional.Media-2044252.shtml.
8. David Niven, S. Robert Lichter, and Daniel Amundson, "The Political Content of Late Night Comedy," *Press/Politics*, 8 (2003): 118–133.
9. "Under the Radar and Over the Top: Online Political Videos in the 2004 Election," *Institute for Politics, Democracy & the Internet*, October 20, 2004. http://www.ipdi.org/UploadedFiles/under_the_radar_and_over_the_top.pdf.
10. Ibid.
11. "The JibJab Story" (n.d.). http://www.jibjab.com/about/.
12. Robert Strauss, "Laugh Early and Often," *New York Times*, October 31, 2004, Section 14NJ, Column 1; *New Jersey Weekly Desk*, 4.
13. J. Patrick Coolican, "Read, Rinse, Repeat," *Houston Chronicle*, July 21, 2004, 1; Kevin Maney, "This News Was Made for You and Me and the Rest of the World," *USA Today*, July 28, 2004, 3B.
14. Robert Strauss, "Laugh Early and Often"; Margaret Hickman and Amy Lavergne, "Did You Hear the One...," *Texas Journalist*, Election Special, November 1, 2004. http://journalism.utexas.edu/vote04/humor2.html.
15. Steve Lohr, "A Duet That Straddles the Political Divide," *New York Times*, July 26, 2004, C5; "Political Networking," *CIO Insight*, October 1, 2004, 26.
16. Bill Hendrick, "The Mocking of a President 2004," *Atlanta Journal Constitution*, August 4, 2004, 1E.
17. "The JibJab Story."
18. As of this writing, the clip can still be viewed at www.jibjab.com.
19. David O. Sears, "The Persistence of Early Political Predispositions: The Roles of Attitude Object and Life Stage," in *Review of Personality and Social Psychology*, vol. 4, eds. L. Wheeler and P. Shaver (Beverly Hills, CA: Sage, 1983); David O. Sears, "College Sophomores in the Laboratory: Influence of a Narrow Data Base on Social Psychology's View of Human Nature," *Journal of Personality and Social Psychology* 51 (1986): 515–530.

20. Stephen R. Schmidt, "Effects of Humor on Sentence Memory," *Journal of Experimental Psychology: Learning, Memory, and Cognition* 20 (1994): 953–967; Jim Lyttle, "The Effectiveness of Humor in Persuasion: The Case of Business Ethics Training," *Journal of General Psychology* 128 (2001): 206–216.

21. Dannagal Goldthwaite Young, "Late-night Comedy in Election 2000: Its Influence on Candidate Trait Ratings and the Moderating Effects of Political Knowledge and Partisanship," *Journal of Broadcasting & Electronic Media* 48 (2004): 1–22; Jody Baumgartner and Jonathan S. Morris, "The 'Daily Show Effect': Candidate Evaluations, Efficacy, and the American Youth," *American Politics Research* 34 (2006): 341–367; Dannagal Goldthwaite Young, "When I Think Kerry I Think Flip-Flopper? An Experimental Exploration of the Effects of Political Jokes on Issue and Trait Salience" (paper presentation at the annual meeting of the American Political Science Association, Washington, DC, September 1–4, 2005).

22. Donald T. Campbell and Julian C. Stanley, *Experimental and Quasi-experimental Designs for Research* (Chicago: Rand McNally, 1963).

23. Thirteen percent of the experimental group reported having seen the clip before; these cases were not excluded from the analysis.

24. See the ANES codebook at http://www.electionstudies.org/.

25. George I. Balch, "Multiple Indicators in Survey Research: The Concept 'Sense of Political Efficacy,'" *Political Methodology* 1 (1974): 1–43.

26. Richard. G. Niemi, Stephen C. Craig, and Franco Mattei, "Measuring Internal Political Efficacy in the 1988 National Election Study," *American Political Science Review* 85 (1991): 1407–1413 (1407).

27. Baumgartner and Morris, "The 'Daily Show Effect.'"

28. Young, "Late-night Comedy in Election 2000."

29. Baumgartner and Morris, "The 'Daily Show Effect'"; Young, "When I Think Kerry I Think Flip-Flopper?"

30. J. Scott Long, *Regression Models for Categorical and Limited Dependent Variables* (Thousand Oaks, CA: Sage, 1997).

31. Steven J. Rosenstone and John Mark Hansen, *Mobilization, Participation, and Democracy in America* (New York: Macmillan, 1993), 141.

32. There is no consensus in the literature in this regard. In fact, one body of work suggests that lower efficacy may actually serve to increase participation. See Margaret Levi and Laura Stoker, "Political Trust and Trustworthiness," *Annual Review of Political Science* 3 (2000): 475–507.

33. "Cable and Internet Loom Large in Fragmented Political News Universe."

34. Rose McDermott, "Experimental Methodology in Political Science," *Political Analysis* 10 (2002): 325–342.

35. "Digital Divisions," *The Pew Internet & American Life Project*, October 5, 2005. http://www.pewinternet.org/pdfs/PIP_Digital_Divisions_Oct_5_2005.pdf.

36. Matthew A. Baum, "Sex, Lies, and War: How Soft News Brings Foreign Policy to the Inattentive Public," *American Political Science Review* 96 (2002): 91–109; *Soft News Goes to War: Public Opinion & American Foreign Policy* (Princeton, NJ: Princeton University Press, 2003); "Soft News and Political Knowledge: Evidence of Absence or Absence of Evidence?" *Political Communication* 20 (2003): 173–190; "Talking the Vote: Why Presidential Candidates Hit the Talk Show Circuit," *American Journal of Political Science* 49 (2005): 213–234.

III

Ready for Prime Time?
Televised Political Humor

9

Our First Cartoon President
Bill Clinton and the Politics of Late Night Comedy

*David Niven, S. Robert Lichter,
and Daniel Amundson*

"I'm going to miss Bill Clinton," Conan O'Brien, host of *Late Night*, wrote as Clinton left the White House.[1] "And I don't mean only in a selfish 'He was great for late-night comedians' way. I'm going to miss Bill Clinton in that aching, visceral way."

Unlike most presidents who provided only one main avenue for caricature, "Clinton was wildly generous to the comedic mind." Indeed, O'Brien exalted, "Comedians will soon have to build their own Clinton Presidential Library just to catalog the thousands upon thousands of joke variations made possible by his two terms. He made our job so easy it was a challenge not to feel irrelevant."

As O'Brien suggested, Bill Clinton was the central political figure in late night comedy during his presidency, and even in its immediate aftermath. Here we explore popular conceptions of Bill Clinton through the lens of late night humor. We note the scope of attention Clinton received on late night comedies, the topics for which he was mocked, and the portrayal of his political associates. We do so both to enhance our understanding of Clinton's place in the American zeitgeist, and to closely view the political side of late night comedy, an increasingly prominent presence in modern politics.

Clinton's Place in American Politics

For many scholars, pundits, and observers, President Clinton represents the greatest paradox in modern politics. Confounding the expectations of nearly every commentator alive, Bill Clinton made it through his scandal-plagued second term not only without a significant loss of popularity, but with a nontrivial gain in popularity. As John Zaller put it, "It has never been this clear that it is possible for public opinion and media opinion to go marching off in opposing directions."[2]

Indeed, numerous scholars document the general upward trend in Clinton popularity in the face of sexually related scandals.[3] Arthur Miller notes that Clinton's job approval was higher a year into the investigation of his activities with Monica Lewinsky than it had been at any time prior to the scandal being made public.[4]

Explanations for this anomaly vary. Some point to the importance of a robust economy in satisfying voters' top concern.[5] Generally, however, scholars suggest that the nature of the scandal and the level of attention it received may have shielded Clinton from the consequences of his behavior.[6] To wit, Miller finds that even among Republicans, who were readily inclined to believe the worst about Clinton, there was a belief that media coverage of the scandal was excessive.[7]

Toward that end, some analysts argue that the people's notion of a private/public divide was violated by the investigation into Clinton.[8] That is, even as polls showed a clear majority of Americans thought that Clinton had lied about his private life, a majority approved of his job as president, and opposed the impeachment proceedings.[9] Instead of taking Clinton's private behavior as an indictment of his presidency, most Americans took interest in Clinton's private behavior as an indictment of the system, the media, and of special prosecutor Kenneth Starr.[10] Examining a series of polls taken after the scandal, Miller found that "for most, the scandal was not about the rule of law or punishing a president who had lied under oath or obstructed justice; it was about a zealous special prosecutor."[11]

From this perspective, obsession with his private activities and the negative portrayal of Clinton's accusers only served to emphasize Clinton's greatest political asset with average Americans: his perceived empathy and concern for people in general and, in particular, people in need.[12] Indeed, after the Starr report was released, Clinton maintained the approval of a majority of Americans, while six in ten Americans disapproved of Kenneth Starr.[13] A March 1998 Pew Center poll found 62 percent had a favorable evaluation of Bill Clinton, in contrast with 22 percent for Kenneth Starr, 17 percent for Monica Lewinsky and Paula Jones, and 10 percent for Linda Tripp.[14] Starr, even though he was working with a media hungry for every scandal tidbit, was ultimately seen as, at best, politically self-serving, and at worst, a scandal-monger delighting in the muck and mire.[15]

Quite tellingly, in a December 1998 poll, Americans by a large margin (60 to 34 percent) concluded that the best way to avoid future presidential sex scandals was to leave a president's private life unscrutinized, rather than to elect a president of high moral character.[16] Concomitantly, Robert Spitzer argues that the larger lesson of the Clinton impeachment will be "that Congress will keep the impeachment blunderbuss in its cabinet, precisely because it was so easily used against Clinton."[17]

Late Night in Politics

While Bill Clinton was confounding analysts' expectations, late night comedy programming was increasingly making its mark in our political communication information stream. When the Pew Center asked Americans in 2000 which media sources had provided them information about the presidential candidates, television comedies (such as *Late Night, The Tonight Show, The Late Show,* and *Politically Incorrect*) finished ahead of news magazines, the Internet, C-SPAN, morning news programs, public television news, political talk shows on cable networks, and Sunday morning network talk shows.[18] Indeed, during the height of the presidential election contest in 2000, candidates Al Gore and George W. Bush received more opportunity to speak in their own words on late night comedies than on the major network news programs.[19] Comments from presidential campaign advisors attest to the significance political professionals place on late night portrayals of their candidates. For example, Dan Schnur of the John McCain for President campaign claimed that "Jay Leno is a lot cheaper than polling. [Late night shows] often reflect what voters feel, and their observations have a tremendous effect on how voters view the candidates, much more so than evening news shows"[20]; Alex Castellanos, a consultant who worked for the Bush campaign, asserted that late night has "the power to create conventional wisdom in politics; they'll set how a candidate is perceived in stone."[21]

When George W. Bush appeared on the *Late Show* in October 2000, Letterman said emphatically to Bush, "Listen to me, Governor." Bush answered, "I am listening to you; I don't have any choice." That same month when Letterman drew laughs declaring to his show's audience that "The election will be decided here," there was already a growing array of observers, experts, and involved parties who agreed with his sentiment. Indeed, one writer proclaimed that his influence over popular culture and, ultimately, political judgments meant that "Letterman is the Walter Cronkite of our generation."[22] Academics too, when consulted by the media, were anything but dismissive of the role of late night humor in our politics.[23]

All this attention does not mean that a wide array of viewpoints was presented on late night television programming. There is no shortage of evidence demonstrating that the traditional news media value negative stories over positive stories when covering politics.[24] Studies of the portrayal of politics and public figures in television entertainment also tend to find a preponderance of negative depictions. S. Robert Lichter, Linda Lichter, and Daniel Amundson, for example, studied four decades of prime-time series television's portrayal of the public sphere and found a "jaundiced view of government" with politicians often shown as "corrupt evildoers" and the "handmaiden of special interests."[25] Concomitantly, previous studies on the political content of late night comedy have found that the jokes were *overwhelmingly negative* and *targeted at the personal characteristics* of the candidates rather than on the issues.[26] In other words, such studies suggest the misadventures of Bill Clinton represented something close to a late night comedic ideal.

The significance of this tendency is suggested in research that finds humor is a particularly effective means of communicating political messages. Eron Berg and Louis Lippman, for example, observe that messages with humor are more easily remembered.[27] William Benoit, Andrew Klyukovski, and John McHale conclude that political humor has great potential influence because of its ability to make weighty political topics more accessible.[28] Jim Lyttle suggests that ironic humor enhances the persuasiveness of a message, in part by providing a distraction from counterarguments.[29] Bryan Whaley and Rachel Holloway add that use of humor can aid in making a political point not only forcefully, but concisely.[30]

Data on Late Night Politics

With a database including every joke told on the *Late Show*, the *Tonight Show*, and *Late Night* from 1996 to 2001, and every joke told on *Politically Incorrect* from 1998 to 2001, we consider the political state of late night comedy through the depiction of its central target of that era, Bill Clinton, and those with whom he was closely associated. The database was built with the efforts of a team of trained coders who were asked to record the target and subject of monologue jokes and other comedy material during first-run episodes of the four programs.

We turn now to the data on late night political jokes to explore four main areas: (1) the amount of attention paid to Bill Clinton during his second term, (2) the subjects associated with Clinton, (3) the amount of attention paid to Clinton associates, and (4) the implications of late night comedy for Clinton.

Collectively, the four late night shows included 15,528 jokes about U.S. political figures between 1996 and 2001; 5,915 jokes (38 percent) focused directly on Bill Clinton. As Table 9.1 shows, Clinton was not only the dominant political target on these programs, he was the dominant target among all politicians, entertainers, and all other notables. For example, on the *Tonight Show*, Clinton was the number one humor target during each of the last four years of his presidency, and the top humor target for the year 2001, after he had been succeeded by George W. Bush. On Leno's program, Clinton was topped only by his presidential opponent, Bob Dole, in 1996. Similarly, on the *Late Show*, Clinton was the top humor target of 1997, 1998, 1999, and 2001. Here he was topped by Dole in 1996, and then-presidential candidate Bush in 2000. For the period overall, Clinton is far and away the top humor target, with Al Gore (1,157 jokes) second, and George W. Bush (1,118 jokes) third.

While President Clinton's many foibles certainly attracted late night attention, mere fame is the starting point for late night interest. As Jay Leno explains, "The audience has to know what you're talking about or else you'll be sunk. [The host] can't know more than anybody watching. And we've found that once you get past secretary of state—and even that's a stretch—no one knows what you're talking about."[31]

Topics: Libido

While Clinton's dominant position in late night humor is revealing, so too are the topics of the jokes told at his expense. As Table 9.2 lists, Clinton's various sexual escapades were the leading subject of

TABLE 9.1. Number of Bill Clinton Jokes on Late Night Comedies (1996–2001)

	Tonight Show/ Jay Leno			Late Show/ David Letterman			Late Night/ Conan O'Brien			Politically Incorrect/ Bill Maher		
	Jokes	Pol. Rank	Ovr. Rank	Jokes	Pol. Rank	Ovr. Rank	Jokes	Pol. Rank	Ovr. Rank	Jokes	Pol. Rank	Ovr. Rank
1996	250	2	2	345	2	2	62	2	2			
1997	281	1	1	373	1	1	111	1	1			
1998	777	1	1	565	1	1	203	1	1	172	1	1
1999	712	1	1	349	1	1	116	1	1	139	1	1
2000	439	1	1	184	2	2	117	2	2	63	2	2
2001	349	1	1	238	1	1	56	2	2	14	2	2

Pol. Rank is the ranking of Clinton's joke total relative to all other political figures. Ovr. Rank is the ranking of Clinton's joke total relative to all other joke targets.

Data from the Center for Media and Public Affairs, www.cmpa.com.

TABLE 9.2. Topics of Bill Clinton Jokes on Late Night Comedies (1996–2001)

	Tonight Show/Jay Leno	Late Show/David Letterman	Late Night/Conan O'Brien	Politically Incorrect/Bill Maher
1996	Sex Scandal: 118 Whitewater: 30 Ideology/Flip-Flops: 11	Sex Scandal: 97 Weight: 78 Administration: 38	Sex Scandal: 12 Democratic Party: 11 First Family: 9	—
1997	Sex Scandal: 98 Campaign Finance: 45 Social Issues: 16	Sex Scandal: 127 Weight: 85 Personal Habits: 23	Sex Scandal: 29 Weight: 18 Personal Habits: 10	—
1998	Sex Scandal: 670 Whitewater: 28 Personal Habits: 21	Sex Scandal: 409 Whitewater: 62 Weight: 34	Sex Scandal: 167 Whitewater: 9 Honesty: 4 Personal Habits: 4	Sex Scandal: 128 Whitewater: 10 Honesty: 5
1999	Sex Scandal: 410 Personal Habits: 74 Whitewater: 26	Sex Scandal: 232 Personal Habits: 20 Whitewater: 12	Sex Scandal: 61 Personal Habits: 28 First Family: 5	Sex Scandal: 77 Personal Habits: 12 Honesty: 5 First Family: 5 Whitewater: 5
2000	Sex Scandal: 216 Personal Habits: 91 Whitewater: 36	Sex Scandal: 98 Personal Habits: 39 Whitewater: 18	Sex Scandal: 50 First Family: 5 Whitewater: 4	Sex Scandal: 26 Personal Habits: 10 Whitewater: 7
2001	Sex Scandal: 209 Gifts/Items Removed from White House: 24 Honesty: 23	Sex Scandal: 132 Gifts/Items Removed from White House: 35 Whitewater: 15	Sex Scandal: 44 Personal Habits: 4 Pardons: 2 Gifts/Items Removed from White House: 2	Sex Scandal: 4 Whitewater: 3 Gifts/Items Removed from White House: 4

Data from the Center for Media and Public Affairs, www.cmpa.com.

Clinton jokes on every show in every year under study. This was true before there was an intern-related investigation, during the investigation, and years after it. Jokes about his personal habits, largely centered on sexual behavior, were frequently the second most occurring topic.

While the attention to scandals and alleged indiscretions was overwhelming, the tone of the jokes was generally not openly condemning. Instead, the jokes told during the entire period paint the president as a bumbling incompetent in marriage or as some kind of hormonally charged teenager, but rarely as a scoundrel or predator. In fact, some of the jokes seem mildly appreciative of the president's sexual appetites. In 1996, Jay Leno offered, "The other night, Air Force One with the president on board hit major turbulence over the state of New Mexico. Major. Major. The thing was rocking back and forth. In fact, it was so bad, listen to this, President Clinton had to return his flight attendant to her full upright and locked position." That same year, David Letterman had this on the subject, "Clinton said that when he was a teenager down there in Arkansas, Bill Clinton, our president, said when he was a teenager he was in bed every night at 9:00, in bed every night at 9:00—and some nights earlier if the girl was drunk." In 2000, David Letterman offered, "President Clinton says he wants $30 million from Congress for contraception and family planning. Thirty million dollars from Congress for contraception? It sounds to me like somebody's going to go dating again." In 2001, Jay Leno continued the theme, "At the New York primary, President Clinton cast his first vote ever for his wife. Of course, while he was pulling the lever, he was thinking of another woman."

This suggestion of disdain or revulsion from his wife was a frequent implication of these jokes. For example

> Jay Leno (2000): A North Carolina jury has awarded a husband $30,000 after another man stole his wife. Guy got 30 grand for losing his wife. Today Clinton said, "Hey, how do I get in on that deal? 30 grand! Get me a new truck."

> Jay Leno (1998): Did you see Clinton? He was pretty funny. I think he got the biggest laugh when he turned to Kenneth Starr and he said, "Take my wife, please."

Over the years, all programs ran some version of this joke with the common punch line: Conan O'Brien (2000), "Today—it's been reported that in preparation for her speech at the Los Angeles Democratic Convention, Hillary Clinton—get this—hired a makeup artist who charges $6,000 a visit. Apparently, the makeup artist made her look so different, President Clinton accidentally hit on her."

Occasionally the sex-related humor encompassed another of Clinton's major appetites, as was the case in this 1996 Jay Leno joke, "A Swiss company has announced it is now making 100 percent safe breast implants made from vegetable oil. That is going to take a lot of willpower for Clinton to pass up, don't you think? I mean, a woman with large breasts who smells like a french fry." That same year, David Letterman offered, "Sharon Stone is giving this interview, and she's saying about President Clinton…Sharon Stone is saying that if he was not married, she, Sharon Stone, would be on President Clinton like white on rice. And you know two things were going through his mind at that point. Two things. First of all, President Clinton is saying, 'mmm, Sharon Stone.' Number two, 'mmm, rice!'"

Topics: Weight

In fact, weight was the topic that drew the second most attention from David Letterman, although not from the other programs. A 1996 Letterman Top Ten list gave one of his personal New Year's resolutions as, "Stop disrespectfully referring to President Clinton as 'Tubby' and start referring to him as 'Fat Boy.'" A 1997 Letterman list presented the Top Ten signs Clinton is losing weight, including "It's been six weeks since he accidentally bit off one of his fingertips" while eating. Another Letterman take on the subject from 1996, "The White House is infested with rats. Isn't that amazing? So here's what they tried to do. They call in one of those exterminators, and they place literally dozens and dozens and dozens of traps all over the White House, but the problem—it's obvious—you know, Clinton keeps stealing the cheese." Conan O'Brien joined in on the fun in 1997, "In South Carolina, a waiter was arrested for leaving President Clinton a threatening note. Seriously. Yeah, and apparently, the note said, 'I can't carry that much food, fatty!'"

While the jokes are obviously mocking in tone, the area of attack may provoke a sympathetic response from an American electorate notable for its girth. Even David Letterman sounded as if he had qualms about his description of Clinton. In a May 23, 1996 interview with Larry King, Letterman said he "would love to have" Hillary Clinton on his show and "We would love to have her husband Tubby on the show." Moments later, Letterman acknowledged, "You know President Clinton is what, like eight pounds overweight? He's like 6'4" and he weighs 208. He's eight pounds overweight. We pretend that he weighs 360. You know, we're just exaggerating and making jokes." Nevertheless, a few months later when Bob Dole visited the *Late Show* (November 8, 1996) after his defeat in the 1996 election, Letterman said of Clinton, "He's huge. He's very fat. Three hundred pounds. He's still 300 pounds, Bob." To which Dole replied, "I never tried to lift him."

Whitewater and Other Scandals

The other major category of Clinton humor revolved around Whitewater and various questions of propriety. While the jokes regularly stated or implied that the president was facing some kind of trouble, the content of the jokes often provided no information regarding what the president was alleged to have done. Frequently, for example, the president was depicted as being chased by the law.

David Letterman (1996): Some more things about the State of the Union Address. It was interrupted 20 times by applause and two times by subpoenas.

Jay Leno (1996): I watched the news a few minutes ago and it showed President Clinton jogging, you know, with a Secret Service agent. And looking a little closer, I realized he was just trying to outrun a guy serving a subpoena.

Alternatively, the jokes played off a scandal to bring up another subject.

Jay Leno (2000): And here's something kind of serious. The committee of the Arkansas Supreme Court has recommended that President Clinton be disbarred and lose his law license. This is the worst setback for Clinton, well, since the Ten Commandments.

David Letterman (1998): Let me see if I have this correct. Hillary, earlier this week, had to testify about the Whitewater thing. Did some testifying, Hillary did. Tomorrow, President Big Shot, White Thighs, Tubby, Bubba...will be testifying in the Paula Jones case down there in Washington, and next week, Hillary and Bill will be testifying in the Congressional mixed doubles hearings.

Other Clinton Characters

While Clinton was the dominant single figure in late night humor, a number of close Clinton associates and adversaries also had a significant place in the late night universe. Indeed, 2,362 jokes were told at the expense of figures whose public persona was derived from their relationship to Clinton. That is, they were known for being related to Clinton, personally associated with Clinton, or involved in a scandal with Clinton (either as accuser, accomplice, or prosecutor). Together with the jokes told directly about Clinton, this represents a clear majority of all jokes on U.S. political figures.

As Table 9.3 shows, the more than 2,300 jokes told at the expense of Clinton family, friends, and accusers demonstrate the rolling waves of scandal attention the president received. Moreover, virtually every member of the list was depicted as a source of embarrassment to the president. First lady and future U.S. senator Hillary Rodham Clinton was depicted as a shrew of dubious integrity. Following

TABLE 9.3.   Number of Jokes on Bill Clinton Associates on Late Night Comedies (1996–2001)

	1996	1997	1998	1999	2000	2001	Total
Hillary Rodham Clinton	126	74	101	290	185	91	867
Monica Lewinsky	0	0	303	343	100	18	764
Paula Jones	2	37	89	34	34	0	196
Linda Tripp	0	0	89	76	10	1	176
Kenneth Starr	0	4	145	16	2	1	168
Dick Morris	72	6	0	1	0	0	79
Roger Clinton	3	8	4	4	1	26	46
Chelsea Clinton	0	10	1	0	4	1	16
Hugh Rodham	0	0	0	0	0	15	15
Vernon Jordan	0	0	9	3	0	0	12
Susan McDougal	1	1	4	2	0	0	8
Gennifer Flowers	4	1	1	1	0	0	7
Buddy the dog	0	0	0	1	0	1	2
James McDougal	0	2	0	0	0	0	2
Kathleen Willey	0	0	1	1	0	0	2
Tony Rodham	0	0	0	0	0	1	1
Total	208	143	747	772	336	155	2,361

Data from the Center for Media and Public Affairs, www.cmpa.com.

her are figures in various Clinton scandals, including a number of women the president was alleged to have had inappropriate contact with (Monica Lewinsky, Paula Jones, Gennifer Flowers, Kathleen Willey), major figures in the subsequent investigations (Linda Tripp and Kenneth Starr), Clinton relatives who were depicted as involved in some form of nefarious behavior (Roger Clinton, Hugh Rodham, Tony Rodham), figures from the president's Whitewater investment deal (Susan and Jim McDougal), and an advisor involved in his own separate sexual scandal (Dick Morris). About the only close Clinton associates not depicted as an embarrassment to the president were his daughter, Chelsea Clinton, and his late dog, Buddy.[32]

Hillary Rodham Clinton Jokes

In contrast to the "forgivable indiscretions" angle that seemed to characterize much of the Bill Clinton comedy, Hillary Clinton's portrayal often blamed her for her husband's behavior.

> David Letterman (1998): They're talking about impeachment, and I think that's silly. I think it's premature. Look at it this way. President Clinton is going on vacation for a month in August with Hillary. Now, isn't that punishment enough.

> Jay Leno (1998): Now, Hillary has the main role in the retelling of a classic children's tale. This one is called, "Frosty, the First Lady."

> David Letterman (1998): President Clinton is on the horns of a dilemma. You know what I'm saying? Let me describe this dilemma. Because if he says that he didn't have sex with Monica Lewinsky, he faces impeachment. On the other hand, if he says he did have sex with Monica Lewinsky, well, God, he faces Hillary.

In something of a contradiction, when not being painted as a shrew, she is castigated for putting up with the president. In fact, Jay Leno apparently liked this joke so much he could not stop using it. In February 1998 he said, "Democratic chairman and Colorado Governor Roy Romer admitted today he had a 16-year affair with his Democratic Party assistant. And out of force of habit, Hillary announced she's standing by him"; and in December of 1998 Leno said, "Speaker-elect Louisiana Congressman Bob Livingston has admitted to numerous affairs during his 33-year marriage. And out of force of habit, Hillary said she was standing by him."

Monica Lewinsky Jokes

Jokes centered on Monica Lewinsky, as opposed to those focused on Bill Clinton, also seem to have a much sharper, nastier edge. While Clinton jokes often take delight in his excesses, Lewinsky jokes portray her as some kind of gutter-dweller.

Late night jokes suggested sexual indiscretions were the center and purpose of Ms. Lewinsky's life.

> Jay Leno (1998): CNN reported today that Monica Lewinsky met face-to-face with Kenneth Starr. That's the first time Monica ever met anyone in Washington face-to-face.

> Jay Leno (1998): A man who claims he was once Monica's first boyfriend said she told him she had read a manual about oral sex, and she wanted to be the best at it. You see that—just a starry-eyed kid with a dream. A dream that took her all the way to the top.

> Jay Leno (1998): Monica Lewinsky was subpoenaed. She's supposed to appear in a federal court tomorrow, but it's been put off till next week. According to her lawyer, she can refuse to testify if she wants to, but let's face it, you know, saying no is not this woman's strong point.

> David Letterman (1998): Monica is very nervous, because, you know, she's got to tell 23 strangers, 23 complete strangers, all about her sex life. You know, and I'm thinking, "Yeah, but knowing Monica, they won't be strangers for long."

> Jay Leno (1998): The winds were so strong today in Brentwood, they actually blew Monica Lewinsky into an upright position.

While few Clinton jokes suggested that his sexual activities had hurt anyone (or at least hurt anyone who didn't deserve it), Lewinsky was portrayed as ruining her family's life. David Letterman in 1998, "Monica Lewinsky is taking her dad out to brunch on Father's Day. Yep. She's going to try to repay him for squandering his life savings for her legal defense fund. The least she can do." Other jokes implied Lewinsky had herpes, referred to her as a "large-mouthed bass" or a "wide-mouth can of beer."

Even jokes directed toward her weight seemed stronger than the many jokes told on Clinton's figure.

> Jay Leno (1998): Now the latest news reports say that Monica Lewinsky has put on 50 pounds. Did you see that? 50 pounds. If this keeps up, she may drop to her knees just from the weight.

> David Letterman (1998): I think it's good her affair with the president is over, because now I'm not sure if she'd fit under the desk.

> David Letterman (1998): She's put on so much weight, the other day she went out in a yellow dress, and three guys tried to hail her.

Similar derogatory jokes were told at the expense of virtually all the women who accused the president of inappropriate contact. The late night reaction to Lewinsky and the other women linked to President Clinton is summed up in this 1998 Letterman joke, "They're already talking about in the worst possible case scenario for President Clinton. Maybe he could invoke the insanity defense, you know? 'Okay, it's true. I'm nuts. Everything happened. It's because I'm insane.' You know, if you think about it, there's Gennifer Flowers, Monica Lewinsky, Paula Jones. He's got a pretty good case."

Two factors may help explain the decided imbalance in the portrayal of Clinton and Lewinsky. First, psychological research suggests men and women understand, define, and react to infidelity quite differently.[33] And, these jokes are written, selected, and performed by a staff that is almost exclusively male. During the years under study, the writing staffs of late night shows ranged from 86 to 100 percent male.[34]

Kenneth Starr Jokes

Kenneth Starr was the center of hundreds of jokes maligning both himself and his investigation of Bill Clinton. Among the less scathing were those that centered on the length and cost of the investigation.

> David Letterman (1998): Starr has announced that he is going to start investigating his own office for news leaks. Oh great, there's another four years and $30 million.

> Jay Leno (1998): They asked Ken Starr what people will say about this investigation 30 years from now? He said, "The same thing they are saying now. When is it going to end?"

More damning were the many jokes suggesting Starr was on a sexual witch hunt.

> David Letterman (1998): President Clinton is over there, and he sees Boris Yeltsin and they meet, and they give each other what has been

described by the press as "an extended bear hug" and then minutes later, Yeltsin was subpoenaed by Kenneth Starr.

David Letterman (1998): Clinton goes to Ireland, and you know, this poor guy can't get a break. Bad luck follows him wherever he goes. He kisses the Blarney Stone, and as soon as he was done, Kenneth Starr subpoenas the damn thing.

Jay Leno (1998): In Washington, it was so cold, Ken Starr had to scrape the ice off windows to look in people's bedrooms.

Among the more personally oriented jokes were many that suggested Starr is an unpleasant person. David Letterman referred to Starr as a "nosebleed" in five different jokes. Jay Leno in 1998 referred to him alternatively as a snake ("In Washington it was so hot, Ken Starr shed his skin") or an unspecified reptile ("Today in Washington it was so hot, people were gathering around Ken Starr just so they could be near a cold-blooded reptile"). A number of jokes portrayed Starr as a social misfit: Jay Leno (1998), "This Ken Starr guy, I'm sorry. This guy is a loser, isn't he? Please, 40 million bucks to get one woman to talk dirty to you"; Jay Leno (1998), "This Kenneth Starr—he is annoying. Isn't this guy? He is just creepy. How many think all Kenneth Starr needs is a good Lewinsky. That would just straighten him out."

Finally, late night comedians explained Starr's decisions as motivated by hatred: Conan O'Brien (1998), "According to Republican Senator Arlen Specter, the American public believes Kenneth Starr is out to get President Clinton. That's what he said.... And in response, Kenneth Starr said, 'That's ridiculous. I have no personal animosity towards that fat horny pig.'"

Effects on Opinion of Clinton

Given the thrust of the results presented, featuring (1) Bill Clinton as the central comedic figure of late night, and (2) Clinton treated less harshly than those around and against him, it is perhaps not shocking to see the pattern revealed in Table 9.4. That is, in short, Bill Clinton had a higher approval rate among those who said they had learned something about politics from late night television comedy than among those who said they had not. In other words, those who had paid more attention to programs making fun of Bill Clinton

TABLE 9.4.   Approval of Bill Clinton's Job Performance
as President by Political Comedy Consumption (2000)

	Has Learned About Politics from Late Night Comedy (n = 740) (%)	Has Not Learned About Politics from Late Night Comedy (n = 534) (%)
Approve	58.1	51.5
Disapprove	34.5	38.6
Don't Know	7.4	9.9

Difference between columns is statistically significant using chi-square; p < .01.

Data from the Pew Research Center poll, "The Tough Job Communicating with Voters (February 5, 2000), http://people-press.org/dataarchive/.

thousands of times during his second term were more likely to think he was doing a good job as president.

Before one draws the inference that late night was independently doing the president some good, it would be useful to more carefully examine this result. For example, if Democrats watch more late night programming than Republicans, this result could reveal little about the effect of the shows and only something about the makeup of the audience. When the results in Table 9.4 are broken down by party, however, the implications remain clear. For example, among only those who identify themselves as Republicans, Bill Clinton's approval rating among late night watchers was 18.6 percent higher than among non-late night watchers (difference significant using chi-square; $p > .01$). Clinton's approval rating was also marginally higher among independents who watched late night versus independents who did not.

As discussed earlier, the many scandals of Bill Clinton did not seem to harm him in the polls. Here, the many thousands of jokes about the many scandals of Bill Clinton did not seem to harm him in the polls. Why? While there were thousands of jokes about Clinton, they did not revolve around major issues or matters of great political substance. While there were thousands of jokes about Clinton, many were somewhat sympathetic to Clinton. While there were thousands of jokes about Clinton, there were many vituperative jokes about his accusers, his wife, and his paramours. In sum, in the morass of negativity that is media coverage of politics in general, and late night comedy politics specifically, several thousand negative jokes about Bill Clinton hardly seem harmful, and may have been helpful.

Conclusion

Bill Clinton, without doubt, was the central figure in late night comedy just as comedy assumed a more central role in the political arena. For perspective, George W. Bush's second term has seen his popularity plummet and his late night jokes skyrocket, doubling from 2005 to 2006. Yet, Bush remains a far less frequent target of jokes than Clinton was at his peak.

We advance the discussion about the politics of late night comedy with a systematic look at the treatment of its long-time leading target. We find that the jokes told at President Clinton's expense over his second term focus on his sexual habits, his weight, and his various scandals. But perhaps as notably, we find that the more than 2,300 jokes directed toward Clinton's family and Clinton's accusers were less forgiving. We find, ultimately, that despite his many failings, and despite this vast quantity of late night television attention to his foibles, viewers of late night comedy were somewhat more likely to approve of Clinton's presidency.

Conan O'Brien spoke to this strange relationship between Bill Clinton, late night comedy, and the American people when he wrote that "Clinton was the first cartoon president. He ran off cliffs, was crushed by anvils and flattened by turn-of-the-century trains. Yet, moments later, we always saw him, just like Wile E. Coyote or Daffy Duck, completely reassembled and eagerly pursuing his next crazy scheme. Essentially, people love cartoon characters because they cannot be hurt. They defy the rules of Greek tragedy.... And so we never turned him off. We sat and watched, grinning and glassy-eyed, waiting expectantly to see what the funny man with the fat red nose would do next." [35]

Notes

1. Conan O'Brien, "What I'll Miss About Bill Clinton," *Time*, January 8, 2001, 80.
2. John Zaller, "Monica Lewinsky's Contribution to Political Science," *PS* 31 (1998): 186.

3. Gary Jacobson, "Impeachment Politics in the 1998 Congressional Elections," *Political Science Quarterly* 114 (1999): 31–51; Arthur Miller, "Sex, Politics, and Public Opinion: What Political Scientists Really Learned from the Clinton-Lewinsky Scandal," *PS* 32 (1999): 721–729; Molly Sonner and Clyde Wilcox, "Forgiving and Forgetting: Public Support for Bill Clinton during the Lewinsky Scandal," *PS* 32 (1999): 554–557; Zaller "Monica Lewinsky's Contribution to Political Science."
4. Miller, "Sex, Politics, and Public Opinion."
5. Zaller, "Monica Lewinsky's Contribution to Political Science"; Thomas Cronin and Michael Genovese, "President Clinton and Character Questions," *Presidential Studies Quarterly* 28 (1998): 892–897.
6. Paul Quirk, "Coping with the Politics of Scandal," *Presidential Studies Quarterly* 28 (1998): 898–902.
7. Miller, "Sex, Politics, and Public Opinion."
8. Kathleen Hall Jamieson and Sean Aday, "When Is Presidential Behavior Public and When Is It Private?" *Presidential Studies Quarterly* 28 (1998): 856–860; Marcia Lynn Whicker, "The Clinton Crisis and the Double Standard for Presidents," *Presidential Studies Quarterly* 28 (1998): 873–880; Juliet Williams, "The Personal Is Political: Thinking Through the Clinton/Lewinsky/Starr Affair," *PS* 34 (2001): 93–98.
9. Miller, "Sex, Politics, and Public Opinion."
10. Jacobson, "Impeachment Politics in the 1998 Congressional Elections."
11. Miller, "Sex, Politics, and Public Opinion," 728.
12. Ibid.
13. Sonner and Wilcox, "Forgiving and Forgetting."
14. Ibid.
15. Katy Harriger, "The President and the Independent Counsel: Reflections on Prosecutors, Presidential Prerogatives, and Political Power," *Presidential Studies Quarterly* 31 (2001): 338–348.
16. Sonner and Wilcox, "Forgiving and Forgetting."
17. Robert Spitzer, "Clinton's Impeachment Will Have Few Consequences for the Presidency," *PS* 32 (1999): 543.
18. "The Tough Job of Communicating with Voters," *The Pew Research Center for the People and the Press*, February 5, 2000. http://people-press.org/reports/display.php3?ReportID=46. Respondents who reported sometimes learning something about the presidential campaign or candidates from these sources: television comedy (58 percent), news magazines (54 percent), morning news shows (53 percent), cable talk shows (52 percent), public television (50 percent), Sunday network talk shows (47 percent), C-SPAN (43 percent), and the Internet (33 percent). Also suggesting the significance of late night programming is previous research finding that late night shows such as David Letterman's are a frequent source of conversation for viewers;

see Richard Schaefer and Robert Avery, "Audience Conceptualizations of Late Night with David Letterman," *Journal of Broadcasting and Electronic Media* 37 (1993): 253–272.

19. "Journalists Monopolize TV Election News," *Center for Media and Public Affairs*, October 30, 2000. http://www.cmpa.com/election2004/JournalistsMonopolize.htm.

20. Bernard Weintraub, "The 2000 Campaign: The Comedians," *New York Times*, January 19, 2000, A16.

21. Ibid.

22. Michael Heaton, "Why Is Letterman Our Cronkite?" *Plain Dealer*, November 3, 2000, 2.

23. Scott Shepard, "Talk Shows: The Last Word in Campaigning," *Atlanta Journal and Constitution*, November 1, 2000, 3A.

24. David Niven, "Bias in the News: Partisanship and Negativity in Coverage of Presidents George Bush and Bill Clinton," *Harvard International Journal of Press/Politics* 6 (2001): 31–46.

25. S. Robert Lichter, Linda Lichter, and Daniel Amundson, "Government Goes Down the Tube: Images of Government in TV Entertainment, 1955–1998," *Harvard International Journal of Press/Politics* 5 (2000): 97–98.

26. Daniel Amundson and S. Robert Lichter, "Heeeeeere's Politics," *Public Opinion* 11 (1988): 46–47; L. Duerst, Glory Koloen, and Geoff Peterson, "It May Be Funny, But Is It True: The Political Content of Late-Night Talk Show Monologues" (presented at the annual meeting of the American Political Science Association, San Francisco, August 30–September 2, 2001); Thomas Dye, Harmon Zeigler, and S. Robert Lichter, *American Politics in the Media Age* (Pacific Grove, CA: Brooks/Cole, 1992); Verena Hess, "The Role of Political Comedy in the 2000 Election Campaign: Examining Content and Third-Person Effects" (presented at the annual meeting of the American Political Science Association, San Francisco, August 30–September 2, 2001); David Niven, S. Robert Lichter, and Daniel Amundson, "The Political Content of Late Night Comedy," *Harvard International Journal of Press/Politics* 8 (2003): 118–134.

27. Eron Berg and Louis Lippman, "Does Humor in Radio Advertising Affect Recognition of Novel Product Brand Names?" *The Journal of General Psychology* 128 (2001): 194–205.

28. William Benoit, Andrew Klyukovski, and John McHale, "A Fantasy Theme Analysis of Political Cartoons on the Clinton-Lewinsky-Starr Affair," *Critical Studies in Media Communication* 18 (2001): 377–394.

29. Jim Lyttle, "The Effectiveness of Humor in Persuasion: The Case of Business Ethics Training," *The Journal of General Psychology* 128 (2001): 206–216.

30. Bryan Whaley and Rachel Holloway, "Rebuttal Analogy in Political Communication: Argument and Attack in Sound Bite," *Political Communication* 14 (1997): 293–305.
31. Weintraub, "The 2000 Campaign."
32. Even though Chelsea Clinton was not personally the source of any embarrassment for the president, even she was used as a setup for a joke about the president's sex life: David Letterman (2000), "Top Ten good things about dating the president's daughter. 10. When President says 'Don't do anything I wouldn't do,' You can pretty much go nuts."
33. Arnie Cann, Jessica Mangum, and Marissa Wells, "Distress in Response to Relationship Infidelity: The Roles of Gender and Attitudes about Relationships," *Journal of Sex Research* 38 (2001): 185–190.
34. Based on the authors' calculation derived from rosters of the writing staffs of each show.
35. O'Brien, "What I'll Miss About Bill Clinton."

10

Political Punditry in Punchlines
Late Night Comics Take on the 2004 Presidential Debates

Josh Compton

The "spin room," a holding tank for spokespersons eager to tout their respective candidates to reporters, is a fixture of contemporary political debates. Ann McFeatters, Washington bureau chief of the *Pittsburg Post-Gazette*, observes, "The goal is to 'spin' the media and public perception on who won, regardless of what happened. And it often works."[1] Despite the predictable agendas in spin room rhetoric, mediated postdebate analysis can be quite impacting.[2] But conventional postdebate punditry is not the only place viewers can get a take on the night's proceedings. During post-prime time, another type of political punditry appears: late night political comics offer their analysis, commentary couched in comedy.

This chapter returns to the first presidential debate of 2004, surveying some of the late night humor that prefaced and then followed the match between George W. Bush and John Kerry. I then discuss the idea that late night comedic postdebate analysis warrants closer scrutiny from scholars to assess both the content and potential effects of this political punditry in punchlines.

Late Night Political Humor

Interest in political humor on late night TV spiked during and immediately after Campaign 2000, an election campaign that "completely obliterated the line that once separated pure campaign discourse and parody."[3] *Saturday Night Live* (*SNL*), *The Daily Show*,

The Tonight Show, and *The Late Show* were among the obliterating forces, offering political parodies, tongue-in-cheek analyses, and a slew of political zingers. According to the Center for Media and Public Affairs (CMPA), late night television comedians Jay Leno and David Letterman rattled off 31,543 political jokes in a decade's time.[4] Perhaps showing the unique resiliency of political humor, the CMPA noted that late night humor "bounced back" four months after the tragic events of 9/11: Jay Leno, David Letterman, and Conan O'Brien were telling more than nine political jokes each night, 38 percent more than they were telling before 9/11.[5]

The topics of late night jokes are regularly political, but what about their tone? Content analyses suggest that it's overwhelmingly negative.[6] David Niven, Robert Lichter, and Daniel Amundson's analysis of 13,301 late night jokes led them to conclude

> In most years, nine out of ten political jokes are not directed toward a political issue but more likely to a personal foible of a political leader. According to late night shows, presidents and presidential candidates are incredibly old, fat, dumb, lecherous, or prone to lie.[7]

Not only are late night jokes increasingly political, they are also increasingly nasty: this is the attack politics of late night comedy. But do these jokes have any effect?

It appears they do. Viewers, especially ones with less political knowledge, pick up on politicians' traits that are ridiculed by late night comics.[8] There is even some evidence that they might be learning something,[9] or at least *think* they are learning something.[10] Besides evaluations of candidates and political knowledge, other studies have assessed late night comedy's potential influence on cynicism[11] and normative political outcomes.[12] When we also consider that 61 percent of young adults report regularly or sometimes learning campaign information from television comedy (late night talk shows and/or comedy shows like *SNL* and *The Daily Show*),[13] it's reasonable to conclude that the laughing matters.

Of the many possible directions for future late night comedy research, focusing on how it characterizes specific political events is particularly promising. In these moments, the late night comedy is not just political, but it's topically political. Perhaps no event demonstrates this better than the presidential debates. The Racine Group, a collection of scholars with expertise in political campaign debates, noted that debate content "matriculates to other forums, including non-traditional outlets, such as late-night talk shows…and comedy."[14] Michael Pfau's analysis of the "subtle effects" of political debates includes a call to explore programs like these when assessing debate effects.[15]

Presidential debates offer unique moments in election campaigns. The Racine Group noted: "Because they command the attention of the public, the media, and the candidates, televised political debates have become a permanent aspect of America's political landscape."[16] Most importantly, debates matter, as a mountain of research[17] and a recent meta-analysis[18] attest. But just because they are important and impacting does not mean that they are immune from late night ridicule. Pre- and postdebate, the late night comics weigh in, adding to what television critic Kay McFadden calls "the distortion that occurs as information proceeds from news to spin to entertainment."[19]

Late night comedy hit the 2000 presidential debates full force, with the presidential debates in *Saturday Night Live*'s comedic crosshairs.[20] Chris Smith and Ben Voth explored these debate parodies in their rhetorical analysis, "The Role of Humor in Political Argument: How 'Strategery' and 'Lockboxes' Changed a Political Campaign."

> With Will Ferrell playing a goofy, squinty-eyed George Bush and Darrell Hammond embodying a sly, overbearing Al Gore, SNL's parody of the debate painted the candidates, not as respectful politicians, but as comic clowns.[21]

Smith and Voth's Burkean analysis examined not only the parodies, but also the candidates' reactions to the comic characterizations, arguing that late night comedy functioned as an influential form of political argument.

But while *Saturday Night Live* is known for its spot-on impersonations and sharp political humor, late night talk show hosts' takes on the debate are more of the "badoom-boom formula."[22] Monologue jokes do not permit much extended satire. Instead, zingers and one-liners are the tools of their presidential debate banter. Myles Martel called the kind of postdebate analysis by traditional, conventional political commentators "meta-debating."[23] To others, it's known as just spin. So what can we call the postdebate analysis by nontraditional political commentators, late night comics? "Meta-musing debating"? Or maybe, "jest-spin"?

Whatever we call it, people are watching. Even the news media turn to the jokesters for their takes. One journalist observed

When the first debate between George W. Bush and John Kerry finished
at 10:30 pm, a fair proportion of the 62.5 million viewers did not bother
with the traditional post-debate analysis by cable and network news outlets. Instead, they hit the remote to find out what late-night jokesters like
Dave Letterman, Jay Leno, Conan O'Brien and Jon Stewart thought.[24]

Similarly, another recalled: "After the great men had finished yam-
mering in Florida Thursday night, I did what any sensible political
columnist does these days: I turned to the late-night comedians for
their take on the affair."[25]

Late night comics did not wait for the first debate to begin mocking it. They began setting the stage beginning September 13, more
than two weeks before George W. Bush and John Kerry faced off.
Instead of taking aim at either of the candidates, they targeted the
debates themselves.

The debate format caused some discord between the campaigns.
The Commission on Presidential Debates, formed in 1987 by Republicans and Democrats for bipartisan involvement, had recommended
three 90-minute debates, and set dates, locations, and moderators.[26]
But the details proved messy, with both campaigns organizing teams
of big-name negotiators to work things out.[27] The *New York Times*
called these negotiations "the predebate debates," and highlighted
their importance in ironing out details that would cater to each
candidate's strengths.[28] The result? Thirty-two pages of rules. Even
the lecterns were dictated: "fifty inches from the stage floor to the
outside top...facing the audience and...forty-eight inches from
the stage floor to the top of the writing surface facing the respective
candidates."[29]

This pre-debate debating was not limited to the campaigns' negotiation teams. Late night talk show hosts chimed in, too, in their
monologue jokes. Jay Leno's quip began a consistent theme among
the comics.

Both sides are arguing about the formats of the big presidential debates....
Bush wants to sit, Kerry wants to stand.... You know, split the difference.
Make them squat.[30]

Referencing the thirty-two pages of agreed-upon debate rules (and
the tabloid-trendy reports of Jennifer Lopez's marriage to Marc
Anthony), David Letterman said "it's like being a J-Lo husband."

Jay Leno and David Letterman also "previewed" the debate categories. Leno was first, with: "The first debate will cover the 1960s. The

second debate will cover the early '70s. And the third debate, if there's time, some topical issues."[31] While Leno's joke mocked the priorities of the two campaigns—much of their rhetoric was swirling around controversies related to George W. Bush's National Guard service and John Kerry's time in Vietnam in the late 1960s and early 1970s—Letterman's punchline format was to give two "real" categories, followed by a humorous third. From Letterman, viewers learn: "There will be three debates, and each debate will have a category, and the categories will be domestic policy, foreign policy, and movie sidekicks."[32] Later, Letterman labeled the third category "girl groups from the '60s,"[33] "sitcom neighbors,"[34] and finally, "one-hit wonders."[35]

The bipartisan Commission on Presidential Debates may have offered official recommendations, and the campaigns' negotiation teams may have hammered out the details. But the bi-comedic quips of two of the most political late night talk show hosts were adding their two cents, too, with millions of viewers tuning in and getting an early picture of the upcoming presidential debates.

While ridiculing the debate formats and rules were common joke topics for Jay Leno and David Letterman, a preponderance of their jokes took aim at the debaters, and sometimes, both of them at the same time. A handful of these referenced the particularly busy 2004 hurricane season (Hurricanes Charley, Frances, and Ivan, among others). Consider this montage of hurricane-themed jokes that took swipes at George W. Bush and John Kerry.

> David Letterman: The first presidential debate will be in Florida. Haven't those people suffered enough?[36]

> David Letterman: The first Kerry-Bush debate takes place Thursday in Miami, and today thousands of local residents began evacuating.[37]

> Jay Leno: You know where the first debate is being held? Miami...I mean, first hurricanes. Now Bush and Kerry going down there? Haven't these people suffered enough?[38]

In jokes like these, neither candidate is promoted over the other. Both are ridiculed. But this type of joke was far less common than jokes that targeted one or the other of the candidates.

John Kerry was pummeled for being rich, aloof, and inconsistent. Consider Jay Leno's observations.

> Kerry just can't seem to shake this rich guy image, you know? Like today, he challenged President Bush to three debates and a yacht race.[39]

> Kerry's advisers are now working hard to try and prepare him for the debates. You know, they told him he has to try and connect with regular people.... They told him, if you need a glass of water, don't yell, "Jeeves!"[40]

> Debate experts say President Bush could win if he does not get off-message. And then they say Kerry could win if he *gets* a message.[41]

A few jokes, including Jay Leno's, took aim at John Kerry's appearance: "They say this debate is helping the economy. In fact, this week, millions of people are buying those big-screen TVs so they can see Kerry's entire head."[42]

John Kerry's famously wealthy wife was not immune to late night mocking. Both Jay Leno and David Letterman mentioned her by name and referenced her wealth. In a nod to Oprah Winfrey's well-publicized gesture of giving cars away to audience members of her talk show, Leno quipped: "They say John Kerry already has begun preparing for the debates.... He figured he'd start off by having his wife buy everyone in the audience a new car,"[43] while Letterman remarked: "The candidates must remain at least ten feet apart. And they cannot talk directly to one another. It's actually based on the John Kerry–Teresa Heinz prenup agreement."[44]

George W. Bush was characterized as ignorant and an "underdog" in the debates. Jay Leno and David Letterman took swipes, as did Conan O'Brien. Leno remarked: "President Bush and John Kerry have agreed on three debates. Kerry wanted more, but Bush said no, he thought three was a good, even number,"[45] and later

> Kerry tried to lower expectations of himself. He said... "Bush has never lost a debate, and he's a formidable opponent." And then Bush lowered expectations of himself when he said, "Hey, what does 'formidable' mean?"[46]

Letterman remarked

> President Bush, here's his strategy, he's seeking to portray John Kerry as confused.... You think about it, you know you're in trouble when you're running against George Bush and you're the one who looks confused.[47]

O'Brien added: "President Bush won the coin toss before the debate, and as a result, at the end, he was allowed to have the last word.... Not surprisingly, the word was 'courageosity.'"[48]

Jokes that portrayed Bush as the "underdog" in the debate included this one from Leno: "A week from now, John Kerry will debate President Bush in Florida. Right now, Kerry has a bad cold and can barely understand what he's saying. So it looks like it should be a fair fight."[49]

Some of the jokes could be perceived as not only attacking one of the candidates, but also of promoting one over the other. For example, one of Leno's jokes about George W. Bush's intelligence also credited John Kerry, noting that the

> experts say Kerry can't look like a know-it-all, and Bush can't appear too simplistic.... So the entire presidential race comes down to this. The smart guy has to look a little dumber, and the dumb guy has to look a little smarter.[50]

Similarly, Letterman offered this quip: "Bush is concerned about the lectern, Bush is worried about the room temperature, he's worried about lighting, and Kerry is making the mistake of concentrating on the issues."[51]

This cursory review of some of the jokes surrounding the first presidential debate represents four main types: jokes that poke fun at the debates, jokes that ridicule both candidates at the same time, jokes that ridicule one specific candidate, and jokes that derogate one candidate while promoting the other. This cacophony of late night debate humor began weeks before the first debate.

Did the late night discourse change after the first debate? Yes and no. In some ways, late night comics confirmed what they predicted. But a few new jokes also cropped into the postdebate, late night analysis.

After the first debate, many political commentators and public opinion polls indicated a strong win for John Kerry. Scot Lehigh of the *Boston Globe* announced: "Last night, John Kerry won as clear a debate victory as we've seen since Ronald Reagan outdueled Jimmy Carter in 1980."[52] A *New York Times/CBS News* poll indicated that more people thought John Kerry looked more presidential than the president.[53] Echoing this perception, the late night jokesters turned most of their attention toward George W. Bush and his lackluster performance. Leno joked: "Political experts say Bush was off his game the other night. They said he looked distracted, confused, at a loss for words. Off his game? That is Bush's game."[54] Letterman's take? "Experts are saying that if this was a game show, Bush would have gone home with a handshake and a quart of motor oil."[55]

Perhaps as damaging, if not more so, for George W. Bush, late night comics also mentioned some issues. Referencing a well-publicized Homeland Security incident with a former musician, Letterman said: "Last night's debate was on foreign policy, and if you saw it you know Bush spent the entire night gloating about the arrest of Cat Stevens."[56] Referring to a charge that George Bush, Sr. "pulled some strings" to keep his son out of active military service, Letterman joked: "But that's it for George Bush. He will not have to be in the next debate because his dad got him out of it."[57]

Jay Leno and Conan O'Brien, consistent with pre-debate jokes, again made fun of George W. Bush's intelligence. Leno joked

> You can see where President Bush made some mistakes during the debate, like when he said, "I know how this world works." You think that's true? You think maybe President Bush doesn't even know how the magic wallet works?[58]

O'Brien quipped: "Last night was the first, the very first presidential debate, and it lasted a full 90 minutes.... Or, as President Bush calls it, three *Sponge Bobs*."[59]

Some jokes that were borderline favorable toward George W. Bush used the "praise" as setups for the zingers. And in these cases, the zinger was usually alcohol-related.

> Jay Leno: People underestimate President Bush when it comes to debating. He is pretty good at it. Back in college, he was able to argue both sides of that "tastes great, less filling" debate.[60]

> David Letterman: This is just my observation, at the debate, Bush appeared confident, he appeared relaxed, he appeared calm. That's right, he's drinking again.[61]

From specific mentions of his lackluster performance to jabs about his competence, George W. Bush was declared the loser of the first matchup. In many ways, this postdebate analysis is consistent with how the comedians set the stage prior to the debate: Bush was projected to be a bad debater, and, after the debate, the comedians concluded that was indeed the case.

While most of the jokes targeted George W. Bush, a few made fun of both candidates. Jay Leno called the debate "the big head versus the airhead,"[62] said the networks were calling it "Rich White Guy Survivor,"[63] and asked: "Did you watch the rich white guy who went to Yale and wore the red tie, or the rich white guy who went to Yale and wore the blue tie?"[64] Referencing the thirty-two pages of debate rules again, he asked: "You know the one rule they should've put in? No lying!"[65]

The comics may have gone a little easier on John Kerry after his strong showing in the debate, but he did not completely escape mockery. Referring to the rule forbidding candidates from leaving their respective podiums, Jay Leno noted this was "especially tough on Kerry—not being allowed to change position."[66] John Kerry's wealth was also mentioned. Leno noted: "Kerry's people have been advising him, keep it simple. They say Kerry gets the biggest payoff when he uses the shortest sentence. Like when he said, 'I do,'"[67] and said that John Kerry won the coin toss because "his wife owns all the coins."[68] Comics took aim at John Kerry's appearance, too. When describing the lights installed on each candidate's podium to give time signals, Leno said: "For Kerry, they actually used a tanning light."[69] A few days later, Leno said that "the terror alert on John Kerry's face has gone from orange back to pasty white" and that he hoped Kerry's win "doesn't give him a swelled head."[70] Yet the prevailing perception that John Kerry had won overshadowed these light barbs, with David Letterman calling Kerry "so confident that he's windsurfing again"[71] and had "even picked up the support of one of the Bush twins."[72]

Over the next few weeks, we would see similar jokes lobbed before and after the second and final debate. George W. Bush would again be stamped incompetent. David Letterman quipped, "I watched the debates, and frankly Bush did look confused, at one point he tried to buy a vowel."[73] Bush's image as a bad debater would also continue in late night joking. For example, Jay Leno said that it was raining so hard, "cars were spinning out of control like President Bush in the debate."[74] A few of the jokes would also approach some issues, including war in Iraq. Consider this one from Leno

> President Bush apparently had a hard time getting past reporters and leaving the auditorium...last week after the debate. He couldn't get out of the auditorium. Literally, the President—isn't that amazing? Bush not having an exit strategy?[75]

But this type of issue-related joke was rare, and even those that did broach some issues spoke in generalities to set up a punchline.

John Kerry's performances in the debates, sometimes praised by the comics themselves, did not earn him total reprieve from continuing ridicule. Jay Leno launched this extended joke

> Tomorrow night's debate...will be before an audience made up entirely
> of undecided voters, which creates a huge dilemma for John Kerry. Does
> he sit on the stage beside President Bush, or does he sit in the audience
> with all of the other people who can't make up their minds?[76]

And in another joke, Leno again returned to the idea that Kerry was
aloof and detached:

> Some people are now saying that the questions at the end of the debate the
> other night actually helped John Kerry 'cause they made him look more
> human. Well that, and you know, taking the bolts out of his neck.[77]

Echoing themes from pre-debate late night mockery, Kerry continued to be portrayed as inconsistent and aloof.

Future Directions

After the first debate between John Kerry and George W. Bush,
political analyst Jack Pitney observed: "We're now at the point where
comedy shows are the true debate referees."[78] Whether or not Jay
Leno, David Letterman, and the like are "true debate referees" may
be arguable, but the idea that they are offering their own pre- and
postdebate spin is not.

Because televised debates warrant continued scholarly attention,[79]
and late night comedy is a growing force in politics, examining the
two together could yield particularly insightful scholarship. Indeed,
looking at late night comics' analysis (jest-spin?) would help answer
some calls for future research made by debate scholars.

> [I]t is shaped by pre-debate attempts to raise or lower expectations, by
> post-debate "spinning," and by media analysis and commentary over the
> days following the debate. Which of these components...shape audi-
> ences' perceptions of the debate, and why, is important to know in order
> to account for the effects that debates can be shown to produce.[80]

Late night comics' characterizations of the presidential debates
could explore each of these areas, from pre-debate predictions to
postdebate analysis.

First, consider potential impacts of pre-debate joking. Journalists
call it "the expectations game," when campaigns try to lower expectations of their candidates by pumping up the skills of the opponent. In 2004, well before the first debate, both campaigns touted the

other. Matthew Dowd, George W. Bush's chief campaign strategist, called John Kerry "the best debater since Cicero."[81] Tad Devine, John Kerry's chief campaign strategist, said: "The fact is, George Bush has never lost a debate."[82] Might late night comedy also play this "expectations game"? Chris Smith and Ben Voth argued that *SNL*'s debate parodies during Campaign 2000 might have. "After SNL ran their parody of the first debate," they noted, "the expectations of Bush's level of performance was drastically lowered."[83] The sample of jokes surveyed here suggest an "expectations game" in late night comedy monologue jokes as well. In this case, it may not have helped Kerry much. Many of the jokes touted Kerry's debating skills and questioned Bush's aptitude. At least one called the Kerry campaign out on its strategy to lower expectations for his own performance and then lowered expectations of Bush.

> Kerry tried to lower expectations of himself. He said... "Bush has never lost a debate, and he's a formidable opponent." And then Bush lowered expectations of himself when he said, "Hey, what does *formidable* mean?"[84]

If the "expectations game" works, do comic versions influence viewers? Future research should find out.

We have evidence that traditional postdebate analysis matters,[85] but does postdebate comedic analysis change the way people think? Chris Smith and Ben Voth wondered if *Saturday Night Live*'s debate parody did this: "Voters seeking to understand the substance of ideas in the debate may have found the parodies of the debate to be a useful organizing tool for their inherent complexities."[86] Could the one-liners in Leno's and Letterman's jokes have impacted how people perceived the debates and/or the candidates? Will the inevitable jokes told before and after the next presidential debates make a difference? Investigating this particular type of "debate coverage" (using, for example, William Benoit's Functional Theory of Political Campaign Discourse[87]) would help answer these and other questions.

Of course, whether debate-topical jokes actually affect perceptions of candidates needs to be confirmed. Extant research into effects of late night comedy suggests that it may, especially with those of lower political knowledge.[88] Honing in on debate-topical jokes may reveal stronger effects: late night joking is overwhelmingly image based,[89] and the relational impacts of presidential debates are particularly impacting.[90]

Besides potential effects research looking into this unique postdebate analysis, future research should also look into the tone and nature of these topical jokes. We have content analyses to which we can compare debate-topical jokes with general political humor.[91] Additionally, scholars should take a closer look at the noncandidate-specific debate jokes. When Jay Leno jokes, "You know who won tonight's debate? Anybody that watched baseball,"[92] does this derogate both candidates, increase voter cynicism, decrease interest in the campaign, or some of each? What about jokes that spoke of neither candidate, but instead, the debates themselves, e.g., format, categories, rules? Political scientists and political communication scholars continue to warn of growing cynicism,[93] and research has found a link to late night comedy and cynicism.[94] Downplaying presidential debates in general may contribute to this growing skepticism toward campaigns and elections. Comics are doing more than "turn[ing] the candidates into walking punchlines,"[95] they are turning debate activities themselves into punchlines as well.

The sample of debate jokes mentioned in this chapter did not include other late night comedic takes on the debates. Comedy Central's Jon Stewart, host of *The Daily Show*, had 2.5 million viewers tune in to his show after the first debate, a record.[96] Although, some critics lamented that *SNL*'s debate parodies of 2004 were not as sharp as they were in 2000,[97] *Saturday Night Live*'s 2004 postdebate show was the most watched season premiere in three years.[98]

Rong Xiaoqing of *South China Morning Post*, mused: "[I]t does make one wonder, in some future election, whether the comedians will not only decide the election, but end up winning it."[99] Both claims, that comedians are deciding elections and may eventually win them, remain, appropriately enough in the context of this chapter, debatable. Continuing research into this unique form of late night political punditry will clarify what role, if any, comics play in influencing perceptions of presidential debates.

Notes

1. Ann McFeatters, "Canning the Candidates," *Pittsburgh Post-Gazette*, October 3, 2004.
2. Susan A. Hellweg, Michael Pfau, and Steven R. Brydon, *Televised Presidential Debates* (New York: Praeger, 1992).
3. Michael Pfau, "The Subtle Nature of Presidential Debate Influence," *Argumentation & Advocacy* 38 (2002): 251.
4. "Jay Leno's Greatest Hits," *The Center for Media and Public Affairs* [press release], April 30, 2002.

5. "Late Night Humor Bounces Back from September 11," *The Center for Media and Public Affairs* [press release], February 2, 2002.

6. Michael Nitz, Alyson Cypher, Tom Reichert, and James E. Mueller, "Candidates as Comedy: Political Presidential Humor on Late-Night Television Shows," in *The Millenium Election: Communication in the 2000 Campaign*, eds. Lynda Lee Kaid, John C. Tedesco, Dianne G. Bystrom, and Mitchell S. McKinney (Lanham, MD: Rowman & Littlefield, 2003), 165–175; David Niven, S. Robert Lichter, and Daniel Amundson, "The Political Content of Late Night Comedy," *Press/Politics* 8 (2003): 118–133; Dannagal Goldthwaite Young, "Late-Night Comedy in Election 2000: Its Influence on Candidate Trait Ratings and the Moderating Effects of Political Knowledge and Partisanship," *Journal of Broadcasting & Electronic Media* 48 (2004): 1–22; "Daily Show Viewers Knowledgeable About Presidential Campaign," *Annenberg Public Policy Center*, September 21, 2004. http://www.annenbergpublicpolicycenter.org/naes/2004_03_late-night-knowledge-2_9-21_pr.pdf.

7. Niven, Lichter, and Amundson, "The Political Content of Late Night Comedy," 130.

8. Young, "Late-Night Comedy in Election 2000"; Dannagal Goldthwaite Young, "Late-Night Comedy and the Salience of the Candidates' Caricatured Traits in the 2000 Election," *Mass Communication & Society* 9 (2006): 339–366.

9. Some of Matthew Baum's research (including Matthew A. Baum, "Soft News and Political Knowledge: Evidence of Absence or Absence of Evidence?" *Political Communication* 20 [2003]: 173–190) suggests that some viewers do learn political information from soft news. Other scholars have cast doubt on what kind of knowledge is gained, if any, from soft news. See Markus Prior, "Any Good News in Soft News? The Impact of Soft News Preference on Political Knowledge," *Political Communication* 20 (2003): 149–171.

10. Barry Hollander, "Late-Night Learning: Do Entertainment Programs Increase Political Campaign Knowledge for Young Viewers?" *Journal of Broadcasting & Electronic Media* 49 (2005): 402–415.

11. Jody Baumgartner and Jonathan S. Morris, "The Daily Show Effect: Candidate Evaluations, Efficacy, and American Youth," *American Politics Research* 34 (2006): 341–367.

12. Michael Pfau, J. Brian Houston, and Shane M. Semmler, "Presidential Election Campaigns and American Democracy: The Relationship Between Communication Use and Normative Outcomes," *American Behavioral Scientist* 49 (2005): 48–62; Patricia Moy, Michael A. Xenos, and Verena K. Hess, "Communication and Citizenship: Mapping the Political Effects of 'Infotainment,'" *Mass Communication & Society* 8 (2005): 111–131.

13. "Cable and Internet Loom Large in Fragmented Political News Universe," *The Pew Research Center for the People and the Press*, January 11, 2004.

14. The Racine Group, "White Paper on Televised Political Campaign Debates," *Argumentation & Advocacy* 38 (2002): 212.

15. Pfau, "The Subtle Nature of Presidential Debate Influence."

16. The Racine Group, "White Paper on Televised Political Campaign Debates," 200.

17. See The Racine Group, "White Paper on Televised Political Campaign Debates," for an extensive review of debate research.

18. William L. Benoit, Glenn J. Hansen, and Rebecca M. Verser, "A Meta-Analysis of the Effects of Viewing U.S. Presidential Debates," *Communication Monographs* 70 (2003): 335–350.

19. Kay McFadden, "Post-Debate Pundits Favor Kerry, But It's Only Act I," *Seattle Times*, October 2, 2004.

20. Pfau, "The Subtle Nature of Presidential Debate Influence."

21. Chris Smith and Ben Voth, "The Role of Humor in Political Argument: How 'Strategery' and 'Lockboxes' Changed a Political Campaign," *Argumentation and Advocacy* 39 (2002): 110–129.

22. Alexander Rose, "When Politics is a Laughing Matter," *Policy Review* 110 (2001/2002): 62.

23. Myles Martel, *Political Campaign Debates: Images, Strategies, and Tactics* (New York: Longman, 1983).

24. Phillip Coorey, "Campaign Comics are the Election Winners," *Daily Telegraph*, November 1, 2004.

25. Norman Webster, "Kerry Cleaned Bush's Clock," *Gazette*, October 2, 2004.

26. Marc Sandalow, "Bush Plays Debate Card Close to Vest," *San Francisco Chronicle*, September 15, 2004.

27. Scott Shepard, "Both Parties Jockey for Edge in Debates," *Atlanta Journal-Constitution*, September 13, 2004.

28. Jim Rutenberg, "Campaigns Enlist Big Names to Set Debates' Details," *New York Times*, September 10, 2004.

29. Marlon Manuel, "Fine Print Defines Every Detail," *Atlanta Journal-Constitution*, September 30, 2004.

30. "Late Night Political Humor," *Frontrunner*, September 13, 2004.

31. Ibid., September 22, 2004.

32. Ibid., September 23, 2004.

33. Ibid., September 24, 2004.

34. Ibid., September 29, 2004.

35. Ibid., September 30, 2004.

36. Ibid., September 22, 2004.

37. Ibid., September 28, 2004.

38. Ibid., September 26, 2004.
39. Ibid., September 14, 2004.
40. Ibid., September 28, 2004.
41. Ibid., September 29, 2004.
42. Ibid., September 30, 2004.
43. Ibid., September 22, 2004.
44. Ibid., September 28, 2004.
45. Ibid., September 23, 2004.
46. Ibid., September 28, 2004.
47. Ibid., October 1, 2004.
48. Ibid., October 1, 2004.
49. Ibid., September 24, 2004.
50. Ibid., September 30, 2004.
51. Ibid., September 29, 2004.
52. Scot Lehigh, "A Presidential Kerry," *Boston Globe*, October 1, 2004.
53. Richard Stevenson and Janet Elder, "Poll Finds Kerry Assured Voters in Initial Debate," *New York Times*, October 5, 2004.
54. "Late Night Political Humor," *Frontrunner*, October 5, 2004.
55. Ibid., October 5, 2004.
56. Ibid., October 4, 2004.
57. Ibid., October 4, 2004.
58. Ibid., October 6, 2004.
59. Ibid., October 4, 2004.
60. Ibid., October 1, 2004.
61. Ibid., October 1, 2004.
62. Ibid., October 4, 2004.
63. Ibid., October 4, 2004.
64. Ibid., October 4, 2004.
65. Ibid., October 1, 2004.
66. Ibid., October 1, 2004.
67. Ibid., October 1, 2004.
68. Ibid., October 4, 2004.
69. Ibid., October 1, 2004.
70. Ibid., October 5, 2004.
71. Ibid., October 5, 2004.
72. Ibid., October 5, 2004.
73. Ibid., October 14, 2004.
74. Ibid., October 21, 2004.
75. Ibid., October 13, 2004.
76. Ibid., October 8, 2004.
77. Ibid., October 18, 2004.
78. In Carolyn Lochhead, "Accusations Fly in Sharp Debate," *San Francisco Chronicle*, October 9, 2004.

79. The Racine Group, "White Paper on Televised Political Campaign Debates"; Hellweg, Pfau, and Brydon, *Televised Presidential Debates.*

80. The Racine Group, "White Paper on Televised Political Campaign Debates."

81. Shepard, "Both Parties Jockey for Edge in Debates."

82. Ibid.

83. Smith and Voth, "The Role of Humor in Political Argument," 123.

84. "Late Night Political Humor," *Frontrunner*, September 28, 2004.

85. Hellweg, Pfau, and Brydon, *Televised Presidential Debates.*

86. Smith and Voth, "The Role of Humor in Political Argument," 124.

87. William L. Benoit and Heather Currie, "Inaccuracies in Media Coverage of the 1996 and 2000 Presidential Debates," *Argumentation & Advocacy* 38 (2001): 28–39.

88. Young, "Late-Night Comedy in Election 2000"; Young, "Late-Night Comedy and the Salience of the Candidates' Caricatured Traits in the 2000 Election."

89. Nitz, Cypher, Reichert, and Mueller, "Candidates as Comedy: Political Presidential Humor on Late-Night Television Shows"; Niven, Lichter, and Amundson, "The Political Content of Late Night Comedy"; Young, "Late-Night Comedy in Election 2000."

90. Pfau, "The Subtle Nature of Presidential Debate Influence."

91. Nitz, Cypher, Reichert, and Mueller, "Candidates as Comedy: Political Presidential Humor on Late-Night Television Shows"; Niven, Lichter, and Amundson, "The Political Content of Late Night Comedy"; Young, "Late-Night Comedy in Election 2000"; "Daily Show Viewers Knowledgeable About Presidential Campaign."

92. "Late Night Political Humor," *Frontrunner*, October 14, 2004.

93. Joseph Cappella and Kathleen Hall Jamieson, *Spiral of Cynicism* (New York: Oxford University Press, 1997); Kathleen Hall Jamieson and Paul Waldman, *The Press Effect: Politicians, Journalists, and the Stories That Shape the Political World* (New York: Oxford University Press, 2002).

94. Baumgartner and Morris, "The Daily Show Effect: Candidate Evaluations, Efficacy, and American Youth."

95. Jill Vejnoska, "Campaign Comedy," *Atlanta Journal-Constitution*, February 2, 2004.

96. Coorey, "Campaign Comics are the Election Winners."

97. Phil Rosenthal, "What Are You Looking At?" *Chicago Sun-Times*, November 1, 2004.

98. Ibid.

99. Rong Xiaoqing, "Funny Election," *South China Morning Post*, October 30, 2004.

11

A Culture War in TV Land? The Sitcom Viewing Habits of Bush and Kerry Voters

Peter L. Francia

The 2000 and 2004 presidential elections were two of the most closely contested races for the White House in American history. In their aftermath, political observers began discussing how polarized the electorate had become. Some labeled the United States the "forty-nine percent nation" or the "fifty-fifty nation."[1] Many journalists went further, arguing that there was a divisive culture war in the United States.[2] The reported cultural divisions separating Democrats and Republicans prompted caricatures of the two sides. In the words of one writer, Republican voters who supported President George W. Bush were "ignorant, racist, fascist, knuckle-dragging, NASCAR-obsessed, cousin-marrying, road-kill-eating, tobacco-juice-dribbling, gun-fondling, religious fanatic, rednecks." Democratic voters who supported the party's 2004 presidential nominee John Kerry were "godless, unpatriotic, pierced-nose, Volvo-driving, France-loving, leftwing Communist, latte-sucking, tofu-chomping, holistic-wacko, neurotic vegan, weenie perverts."[3]

While such extreme stereotypes grossly exaggerate reality, several studies have reported that there are significant cultural divisions in American society.[4] In the seminal book, *Culture Wars: The Struggle to Define America*, James Davison Hunter argues that Americans are deeply split by two competing worldviews: progressivism and orthodoxy.[5] Those adhering to progressivism believe in policies that will bring about social change. In contrast, those adhering to orthodoxy oppose social change and are deeply committed to maintaining existing traditions. According to Hunter, these values fundamentally divide Americans.

One arena that has been a battleground for the clash of different cultural values has been the perpetual debate over the content of Hollywood entertainment.[6] Television programs, especially sitcoms, often have been a stage for this conflict. During the early days of television, sitcoms generally reinforced the traditional or orthodox values that dominated the conservative 1950s. As times began to change, more controversial programs began to appear, along with a shift toward sitcoms that reflected the emerging progressive values of the late 1960s and 1970s. For example, near the time of the *Roe v. Wade* decision, the sitcom *Maude* devoted an episode to covering the morality of abortion. In 1992, then vice president Dan Quayle criticized the sitcom *Murphy Brown*, for the lead character's decision to have a child outside of wedlock. More recently, sitcoms such as *Ellen* have addressed controversial issues related to homosexual relationships.

In a polarized political climate, the controversial nature of many sitcoms may attract some viewers, while turning off or even offending others. If so, television viewing may be growing polarized along partisan lines. In an era of cable and satellite television with an unprecedented number of television programs to view, television audiences have become increasingly fragmented.[7] It would therefore seem plausible that with so many choices, Democrats and Republicans may watch different programs that appeal to their different political sensibilities.

If there are partisan differences in television viewing, this would represent an important development in the broader culture war. Indeed, television has been a dominant part of American culture since the 1950s.[8] Moreover, when one considers that the average American household tuned into television an average of eight hours and eleven minutes per day in 2004–2005,[9] it is easy to conclude that television plays a dominant role in American culture. Politicians, social activists, and members of various political organizations also perceive sitcoms as more than simply entertainment. To them, the portrayal of the family in television sitcoms can influence and have an impact on the real-life American family. As Lynn Spigel explains, "As the case of Quayle demonstrates, the public often assumes that television fictional representations of the family have a strong impact on actual families in America. For this reason people have often assumed that these fictional households ought to mirror not simply family life in general, but their own personal values regarding it."[10] Thus, the television viewing habits of Democrats and Republicans are not a trivial matter. Television viewing habits provide insight into American values, and have broad implications for the culture war and in understanding how polarized Americans have become.

In the pages that follow, I review the controversy surrounding the culture war, and then discuss how television sitcoms often have been a part of this larger conflict. For obvious reasons related to the scope of this project, not every sitcom could be mentioned or discussed in this chapter. However, the chapter does offer a broad and comprehensive overview of top-rated sitcoms that best illustrate the political or social themes related to the culture war. After discussing the role of sitcoms in the culture war, I turn to the question of whether there are partisan differences in television viewing habits. Using survey data from the Pew Research Center for the People and the Press, the findings confirm that there are some significant partisan differences, even when controlling for various socioeconomic and demographic factors. I conclude with a discussion about the implications of cultural polarization for American politics.

Television Comedy in an Era of Orthodox Values

The 1950s and early 1960s is an era often defined as a time of conformity and traditional values.[11] During this period, home ownership and suburban communities exploded and the country experienced a rapidly growing birthrate, referred to as the "baby boom." Women were expected to marry, have children, and perform domestic work. Men held jobs outside of the home and provided the family income. As Edward P. Morgan explains, "Fathers [of the 1950s] were caught up in the rat race, while middle-class mothers were encouraged to abandon their wartime employment for the new fulltime job as housewife and primary parent."[12]

Fitting these times were a number of television sitcoms that reinforced traditional gender roles and the orthodox "family values" of the era. As Spigel writes, "The introduction of television after World War II coincided with a steep rise in mortgage rates, birth rates, and the growth of mass-produced suburbs. In this social climate, it is no wonder that television was conceived as, first and foremost as a family medium."[13]

The first television sitcom to dominate the Nielsen ratings was *I Love Lucy*.[14] The show aired on CBS and was an enormous success throughout much of the 1950s, earning the highest Nielsen ratings for four seasons: 1952–53, 1953–54, 1954–55, and 1956–57. *I Love Lucy* centered on the everyday lives of Lucy Ricardo (Lucille Ball), her musician husband, Ricky Ricardo (Desi Arnaz), and their landlords and close friends Fred and Ethel Mertz (William Frawley and Vivian Vance). Many of the storylines poke fun at Lucy's never-ending ineptitude. Perhaps the best remembered episode (rated the second greatest television episode of all time by *TV Guide* in 1997) is titled "Lucy Does a Commercial," in which Lucy earns a role in a commercial as the salesperson for the tonic "Vitameatavegamin," which contains not only vitamins, meats, vegetables, and minerals, but also 23 percent alcohol. After several rehearsals, Lucy becomes inebriated from the tonic, causing her to scramble her words ("little bottle" to "bittle lottle").[15]

Although most *I Love Lucy* episodes said little, if anything, about American politics, there were occasional moments that touched on issues pertinent to the culture war. The episode entitled "Lucy in the Candy Factory" is best remembered for a scene in which Lucy frantically stuffs candy in her mouth to keep pace with a rapidly moving conveyor belt. However, few remember that the premise of the episode centers on a wager that Lucy and Ethel make with Ricky and Fred that involves a reversal of traditional gender roles. In the episode, Lucy and Ethel challenge Ricky and Fred to spend a day doing domestic work, and the men challenge the women to spend a day in the workforce. The result of the wager is consistent with the prevailing attitudes about gender roles in the 1950s. Ricky and Fred fail miserably in handling the domestic work, while the women are terribly unsuccessful at their jobs in the candy factory. The scene of Lucy stuffing candy in her mouth only punctuates the overriding message of the episode: women belong in the kitchen as homemakers and men in the workplace as the wage earners and providers.

I Love Lucy was not alone in reinforcing the orthodox values of the era. Some programs, such as *Father Knows Best* (1954–62), advertised orthodox values in the title itself. Others, such as *Leave It to Beaver* (1957–63) and *The Donna Reed Show* (1958–66), further reinforced fixed family roles.[16] These shows also were all staged in white-dominated, suburban, middle-class settings. Minorities, notably African Americans who had organized the civil rights movement to end racial injustice at this time, received virtually no attention in the sitcoms of this period.

Television Comedy in an Era of Progressive Values

As the 1960s began, various social movements began to challenge the conformity of the 1950s. The civil rights movement, which succeeded in desegregating public schools in the South during the 1950s, began a strong push for voting rights and political power for African Americans in the 1960s. Women also demanded equal rights. In 1963, Betty Friedan published her best-selling book, *The Feminine Mystique*, which challenged the prevailing gender stereotypes that women could only discover true happiness in their role as a wife, mother, and homemaker. Friedan's book sparked the "second wave" of the feminist movement, which focused on winning full social and economic equality for women.[17]

Perhaps the most radical of all movements for change came from the counterculture movement. With its popular slogan to "turn on, tune in, and drop out," the counterculture movement encouraged a generation to reject traditional sexual mores such as monogamy, and to experiment with illicit drugs such as LSD ("tuning in"), and to disengage from mainstream society. These movements were all immensely controversial for the times, and would influence the direction of television sitcoms in the years to come.

Indeed, television would become a stage for the emerging culture war of the late 1960s and early 1970s. Perhaps no show better showcased the culture war than Norman Lear's *All in the Family* (which was an adaptation of the British sitcom, *Till Death Us Do Part*). *All in the Family* aired from 1971 to 1979, and was the top-rated show for five consecutive seasons (1971–76)—a feat matched only by *The Cosby Show* (1985–90).[18] *All in the Family* wrapped politics and social commentary into comedy, and revolutionized sitcoms with its willingness to confront culturally and politically explosive issues, such as racism and bigotry, sexism and rape, and even religion and homosexuality. Virtually no subject on the show was taboo.

All in the Family was set in the New York borough of Queens, and focused on the Bunker family. The original cast included four primary characters: Archie and Edith Bunker (Carroll O'Connor and Jean Stapleton), their daughter Gloria (Sally Struthers), and Gloria's husband, Mike Stivic (Rob Reiner). Archie Bunker serves as the show's lead character. He works on the loading docks and represents the stereotypical blue-collar worker of the times. Archie is from the older,

World War II generation that often struggled to make sense of the protest and social movements occurring throughout the United States during the 1960s and 1970s. His values are traditional, religious, and conservative, but also bigoted. He has no inhibitions about using racist, anti-Semitic or sexist epithets.

Archie's racist, anti-Semitic, sexist, and other bigoted views, however, do not go unchallenged on the show. He frequently engages in spirited arguments with his college-aged daughter, Gloria, and his son-in-law, Mike, whom he labels a "meathead" for his liberal views. Mike and Gloria represent the voice of a younger, rebellious, and more egalitarian generation. Mike, in particular, is the most vocal critic of Archie's political and social views. He is college educated, an atheist, an advocate of civil rights, and an opponent of the Vietnam War. His views are equally as strong as Archie's, leading to many heated arguments in the Bunker home that paralleled the real-life political, social, and cultural divisions of the late 1960s and 1970s. Mike articulates his positions considerably better than Archie does; however, Archie financially supports him. This provides an important contrast. To traditionalists, Mike's high-minded intellectualism was based on his naiveté of life in the "real" world. Archie, while often quite abrasive, was still the breadwinner of the family.[19]

Other television sitcoms followed the controversial format of *All in the Family*. Another Norman Lear production, *Maude*, a spin-off of *All in the Family*, was equally as political and perhaps even more hard-hitting in its social commentary. Aired from 1972 to 1978 on CBS, *Maude* entered the top ten of the Nielsen ratings during its first four seasons. Similar to *All in the Family*, the show centers on four family members: Maude Findlay (Beatrice Arthur), who is the cousin of Edith Bunker from *All in the Family*, her husband, Walter Findlay (Bill Macy), her divorced daughter Carol (Adrienne Barbeau), and Carol's son Phillip (Brian Morrison, 1972–77; Kraig Metzinger, 1977–78). However, unlike *All in the Family*, the show is set in the upper-middle-class suburb of Tucahoe, New York, as opposed to the working-class Queens neighborhood in *All in the Family*, and the main character, Maude, has political views that are diametrically opposite those of Archie Bunker. Maude is a self-described "FDR Democrat" who is unabashedly liberal. The show tackled political issues related to race, class, and gender.

However, the show is perhaps most remembered for a controversial two-part episode on abortion. Maude, who is 47 years old, discovers that she is pregnant. After deep reflections and deliberation with her husband, Walter, Maude decides to have an abortion, which at the time had only recently been legalized in the state of New York. Walter also discusses openly the possibility of seeking a vasectomy—a topic that some considered at the time to be inappropriate for network television.[20]

While *All in the Family* and *Maude* are widely recognized as trailblazers in bringing controversial social issues to network television in a comedic format, they were not the only sitcoms of the 1970s to make political and social statements that reflected the changing times of the 1970s. In the wake of the civil rights movement, sitcoms portrayed African American families in shows such as *Sanford and Son* (1972–77), *Good Times* (1974–79, a spin-off of *Maude*), and *The Jeffersons* (1975–85, a spin-off of *All in the Family*). *Sanford and Son* centers on the lives of junk dealer Fred Sanford (Redd Foxx) and his adult son Lamont (Demond Wilson). The show takes place in the Watts section of Los Angeles. While never designed to be overtly political, *Sanford and Son* did occasionally address issues related to race. Indeed, it was one of the first shows to spoof white characters. One of the show's recurring white characters was a police officer, "Swanny" Swanhauser (and later "Hoppy" Hopkins), who often seemed out of his element in Watts as evidenced by his frequent mangling of phrases (e.g., "torn off" rather than "ripped off"). This portrayal had political undertones. Swanny and Hoppy were symbols of the out-of-touch police forces that patrolled much of inner-city America. This caricature seemed particularly poignant given that the show took place in Watts, an area notorious for the "Watts Riot" against police in 1965.

Good Times portrayed the life of the Evans family, and was one of the first to depict the lives of a poor, African American family trying to survive and make ends meet in the inner city of Chicago. *The Jeffersons* also centers on the lives of an African American family, although under very different financial circumstances. The main character, George Jefferson (Sherman Hemsley), and his wife, Louise Jefferson (Isabel Sanford), live in a luxury apartment on the Upper East Side of Manhattan (after moving from the working-class Queens neighborhood of the Bunkers).

All three shows were revolutionary for placing African American actors in lead roles, although some took issue with Hollywood's portrayal of the characters. Two of the cast members of *Good Times*, Esther Rolle (who played the family's mother, Florida Evans) and John Amos (who played the family's father, James Evans), were critical of the show's story lines for placing too much emphasis on the clownish behavior of J. J. Evans, the eldest son in the family, played by Jimmie Walker.[21] Others complained about both Fred Sanford's and George Jefferson's volatile antics and bigoted views.[22] Rather than debunking stereotypes of African Americans, some argued that these shows only reinforced them.[23]

Other sitcoms of the era focused on the conditions of women. The sitcom *Mary Tyler Moore* portrayed a single woman, Mary Richards (Mary Tyler Moore), who moved to Minneapolis to work as an associate producer for local news station WJM-TV. Unlike *All in the Family* and other shows from this period, *Mary Tyler Moore* (which aired from 1970 to 1977) rarely tackled the controversial political issues of the day. In fact, producers for the show often deliberately avoided it. The show's producers, for example, decided to make Mary Richards a character that arrives in Minneapolis following a broken engagement rather than a divorce, as originally planned. Yet, while the specific premise of each show rarely touched on hot-button political issues, the very concept and general premise behind *Mary Tyler Moore* made a very bold political and social statement: women could be independent and find happiness in a career without being married and having children.

Going one step further, *One Day at a Time*, which aired from 1975 to 1984, centers on Ann Romano (Bonnie Franklin), who divorces her husband and takes her two children, Julie and Barbara, to her hometown of Indianapolis to "find herself." Similar to *Mary Tyler Moore*, the overarching theme of *One Day at a Time* is women's liberation and independence.[24] This theme is captured in Ann's efforts to work and raise a family on her own terms. Indeed, television portrayals of single-parent families that experienced divorce were hardly uncommon throughout the 1970s (e.g., *Alice*, 1976–85, and *What's Happening*, 1976–79).[25] As Paul Cantor observes, "American television genuinely began to move away from the nuclear family as the norm and suggest that other patterns of child rearing might be equally valid or perhaps even superior." This development, according to Cantor, "expressed the ideological bent of Hollywood and its impulse to call traditional family values into question."[26]

Finally, themes related to the "sexual" revolution of the late 1960s and 1970s were featured during this era. *Three's Company* (1977–84), which topped the Nielsen ratings in 1978–79, revolved around the controversial premise of three people—two women and one man—sharing an apartment together. This was a sharp break from the sitcoms of the 1950s and early 1960s when married couples did not even share a bed (including cast members such as Lucille Ball and Desi Arnaz, who were married in real life). The characters in *Three's Company* were never romantically linked, although the show derived much of its humor from sexual double entendres that some organized groups, such as the National Federation for Decency, considered too risqué for network television.[27]

Another show of the era, *Soap* (1977–81), addressed homosexuality. One of the show's regular characters, Jodie Dallas, played by Billy Crystal, was openly gay. At the time, the show was heavily criticized by some conservatives for Crystal's character and other controversial "soap opera" storylines. ABC received some 32,000 letters in protest of the Crystal character in 1977. In response, the National Gay Task Force threatened a sponsor boycott if ABC gave in to pressure to alter or remove the Crystal character from the show.[28]

As the 1970s came to a close, another new era would begin. The election of Republicans Ronald Reagan in 1980 and 1984, and later his Vice President George H. W. Bush in 1988 to the White House, and the landslide victory of congressional Republicans during the 1994 election, ushered in a reenergized conservative political era that would pit its orthodox supporters against the progressive voices of the 1960s and 1970s. These developments, not surprisingly, would begin another new period for television sitcoms.

Television Comedy in an Era of Competing Values

The top-rated show for much of the 1980s was *The Cosby Show* (1984–92). In sharp contrast to the inner-city conditions of *Good Times*, *The Cosby Show* portrayed an upper-middle-class African American family, the Huxtables, living in Brooklyn, New York. Much like the programs of the 1950s, most subjects on the show dealt with family-specific problems as opposed to broader social and political controversies.

Some criticized the show for this approach, specifically for its unwill-ingness to address pressing political problems such as the AIDS-HIV epidemic, poverty, and racism, or for suggesting that blacks who fail to achieve in society have only themselves to blame.[29] Others hailed the show as groundbreaking for its positive portrayal of an African American family and its "color-blind" approach to race relations.[30] Many of these themes played to traditional orthodox values.

However, the show touched on some progressive values as well. Claire Huxtable (Phylicia Rashad), the mother of the family, was a successful attorney and strong voice in the Huxtable home. *The Cosby Show* also sent a message that many progressives had champi-oned in the 1960s and 1970s: African Americans could integrate and thrive in mainstream American society. This cross-appeal made *The Cosby Show* immensely popular during the 1980s when Americans were weary of the rebellious 1960s and 1970s, but also unwilling to turn back the clock completely to the 1950s.

Other shows of the 1980s also found a balance in values, and even family politics. *Family Ties* (1982–89), which focused on the Keaton family, turned the generational conflicts of the 1960s and 1970s on their head. The parents, Steven (Michael Gross) and Elyse (Meredith Baxter-Birney), have three children: Alex, Mallory, and Jennifer. The twist is that the parents are not the conservatives in the family, but instead are liberal Democrats, while their son Alex (Michael J. Fox) is a Republican. (The other two children are Mal-lory, played by Justine Bateman, who is obsessed with shopping and her social life, and Jennifer, played by Tina Yothers, a tomboy who enjoys sports.)

In addition to the political balance of the characters on the show, *Family Ties* played to both orthodox and progressive values. Like *The Cosby Show*, the mother, Elyse, is a strong female figure. Her marriage is not a traditional, male-dominated relationship, but an equal partnership with Steven. Elyse also has a successful career as an architect. However, she is not consumed by her work and is a devoted wife and mother. Elyse even becomes pregnant on the show and gives birth to her fourth child, Andrew. The show was popular throughout the 1980s, reaching number two in the Nielsen ratings in 1985–86 and 1986–87. President Ronald Reagan even called it his "favorite show."[31]

By the late 1980s and early 1990s, however, the idealized, mod-ern families of the Huxtables and the Keatons begin to fade from television. In their place, the dysfunctional family became the norm. Comedies such as *The Simpsons* and *Married with Children* returned back to the days of stay-at-home mothers (Marge Simpson and Peggy Bundy), but with idiotic and bumbling fathers (Homer Simpson and Al Bundy) who sharply contrast with the sage-like fathers of the 1950s.

Other television sitcoms began to present families with serious problems, and to offer social commentary on the pressing social issues of the times. Perhaps the best example was the Connor family of the popular show, *Roseanne* (1988–97), which topped the Nielsen ratings (along with *The Cosby Show*) in 1989–90. The Connors are a working-class family who endure numerous economic hardships. The lead character Roseanne (Roseanne Barr) and her husband, Dan (John Goodman), both lose or change jobs at various junctures in the show. These difficult economic times for the Connor family paralleled the fears and financial uncertainty of many working-class Americans during this time. The show, however, largely centers on Roseanne and her dominating personality, which contrasts with Dan's easygoing nature. This often provokes disagreements and conflict between the two characters. Unlike the near-flawless marriages in many other earlier sitcoms, Dan and Roseanne experienced real difficulties in their relationship during the show's nine seasons. *Roseanne* also covered controversial political issues, including spousal abuse, alcoholism, and homosexuality.[32]

The show *Murphy Brown* drew perhaps the most controversy of all when it became the focus of a real-life political debate and a symbol of the culture war over "family values." The show focuses on the life of Murphy Brown (Candice Bergen), a single woman who works as an investigative journalist for the news magazine *FYI*. During the 1991–92 season, Murphy becomes pregnant and gives birth to a child. This was followed with real-life criticism from Vice President Dan Quayle, who took issue with the show for minimizing the importance of a father's role in raising a child. On May 19, 1992, at the Commonwealth Club in San Francisco, Quayle observed, "It doesn't help matters when prime time TV has Murphy Brown—a character who supposedly epitomizes today's intelligent, highly paid, professional woman—mocking the importance of fathers by bearing a child alone and calling it just another 'life style choice.'"[33] Quayle's comments touched off a national debate that made its way into the 1992 presidential campaign. Democrat Bill Clinton labeled

Quayle's comments "cynical election year politics," while another Democrat, the Reverend Jesse Jackson, responded with even harsher words: "No exam-cheating, pot-smoking, draft-dodging, privileged-youth vice president in a 'Bush the Blamer' administration can speak with moral authority about abandoned moral values and assuming personal responsibility."[34]

Conservative opposition intensified in 1997 when Ellen Morgan (Ellen DeGeneres), the lead character of the popular sitcom *Ellen*, revealed that she was homosexual. Conservative leaders, such as the Reverend Jerry Falwell, labeled the lead actress as Ellen "Degenerate" and called on General Motors, Chrysler, and Johnson & Johnson to end their sponsorship of the show.[35] While many gay activists hailed Ellen's decision to "come out" as an enormous breakthrough for gay acceptance,[36] the show's ratings plummeted shortly after DeGeneres's announcement and ABC dropped the show in 1998.

As the nation entered the new century, cultural issues, such as gay rights and family values, remained salient.[37] At the same time, partisan political warfare reached new heights. In the 2000 presidential election, George W. Bush captured the state of Florida by a mere 537 votes, giving him an Electoral College majority over Democrat Al Gore by a 271 to 266 margin—this despite losing the popular vote to Gore by roughly a half-million votes. Bush's victory required the intervention of the U.S. Supreme Court to settle disputes surrounding the standards for recounting votes in Florida. When the court ended the Florida recount with a divided five-to-four decision in *Bush v. Gore*, Gore supporters charged that a conservative Supreme Court had "stolen" the election.[38] By comparison, many Bush partisans saw Gore as little more than a "sore loser" who refused to accept defeat graciously.[39]

Likewise, Democrat John Kerry was narrowly defeated by Bush in the 2004 presidential election, losing the decisive state of Ohio by roughly 120,000 votes. Kerry did not concede defeat until the day after the election, and many Kerry supporters later raised charges of election improprieties in Ohio. This prompted a brief but failed challenge from Democratic Congresswoman Stephanie Tubbs Jones and Democratic Senator Barbara Boxer to the official counting of Ohio's electoral votes.

Both elections made clear that the nation was evenly and bitterly divided at the polls. These divisions, however, likely underscore other deeper cultural differences. As documented above, television sitcoms have served as a vehicle for social and political commentary. This raises the possibility that partisan divisions might also be present in television viewing habits.

Television Sitcoms and the Culture War in the New Century

Many top sitcoms in the new century address subjects pertinent to the culture war. The very premise behind three shows—*Desperate Housewives, Sex and the City,* and *Will and Grace*—make them likely candidates to attract more progressive viewers who voted for Kerry. *Desperate Housewives* traces the lives of four women on the fictional Wisteria Lane. The show takes a deeply cynical view of traditional upscale suburban family life, and focuses its comedy on the sexual escapades of the four women. Likewise, *Sex and the City,* an HBO sitcom, focuses on the sex lives of four single women living in New York City. The adult sexual dialogue and the active sex lives of the four female characters made the show groundbreaking to some, but offensive to others.[40]

Will and Grace focuses on the lives of Will Truman (Eric McCormack) and Grace Adler (Debra Messing). The controversy of the show surrounds Will, who is openly gay and has relationships with men on the show. While Grace is heterosexual, her love life is checkered throughout the show. During the show's run, she gets married and divorced, and even discusses having a child with Will through in vitro fertilization. The show is untraditional in almost all respects.

Perhaps not surprisingly, the three shows are significantly more likely to attract Kerry voters than Bush voters (see Table 11.1; for information about the data used in this chapter, please refer to the Appendix). Among Bush voters who watch at least one television program on a regular basis, some 14 percent report they watch *Desperate Housewives* compared to 22 percent of Kerry voters. Significant differences were also present for *Sex and the City* and *Will and Grace,* with Kerry voters more likely than Bush voters to watch the two programs.

Two other sitcoms, *The Bernie Mac Show* and *Girlfriends,* have lead characters who are African American. The premise of *The Bernie Mac Show* centers on Bernie Mac's trials and tribulations as a parent. Bernie Mac is married, but the children come from his sister who leaves them with Bernie when she enters drug rehabilitation.

TABLE 11.1. Television Comedy Viewing among Bush and Kerry Voters (2005)

Program	Bush Voter (%)	Kerry Voter (%)
Desperate Housewives‡		
Watches regularly	14	22
Does not watch regularly	86	78
Sex and the City*		
Watches regularly	10	17
Does not watch regularly	90	83
Will and Grace‡		
Watches regularly	19	24
Does not watch regularly	81	76
The Bernie Mac Show*		
Watches regularly	8	17
Does not watch regularly	92	83
Girlfriends*		
Watches regularly	1	14
Does not watch regularly	99	86
The Simpsons*		
Watches regularly	16	28
Does not watch regularly	84	72
Everybody Loves Raymond†		
Watches regularly	49	39
Does not watch regularly	51	61
N	539	534

Percentages and statistics were computed by the author. Analysis includes only respondents who reported watching at least one television program on a regular basis.

*p < .001; †p < .01; ‡p < .05.

Pew Research Center for the People and the Press, March 2005 News Interest Index.

The sitcom *Girlfriends* centers on the lives of four African American women in Los Angeles. The show focuses on the everyday concerns of the characters and extends into broader social themes, such as the role of women in society. It is a show summarized as "for and about the black middle class."[41]

Given that African Americans disproportionately support Democrats over Republicans, both *The Bernie Mac Show* and *Girlfriends* should be more likely to attract Kerry voters, and indeed they do. More than twice as many Kerry voters watch *The Bernie Mac Show* compared to Bush voters. The differences are even more pronounced for *Girlfriends*. A scant 1 percent of Bush voters regularly watch *Girlfriends* compared to 14 percent of Kerry voters.

Aside from the race factor, other factors may also be at play in explaining the differences between Bush and Kerry voters. *The Bernie Mac Show* might turn off Bush voters because of its focus on an untraditional family. Bernie Mac is not the biological father of the children and his sister is a drug addict—a far cry from the Ward family in *Leave It to Beaver* or the Anderson family in *Father Knows Best*. Likewise, the strong female characters and the social commentary in *Girlfriends* would make the show less than appealing to conservatives who supported Bush.

Everybody Loves Raymond and *The Simpsons*, two additional popular shows, feature more traditional, but somewhat dysfunctional, families. *The Simpsons* is an animated series that bases its humor around the exploits of its five family members: the parents Homer Simpson and Marge Simpson, and the children Bart, Lisa, and Maggie Simpson. Homer is hapless and irresponsible, often ignoring or exploiting his family. Marge provides the moral compass for the family, but she is often left disappointed by Homer's repeated failures. Bart, the oldest child, is an irrepressible prankster who often finds himself in trouble, while Lisa is a bright and gifted child who behaves more like an adult than someone in the second grade.

The show's theme is to poke fun not only at the Simpson family's misadventures, but more generally at family life in middle America—a theme unlikely to be popular with Americans who have orthodox values. Moreover, while the show pokes fun at both Democrats and Republicans, there is more anti-Republican bias.[42] Some also take issue with its negative portrayal of the American family. In 1992, President George H. W. Bush remarked, "We need a nation closer to *The Waltons* than *The Simpsons*."[43] However, Paul Cantor adds that for all of the criticism, *The Simpsons* does have some traditional appeal in that it "ends up celebrating the nuclear family as an institution."[44] The show attracts a healthy percentage of Bush voters (16 percent), although it still attracts a much larger percentage of Kerry voters (28 percent).

Everybody Loves Raymond features an extended family. The lead character, Ray Barone (Ray Romano), a sportswriter, is married and has three children. Ray's parents, Frank and Marie (Peter Boyle and Doris Roberts), live across the street and serve as an unending source of aggravation for Ray and his wife Debra, (Patricia Heaton). Robert (Brad Garrett) is Ray's older brother. He is fiercely jealous of Ray because their mother often goes out of her way to favor Ray. Family bickering, squabbles, and rivalries provide the show with its source of humor. *Everybody Loves Raymond* rarely touches on any controversial political subjects, and instead focuses on everyday difficulties associated with parenting and family relationships. The show's absence of politics and social commentary would seem to make political affiliations irrelevant. However, the absence of political commentary is in some ways a conservative statement, which may explain why Bush voters (49 percent) are more likely than Kerry voters to watch the show regularly (39 percent).

Differences between Bush and Kerry voters remain statistically significant for most of the shows even when controlling for various factors, such as race, gender, marital status, income, education, church attendance, and age (see Table 11.2; for a complete look at the full multivariate statistical results, see Table 11A-1 in the Appendix). Kerry voters are 1.5 times more likely than Bush voters to watch *Desperate Housewives* on a regular basis, holding all other factors (race, gender, marital status, income, education, church attendance, and age) constant. They were also 2.3 times more likely than Bush voters to watch *Sex and the City*, 2.1 times more likely than Bush voters to watch *The Bernie Mac Show*, 6.3 times more likely than Bush voters to watch *Girlfriends*, and 1.6 times more likely than Bush voters to watch *The Simpsons*.

Differences between Bush and Kerry voters were not statistically significant for *Everybody Loves Raymond* and *Will and Grace* when controlling for other factors. However, a separate analysis conducted

TABLE 11.2.   Predicted Likelihood of Viewing Television Comedies

Program	More Likely to View	Odds Ratio
Desperate Housewives	Kerry voter	1.5 times more likely
Sex and the City	Kerry voter	2.3 times more likely
Will and Grace	Kerry voter	NS
The Bernie Mac Show	Kerry voter	2.1 times more likely
Girlfriends	Kerry voter	6.3 times more likely
The Simpsons	Kerry voter	1.6 times more likely
Everybody Loves Raymond	Bush voter	NS

NS = not statistically significant. Odds ratios are based on multivariate logistic regression estimates, which include controls for race, gender, marital status, income, education, and age. For the complete results, see Table 11A-1.

Pew Research Center for the People and the Press, March 2005 News Interest Index.

TABLE 11.3.   Favorite Television Programs (2004)

	Comedy	Reality	Drama
Republicans	1. *Everybody Loves Raymond*	1. *Amazing Race*	1. *JAG*
	2. *8 Simple Rules*	2. *Last Comic Standing*	2. *Without a Trace*
	3. *2½ Men*	3. *The Simple Life*	3. *Joan of Arcadia*
Democrats	1. *Will & Grace*	1. *Extreme Makeover*	1. *Judging Amy*
	2. *Quintuplets*	2. *For Love or Money*	2. *Crossing Jordan*
	3. *2½ Men*	3. *Last Comic Standing*	3. *Law & Order*

Initiative Media Worldwide.

by Initiative Media Worldwide had respondents rate their favorite television shows (as opposed to reporting whether they watched a specific program regularly). Interestingly, the results of this survey showed that *Everybody Loves Raymond* was the "favorite" comedy program for Republicans, whereas *Will and Grace* ranked as the "favorite" comedy program for Democrats (see Table 11.3).

Finally, it is worth noting that there were no partisan differences for non-comedy programs. Most non-comedy programs do not attract Kerry voters more than Bush voters, or vice versa. Five of the eight non-comedy programs (*American Idol, CSI: Crime Scene Investigation, Seventh Heaven, Fear Factor,* and *24*) show no statistically significant differences for Bush and Kerry voters.[45] Television sitcoms thus appear to occupy a special place in the culture war that divides Democrats and Kerry voters from Republicans and Bush voters.

Conclusion

The "fifty-fifty nation" is a term that has come to define the political divisions of the United States in the aftermath of the competitive and polarizing 2000 and 2004 presidential elections. This chapter, however, concludes that Americans may be divided in even more fundamental ways than at the polls. It recounted how television sitcoms have been a stage and a battleground for the culture war, and the results indicate that Bush and Kerry voters turn to different television sitcoms to find humor.

The results also suggest that television sitcoms are more than just laughing matters. Sitcoms very often provide serious social commentary, which can play a significant role in the ongoing cultural debate of the nation. Democrats and Republicans appear to recognize this and have responded by choosing different programs to watch. In an era of cable and satellite television, Democrats and Republicans will likely continue to find humor from different sources to accommodate their different sets of values. This undoubtedly should allow more Americans to find and enjoy entertainment that suits their values. On the downside, it may also further polarize Americans, giving a much larger meaning to the "fifty-fifty nation."

Acknowledgment

The author thanks Kali Chrysovergis, Julie Francia, and Nancy Spalding for their helpful comments and suggestions.

APPENDIX

Data

This study relied on the March 2005 News Index Survey/Entertainment Media Survey data from the Pew Research Center for the People and the Press. The survey asks a random sample of Americans a series of political and media questions, as well as the televisions programs that they watch regularly. It includes seven sitcoms or comedy dramas: *Everybody Loves Raymond*, *The Simpsons*, *Desperate Housewives*, *Sex and the City*, *Will and Grace*, *The Bernie Mac Show*, and *Girlfriends*. It was conducted via telephone interviews by Princeton Research Associates International from March 17–21, 2005. The results of the survey are based on a nationally representative sample of 1,505 adults (eighteen years of age or older) in the continental United States. The margin of sampling error for the data is ±3%. For more information about the survey, see http://people-press.org/reports/display. php3?PageID=941.

Methods and Analysis

The results in Table 11.2 and Table 11A-1 are based on logistic regression analysis because of the binary nature of the dependent variable.[46]

TABLE 11A-1. Logistic Regression Estimates of Television Comedy Viewing

Variables	Everybody Loves Raymond	Simpsons	Desperate Housewives	Sex and the City	Will and Grace	Bernie Mac	Girlfriends
Kerry voter	-.121 (.141)	.448‡ (.204)	.376‡ (.175)	.829‡ (.221)	.255 (.176)	.726† (.259)	1.838* (.571)
Socioeconomic/demographic controls							
White	.300 (.202)	-.204 (.258)	.152 (.248)	.372 (.310)	-.063 (.238)	-1.271* (.262)	-3.100* (.449)
Female	.226* (.133)	-1.014* (.197)	.649* (.172)	.100 (.208)	.624* (.174)	-.204 (.235)	.081 (.381)
Married	.128 (.161)	-.533‡ (.212)	-.126 (.195)	-.829‡ (.231)	-.512† (.189)	-.301 (.262)	-.748‡ (.401)
Income	.016 (.039)	-.095‡ (.055)	.076 (.049)	.220* (.061)	.065 (.049)	-.017 (.066)	-.236‡ (.107)
Education	-.091‡ (.046)	.058 (.068)	.067 (.060)	.042 (.074)	-.008 (.060)	-.211† (.080)	-.126 (.135)
Church attendance	.052 (.044)	-.212* (.063)	-.047 (.055)	-.111‡ (.069)	-.180* (.055)	.025 (.078)	.172 (.130)
Age 18–34	-.294 (.220)	2.296* (.364)	.706† (.293)	.530 (.348)	.601‡ (.273)	.875‡ (.387)	.876 (.638)
Age 35–49	-.385‡ (.195)	1.161* (.367)	.615† (.270)	-.039 (.341)	.087 (.262)	.744‡ (.366)	.767 (.616)
Age 50–64	-.455† (.190)	.581 (.375)	.517‡ (.266)	.205 (.325)	.012 (.258)	-.186 (.407)	.103 (.691)
Constant	-.183 (.394)	-.975 (.581)	-3.055 (.520)	-3.464 (.642)	-1.281 (.489)	-.807 (.660)	-1.796 (1.148)
N	1,037	1,037	1,037	1,037	1,037	1,037	1,037
Percent correctly predicted	58%	85%	80%	87%	80%	90%	96%

Coefficients are based on logistic regression estimates. Standard errors are in parentheses. Analysis includes only respondents who reported watching at least one television program on a regular basis.

p < .001; †p < .01; ‡p < .05, one-tailed.

Pew Research Center for the People and the Press, March 2005 News Interest Index.

For the analysis, the primary explanatory variable is a dummy measure that designates a 1 if the respondent voted for Kerry and a 0 if the respondent voted for Bush. The controls for race, gender, and marital status are also coded as dummy variables. Income, education, and church attendance are interval variables. Age is divided into different cohorts with each cohort dummy coded.

Notes

1. Michael Barone, "The 49% Nation," *Almanac of American Politics 2002* (Washington, DC: National Journal, 2001), 21–45. See also "The Creaking of the Logs," *Economist*, February 2, 2002.
2. Jill Lawrence, "Values, Votes, and Points of View Separate Towns—and Nation," *USA Today*, June 2, 2002. See also E. J. Dionne, Jr., "One Nation Deeply Divided," *Washington Post*, November 7, 2003. For a different perspective, see Suzanne Fields, "Moderates in the Middle; The Divided Electorate is Not Polarized," *Washington Times*, December 14, 2000.
3. Quoted in James Q. Wilson, "How Divided Are We?" *Commentary Magazine*, February 2006.
4. John Kenneth White, *The Values Divide* (Chatham, NJ: Chatham House, 2003). See also Peter L. Francia and Jody C Baumgartner, "Victim of Victor of the 'Culture War?' How Cultural Issues Affect Support for George W. Bush in Rural America," *American Review of Politics* 26 (2006): 349–367. For a different perspective, see Morris P. Fiorina, Samuel J. Abrams, and Jeremy Pope, *Culture War? The Myth of a Polarized America* (New York: Longman, 2005).
5. James Davison Hunter, *Culture Wars: The Struggle to Define America* (New York: Basic Books, 1991).
6. Ibid., chapter 9. See also Lynn Spigel, *The Revolution Wasn't Televised* (New York: Routledge, 1997).
7. Richard Davis and Diana Owen, *New Media and American Politics* (New York: Oxford University Press, 1998).
8. Karal Ann Marling, *As Seen on TV: The Visual Culture of Everyday Life in the 1950s* (Cambridge, MA: Harvard University Press, 1994).
9. "Nielsen Reports Americans Watch TV at Record Levels," *Nielsen Media Research*, September 29, 2005. http://www.nielsenmedia.com/newsreleases/2005/AvgHoursMinutes92905.pdf.
10. Lynn Spigel, "Family on Television," *The Museum of Broadcast Communications*. http://www.museum.tv/archives/etv/F/htmlF/familyontel/familyontel.htm.

11. Lynn Spigel, *Make Room for TV: Television and the Family Ideal in Postwar America* (Chicago: University of Chicago Press, 1992). See also Irene Taviss Thomson, "Individualism and Conformity in the 1950s vs. the 1980s," *Sociological Forum* 7 (1992): 497–516.

12. Edward P. Morgan, *The 60s Experience: Hard Lessons about Modern America* (Philadelphia: Temple University Press, 1991).

13. Spigel, "Family on Television."

14. Casting information and the summary of sitcom plots discussed throughout this chapter come from the author's own viewing of various programs, as well as the Web site www.answers.com. Information about Nielsen ratings comes from the Wikipedia, http://en.wikipedia.org/wiki/Nielsen_Ratings.

15. For a more detailed account of this episode and other perspectives about *I Love Lucy*, see Lori Landay, "Millions 'Love Lucy': Commodification and the Lucy Phenomenon," *NWSA Journal* 11 (1999): 25–47. See also Lori Landay, "I Love Lucy: Television and Gender in Postwar Domestic Ideology," in *The Sitcom Reader: America Viewed and Skewed*, eds. Mary M. Dalton and Laura R. Linder (Albany, NY: SUNY Press, 2005).

16. Judy Kutulas, "Who Rules the Roost? Sitcom Family Dynamics from the Cleavers to the Osbournes," in *The Sitcom Reader: America Viewed and Skewed*, eds. Mary M. Dalton and Laura R. Linder (Albany, NY: SUNY Press, 2005).

17. Patricia Bradley, *Mass Media and the Shaping of American Feminism, 1963–1975* (Oxford: University of Mississippi Press, 2003).

18. After 1979, the show was reorganized and renamed *Archie Bunker's Place*, which CBS aired until 1983.

19. For more information about *All in the Family*, see Josh Ozersky, *Archie Bunker's America: TV in an Era of Change, 1968–1978* (Carbondale: Southern Illinois University Press, 2003).

20. For more information about *Maude*, see the Web site of the Museum of Broadcast Communications, http://www.museum.tv/archives/etv/M/htmlM/maude/maude.htm.

21. Renee Graham, "Rolle Plays an Enduring Role," *Boston Globe*, May 21, 1995.

22. Dorothy Gilliam, "The Racial Trap in Black Sitcoms; The Trap of Black Sitcoms," *Washington Post*, May 14, 1978.

23. Robin R. Mean Coleman and Charlton D. McIlwein, "The Hidden Truth in Black Sitcoms," in *The Sitcom Reader: America Viewed and Skewed*, eds. Mary M. Dalton and Laura R. Linder (Albany, NY: SUNY Press, 2005).

24. Lauren Rabinovitz, "Sitcoms and Single Moms: Representations of Feminism on American TV," *Cinema Journal* 29 (1989): 3–19.

25. Ella Taylor, *Prime-Time Families: Television Culture in Post War America* (Berkeley: University of California Press, 1989).

26. Paul A. Cantor, "The Simpsons: Atomistic Politics and the Nuclear Family," *Political Theory* 27 (1999): 734–749.

27. Bruce Fretts, "Remember When?" *St. Petersburg Times*, June 5, 1992.

28. Ibid.

29. Sut Jhally and Justin Lewis, *Enlightened Racism: The Cosby Show, Audiences, and the Myth of the American Dream* (Boulder, CO: Westview, 1992).

30. Robert E. Johnson, "TV's Top Mom and Dad," *Ebony* 41 (1986): 29–34. See also Herman Gray, "Television, Black Americans, and the American Dream," *Critical Studies in Mass Communications* 6 (1989): 376–386. For an excellent summary of the many controversies surrounding *The Cosby Show*, see Leslie B. Inniss and Joe R. Feagin, "The Cosby Show: The View from the Black Middle Class," *Journal of Black Studies* 25 (1995): 692–711.

31. Peter M. Nichols, "Television; In a Sitcom for Its Time, Teenagers Knew Best," *New York Times*, July 5, 1998.

32. For an excellent analysis of the working-class themes in *Roseanne*, see Julie Bettie, "Class Dismissed? Roseanne and the Changing Face of Working-Class Iconography," *Social Text* 45 (1994): 125–149.

33. Reuters, "After the Riots; Excerpts from Vice President's Speech on Cities and Poverty," *New York Times*, May 20, 1992.

34. Maureen Downey, "Quayle Comment Sparks Anger of Single Mothers," *Atlanta Journal-Constitution*, May 22, 1992. For a pro-Quayle perspective, see Barbara Dafoe Whitehead, "Dan Quayle Was Right," *Atlantic Monthly*, April 1993.

35. Associated Press, "Falwell Urges Boycott of 'Ellen,'" *Chicago Sun Times*, March 27, 1997.

36. Michael Szymanski, "GLAAD to See 'Ellen' Coming Out," *USA Today*, March 18, 1997.

37. "National Exit Poll Results: Presidential Election," *Washington Post*, November 2, 2004.

38. Kevin Merida, "Standing Up to be Counted; Some Gore Supporters Simply Grieve," *Washington Post*, December 23, 2000. See also Dean E. Murphy, "The 43rd President: The Voters—New York; Some Americans Seem Ready to Move On, but Others Aren't So Sure," *New York Times*, December 14, 2000.

39. Noemie Emery, "First Principles in Florida; Conservatives Believe in Rules; Liberals Want to be 'Fair,'" *Weekly Standard*, December 11, 2000.

40. Gary Levin, "All You Ever Wanted to Know About 'Sex'; Critics Single Out Risque Couplings, but Women Drawn to Life in the City," *USA Today*, June 2, 2000.

41. Phil Kloer, "UPN Introduces Viewers to Attractive 'Girlfriends,'" *Atlanta Journal-Constitution*, September 11, 2000.

42. Cantor, "The Simpsons."

43. Fretts, "Remember When?"

44. Cantor, "The Simpsons."

45. Because of space considerations, these results are not included.

46. Scott Menard, *Applied Logistic Regression Analysis* (Thousand Oaks, CA: Sage, 1995).

12

The ABCs of the *The Simpsons* and Politics
Apathy of Citizens, Basic Government Leaders, and Collective Interests

Nicholas Guehlstorf, Lars Hallstrom, and Jonathan Morris

The sharp wit and irreverent humor of the animated series *The Simpsons* has not only inspired a generation of loyal viewers, but has also stimulated a noteworthy amount of scholarly interest. It is intriguing that a single televised cartoon can capture the attention of American popular culture while simultaneously receiving the praise of a Shakespeare scholar as the best modern program to strategically layer comedy.[1] In fact, many casual viewers would maintain that *The Simpsons* is the longest-running sitcom in the United States because the writers use dual-edged jokes, parodies, and wordplays to entertain different audiences. It is the contention of this chapter that the cartoon citizens and exploits of Springfield can provide meaningful assessments of and for modern citizens.[2] In fact, current research that has examined *The Simpsons* from the perspective of religion,[3] philosophy,[4] and civic culture[5] asserts that the series educates while it entertains.

The purpose of this chapter, however, is to analyze how the political humor of *The Simpsons* comments on American political institutions and actors, democratic citizenship, and civil society. Others have addressed this topic, if only tangentially. For instance, Cantor observes that instead of mindless jokes and plots about domestic and communal disagreement, the political satire of *The Simpsons* actually encourages traditional family and societal values.[6] Similarly, researchers have claimed that the show aids in relationship building[7] and discerning individual power interactions in political life.[8]

It is our goal to contribute to this literature by mapping out how the writers of *The Simpsons* make politics funny in a way that resonates with audiences of varying levels of political sophistication. In turn, we hope to offer some insight into the reasons why *The Simpsons* is politically relevant, sophisticated, and highly critical of the current state of the democratic process in America.

We identify three different categories of political humor in *The Simpsons*. These groupings are (1) humor about elites and leadership; (2) comedy targeting the irrationality of the American mass public, particularly when a collective action is taken; and (3) obscure and humorous political references that are disconnected with the episode but offer gratification to politically and historically informed viewers. We argue that *The Simpsons'* criticism of the uninformed, irrational, and disengaged American public is harsher, more frequent, and more sophisticated than that of elites. Furthermore, our analysis suggests that humor revolving around collective action is less about leaders and leadership and more about the followers—particularly regarding the ease with which collective action denigrates quickly into irrational and often violent mob rule.

Political Humor of the Obvious: Marking and Mocking Elites in *The Simpsons*

The most noticeable category of Simpson's humor is the often-repeated and indeed stereotypical satire and critique of elites, whether political (the Kennedy-esque Springfield Mayor "Diamond" Joe Quimby), industrial (the ancient nuclear power plant owner C. Montgomery Burns), media (local television news anchor Kent Brockman), or entertainment (such as the TV and film fixtures Krusty the Klown and the Schwarzenegger-like Rainier Wolfcastle). Other elites, drawn from the sociopolitical and cultural events of the day, are lampooned as well, including past and current presidents, political hopefuls, congressional leaders, and foreign heads of state.

In these stereotype-based portrayals of elites, *The Simpsons* depicts elected officials as corrupt, the media as self-obsessed, bureaucrats as incompetent, and political institutions as ineffectual. This depiction appeals to the majority of Americans, as almost everyone (nuclear technician, bar owner, or housewife) at least partially believes the stereotypical notion that politicians abuse the system for personal gain, or that bureaucrats have the tendency to become complacent and abuse power.

A good example of *The Simpsons'* political humor that coincides with popular negative perceptions of politics and political leaders is found in the episode "Mr. Lisa Goes to Washington." In this season 3 plot, Springfield's "typical" congressman Bob Arnold is seen taking a bribe to allow the logging of a natural forest. As a corrupt legislator, he brusquely notes that "logging isn't like burying toxic waste...people will notice." In fact, the episode is filled with scenes of representatives wasting taxpayer money, getting drunk before voting, and abandoning all morals in pursuit of money and power. Although Lisa eventually exposes Springfield's corrupt congressman (who is expelled by the House of Representatives and jailed), she loses her innocence about democracy and begins to see the representatives on Capitol Hill as fattened pigs feeding at the trough of the rich.

Similarly, other politicians, both real and imagined, have been included, spoofed, and satirized on the show. Multiple U.S. presidents have been portrayed, and the underlying commentary on political leadership is generally the same: corrupt, inept, and prone to the same weaknesses as the rest of us. President Ford, for example, became fast friends with Homer because they both had a love for "nachos and beer." In an episode placed in the future ("Bart to the Future," season 11, episode 17), Lisa is the newly elected president who must deal with the exploits of her slacker brother, thus lampooning presidential brothers such as Billy Carter and Roger Clinton. In this episode, even the virtuous Lisa fools the public into accepting a tax increase by calling it a "temporary refund adjustment." As noted above, such depictions are blatant stereotypes. However, it is doubly clever since it provides ready laughs and gives viewers a chance to reinforce perspectives they already hold about political and social elites.

All of the negative clichés regarding corrupt politicians are exemplified in the dishonest, amoral, and devious Mayor "Diamond" Joe Quimby, a politician who frequently makes public decisions solely in order to get reelected. In episode 15 of season 3 titled "Homer Alone," Mayor Quimby allows Marge Simpson to be released from jail in order to keep the "chick vote." Quimby also declares "Marge Simpson Day" in order to pander, and then privately mentions to his security guard that the public is "like trained seals...toss them a fish and watch them slap their fins together." Not surprisingly, Quimby's selfishness goes far beyond his penchant for political survival. In dozens of episodes, Diamond Joe is shown taking bribes and kickbacks as well as endlessly philandering. Again, although the humor is obvious, it is also shrewd and multifaceted. In explaining why the mayor is having an extramarital affair at a sleazy hotel, one police officer tells Bart Simpson that Diamond Joe is "polling the electorate."

Beyond elected officials, other government officials and elites are criticized as well. Selma and Patty Bouvier, the elder sisters of Marge Simpson, are Department of Motor Vehicles (DMV) employees who make agency decisions motivated by personal favoritism and spite. Often, the sisters show complacency toward their jobs and DMV customers, and are quick to abuse their power for personal gain or amusement. For example, in season 3, episode 22, "The Otto Show," Selma Bouvier fails Otto on his driving test primarily because he insulted her femininity. However, at the end of the episode Otto retakes the test and passes. Despite Otto's utter incompetence behind the wheel, he is passed by Selma because of their shared hatred of Homer.

The presentation of law enforcement officers in *The Simpsons* demonstrates similar characteristics. The officers of the Springfield Police Department are typically self-interested and self-important and usually easily corruptible. Most notably, Police Chief Wiggam is often targeted as a particularly inept, bumbling, and corrupt fool of a police officer who is rarely capable of deliberately solving a crime, yet who continues to be "in the right place at the right time." This is best demonstrated in season 5, episode 2, when would-be murderer "Sideshow" Bob Terwilliger is serendipitously apprehended because the boat landing for the outlaw coincides exactly with the brothel being visited by Wiggam and his colleagues. In another episode Chief Wiggam is actually fired for his incompetence but reinstated after his replacement is found to be too tough on crime.

The lampooning of elites goes beyond the obvious choices of municipal officials, congressmen, and police officers. *The Simpsons* identifies and mocks the abilities, decisions, and actions of virtually all those in a position of leadership. Few influential positions in American society have escaped the pens of these writers. Examples abound throughout the eighteen-year history of the show of how normal individuals can become petty and corruptible when placed in positions of power. For example, public school teachers Edna Crabapple (Bart's

teacher) and Lynda Hoover (Lisa's teacher) are often portrayed as disinterested and uncaring, which often negatively affects the learning
process. In season 3, episode 18, Lisa plays an uncharacteristic prank
on the Springfield Elementary faculty by stealing all of the "Teacher's
Edition" textbooks, which contain the answers. As a result, the school
is crippled, exposing the teachers as frauds.

Such issues continue at the administrative level. Principal Seymour Skinner retains his position despite the apparently never-ending series of accidents and issues occurring at Springfield Elementary
(which range from a pet boa constrictor consuming a number of
young children, to vandalism, to the flooding of the school gym with
rendered animal fat). Additionally, School Superintendent Chalmers,
while gruff on the surface, is apparently easily placated, and rarely,
if ever, takes steps to discipline faculty or reform administration of
the school.

The mass media are consistently criticized as well. Local television
news anchor Kent Brockman is the prototypical self-aggrandizing
and chronically self-centered news personality, a clear parody of the
modern-day network and cable newsperson. Brockman's antics have
included throwing a Dan Rather-like tantrum because someone
stole his pastry, taking news tips from his preteen daughter, and even
offering to help imprison his fellow human beings for an alien race of
giant ant people. Also, Brockman's sleazy television newsmagazine
show, "Eye on Springfield," is an obvious parody of the "softening" of
television news, where policy and event-oriented news is abandoned
in favor of entertainment-based programming.

Beyond Kent Brockman, *The Simpsons* takes aim at other media
as well. For example, in "Mr. Spritz Goes to Washington" (season
14, episode 14), Krusty the Klown runs for Congress and debates his
opponent on Fox News. In a farcical presentation of Fox News' perceived ideological bias toward the right, the scrolling "ticker" at the
bottom of the screen reads, "Do Democrats cause cancer? Find out
at Foxnews.com.... Rupert Murdoch: Terrific Dancer.... Dow down
5000 points.... Study: 92 percent of Democrats are gay.... JFK post-
humously joins Republican Party.... Oil slicks found to keep seals
young, supple.... Dan Quayle: Awesome." In fact, Matt Groening
claims that Fox News threatened a lawsuit over the parody. While
spokespersons from Fox News denied such as threat, the Fox network did actually issue a rule forbidding *The Simpsons* from parodying their scrolling ticker in future episodes. The reasoning was that

the audience may accidentally interpret the ticker as real news, as opposed to a joke.[9]

Medicine and the law have also been targeted by *The Simpsons* as well. Dr. Nick Riviera is portrayed as a chronically malpracticing physician whose missteps often maim or kill his patients. Similarly, Dr. Julius Hibbert, although competent, often crosses ethical lines by dabbling in the medical black market, frivolously administering drugs, and ignoring his Hippocratic Oath in order to satisfy the medical insurance industry. Of course, the show's mocking of powerful elites would not be comprehensive if they did not poke at the legal community. Lionel Hutch plays the stereotypical heartless lawyer who, despite his ineptitude, is continually hired to represent Homer and Marge when they encounter legal woes. Not only is Hutch portrayed as an unethical letch who continually chases dollars and ambulances, but on occasion as a substance abuser and fugitive from the law.

Ultimately, there is an interesting message underlying this commentary that perhaps echoes Joseph Schumpeter's theory of "competitive elitism."[10] That is, although much of the influence exercised in political, economic, and social terms is exercised due to the capitulation of the public, very rarely do elites change, learn, or modify their behavior. Instead, they retain power over the apathetic masses who mock their decision making. Why is this? When punished for their shortcomings (by the loss of an election, an appointment, or a nuclear power plant), characters such as Quimby, Krusty, Burns, and Wiggam inevitably rebound and return to power. While such elites are quite average, they serve a function. Not only do they provide commentary on the influence that they (and their counterparts in the non-cartoon world) wield, they provide a second avenue of commentary on the status of conventional modern citizenship. Homer, Barney, Moe, and even Marge usually fail to act upon the inabilities and corruption of elites, and when they do, it is rarely through political or legal avenues, but rather through individual action.

For example, Homer has served as a self-appointed safety watchdog, Marge a steroid-using bodybuilder and police officer, and Lisa as the "Environmental Teacher" of Mr. Burns. As a result, their functionality remains the same, reinforced by the fact that Homer ends his safety role to return to the power plant, Marge quits both bodybuilding and the police force, and Lisa's environmentalism is thwarted by Burns's desire for profit. Despite events that should lead to change and reform, and even individual attempts to rectify such wrongs, the permanence of elites and their influence is a major underpinning of the elite criticism in *The Simpsons*. It is also a major counterpart to the more prevalent, yet often subdued critique of the masses presented by Groening et al.

Mob Rule and Tyranny of the Majority in *The Simpsons*

"That's Why We Have Elected Officials, Honey...
So We Don't Have to Think"
—*Homer J. Simpson*

The second category of humor, while sometimes more subtle than the first, occurs with greater frequency and often with more venom. Since the earliest seasons of *The Simpsons* (which first aired as a short cartoon on the *Tracey Ullman Show*), the writers have been quick to identify political shortcomings of U.S. citizens. In addition to presenting individuals such as Homer Simpson, Barney Gumble, and the ever-connected Lenny and Carl in all of their apolitical glory, *The Simpsons* frequently points to the ease with which a group of citizens (whether in a town hall meeting or a protest) find the lowest common denominator and move to irrational mob rule.

Groening et al. present a distinctly Madisonian perspective on the state of American politics, in their representation of both elites and the masses. Not only do they draw attention to the obvious weaknesses of elites and their authority (tyranny of the minority), they are unafraid to demonstrate the potential for quick degeneration of rule of law into the base rule of the majority. It should be noted that we identify this type of comedy as targeted not because Groening et al. have a political agenda, ideological bias, or even casual impact on their viewers. Rather it is labeled as targeted because *The Simpsons* is making a clear statement—through satire—about the politically ignorant masses. An early example of this type of humor is in season 1's "The Crepes of Wrath" (episode 11). In introducing the Albanian exchange student to the school, Principal Skinner says, "You may find his accent peculiar; certain aspects of his culture may seem absurd, perhaps even offensive.... I want you to give him the benefit of the doubt. This way, and only this way, can we hope to better understand our backward neighbors throughout the world."

This commentary, of course, is not a criticism of non-American cultures. Instead, it serves as a satirical illumination of the American public's tendency to dismiss foreign cultures as primitive or inferior. Although poking fun at another culture might be an obvious gag, the show often highlights the inadequacies of American citizens even while they parody Germany (embodied in Uter, the obese, chocolate-obsessed, lederhosen-wearing pupil in Springfield Elementary), France (embodied in a snooty waiter at the Quimby estate), Scotland (perpetually stereotyped in groundskeeper Willie, the shack-dwelling kilt wearer from Glasgow); and even Canada, a country whose citizens, despite having invented the sport of basketball, are depicted as so unskilled that both Bart and Milhouse can play for the national team.

U.S. citizens are consistently portrayed as politically apathetic, ideologically unsophisticated, ignorant of other nations or cultures, unmotivated, and generally disinterested in the American political process, particularly at the national level. A ready example is seen in the first episode of season 3, "Stark Raving Dad," when Dr. Marvin Monroe is about to give Homer a sanity test, and Homer suggests that his son take the exam. Although Bart replies with, "Dad, maybe you should take this test." Homer rejoins, "Son, it's just like the time I let you vote for me.... Remember that absentee ballot?" In the episode "Two Cars in Every Garage and Three Eyes on Every Fish" (season 2, episode 4), Mr. Burns's run for governor is foiled by the Simpson family. At the end of his campaign, he remarks that "this anonymous clan of slack-jawed troglodytes [the Simpsons] has cost me the election, yet if I were to have them killed, I would be the one to go to jail.... That's democracy for you!" Here, the joke is first about the tyranny of seemingly unfeeling and merciless conservative leaders, but on closer inspection, it becomes apparent that it mocks a tyranny of the majority where elections are won and lost on a brief sound bite.

The lack of sophistication among the mass public often leaves them open to manipulation by Springfield elites. One of the best examples is found in the explicitly political episode, "Sideshow Bob Roberts" (season 6, episode 5), where a newly paroled Sideshow Bob becomes the Republican challenger to Democratic incumbent Mayor Quimby. While much of the episode is filled with conventional portrayals of political pandering and hyper-stereotypical demonization of the Republican Party, the mass public are painted as incompetent sheep. Angry senior citizens, for instance, are a self-interested voting block that questions Quimby's proposed new expressway: "What's in it for us? Give us something we like or we'll ride you out of town on a rail!" Ultimately, the seniors are appeased simply by naming the expressway after their favorite television show, *Matlock*. Early in the episode, a Rush Limbaughesque talk radio host calls for the public to "do everything they can to get [Sideshow Bob] released from jail." In typical knee-jerk fashion, bar owner Moe reacts by telling his patrons, "Alright, you heard the man." He then begins passing out grenades. The call to action is then clarified by an uncharacteristically lucid Barney, who tells Moe, "I think he meant through non-violent grassroots political action."

The mass public's political ineptitude is especially highlighted when they are bamboozled by the most rudimentary political pandering. As mentioned before, elites are not often painted in a flattering light. Thus, their ability to effectively manipulate the public makes the masses appear even more mindless. In the episode "Mr. Lisa Goes to Washington," Springfield's corrupt congressman visits with Lisa in his office, and uses the situation for a photo-op. As the photographer snaps pictures, he slyly states under his breath that these types of photographs are always popular in "the sticks." The next scene shows Moe and Barney reading the newspaper with the photo of the congressman and Lisa with the headline, "Never too Busy." In an admiring tone, Moe observes, "Aw, isn't that nice. Now there's a politician who cares." Equally impressed, Barney chimes in that, "If I ever vote, it will be for him."

A second example occurs when Mr. Burns runs for governor and subsequently convinces the majority of voters that he would indeed be an ethical and trustworthy public official. His duplicity is exposed only when Marge serves him a mutated fish—contaminated by his nuclear power plant—for dinner. With the press present, Burns refuses to eat it. In "Trash of the Titans," (season 9, episode 22), Homer runs for trash commissioner of Springfield. Initially, Homer's campaign falls flat, as he possesses no understanding of the position for which he is running. Candidate Homer then revamps his campaign to appeal to the laziness of the American voter, promising that, under his administration, the trash department will change into a free butler and maid service. His campaign slogan becomes, "Can't someone else do it?" Homer's opponent, Commissioner Ray Patterson, mistakenly attempts to use logic to appeal to the voters and states: "If you want an experienced public servant, vote for me. But if you want to believe a bunch of crazy promises about garbage men cleaning your gutters and waxing your car, then by all means, vote for this sleazy lunatic [Homer]." Ultimately Homer is able to win in a landslide over a capable, accomplished, and well-liked incumbent by promising benefits to the public that he obviously cannot deliver.

In "Marge vs. the Monorail" (season 4, episode 12), the entire town of Springfield is duped into spending $3 million on an unnecessary monorail system simply because a skilled con man taunts them with the sales pitch, "I come before you good people tonight with an idea. Probably the greatest.... Aw, it's not for you. It's more of a Shelbyville idea." The con man, Lyle Lanly, then leads a musical sales pitch (derived from the musical *The Music Man*) that hooks Springfield. When Marge attempts to question the appropriation, Bart observes, "Sorry Mom, the mob has spoken."

James Madison, chief writer of *The Federalist Papers* and significant contributor to the U.S. Constitution, was well aware of the threat of tyranny of the majority rule. In the *Federalist* No. 10, he explicitly states that "[w]hen a majority is included in a faction, the form of popular government, on the other hand, enables it to sacrifice to its ruling passion or interest both the public good and the rights of other citizens." Madison, a supporter of minority rights, faced many intellectual problems in getting protection for minority factions. In *Federalist* No. 51 he stresses that "[i]f a majority be united by a common interest, the rights of the minority will be insecure." Following the ideas of classical liberalism more than many of his fellow Federalists, Madison endorsed a pluralist solution of checks and balances between government branches and multiple centers of influence. Thus, instead of one majority faction always winning, any number of minorities can vie for influence on a contested political issue. Madison reconciled his fear of the "tyranny of the majority" with his classical liberalism roots by calling for a semi-democratic rule with elite rule and minority rights. Through compromise, Madison believed the federal government, as a trustee, could control multiple centers of influence and destroy majorities in government.

Although *The Simpsons* often points (typically through Homer and his confreres) to the political inadequacies of citizenship, the criticism of Groening et al. frequently extends to the mass public, and is most evident in his frequently occurring depiction of collective action gone awry. On a number of occasions, the people of Springfield degenerate into an angry mob intent on inflicting immediate justice or retribution. Consistent with the concerns of James Madison, Groening depicts the citizens of Springfield as most dangerous when they are impassioned, and most easily impassioned by the basest of desires and issues. Holding true to the Madisonian concern of tyranny of the majority, the Springfield mob almost never exercises restraint or deliberation—in fact, it even revels in its absence. And, in many instances, minority rights are subsequently trampled.

The factors that lead to the formation of the angry mob on the show vary. In "Rosebud" (season 5, episode 4), Mr. Burns finds that Maggie Simpson is in possession of his childhood teddy bear, "Bobo." Initially, Burns attempts to buy the bear from Homer. When Homer refuses to sell, the clever Mr. Burns purposefully instigates a mob by shutting down the television stations and cutting off Springfield's supply of beer. He then turns this mob on Homer by telling the public, "And if the rest of you beer-swilling tube-jockeys out there have a problem with [cutting of television and the beer supply], talk to Homer Simpson." Eventually, the mob storms the Simpsons' home, and forcibly takes the teddy bear from Maggie. Again, in a turn of satirical irony, the mob decides to return the bear to Maggie when she begins to cry. Feeling guilty, Dr. Julius Hibbert sulks that, "We've given the word 'mob' a bad name."

In other instances, the mob forms as a result of some trauma or perceived injustice. In season 1's "The Telltale Head" (episode 8), Bart removes the head from the statue of local hero and town founder, Jebediah Springfield, in an effort to impress some of his older hooligan classmates. Initially, the town's response to the beheading is sorrow, but that melancholy quickly turns to rage. By the end of the episode, the citizens of Springfield have formed an angry mob that chases Bart through the street with the intent of killing him. In "Bart's Inner Child" (season 5, episode 7), the entire town of Springfield adopts Bart's carefree approach to life and work (at the behest of self-help guru Brad Goodman). The result is a quick erosion of public safety and order and a mob quickly forms amidst the chaos. Bart is made the scapegoat, and must once again flee a murderous town rampage.

The mob's irrationality is parodied in a unique manner in season 4's "Whacking Day" (episode 20). In a caricature that loosely mirror's Shirley Jackson's short story, "The Lottery," this episode chronicles Springfield's annual Whacking Day, which is a day of *planned* mob violence. All of the town's frustrations are excised by beating snakes to death with clubs (according to Homer, it is "the greatest day of the year"). The violence of Whacking Day is embraced by religion (Reverend Lovejoy falsely quotes the Bible, "Whack ye, all the serpents that crawl on their bellies, and thy town shall be a beacon unto others"), political leaders (Richard Nixon was a "guest whacker" in the 1950s, and Mayor Quimby presides over the festivities), and even the usually temperate Marge Simpson (who is sexually aroused by Homer's participation in the event) endorses the event. Only Lisa Simpson is critical of the barbaric holiday. When she begs Homer not to "lower [himself] to the level of the mob," he cheerfully retorts, "Lisa, maybe if I'm part of that mob, I can help steer it in wise directions. Now, where's my giant foam cowboy hat and air horn?"

Even when collective action seems harmonious and well conceived, the outcome is typically undesirable. In "Hurricane Neddy" (season 8, episode 8), the town joins together to rebuild Ned Flanders's house, which was destroyed by Hurricane Barbara. The effort, however, is so poorly executed that the reconstructed house collapses, sending Flanders into a tirade. Similarly, in "Homer the Vigilante" (season 5, episode 11), Homer is appointed head of a neighborhood watch program and charged with the task of recovering personal and public items that were stolen by the self-described "Cat Burglar" (including Springfield's prize possession, the world's largest cubic zirconium). Of course, Homer's watch program quickly descends into an irrational and violent vigilante group that carries weapons, starts fires, and randomly beats innocent people. In discussing the events of an evening of vigilante work, Homer recounts, "So I said to him, look, buddy, your car was upside down when we got here. And as for your Grandma, she shouldn't have mouthed off like that!" When Lisa attempts to remind Homer that the original goal of his group was to recover her stolen saxophone and other items, the following exchange takes place.

> *Homer:* Lisa, the mob is working on getting your saxophone back. But we've also expanded into other important areas. (Reads from a list) Literacy programs, preserving our beloved covered bridges, world domination....
>
> *Lisa:* World domination?
>
> *Homer:* Oh…that might be a typo. (*Thinks to himself,* "the girl knows too much.")

Homer's vigilante group, of course, becomes both consumed and corrupted with power, and has no role in the eventual capture of the Cat Burglar (Grandpa Simpson actually catches the criminal). In the end, the clever Cat Burglar easily escapes from jail by sending the gullible (and greedy) citizens of Springfield on a wild goose chase in search of a fictitious buried treasure.

The notion of faction that can aid, via the American democratic model of pluralism, a democratic republic, is best exemplified by interest groups. Satirizing the free rider problem, collective bargaining, and interest group liberalism is a common theme in *The Simpsons*. In episode 5 of season 9, "The Cartridge Family," Homer exemplifies National Rifle Association members who are obsessive about owning and playing with firearms, bemoan any restrictions like a waiting period because "they are mad now," and use the Second Amendment to justify even irresponsible gun activities.

Organized labor is lampooned in a season 4 episode, "Last Exit to Springfield" (episode 17). Upon election to the position of union president, Homer asks what the job pays. Lenny replies, "Nothing...unless you're crooked." This same episode also features Mr. Burns's flashback to a childhood moment in his grandfather's industrial plant. In that flashback, Burns's grandfather frivolously mistreats his employees and has a young employee fired for "stealing atoms." As the fired employee is being carried out of the plant, he yells to Burns's grandfather: "You can't treat the working man this way. One day, we'll form a union and get the fair and equitable treatment we deserve! Then we'll go too far and get corrupt and shiftless, and the Japanese will eat us alive!" Along these lines, Homer maintains that misappropriation of union funds and organized crime connections are the only benefits of labor unions. Although the union successfully negotiates a family dental plan, this collective triumph is achieved only by having Homer as the self-interested leader.

In a 1991 interview, creator Matt Groening stated that "If Homer voted, he'd probably vote Republican. Luckily, he doesn't vote."[11] Although some might interpret this quote as political humor targeted at the stereotypical apathetic citizen, some might conclude that Homer does not vote because he is a cartoon character. Often the writers of the show like to remind their viewers that implicit messages of the show should not be interpreted as explicit political encouragement. This is often done by using actual political events, because, as Shakespeare noted, life is a stage. For instance, one of the Springfield

Republicans' strategic ideological plans was to rename everything after Ronald Wilson Reagan. This is not really funny unless one knows there was a federally funded "Ronald Reagan Legacy Project" attempting to attach the fortieth president's name to landmarks in every state in the Union. In the genre of "its only funny because it is true" is the episode "See Homer Run" (season 17, episode 6), where Major Quimby faces a recall election that includes hundreds of candidates running for mayor. In fact, the character Rainer Wolfcastle mocks the actual bodybuilding actor who won the Gray Davis California recall election. While the plot of the episode is about lack of citizen efficacy and the power of name recognition and popularity, the sophisticated humor for a few serves little comedic purpose.

Obscure Political Humor

Finally, the third grouping of political humor is less concerned with political critique, commentary, or thematic observation. Instead, it appears to exist largely for the satisfaction of the writers themselves. However, in doing so it also provides a sense of gratification (for "getting it") for a select grouping of viewers at a level of obscurity and political knowledge far removed from that of the typical viewer of cartoons. The presence of these political references, while rarely relevant in the context of an episode, contribute to the political humor of *The Simpsons* by giving a small group of viewers yet another level of comprehension and implied intent. Viewers who note or understand these references are literally able to say, like Homer, that the show is funny on many different levels.

Selective political Simpsons humor is for the relatively few viewers who are very sophisticated and confident in their knowledge of political history, public policy, and current events. For instance, episodes will mock Carter's "Malaise" speech or Nixon's "Checkers" speech for few laughs and almost no meaning, since the humor is rarely, if ever, related to the episode into which it is placed. Principal Skinner, for instance, in (season 13, episode 11) "The Bart Wants What It Wants," justifies stealing public resources to Lisa by awkwardly testifying: "Welcome to Dick Cheney's America." This type of humor appears seemingly at random and serves primarily to appeal to historically and/or politically informed viewers.

There are many examples of this selective humor. In "I Married Marge" (season 3, episode 12), Homer recalls the idealistic days of Reagan and the 1980s and cites the candidacy of John Andersen for no apparent reason. In a different flashback episode, "Lisa's First Word" (season 4, episode 10), Homer takes advantage of the 1984 Soviet boycott of the Los Angeles Summer Olympics to acquire free meals from Krustyburger (parodying what happened to McDonald's). The third season's "Treehouse of Horror II" (episode 7) features a short story in which Lisa is granted her wish of world peace. To demonstrate peace unfolding, representatives from Great Britain and Argentina are shown hugging. The British representative says, "Sorry about the Falklands, old boy." The Argentinean replies, "We kind of knew they were yours anyway."

Although there are full episodes dedicated to demonstrating the failure of Lisa's naive environmentalism, such as her attempt to change the corporate polluter Burns into an organic green producer, most of the green humor is selective at best. In fact, countless references make a mockery of green politics. While many of the pranks about individuals, groups, or politicians who are passionate about the environment are amusing for all viewers, there are many sophisticated references that are appreciated only by a few. This obscure humor, however, is profound for green citizens watching the show because they deride actual events. For instance, in one episode Homer commits the ecological massacre of cutting down an entire old growth forest because his cartoon persona is not in concert with "real" Hollywood environmental activists. This dual-edged sword is poking fun of celebrity protesters who are ridiculed by environmental groups for being symbolically interested in high-profile issues. Furthermore, in referencing the real-world biological event of rabbits in Australia, Bart violates the science of ecology by introducing a "nonnative or invasive species" to a foreign biological ecosystem by taking his pet frog to Australia where it multiplies exponentially because it has no enemies. Similarly, in "Brawl in the Family" (season 13, episode 7), the school bully taunts a harmless owl by chanting, "Stop endangering yourself!"

This third-level stage of humor is well illustrated by the show's constant mocking of Lisa's decision not to eat meat. In the episode "Lisa's Wedding" (season 6, episode 19), she has a vision of her future where she studies the environment, is "utterly humorless about...vegetarianism," and loves the Rolling Stones "not for their music, but for their tireless effort to preserve historic buildings." Next, in the installment "Lisa the Vegetarian" (season 7, episode 5), she is overwhelmed by the plight of the self-righteous vegetarian until she realizes that Apu and close to 1 billion people of his country do not eat animals, not because of environmental ethics but as a result of culture and religion. Lastly, in "Lisa the Treehugger" (season 12, episode 4), she meets an environmental activist who works for the group Dirt First! and eventually plays the real-life civil disobedient of Earth Firster Julia "Butterfly" Hill by tree-sitting for a number of days.

Conclusion

The notion of a tyrannical majority has existed since the beginning of political theory and practice, having over the centuries gained a definite negative but subjective connotation. Aristotle, for instance, feared a governmental system of democracy for it would be susceptible to tyrannical rule. In fact, any good American civics lesson would explain that our Founding Fathers had reason to be concerned about the tyranny of a majority rule. The framers of the Constitution were, or course, a white minority of wealthy, well-educated, slave-owning elite men. Although the framers borrowed from democratic principles, they feared that the uneducated masses would be unfit to take part in any form of direct democracy. Thus, it would be more suitable for the political elites to act as sophisticated and temperate representatives, who would enact legislation on behalf of the masses.

The targeted humor of The Simpsons asserts via comedy that even in a representative democracy, it is still possible for a tyranny of the majority. This is, of course, a topic that is addressed by serious political scientists from Phillip Converse[12] to Robert Putnam.[13] Rather than profound philosophers and statesmen like Aristotle, Madison, Schumpeter, or Mill who offered solutions, however, Groening conveys his perspective on the masses through his humor. Lest we forget that while The Simpsons is politically relevant, it does not advocate any specific politics. Like true liberal education and many distinguished and well-respected political theorists, it is simply developing critical or independent thought. This is best illustrated in "Bart Gets an Elephant" (season 5, episode 17), where the Republican Party claims "We're pure evil" and the Democrats self-assert that "We can't govern" and/or "We hate life and ourselves."

While Groening equally mocks both political parties, he is encouraging viewers to observe the shortcomings of the current political system and consider third parties and support for new platforms. Similarly, it can also prompt viewers to reconsider their own perspectives on the environment and environmental activism, their possible dismissal of veganism, or even the importance of televised sports to the American male. Quite simply, *The Simpsons* from 1989 to present is more than a cartoon about some dim-witted nuclear technician who lives with his wife and their three kids. While the sitcom is not an animated political strip, it does make some political jokes and social messages that can amuse the viewer on multiple levels. This is best seen in jokes that appear to operate simultaneously on all three dimensions we have discussed, such as the seemingly banal dialogue between Kent Brockman and Leeza Gibbons while commenting on a Thanksgiving Day parade in "Homer vs. Dignity" (season 12, episode 5):

> *Kent:* Here's a float saluting the Native Americans, who taught us how to celebrate Thanksgiving.
> *Leeza:* Interesting side note on this float: the papier-mâché is composed entirely of broken treaties.
> *Kent:* They're such good sports.

Notes

1. Paul Cantor, "In Praise of Television: the Greatest TV Show Ever," *The American Enterprise* 8 (1997): 34–37.
2. Our argument generally follows that found in Andrew Wood and Anne Marie Todd, "'Are We There Yet?': Searching for Springfield and the Simpsons' Rhetoric of Omnitopia," *Critical Studies in Media Communication* 22 (2005): 207–222.
3. Mark I. Pinsky, *The Gospel According to the Simpsons: The Spiritual Life of the World's Most Animated Family* (Louisville, KY: Westminster John Knox Press, 2001); Lisa Frank, "The Evolution of the Seven Deadly Sins: From God to the Simpsons," *Journal of Popular Culture* 35 (2001): 95–105.
4. William Irwin, Mark T. Conard, and Aeon J. Skoble, eds., *The Simpsons and Philosophy: The D'Oh! of Homer* (Chicago: Open Court, 1999); Brian Ott, "'I'm Bart Simpson, Who the Hell are You?' A Study in Postmodern Identity (Re)Construction," *Journal of Popular Culture* 37 (2003): 56–82.

5. Chris Turner, *Planet Simpson: How a Cartoon Masterpiece Defined a Generation* (Cambridge, MA: Da Capo Press, 2004); Steven Keslowitz, The Simpsons and Society: An Analysis of Our Favorite Family and Its Influence in Contemporary Society (Tucson, AZ: Hats Off, 2003).

6. Paul Cantor, "The Simpsons: Atomistic Politics and the Nuclear Family," *Political Theory* 27 (1999): 734–749.

7. Polly Schulman, "Men Know from Homer, Women from Marge," *Psychology Today* 36 (2003): 32–34, 36.

8. Margaret Betz Hull, "Postmodern Philosophy Meets Pop Cartoon: Michel Foucault and Matt Groening," *Journal of Popular Culture* 34 (2000): 57–67.

9. "This Just In: Fox News Humourless," *Gazette* (Montreal, Quebec), October 30, 2003, A26.

10. David Held, *Models of Democracy*, 2nd ed. (Stanford, CA: Stanford University Press, 1996).

11. "Politics in *The Simpsons*," Wikipedia. http://en.wikipedia.org/wiki/Politics_in_The_Simpsons.

12. Phillip Converse, "The Nature of Belief Systems in Mass Publics," in *Ideology and Discontent*, ed. David Apter (London: Free Press of Glencoe, 1964), 206–261.

13. Robert D. Putnam, *Making Democracy Work: Civic Traditions in Modern Italy* (Princeton, NJ: Princeton University Press, 1993); Robert D. Putnam, "Bowling Alone: America's Declining Social Capital," *Journal of Democracy* 6 (1995): 65–78.

13

Saturday Night Live and Presidential Elections

Ben Voth

Saturday Night Live (SNL) is one of the more important traditions of contemporary American political humor. At least as far back as Chevy Chase's depictions of Gerald Ford, *SNL* has translated the serious realm of politics into something the public could laugh about. More recently, *SNL* has played a noticeable public role in the last two U.S. presidential elections. Both elections were close, and a variety of factors may have swayed the ultimate outcomes. Humor provided by outlets like *SNL* was arguably an important factor. This analysis provides a rhetorical study of *SNL*'s parodies of presidential debates for the elections of 2000 and 2004. This study concludes that *SNL*'s powerful role in defining in the 2000 presidential candidates declined considerably in the 2004 process. From a comparative perspective of the two political seasons (2000 and 2004), it is possible to see how *SNL* demonstrates the effective and ineffective rhetorical ranges of humor in politics.

While focusing on *Saturday Night Live*'s parodies of presidential debates, it is important to recognize the significant role that these political debates play in shaping public opinion and electoral behavior in the United States. The public contrast on television of direct arguments from candidates represents a pivotal event in the overall presidential election process.[1] There is an immediate effort on the part of analysts to determine winners in these debates. Such debates and the perceived outcome do have a significant impact on the presidential campaigns themselves. The importance of these campaign events is confirmed by the tens of millions of viewers who tune in to the debates that typically run during October, just a month before the election. In 2004, a record number of individuals tuned in to the first presidential debate between John Kerry and George W. Bush, surpassing records set in 2000.[2] Interestingly, viewership of presidential debates drops off precipitously after the first of typically three debates. The American electorate has shown reluctance to take repeated doses of the bitter pills offered in presidential debates. Consequently, the first debate is by far the most important of these events.

Given the heightened drama surrounding presidential debates, it is not surprising that satirists and humorists are focused on these moments. Consequently, the *SNL* parodies of the first presidential debates for 2000 and 2004 are rhetorically significant. These parodies frame public discussion of winners and losers from the debate and help establish important public themes of analysis for what remains of the campaigns in the month before an election. Put simply, these parodies may influence the public's feelings about the candidates. It is, therefore, useful to focus a rhetorical study on *SNL*'s use of humor in presidential elections at the critical juncture of the first presidential debate.

Rhetorical Analysis

This review employs a rhetorical analysis. Rhetorical study provides a situational review of persuasion strategies in order to assess the role of these strategies in creating public outcomes. The outcomes in this case concern the election. Aristotle has defined rhetoric as the faculty of observing in any given situation all available means of persuasion.[3] In this rhetorical analysis, an assessment will be made of how humor functions strategically within the situation of a presidential election.

To complete a strategic analysis, a more precise rhetorical theory is needed. Noted rhetorical theorist Kenneth Burke provides important insights into how humor functions as a rhetorical strategy. Burke suggests that the symbolic world is divided between the tragic and comic frames. Frames are the symbolic structures humans use to impose order upon their lives. Cheree Carlson notes that frames are the constructs humans use to view, group, and interpret experiences with reality.[4] These frames, in turn, determine the symbolic actions and choices humans make from these experiences. Burke argues that humans categorize their actions and choices through the major poetic frames of epic, tragedy, comedy, elegy, satire, burlesque, and the grotesque. He further explains these frames in terms of acceptance and rejection. Frames of acceptance, such as comedy and epic, single out relationships as friendly and, therefore, capable of mutual dialogue and understanding.[5] However, rejection frames, such as burlesque and tragedy, define the human situation as unfriendly and incapable of understanding. These frames emphasize their relation to authority and attempt to resist action that could potentially threaten that authority. Politics represents a tragic rhetorical frame. Political contests end decisively with winners and losers. The serious symbols exchanged between campaigns will bring one individual to power and bring to an end the quest of another. The comic frame works upon absurdity and urges contestants to consider alternatives to their dualistic framing.

Christiansen and Hansen suggest that the frame of impulse in Western society is tragedy.[6] The tragic frame holds that any violation of social principles must inevitably lead to punishment and the acknowledgement of guilt. Tragic action condemns and ridicules rather than attempts to expose and correct transgressions. The victim of tragic action is left to suffer the impulses of those in the tragic perspective either through mystification, scapegoating, or banishment. Authority and its hierarchy are upheld through this victimization by symbolically ridding society of wrongdoing and preserving social order.[7] This victimization ultimately leads tragedy to a form of what Burke identifies as relativism, whereby only one point of view is seen. Isolating one vantage point leaves other points of view incapable of observation, thus creating a skewed and biased portrayal of reality. This flawed perspective, in turn, leads to drawing inaccurate judgments because other equally important and valuable perspectives are not taken into consideration.

The recent and increasing partisan bitterness of political argument in the United States has created a public exigence for the realm of comic relief. Like water on a too hot political day, comedy arrives in the communication scene as an increasingly popular commodity. Consequently, the comedic parodies of *Saturday Night Live* have an intrinsic appeal to the American electorate. Voters are burned by tragic appeals common with presidential campaigns that now last more than a year administered in tart daily doses by the media. Whereas the tragic frame leads to chaos in order to criticize and condemn the tragic actor, action in the comic frame seeks exposure and reconciliation of the actor's errors. The comic perspective of *Saturday Night Live* is somewhat unique compared to its rivals from the week-nights. Lorne Michaels, creator and producer of *SNL*, notes that the political parodies on *SNL* are not created or executed with the same malicious demeanor as other humorists, such as Dave Letterman, who made no effort to hide his ill feelings toward candidate Bush. Michaels further commented, "*SNL*'s spoofs tend to be more affec-tionate and goofy than mean."[8] Michael's comment illustrates how rhetoric in the comic frame transcends traditional tragic thought of victimizing the actor. Instead, comic rhetoric attempts to ease ten-sions by constructing a distinctive form of social criticism that only seeks exposure and reconciliation of error.[9]

An additional element of insight within Burke's overall work is a notion of perspective by incongruity. Humor provides a comic cor-rective by juxtaposing irreconcilable contrasts that compel a viewer to seek comic relief to the contradiction. The incongruity is a gentle but firm symbolic reminder that the tragic frame of representation is inherently an exaggeration. The tragic appeals involve hyperbole that can be readily identified in a comic portrayal highlighting the exaggerated features of an appeal. A father who finds his young child unexpectedly disrupting his tool set being used on an important proj-ect may experience a sense of comic relief as he realizes that there are things more important than "the important project." The juxtaposi-tion of the playful child's disruption with the serious tools creates the perspective by incongruity wherein greater insight is gained by the observer. This is one specific way that the comic frame can solve symbolic problems created in the tragic frame.

Numerous communication and political science studies and anal-yses have recognized the utility and necessity of humor in the politi-cal arena.[10] In fact, there is a strong trend of increasing use of humor in political discourse. Experts notice that politicians are using humor to their own advantage, rendering humor as a device rather than becoming mere objects of derision in comedic treatments. In Ameri-can political discourse, *SNL* is a longtime tradition for the integra-tion of humor and politics in American entertainment. The dramatic presidential elections of 2000 and 2004 provided significant insights into how humor and argument work together to produce rhetori-cal results in the campaign process. *Saturday Night Lives*'s influence on the two elections was quite different—with 2000 being a water-shed moment while 2004 was a relatively low-impact event. From these two elections we can make rhetorical assessments as to how the comic frame works and does not work as political argument.

2000 Situation and Analysis

Many critics and scholars have pointed to the first presidential debate as the defining moment in the 2000 election. John Buell suggests, "For many citizens, the first televised debate is their only political participation."[11] In fact, Nielsen Media Research concluded that 10 million more viewers watched the first debate than the second or third debate.[12] In regards to the 2000 election, Carl argues that the first debate probably would not decide the race, but it would set the tone for the events left to unfold. In other words, the debate in Boston would not be the final determinant in deciding the next president of the United States, but it would provide a means for the voting public to sharpen their impression of the candidates, and it would define how the candidates would shape the rest of their campaign. This prediction as articulated by William Carl certainly proved true as the candidates used the first debate as a foundation and model for how they would present themselves in the final two debates.[13] However, the importance attributed to the first debate in the 2000 did not necessarily come from the debate itself; rather, it stemmed from the events surrounding the debate. Largely attributable to the influence of *Saturday Night Live*, the first debate created an interpretive mold and precedent for humor in the political sphere. This humor would set the tone for the final two debates in the 2000 race. Collins claims that in an attempt to convey what is on the mind of voters, "*Saturday Night Live* has been the hardest-hitting forum of all."[14] Boedeker suggests that by providing liberating and therapeutic laughter in surreal circumstances, "The clearest winner in this year's presidential election is *Saturday Night Live*."[15] Clearly, the manner in which *SNL's* rhetoric and influence operated as a legitimate political argument is worthy of further analysis.

The *SNL* parody of the first debate contained numerous memorable moments that captured the public imagination. Most significant was perhaps at the conclusion of the debate where Chris Parnell asked each candidate for purposes of brevity to sum up their campaigns in one word. The Gore character, played by Darrell Hammond, chose "Lockbox," while the Bush character, played by Will Ferrell, chose

"Strategery." To this day, those terms are etched in the American political lexicon. The brilliant conclusion of the skit tended to highlight public hunger for reductionism and simplicity during the overly dramatic political season. Additionally, the demeanor of the candidates was effectively mimicked by the comedians. The Gore character exuded loud exasperated sighs while the Bush character answered questions and seemed easily distracted, looking aimlessly up at the lights during the debate. The scriptwriting had many memorable lines, including a highly amusing hyperbole of a Gore campaign anecdote involving a constituent suffering from Lyme disease, shark attacks, and epilepsy. According to the Gore character, "under my plan her prescription drugs would be paid for, while under my opponents plan—her house would be burned to the ground." The Bush scripting offered up numerous mispronunciations and awkward inabilities to answer. One tough foreign policy question on Bosnia left Bush suggesting that he would not pronounce the names of the politicians involved because "it's not in our national security interest." The overall parody was publicly captivating. Consequently, it elicited immediate and direct action from the presidential campaigns.

Subsequent to this parody, many thought that Gore the candidate transformed into different characters in each debate in order to respond to criticism that he was either too hard or too soft in previous debates. As a result, many voters began to muse over whether there was a "real" Al Gore or if he was merely a chameleon who repeatedly changed in order to adapt to criticism and remain in a favorable public light. However, regardless of if the electorate saw a "real" Al Gore or maybe that Gore was simply not as appealing as the public originally perceived, it is unimportant when looking at his demise. Gore's problems ensued from attempting to correct his flaws as exemplified by Darrell Hammond's comedic portrayal. The problem with attempting to correct his inadequacies based on Hammond's exaggerated spoofs is that Gore was trying to correct the flaws as inflated by an actor. In doing so, Gore continued to act tragically by trying to cover up his foibles through the subsequent debates rather than realizing that the *SNL* skits were enacted for sheer entertainment purposes and not intended to victimize either candidate. As a result, most believed that Gore tried too hard to adapt to criticism and, consequently, failed to show America his true personality. Moreover, the polls tend to suggest the same.[16]

Perspectives by incongruity, such as those employed in *SNL*'s spoofs, are not meant to have any basis in reality. They are only meant to humorously point out the target's failings so that those errors can be corrected in an appropriate fashion. Consequently, Gore's troubles did not result from failing to accept the role as comic clown. He not only accepted the role, he embraced it, but it was too little too late. Initially, he and his staff were terrified to accept the role as comic fool. Their insistence on having Gore watch the skits and also having a speech writer attempt to edit the script of *SNL*'s "Presidential Bash 2000" illustrate the Gore campaign's incapacity to properly respond to the misgivings exposed through the comic frame. Gore's notable overcompensations in the final debates tend to indicate that he responded in a similarly incongruous perspective that *SNL* originally used to expose his and Bush's errors. In other words, just as *SNL* exaggerated the candidates' errors, Gore employed exaggerated responses to these errors in the final two debates, making his behavior appear artificial and inconsistent. This ultimately fed into already preconceived notions about Al Gore as a person and candidate.

Intended as irreverent mockery of the political process, *Saturday Night Live*'s political parodies in 2000 left an important mark on the political landscape. *SNL*'s antics left a legacy of classic humor, but they will also help denote the 2000 presidential election as one of the strangest in the history of the United States. The 2000 election broke away from these historical precedents defining the autonomy of the political and entertainment spheres and illustrated a novel blending of politics and comedy seldom seen before in such magnitude.[17] In Burke's terms, the 2000 election signaled that certain segments of the American public, particularly young people, were choosing to abandon traditional rhetoric disseminated from a tragic perspective; instead, the public often utilized humor as a primary means of collecting information to organize vast areas of political substance.[18] These peculiarities set up an unusual set of expectations for the next presidential election.

2004 Situation and Analysis

In 2004, the presidential contest between Senator John Kerry and President George W. Bush was framed primarily as debate over national security and the conflict in Iraq. The Kerry campaign principally argued that the Bush administration misled Americans about the war while the Bush campaign principally argued that candidate Kerry vacillated, or "flip-flopped," on security issues. For *Saturday Night Live*, the situation was also different from 2000. Most importantly, the major star of their Bush parodies, Will Ferrell, had graduated from *SNL* and moved on to his own independent career. It was apparent in 2004 that *SNL* was suffering by comparison to its 2000 skits. Most centrally, the ghost of Ferrell's portrayal made it difficult for Will Forte's parody to stick.

Saturday Night Live's 2004 parody of the first presidential debate was similar to its 2000 parody. Jim Lehrer (played by Chris Parnell) led the skit as moderator of the debate. The Kerry parody emphasized the "flip-flop" theme suggested by the Bush campaign. The Kerry character would make frequent contradictory statements back to back about the war. The sentences were accompanied by exaggerated hand gestures comparable to Kerry's original delivery in the debate. Forte's parody of Bush emphasized Bush's exasperated demeanor apparent in debate one. The most frequent line was "it's hard"—in reference to the job of being president. Forte highlighted political difficulties in Iraq by elaborating Bush's backup plan of bringing a strong leader to Iraq if his current policy failed—the new leader...Saddam Hussein. The Kerry character amused the audience by suggesting that his contradictory statements were not flip-flops but pandering, and that "the American public deserves a candidate that knows the difference."

Reaction to the 2004 skit was subdued. The skit received little replay compared to its 2000 counterpart. Moreover, comparisons to the stronger parodies of 2000 were immediate. *Saturday Night Live* was drowning in the larger comedic market of John Stewart, JibJab .com, and various late night comedians. The parody of Bush was particularly weak, relying persistently on a theme of tiredness. The writing of the skit was equally unimpressive. Except for the pandering line, the script elicited few memorable lines that could be compared to the "lockbox" themes of 2000.

Forte's parody of Bush became more nuanced by 2006, exposing the limited range of his original interpretation in 2004. A spring 2006 Katrina parody contained stronger writing and greater emotional range. Forte discussed Bush's desire to "consolidate the national debt with Ditech." He demanded that Vice President Cheney apologize on air for "shooting his friend in the face." The relatively robust performance of these recent skits tended to highlight the limited power of the 2004 parody.

The 2004 parody did not produce the dramatic change in poll position seen in the election of 2000. Bush and Kerry were locked around 48 percent throughout the month of October. The close position continued through to the election results. In 2000, Gore's lead disappeared shortly after the first parody of the presidential debate in October. Bush took the lead for some time after the first parody. The race came close again as the election neared in 2000.

Conclusions

Saturday Night Live's parodies of presidential debates in 2000 and 2004 are important rhetorical artifacts indicating how humor influences the American political process. The two cases are highly contrasted. In 2000, *SNL* produced significant rhetorical impacts, which may have played a role in reversing Gore's polling trajectory toward victory in that presidential season. In 2004, *SNL* suffered by direct comparison to its 2000 work and had little influence on the overall assessment of the candidates. These contrasting cases help confirm what are the necessary and sufficient ingredients for humor to impact the political process.

Saturday Night Live's historic parodies of politics rely on two principal elements: strong content and strong characters. Strong content requires scripts that produce memorable lines. *SNL*'s lines in 2000 about "lockboxes" and "strategery" became definitive. Today the Bush White House has a room called the "strategery" room. The term has no origin other than the decisive *SNL* skit parodying the first presidential debate in 2000. Memorable content was not apparent in 2004. Will Forte's Bush character continually explained that "it's hard" being president. Seth Meyer's Kerry character had one clever line about "pandering" but it did not become dominant public stock like the 2000 material.

Strong characters are also important to *SNL*'s parody power. Will Ferrell stands as a unique icon among political satirists. His role in 2000 ultimately overshadowed the 2004 efforts to depict Bush after he left *SNL*. For most of the American public, Ferrell continues to define the Bush parody despite Forte's growing strength since 2004. Darryl Hammond's 2000 rendering of Gore was considered by many to be "dead-on," and will continue to be one of the more memorable moments of political parodies.

Saturday Night Live does provide a unique comedic artifact for studying how the comic frame resolves the tragic frame of American politics. Because the comedians are playing roles rather than making direct commentary—as in the case of Jon Stewart—*SNL* provides a means of comic correction wherein political players can accept their roles as comic clowns. In the case of 2000, the Gore campaign panicked about the initial depiction of Gore and coached an overreaction for the second debate. This suggests that Gore and other political players recognize the organizing centrality of *SNL*'s political parodies. Political characters such as Gore and Bush now appear on *SNL* as a way to solidify their acceptance and redemption through the comic frame. They help the American electorate understand that "they get it." In so doing, *Saturday Night Live* has become one of the spoonfuls of sugar that helps the bitter medicine of presidential politics go down easier.

Notes

1. William Benoit, Glenn Hansen, and Kevin Stein, "Newspaper Coverage of Presidential Campaigns," *Argumentation & Advocacy* 40 (2004): 246–258.
2. "Third Bush-Gore Debate Draws 37.6 Million Viewers," *Associated Press*, October 18, 2000.
3. Aristotle, *The Art of Rhetoric* Volume XXII, 2006, Loeb Classical Library, Cambridge: Harvard University Press.
4. Cheree Carlson, "Gandhi and the Comic Frame: 'Ad bellum purificandum,'" *Quarterly Journal of Speech* 72 (1986): 446–455.
5. Kenneth Burke, *Attitudes Toward History* (Los Altos, CA: Hermes Publications, 1959).
6. Adrienne E. Christiansen and Jeremy J. Hanson, "Comedy as a Cure for Tragedy: Act Up and the Rhetoric of AIDS," *Quarterly Journal of Speech* 82 (1996): 157–170.
7. Mark P. Moore, "'The Quayle Quagmire': Political Campaigns in the Poetic Form of Burlesque," *Western Journal of Communication* 56 (1992): 108–124.
8. D. Holloway, "Presidents' Parodies Make for Good TV," *Chattanooga Times*, April 11, 2001, E3.
9. Kenneth Burke, *On Symbols and Society*, ed. and Intro. Joseph R. Gusfield (Chicago: University of Chicago Press, 1989).

10. M. Alisky, "White House Wit: Presidential Humor to Sustain Policies, from Lincoln to Reagan," *Presidential Studies Quarterly* 20 (1990): 373–381; Denise M. Bostdorff, "Vice-Presidential Comedy and the Traditional Female Role: An Examination of the Rhetorical Characteristics of the Vice Presidency," *Western Journal of Speech Communication* 55 (1991): 1–27; Cheree Carlson, "Limitations on the Comic Frame: Some Witty American Women of the Nineteenth Century," *Quarterly Journal of Speech* 74 (1988): 310–323; Adrienne E. Christiansen and Jeremy J. Hanson, "Comedy as a Cure for Tragedy: Act Up and the Rhetoric of AIDS," *Quarterly Journal of Speech* 82 (1996): 157–170; Arthur P. Dudden, "The Record of Political Humor," in *American Humor*, ed. A. P. Dudden (New York: Oxford University Press, 1987), 50-75; David Levasseur and Kevin Dean, "The Dole Humor Myth and the Risks of Recontextualizing Rhetoric," *Southern Communication Journal* 62 (1996): 56–72; John Meyer, "Ronald Reagan and Humor: A Politician's Velvet Weapon," *Communication Studies* 41 (1990): 76–88; Mark P. Moore, "'The Quayle Quagmire'"; David L. Paletz, "Political Humor and Authority: From Support to Subversion," *International Political Science Review* 11 (1990): 483–493; Michael Pfau, "The Subtle Nature of Presidential Debate Influence," *Argumentation and Advocacy* 38 (2002): 251–262; Chris Smith and Ben Voth, "The Role of Humor in Political Argument: How 'Stratgery' and 'Lockboxes' Changed a Political Campaign," *Argumentation & Advocacy* 39 (2002): 110–130.
11. John Buell, "Presidential Debates as Corporate Circus," *Bangor Daily News*, October 10, 2000, 1.
12. "Third Bush-Gore Debate Draws 37.6 Million Viewers," *Associated Press*, October 18, 2000.
13. William Carl, "Presidential Debate Shows Why Race Appears to be Tied," *Dallas Morning News*, October 5, 2000, 27A.
14. Monica Collins, "Television; Beat the Press; It's a Sad State of Affairs When 'SNL' Offers More Substance on the Candidates than TV Journalists," *Boston Herald*, November 7, 2000, 047.
15. H. Boedeker, "Comics' Election Coverage Tops TV News," *San Diego Tribune*, November 24, 2000, D7.
16. Pew Research Center, "Presidential Debate Clouds Voters' Choice," October 10, 2000. http://people-press.org/reports/display.php3?ReportID=30.
17. Collins, "Television; Beat the Press."
18. Burke: On Symbols and Society.

14

The Daily Show as the New Journalism
In Their Own Words

Dannagal Goldthwaite Young

When asked about the influence of his critically acclaimed, Emmy-winning comedy show, *The Daily Show* on Comedy Central, Jon Stewart's response is one of unequivocal denial. "We have no power," he stated in a *Newsday* interview. "I would say influence implies results [and] influence implies we have a platform. We don't. No platform. No agenda. No reason for being, other than to entertain ourselves."[1] "I would recommend that you look at the state of the world and you look at the state it would seem that we would like it to be in. And then you tell me if we have any influence," he stated in a *Time* magazine interview.[2] In *Rolling Stone* magazine, Stewart used irony to make his point, "I think we've changed the world dramatically. When we were picked up for broadcast by CNN International—I don't want to say a week later, but maybe two weeks later—the border between Pakistan and India stood down. Direct correlation? I don't know what else you can point to."[3]

Daily Show executive producer Ben Karlin has explained that conversations about *The Daily Show*'s cultural significance hinder the creative process. "When you're a part of something successful and meaningful, the rule book says don't try to analyze it too much or dissect it.... The one thing that you have control over is the content of the show."[4] "It's nice to be unselfconscious when you are working," states Karlin, "and not dealing with abstractions—like ratings or other statistics, which have meaning, but not in a way that positively contributes to the creative process."[5]

Yet, the importance of *The Daily Show* and its host became undeniable in early January 2005. It was then that new CNN president

Jonathan Klein announced that the "head-butting debate show" *Crossfire* would be cancelled.[6] In his reasons for the cancellation of the show, Klein cited the criticisms articulated by Jon Stewart in his infamous appearance as a guest on *Crossfire* in October 2004. That appearance, which circulated widely on the Internet, was a rare moment in which Stewart put aside his comedic persona and instead levied a serious critique of the argumentative program on the show's hosts, Tucker Carlson and Paul Begala. "You have a responsibility to the public discourse and you fail miserably," Stewart said. He asked them to "stop" what they were doing, arguing that the "partisan hackery" on their program was "hurting America." When Klein announced the cancellation of *Crossfire*, he told the *New York Times*, "I agree wholeheartedly with Jon Stewart's overall premise."[7]

Finally unable to ignore or deny his importance in the cancellation, Stewart acknowledged his part at the start of the next night's *Daily Show*. Feigning naiveté, he stated, "I had no idea that if you wanted a show canceled, all you had to do was say it out loud." Stewart's appearance on *Crossfire* and the program's subsequent cancellation confirmed what many journalists, scholars, and even fans already knew: while his influence on elections may be difficult to quantify, his influence on the state of contemporary journalism and emerging models of journalism is palpable.

In interviews with traditional journalists (in between jokes) Stewart has critiqued the state of contemporary journalism and outlined what emerging models of journalism *should* look like. Once assembled, his words describe precisely what *The Daily Show* is: a program that rejects the problematic norms of objectivity, drama, personalized and fragmented news, reacts to the game of politicians rather than embraces it, and stands outside the media pack commenting on the spectacle that the symbiotic relationship between media and politics has become.

Situating both Stewart's comments and *The Daily Show*'s content in the context of Murray Edelman's *Constructing the Political Spectacle*[8] and W. Lance Bennett's *News: The Politics of Illusion*,[9] this chapter outlines how *The Daily Show* serves as an alternative model of journalism—one that is hardly accidental, but a clear illustration of Stewart's specific criticisms of modern journalistic practices. The premise of these observations is consistent with that offered by Geoffrey Baym, that to describe *The Daily Show* as "fake news" is problematic—not only because it assumes some quantifiable distinction between what is "real" news and what is not, but also because it serves to downplay the significance of this important new model of journalism.[10]

Demystifying the Political Spectacle—
Jon Stewart's New Journalism

In an interview with *Rolling Stone*, Jon Stewart was asked what the media's role *should* be in covering politics.[11] In his response, he described Alexandra Pelosi's documentary *Journeys with George*, in which she followed George W. Bush throughout the 2000 presidential campaign with her handheld video camera while serving as a member of the press. In describing the documentary, Stewart articulated his vision of a new journalism that would expose the political spectacle for what it is—a theatrical performance largely orchestrated to advertise and maintain the status of political elites.

> What [*Journeys with George*] really does is, it exposes the media for what they are, which are spectators at a sales pitch. I mean, the most interesting camera shot in the whole thing is not the candidates, it's the pack. *That's what reporting should be. That person standing behind the pack, shooting the pack, that's got to be the new journalism* [emphasis added].[12]

Stewart's words echo the sentiments of Murray Edelman, who described contemporary news as a form of theater. According to Edelman, the spectacle that calls itself news does not reflect political reality, but is merely a construction—an outcome of the motives of politicians and news producers designed to mystify the public rather than enlighten them. Political actors use language and symbols to create a pseudo-reality that helps them maintain power. This construction of reality is then taken as real by news viewers.

Edelman offers several antidotes to remedy this contrived spectacle. Among them are art and counterdiscourses, two textual forms illustrated in the content of *The Daily Show*. According to Edelman, art serves as a potential solution to the problem of politics as spectacle because it rests outside of the symbiotic relationship between media and politics.

> Art is worth attention as an antidote to political mystification because works of art depend for their power upon properties that contrast revealingly with the characteristics of political language. Art helps counter banal political forms and so can be a liberating form of political expression.[13]

As *The Daily Show* is a program designed not to inform, but to entertain, by definition it rests outside of the traditional political realm. As such, the writers and producers of the show are not beholden to interests other than their own, except for the occasional consideration of the network. In addition, because the show makes use of the hyper-mediated digital environment, culling television, newspaper, and the Internet for preexisting material, it is not dependent on official or privileged "access" for its content. Hence the show does not operate under a fear of having that access denied. These factors work together to situate *The Daily Show* firmly outside the sphere of "banal political forms" and instead allow the writers and producers to undermine the norms of political language.

Executive producers Jon Stewart and Ben Karlin have stated that they see the program as situated outside of the sphere in which politics and news reside. "We are separate, we are peripheral, we're a sundae bar... we're reactive, and not actual news," Stewart stated on *Nightline*.[14] As explained by Karlin, they feel no sense of obligation to produce the show in a particular way and do not feel that the program is a public trust.

> I am writing for myself, insofar as the only way I can write something funny is if I think it's funny—not if others will.... Our show is not a public trust. We are responsible to no one but ourselves and the network. I feel an equal measure of pride if I think something is good and no one else does, as I do if something I am a part of is universally beloved.[15]

A second remedy proposed by Edelman is the proposition that "a potential for liberation from political texts and their rootedness in the present lies in the refusal to see any text or any form of discourse as paramount or essential."[16] An example of this is what Edelman refers to as counterdiscourses: "texts that challenge hegemony by undermining its presuppositions and offering alternatives."[17] Stewart's notion of a new journalism that is "behind the pack, shooting the pack" is an example of a text that would undermine the assumption that political reality is what comes through the news camera.

In his discussion with Ted Koppel, Stewart revealed the tension that exists between contemporary journalism and Stewart's ideal model. After Stewart described presidential campaign coverage as a "product launch," Koppel and Stewart debated the existence of a political reality beyond the spectacle.

Koppel: You know, back 40 years ago, we would actually come to these [campaign] events in the expectation that unexpected things were going to happen.

Stewart: But unexpected things used to happen in the world. They don't happen anymore.

Koppel: Oh, sure they do.

Stewart: Very rarely. Very rarely is an event not parsed prior to when it happens. And when it does happen unexpectedly, it's only because the speculation was off cue.

Not only does Stewart offer critiques of journalism when interviewed, but in his work with *The Daily Show*, he illustrates through satire and irony the harm posed by modern news norms. The show challenges the normative assumptions governing journalistic practices and offers a functional alternative. As Baym observes, "Ultimately, it is this disinterest in fact, the construction of televisual spectacle at the expense of understanding, for which the parody pieces [on *The Daily Show*] most criticize mainstream television news."[18] By deconstructing the norms that journalists and viewers generally consider necessary and real, the satirical segments on *The Daily Show* contrast "what is with what ought to be," thereby encouraging us to consider something different—something better.

Jon Stewart versus the Objectivity Trap

One of the central tenets of Jon Stewart's public criticisms of news concerns the legitimacy and value of neutrality and objectivity. In the interview with Ted Koppel, Stewart described how contemporary journalism's norm of objectivity does a disservice to public debate by fostering discourse that fails to substantively engage the issue or push the two sides beyond their talking points. Stewart illustrated, through role-playing, a typical political debate show.

She throws out her figures from the Heritage Foundation and she throws her figures from the Brookings Institute, and the anchor, who should be the arbiter of the truth says, "Thank you both very much. That was really interesting." No, it wasn't! That was Coke and Pepsi talking about beverage truth. And that game is what has, I think, caused people to go, "I'm not watching this."[19]

Here Stewart explicitly rejects the premise that the journalist's role is to present opposing sets of facts from official sources. Instead, he argues that ignoring the underlying truth-value of those "facts" denies viewers an important critical analysis of political life and that instead, the journalist should act as an "arbiter of the truth."

> *Koppel:* Those who watch you say at least when I'm watching Jon, he can use humor to say, "BS." You know, "That's a crock."
> *Stewart:* But that's always been the case.
> *Koppel:* Okay, but I can't do that.
> *Stewart:* No. But you *can* say that's BS. You don't need humor to do it, because you have what I wish I had—which is credibility, and gravitas. This is interesting stuff. And it's all part of the discussion, and I think it's a good discussion to have, but I also think that it's important to take a more critical look. Don't you think?
>
> *Ted Koppel:* No.[20]

Stewart is certainly not the first to raise doubts about whether objectivity in reporting is a tenable or even desirable goal, but he may be among the first to bring this argument into the news itself. David Mindich defined the central elements of objectivity as journalist detachment, nonpartisanship, the reliance on facts, and balance in both number of sources and time allotted to both sides.[21] Many scholars have argued that objectivity in journalism is simply not possible. John Merrill, for example, echoed the sentiments of Walter Lippman (1922) when he argued that objectivity in journalism is unattainable due to the fact that journalism requires selectivity in topics, sources, facts, and details.[22] Others, like Donald McDonald, suggest that the pressures of the newsroom and the ownership of the news-making enterprise conspire to make objectivity impossible to achieve.[23]

Scholars have also explored how objectivity is not necessarily desirable in the production of news. Gaye Tuchman's research illustrated that objectivity in the newsroom was often used strategically to help protect and advance the status of journalists.[24] Mindich explored how the need to balance one side of the story with another can equalize the legitimacy of arguments that are clearly indefensible.[25] Edward Herman and Noam Chomsky argued that objectivity served to maintain the status quo, favoring elite sources and weighting the arguments in favor of those in positions of power.[26]

While the objectivity norm came under fire after McCarthy-ism for failing the public, some argue that no alternative model has emerged to fill the void.[27] In an effort to appeal to as wide of an audience as possible, most news media still prefer to embrace neutrality. And most often, this means taking each side's arguments at face value rather than challenging their underlying truth.

At a Newhouse School forum that aired on C-SPAN in October 2004, Stewart explained that the news media have an obligation to the public that includes abandoning this "objective" approach in favor of coverage that challenges talking points.

> I think there is a responsibility within the media to help. You could create a paradigm of a media organization that is geared towards no bullshit—and do it actively—and stop pretending that we don't know what's going on. And stop pretending that it's a right/left question. I don't buy that the world is divided into bi-chromatic thought like that.[28]

While Stewart's non-humorous comments reveal why he sees the norm of objectivity as a problem, the satirical segments on the show illustrate how problematic objectivity can be. In a segment about the media coverage of the Swiftboat Veterans for Truth allegations about John Kerry's service in Vietnam, Jon Stewart asked comedian-correspondent Rob Corrdry about the role of the journalist in reporting and examining contradictory claims.

> *Stewart:* Here's what puzzles me most, Rob. John Kerry's record in Vietnam is pretty much right there in the official records of the U.S. military and hasn't been disputed over the past 35 years.
>
> *Corrdry:* That's right Jon—and that's certainly the spin you'll be hearing from the Kerry campaign over the next several days.
>
> *Stewart:* That's not a spin thing. That's a fact—it's established.
>
> *Corrdry:* Exactly, Jon, and that established incontrovertible fact is one side of the story.
>
> *Stewart:* That's the end of the story! I mean you've seen the records, haven't you? What's your opinion?
>
> *Corrdry:* I'm sorry, my "opinion"? I don't have "O-pinions" [air quotes]. I'm a reporter, Jon. My job is to spend half the time repeating what one side says and half the time repeating the other. Little thing called objectivity—might want to look it up someday.
>
> *Stewart:* [Incredulous] Doesn't objectivity mean objectively weighing the evidence and calling out what's credible and what isn't credible?

> *Corrdry*: Whoah! Well well well! Looks like someone wants the media
> to act as a filter. [In high-pitched, mocking tone] "Oooh! This
> claim is spurious! Upon investigation this claim lacks any
> basis in reality! [grabbing his nipples] Mmm Mmmm!" Listen
> buddy—not my job to stand between the people talking to me
> and the people listening to me.
> *Stewart*: So, basically you're saying that this back and forth is never
> going to end.
> *Corrdry*: No, Jon. In fact, a new group has emerged. This one composed
> of former Bush colleagues challenging the president's activities
> during the Vietnam era. That group—Drunken Stateside Sons
> of Privilege for Plausible Deniability. They've apparently got
> some things to say about a certain Halloween party in '71 that
> involved trash can punch and a sodomized piñata. Jon, they
> just want to set the record straight. That's all they're out for.[29]

As illustrated in this segment, the practice of objectivity encourages
journalists to give equal weight to all sides, regardless of their merit.
In exaggerated terms, this means that interest groups can inject any
falsehood into the public discourse simply through the process of
allegation. If journalists do not challenge the underlying truth-value
of those claims, then making allegations—no matter how false—
becomes as good as fact.

Stewart later discussed this issue in a *Daily Show* interview with
cable talk show host Chris Matthews in September 2004. He asked
Matthews about the factors inhibiting journalists from pushing public officials beyond their talking points.

> Why is it so hard in this day and age for people such as yourself to ques-
> tion politicians—[Is it] because they're so unaccustomed to it?... It hap-
> pens so infrequently, they don't know what to do?... Can the press then
> maybe take a stronger stand and—what's the word I'm looking for—fact
> check?... Are you worried if you question their talking points, there goes
> your access? You're cut off? You're blackballed?[30]

Stewart followed up with a description of the kind of exchange that
he would like to see. "I think it should be nonpartisan—Democrat,
Republican. Everyone should be questioned on these stupid...talk-
ing points. We should be able to have a normal conversation."

I would argue that this "normal conversation" that Stewart thinks
should exist in the news is one that he has tried to initiate during
the interview segment of *The Daily Show*. Illustrating how objectivity might be overcome, Stewart's interviews offer an alternative in

which truth is assessed and neutrality is abandoned in favor of critical analysis. As Baym points out, "if the insistence on objectivity too easily can become amplification, *The Daily Show* instead engages in subjective interrogation."[31]

One of the clearest, and perhaps most uncomfortable, examples of Stewart's attempt to initiate such a conversation occurred during the August 2, 2004, interview with Republican representative Henry Bonilla. Even executive producer Ben Karlin has admitted that "Representative Henry Bonilla from Texas probably had the least clue [of any guest] of where the hell he was and what the hell he was doing on our show."[32] Unfortunately for Bonilla, who was unfamiliar with the program, he was unaware of Stewart's recent criticism of the influence of partisan "talking points." Only two weeks prior, Stewart had taken up the issue of the pervasiveness of "talking points," illustrating through a montage dozens of Republicans on various news shows reciting, "John Kerry and John Edwards are the first and fourth most liberal Senators in the U.S. Senate"—each one unchallenged by journalists. That segment closed with Stewart's observation: "Talking points—they're true because they're said a lot."

Stewart asked Representative Bonilla, who also served as an RNC Rapid Response team member during the 2004 election, about the source of the "first and fourth most liberal senators" statistic. What followed was a five-minute exchange in which Stewart repeatedly asked about the statistic's source and Bonilla repeatedly attributed the statistic to various "groups" from both the left and the right. Finally Stewart ended the evasive Q&A stating, "Okay, I'll tell you who it is. It's actually called the *National Journal*." Stewart's comments also led Bonilla to admit that the statistics regarding the senators' rankings were not compiled over their entire careers, as the talking points would imply, but rather referred to individual years.[33] In response to his frustration that this particular talking point was going unchallenged by journalists, Stewart used his interview segment as an opportunity to challenge it himself.

An interview with NBC *Nightly News* anchor Brian Williams on *The Daily Show* just after Hurricane Katrina illustrates the contrast between the news norms that embrace objectivity and an alternative model that assessed the truth-value of a given claim. Replying to Stewart's question about the responsibility of local, state, and federal officials for the aftermath of Hurricane Katrina, Brain Williams simply responded, "I'm going to let that one go—I don't do opinions," to which Jon quickly retorted, "I do. I've got one." Stewart then offered pointed criticism of the pattern of response offered by the Bush administration.

When Stewart concluded his critique and asked Williams for input, Williams cautiously cited an observation from people he had met in New Orleans, "How could this happen here?" Williams then referred to "the other refrain" he had heard while in New Orleans, that had this tragedy struck Nantucket, Boston, Chicago, Cleveland, Miami, or Los Angeles, the response would have been different.[34] Williams was able to subtly introduce the issues of class and race, simply by attributing opinions not to himself, but to others. The contrast between the two opposing approaches, the journalist trained to cite only the opinions of others, and Stewart unapologetically offering his own critique, was striking.

Bennett's Content Biases a la Stewart

While Stewart might not wish to be academic in his critique of the media, his public statements and the content of *The Daily Show* illustrate some of the most problematic aspects of news coverage outlined by Lance Bennett in the popular text *News: The Politics of Illusion*. Political communication scholars have long discussed the question of media bias. Bennett argues that the concern over ideological biases (liberal vs. conservative) diverts our attention away from the more pervasive and problematic biases in the news: biases of content. Among the content biases Bennett outlines are personalization, dramatization, and fragmentation. Discussing the news bias of personalization, Bennett writes, "If there is a single most important flaw in the American news style, it is the overwhelming tendency to downplay the big social, economic, or political picture in favor of the human trials, tragedies, and triumphs that sit at the surface of events."[35] Related to this tendency to embrace stories about people and neglect complex issues is the problem of dramatization, the tendency to emphasize emotional stories that grab viewers' attention. According to Bennett, this bias toward the dramatic results in less coverage of complex policy information vital for an informed electorate. Finally, fragmentation can be seen as an extension, or an outcome, of dramatization and personalization. Here the media fragment the news into separate unrelated narratives that are not contextualized for the viewer to make sense of the world. Taken together, these biases result in news coverage that is sensationalist, highlights emotionally compelling stories about people, ignores complex issues of public policy, and leaves each news story floating in space with no connection to larger issues or its relevance in the world.[36]

Each of these biases is largely an outcome of production routines, constraints of time and money, and an underlying economic pressure to make a profit—particularly in the case of television news. Fitting stories into larger contexts, taking time to explain issues and relate them to economics, history, or sociology, and investigating issues beyond mere events all require time, money, and brain power. While Bennett refers to these as content biases resulting from economic pressures and subsequent production routines, Stewart goes one step further, stating unequivocally, "The bias of the media is not liberal—it's lazy. It's sensationalist. But it's not liberal."[37]

The satirical segments on *The Daily Show* use irony to illustrate these "lazy" content biases. As literary scholar Dustin Griffin argues, "The business of the satirist is to insist on the sharp differences between vice and virtue, between good and bad, between what man *is,* and what he *ought to be.*"[38] Or, in the words of Edward and Lilian Bloom, satire "weeps, scolds, and ridicules, generally with one major end in view: to plead with man for a return to his moral senses."[39] By juxtaposing actual news footage with Stewart's own comments, *The Daily Show* uses irony to reveal the gap "between the real and the ideal, between what is and ought to be."[40]

The *Daily Show*'s Deconstruction of Personalization, Fragmentation, and Dramatization

In the October 13, 2004, presidential debate between John Kerry and George W. Bush, Kerry made a statement that dominated headlines in the days after. When asked, "Do you believe homosexuality is a choice?" Kerry replied, "We're all God's children. And I think if you were to talk to Dick Cheney's daughter, who is a lesbian, she would tell you that she's being who she was, she's being who she was born as." The statement was widely criticized by Bush supporters as a political trick and soon the topic of Mary Cheney's sexuality overtook the airwaves. Pointing out the media's obsession with dramatic sensationalized stories about people instead of issues, Stewart used irony to expose the content bias. In a confident and didactic tone, Stewart introduced the program's headlines.

> So now the debates are over, both candidates have staked out their positions on domestic policy, the war on Iraq, the war on terror, and the media can finally help the American people focus in on the important issues that will help them make an informed decision on their choice for president.[41]

The program then cut to nine different clips from news sources ranging from NBC to FOX to CNN, including such well-known newspeople as Wolf Blitzer, Katie Couric, Judy Woodruff, Bill O'Reilly, and Jack Cafferty. In each clip, the reporter referred to Mary Cheney's "sexuality," her being "gay" or a "lesbian." Taken together, in rapid succession, the banality of the topic becomes clear. Mary Cheney's sexuality is not an issue that will "help the American people make an informed decision on their choice for president." Instead, it represents the dysfunctional press bias toward the personal and the dramatic.

Once the camera cut back to Stewart after the montage of news clips, Stewart looked into the camera and pleaded, "Media good! No criticism. Media good! [pointing to himself] Funny monkey! Funny Funny Monkey!"—a direct allusion to his appearance on *Crossfire* in which he criticized the show and told Tucker Carlson that he would not be funny and that he wasn't going to "be his monkey."

Another explicit example of *The Daily Show*'s criticism of mainstream media's affection for the sensational aired just prior to the U.S.'s deadline for Saddam Hussein to comply with U.S. demands. Stewart addressed the overly dramatic coverage of the twenty-four-hour cable news channels by framing it as a contest.

> Which one of these 24-hour news networks has best exploited our emotional vulnerability so far? Let's look at the nominees: [cut to clip from CNN] CNN for its crazy "Showdown" graphic? [cut to clip from Fox] Fox News for its "Terror alert status" warning? (It's high, folks!) [cut back to Stewart] Fine work by both, but there can only be one winner...and the award for most useless news channel dramatic war graphic goes to...the least watched of all the news channels!—MSNBC for its scintillating "Deadline" graphic! [cut to clip of MSNBC with the countdown to the deadline].... [under his breath] ...idiots.[42]

When the camera returned to Stewart, he did his impersonation of a show business executive with finger in the air, gravelly voiced: "Now *that's* sensationalism!" The mock content followed by his showbiz comment satirized how news executives appear to be producing a product designed to entertain and titillate rather than inform.

Finally, a December 2003 episode tackled the issue of press dramatization and the extremes to which newsmakers go to fill the large twenty-four-hour news hole. In mid-December 2003, U.S. soldiers found Saddam Hussein hiding in the bottom of a hole in the ground in a town outside of Tikrit. The press swarmed around the story, particularly the dramatic element of the small dark hole dug in the ground—the ideal subject for *The Daily Show*'s ironic criticism.

> The capture of Saddam Hussein was obviously a huge story, but here's the problem from the point of view of the 24-hour cable news standpoint: it's only one story. It happened and now it's no longer happening. There's still 24 hours to fill. So how are you going to do it?
>
> Well... [cut to various computer models shown on CNN and Fox] 48 hours of nonstop computer simulations that boil down the concept of "guy in hole" to something even the layman can understand. But computers are so cold, impersonal, so... accurate. [Cut back to Stewart] Is there some theatrical cheesy, low budget perhaps way of doing this—ah yes... MSNBC [cut to MSNBC clip of female reporter in high heels and a suit standing in and then crawling down *into* a plywood model of a Saddam's "spiderhole"].[43]

And in an illustration of why Stewart's job must sometimes seem easy, the camera cut back to Stewart who simply placed his face in his hands and shook his head. No words were needed. The content itself was satire.

Illustrating Stewart's criticism of the news' bias toward fragmentation, several *Daily Show* segments have criticized the excessively fragmented nature of CNN's program *The Situation Room*. According to its Web site, *The Situation Room* with Wolf Blitzer is a news program "modeled on the White House Situation Room... which combines traditional reporting methods with the newest innovative online resources, making the entire process of newsgathering more transparent and placing the latest news and information at the viewers' fingertips." The show features its host standing in front of a series of television screens monitoring various events in real time. Blitzer then sends off to correspondents in the different locations for updates during the show.

Stewart does not hide his contempt for the program and the lack of context provided by the format. "You know what the situation room is?" he rhetorically asked Chris Wallace in a *Daily Show* interview. "The guy [Blitzer] got a satellite dish. That's all it is." While covering a story about a woman whose baby was barred from boarding a flight because of safety checks, Stewart cut to footage from *The Situation Room* in which the mother was being interviewed by Wolf Blitzer with a squirming, complaining baby on her lap. Stewart then translated the baby's gibberish for the audience, "It hurts me! Being in *The Situation Room* hurts me! It's too much information that seems like non-sequiturs!"

Indexing: Stewart Comes to Sharpton's Defense

In addition to objectivity and the content biases of personalization, dramatization, and fragmentation, Bennett addresses the problem of the press marginalizing points of view that are not mainstream—a topic that has also been addressed in the content of *The Daily Show*. Bennett's "indexing hypothesis" posits that due to press reliance on official government sources, the range of opinions that appear in the news mirrors those of elites. This reliance on official and elite sources does not make room for opinions in the margins. According to Bennett, indexing refers to "the journalistic practice of opening or closing the news gates to citizen activists (and more generally, a broader range of views) depending on levels of conflict or political difference among public officials and established interests with the capacity to influence decisions about the issue in question."[44] The indexing hypothesis has been examined extensively, and has proved difficult to test or define clearly. However, *The Daily Show* has succeeded in illustrating a form of indexing at work.

During *The Daily Show*'s coverage of the 2004 Democratic National Convention in Boston, Reverend Al Sharpton gave a speech that had not been approved by the Democratic National Committee. *The Daily Show* aired a segment that highlighted how uncomfortable journalists and pundits were with Sharpton's unplanned comments and how quickly they collectively acted to marginalize his sentiments, cutting him off and reporting on his statements as though they constituted an incoherent stream of nonsense.

Stewart's report on Sharpton's speech acknowledged that his speech had some "zingers." Yet the segment also illustrated how Sharpton's speech was, in fact, substantive, cutting to his statement concerning what conservative judges would have done to the civil rights movement: "I suggest to you tonight that if George Bush had selected the court in '54, Clarence Thomas would have never got to law school."

Again contrasting what is with what ought to be, Stewart prefaced journalists' outraged responses by saying, "Al Sharpton's speech was clearly the oratorical highlight of the convention so far and it no doubt made the pundits happy to finally have themselves some unscripted excitement." The montage that followed included such commentators as Bob Novak, Doris Kearns Goodwin, Bill O'Reilly, Judy Woodruff, Wolf Blitzer, and Howard Fineman, all challenging the appropriateness of Sharpton's remarks and, more simply—casting Sharpton and his sentiments aside as irrelevant and even offensive.

O'Reilly: "That's our pal Al Sharpton, doing what Al does."
Blitzer: "He wound up speaking for about 20 minutes."
Kearns Goodwin: "It's grating. You can't bear to listen to it."
Novak: "He's…he's a nasty man."
Woodruff: "Al Sharpton just hijacked this convention."
Guest of Bill O'Reilly: "He still has never held a job."
Fineman: "He could actually *turn off* the black vote."

The segment ended with an interview between Brian Williams (a frequent guest of Stewart) and Al Sharpton.

Williams: Reverend Sharpton, from my vantage point here on the podium, I was able to look over your shoulder at that TelePromTer that just sat there for what seemed like a half hour while you did a riff on whatever you did a riff on.
Stewart: [Incredulous] Riff on whatever you did a riff on?? *You were there!* Yeah, what, what was Al Sharpton scattin' about?[45]

At that point the segment cut back to Sharpton saying, "Our vote was soaked in the blood of martyrs! Soaked in the blood of Goodman, Chaney, and Schwerner! Soaked in the blood of four little girls from Birmingham! This vote is sacred to us!"

This segment reveals how journalists often operate as a pack, marginalizing points of view that fall outside of the established range of acceptable opinion. Sharpton's actual words, while colorful and theatrical, did indeed include substantive critiques of the Bush administration and Republican policies that affect African Americans. These statements juxtaposed with critiques of journalists and pundits made the latter seem reactionary and even petty.

The Daily Show as the New Journalism

While Jon Stewart may want to appear "peripheral" in a way that mini-mizes the appearance of any substantive influence of *The Daily Show*, his location on the periphery may be just the weapon needed to undermine the political spectacle of modern political news. In the rare moments when Stewart has spoken seriously about his thoughts on the press, he has articulated his vision of what journalists *ought* to be doing. That vision includes abandoning objectivity in favor of reporting that chal-lenges the underlying truth-value of the claims of public officials and elites—something that Stewart does during the interview segment of *The Daily Show*. It also includes raising the curtain to reveal the political spectacle in action ("being behind the pack, shooting the pack")—some-thing that the satirical segments of *The Daily Show* do by design.

The fact that these two main tenets of Stewart's criticism of the press are both remedied in the interviews and satirical segments of the show reveals how *The Daily Show* serves as an example of Edelman's (1988) concept of a counterdiscourse as it illustrates a "text that challenges hegemony by undermining its presuppositions and offering alternatives." While Stewart's self-prescribed status as "peripheral" may enable him to demystify the political spectacle, it would be a mistake to dismiss *The Daily Show* as irrelevant due to its lack of formal political legitimacy. Ironically, without the protection offered by its "fake news" label, *The Daily Show* would be unable to play its self-prescribed role as an outsider mocking the political spec-tacle, yet scholars studying *The Daily Show* should be careful to use the "fake news" label accompanied by the same wink and nod that Stewart offers his audience.

Limitations of *The Daily Show*

Before suggesting that *The Daily Show* is the panacea to the deficits of modern political news, the limitations of the show must be acknowl-edged. First and most simply, it is not viewed by enough people (less than 5 percent of the American population) to influence individual opinions or attitudes in a way that would constitute a societal trend. However, among that young, educated, politically sophisticated minority[46] are journalists, politicians, and other young elites who render *The Daily Show* important because of its potential impact on *them* and their likely status as opinion leaders in certain circles. Second, because of Stewart's status as a jester, when he does step outside of his role as comedian, some find it inappropriate—a reaction that could undermine his influence. For example, following his serious appearance on *Crossfire* in which he criticized the program and its format, some were uncomfortable with his abandonment of his comedic role, arguing that he cannot claim to be "just a comedian" and then seriously attack journalists for failing at their jobs.

Third, while Stewart has articulated what journalism *ought* to be and *The Daily Show* often illustrates a new model, it does not always succeed. After his interview with John Kerry, Stewart came under fire for not being tough enough on the Democratic candidate. Stewart acknowledged his overly cautious treatment of Kerry in later comments, stating, "I honestly think it was my discomfort at wanting to be funny....I think I could have been more forthright with him and still done the type of interview that I normally do."[47] Yet, at the same time, the host rejects the contention that *The Daily Show* ought to conform to any semblance of news standards.

> Ultimately I'm judged on whether or not the show is funny. If people get a certain insight from the comedy, that's wonderful, because we're trying to do jokes about things we care about and certainly our point of view is inherent in it. But the idea that somehow we fail when we don't live up to journalistic expectations is a misreading of what it is we're doing.[48]

Finally, it is important to understand what *The Daily Show* does not explicitly discuss when criticizing the flaws of modern journalism. According to Bennett and countless other political communication scholars, at the heart of the problem of the content biases plaguing modern journalism are news economics. While Stewart does critique professional news norms, he does not explicitly discuss the institutional processes that foster those norms. He doesn't talk about the market pressures that are largely responsible for the problematic aspects of journalism that he disdains. Of course, if faced with this criticism, Stewart could again reply that such a critique is "a misreading [of] what it is [we are] doing," and that it is not *his* responsibility to discuss the root of modern journalism's failures.

Despite these limitations, content on *The Daily Show* offers an alternative journalistic model, one that undermines the norms of journalism while simultaneously offering something different—something better. Whether or not this will influence the direction of contemporary journalism depends on where young people turn for political information in the future. If they increasingly turn to the Internet, blogs, and shows like *The Daily Show* for their understanding of politics, it may suggest that journalism in its current form does not resonate with them. In this case, it would behoove journalists to reconsider the norms they assume to be absolute—norms like objectivity, narrative, personalization, and drama.

Notes

1. Verne Gay, "Not Necessarily the News; Meet the Players Who Will Influence Coverage of the 2004 Campaign; You Might Be Surprised," *Newsday*, January 14, 2004, B6.
2. "Ten Questions for Jon Stewart," *Time*, September 27, 2004, 8.
3. John Colapinto, "The Most Trusted Name in News," *Rolling Stone*, October 28, 2004, 58–64.
4. Thomas Goetz, "Reinventing Television," *Wired*, September 2005, 102–105.
5. Personal correspondence with *The Daily Show* executive producer Ben Karlin, May 2004.
6. Bill Carter, "CNN Will Cancel 'Crossfire' and Cut Ties to Commentator," *New York Times*, January 6, 2005, C1.
7. Ibid.
8. Murray Edelman, *Constructing the Political Spectacle* (Chicago: University of Chicago Press, 1988).
9. W. Lance Bennett, *News: The Politics of Illusion*, 5th ed. (New York: Longman, 2003).
10. Geoffrey Baym, "The Daily Show: Discursive Integration and the Reinvention of Political Journalism," *Political Communication* 22 (2005): 259–276.
11. Tom Nawrocki, "Faking the News," *Rolling Stone*, June 26, 2003, 35–38.
12. Ibid., 38.
13. Edelman, *Constructing the Political Spectacle*, 126.
14. *Nightline*, ABC, July 28, 2004.
15. Personal correspondence with *The Daily Show* executive producer Ben Karlin, May 2004.
16. Edelman, *Constructing the Political Spectacle*, 128.
17. Ibid.,129.
18. Baym "The Daily Show."
19. *Nightline*.
20. Ibid.

21. David Mindich, *Just the Facts: How "Objectivity" Came to Define American Journalism* (New York: New York University Press, 1998).

22. John C. Merrill, "Journalistic Objectivity Is Not Possible," in *Basic Issues in Mass Communication*, eds. John C. Merrill and Everett Dennis (New York: Macmillan, 1984), 104–110.

23. Donald McDonald, "Is Objectivity Possible?," *Center Magazine* (September/October 1971): 29–43.

24. Gaye Tuchman, "Objectivity as Strategic Ritual: An Examination of Newsmen's Notions of Objectivity," *American Journal of Sociology* 77 (1972): 660–679.

25. Mindich, *Just the Facts*.

26. Edward S. Herman and Noam Chomsky, *Manufacturing Consent: The Political Economy of the Mass Media* (New York: Pantheon, 1988).

27. Brent Cunningham, "Rethinking Objectivity," *Columbia Journalism Review* 4 (2003).

28. C-SPAN, *Newhouse School Forum with Jon Stewart*, October 14, 2004.

29. Jon Stewart and Ben Karlin (executive producers), *The Daily Show*, August 23, 2004.

30. Ibid., 2004.

31. Baym, "The Daily Show."

32. The *Washington Post*, "The Daily Show," online discussion with executive producer Ben Karlin, washingtonpost.com, September 24, 2004. http://www.washingtonpost.com/wp-dyn/articles/A39427-2004Sep21.html.

33. Stewart and Karlin, *The Daily Show*, August 2, 2004.

34. Ibid., September 8, 2005.

35. Bennett, *News: The Politics of Illusion*, 45.

36. Ibid.

37. C-SPAN, *Newhouse School Forum with Jon Stewart*.

38. Dustin Griffin, *Satire: A Critical Reintroduction* (Lexington: The University Press of Kentucky, 1994), 36.

39. Edward A. Bloom and Lilian D. Bloom, *Satire's Persuasive Voice* (Ithaca, NY: Cornell University Press, 1979), 38.

40. Henri Bergson, "Laughter," in *Comedy*, ed. George Meredith (New York: Doubleday Anchor Books, 1956), 127.

41. Stewart and Karlin, *The Daily Show*, October 18, 2004.

42. Ibid., March 17, 2003.

43. Ibid., December 16, 2003.

44. Bennett, *News: The Politics of Illusion*, 4.

45. Stewart and Karlin, *The Daily Show*, July 28, 2004.

46. "DailyShowViewersKnowledgeableAboutPresidentialCampaign," *Annenberg Public Policy Center*, September 21, 2004. http://www.annenbergpublicpolicycenter.org/naes/2004_03_late-night-knowledge-2_9-21_pr.pdf

47. Colapinto, "The Most Trusted Name in News," 58–64.

48. Ibid., 64.

IV

Does It Really Matter? The Effects of Late Night Televised Humor

15

Late Night Comedy Television Shows as News Sources
What the Polls Say

Paul Brewer and Xiaoxia Cao

Today, the conventional wisdom in the popular media casts shows such as *The Tonight Show, The Late Show, The Daily Show,* and *Saturday Night Live* as key sources of political information for Americans in general and young people in particular. Some observers find this notion "a troubling thought" because they regard late night comedy as a "poor substitute" for more traditional news.[1] Others disagree, arguing that late night comedy provides "an important link between a cynical nation and its government, and, in the process, a viable alternative to traditional news outlets."[2] With this debate in mind, we present a closer look at what Americans have told pollsters about late night comedy on television—how much they watch it, what they think about it, and whether they learn about politics from it.

Late Night Comedy Shows as Soft News Sources

In the past few years, media and politics scholars have begun to pay more attention to what Matthew Baum, among others, has called "soft news" sources—that is, the wide range of media that focuses on entertaining content rather than on public policy content.[3] A variety of late night comedy programs fit this definition, including talk shows (e.g., *The Tonight Show, The Late Show*), sketch comedy shows (e.g., *Saturday Night Live,* [SNL]), and other sorts of programs (e.g., *The Daily Show,* with its mock news format).

As both Baum[4] and Markus Prior[5] have shown, people watch soft news programs primarily for their entertainment value rather than their news value. Nevertheless, late night political comedy shows often contain political content. For example, the hosts of late night shows target politicians with numerous jokes. David Niven, S. Robert Lichter, and Daniel Amundson's content analysis of *The Tonight Show*, *The Late Show*, *Late Night*, and *Politically Incorrect* tallied 13,301 jokes about political figures from 1996 to 2000 (with President Bill Clinton bearing the brunt of more jokes than any other target).[6] Similarly, an Annenberg Public Policy Center content analysis found over 500 political jokes in the monologues on *The Tonight Show*, *The Late Show*, and *The Daily Show* during just one month of the 2004 presidential campaign.[7] For their part, late night sketch comedies often parody politicians; in 2000, Al Gore's campaign aides even used a tape of *SNL*'s parody of the first presidential debate to show the candidate what not to do in the next debate.[8] Last, but not least, numerous figures from the world of politics have been guests on late night talk shows or hosted *SNL*.

Watching Late Night Comedy Shows

To what extent does the public follow late night political comedy? In answering this question, we begin with 1992, a transitional year in both American politics and late night television: Bill Clinton defeated President George H. W. Bush, and *Tonight Show* host Johnny Carson retired, setting off a succession struggle between frequent guest host Jay Leno and *Late Night* host David Letterman. The Pew Research Center's April/May 1992 survey asked how often respondents watched six different late night comedians or comedy programs: "Regularly, sometimes, hardly ever, or never." Judging by the results, one of the most popular of these was Arsenio Hall: 35 percent of the respondents said that they watched him regularly or sometimes (this was not long before Bill Clinton famously played his saxophone on Hall's show). At 33 percent, *Saturday Night Live* rivaled Hall's show in popularity. Johnny Carson was close behind at 30 percent, but only 21 percent of the respondents said that they regularly or sometimes watched Leno, Carson's eventual successor; a roughly similar percentage (24 percent) said the same of Letterman. At 9 percent, Dennis Miller clearly had the smallest audience.

Between 1992 and 1996, the late night comedy landscape shifted considerably. Leno assumed the throne of *The Tonight Show*, Letterman bolted to another network to host *The Late Show* in 1993, and Conan O'Brien replaced Letterman on *Late Night*; *The Arsenio Hall Show* was cancelled; Bill Maher's *Politically Incorrect* and Craig Kilbourn's *The Daily Show* launched on Comedy Central (in 1994 and 1996, respectively). After all these changes had taken place—and as the 1996 presidential election was under way—CBS News and the *New York Times* sponsored four polls (in July, September, early October, and late October) that each included the question, "How often do you watch any of the late night comedians like Jay Leno, David Letterman, and Conan O'Brien: Frequently, sometimes, hardly ever, or never?" Taken together, the late night comedians had a sizable audience: the percentages saying "frequently" ranged from 10 to 14 percent and the percentages saying "sometimes" ranged from 20 to 25 percent.

Six years later, Leno, Letterman, and O'Brien all remained in place. In the meantime, *Politically Incorrect* had moved to ABC in 1997 only to be cancelled in 2002 (as we discuss in more depth below), and Jon Stewart had replaced Kilbourn as the host of *The Daily Show*. In an April 2002 poll, the Pew Research Center asked respondents how often they watched "late night TV shows such as *David Letterman* and *Jay Leno*: Regularly, sometimes, hardly ever, or never." Of the interviewees, 12 percent said that they regularly watched such shows, and 22 percent said that they did so sometimes. In a survey conducted two years later, the distribution of responses was virtually identical. A comparison to the CBS News/*New York Times* results from 1996, then, suggests that the audience for late night comedy shows in general was quite consistent in size for at least an eight-year span. The two Pew Research Center surveys also included a question asking how often respondents watched *The Daily Show*. In April 2002, 2 percent said that they did so regularly and 10 percent said that they did so sometimes; in April/May 2006, the percentages were 6 and 15 percent, respectively. Thus, the audience for *The Daily Show* was small in comparison to the overall late night comedy audience.

Public Opinion about Late Night Comedy Shows and Comedians

Polls conducted over the past decade and a half have included a number of questions assessing public opinion about late night comedy shows and comedians; we could only find one, however, that asked people their opinions about who had the funniest political jokes. The Pew Research Center's April/May 1992 survey included the following question: "Which one of the late night comedians or comedy shows has the best political humor this year—the best jokes about the presidential candidates and the campaign?" Of the six options listed, Johnny Carson—named by 18 percent of the respondents— was the clear winner. Nor was this surprising, for reasons described by Joe Urschel.

> For decades, Johnny Carson was the primary source of political humor on TV, and he helped set the rules with his conduct. He made an effort to apply some kind of equal-time provision with his humor—for every Republican blast, there was one at the Democrats with equal intensity. Anything nasty or personal was rare.[9] Arsenio Hall (12%) and *Saturday Night Live* (10%) had their advocates as well, whereas Leno (7%), Letterman (4%), and Miller (3%) were all far behind in Pew's poll.

Dana Carvey's impersonation of President George H. W. Bush (highlighted by the catchphrase "wouldn't be prudent") was undoubtedly one of *Saturday Night Live*'s most popular pieces of political humor that year; indeed, a CBS News poll conducted in October 1992 found that almost half of the respondents (48 percent) had seen Carvey's impersonation. This survey also included the following question: "Some people say that comedians who impersonate the president— like Dana Carvey on *Saturday Night Live*—are hurting the chances of George Bush being re-elected. Do you think that is true or don't you think so?" Respondents were skeptical about the impact of such humor on Bush's political fortunes: only 14 percent said "true," whereas 70 percent said "not true."[10]

A variety of polls from the past few years have asked respondents to evaluate specific late night comedians; taken as a whole, the results indicate that when Americans know enough to offer an opinion, they tend to view late night comedians in a positive light. A March 2002 Gallup poll, for example, measured whether respondents viewed Jay Leno and David Letterman favorably or unfavorably. Letterman may have lost *The Tonight Show* to Leno, but he won this contest: 67 percent viewed him favorably and only 21 percent viewed him unfavorably, compared to Leno's 59 percent to 30 percent breakdown. Even so, impressions of Leno were favorable by a two-to-one margin.

Polls have also measured public opinion about political humorists Jon Stewart and Dennis Miller. An October 2003 University of

Connecticut poll found that 7 percent of the respondents trusted Stewart "a lot," 16 percent trusted him "some," 13 percent trusted him "a little," and 8 percent trusted him "not at all," with over half of the respondents saying that they did not know or not answering. Two different polls included questions about Miller. A November 2003 Gallup poll found that 41 percent of the respondents viewed him favorably, whereas 20 percent viewed him unfavorably (note that Miller, like Stewart, was evidently not as familiar to the public as Letterman or Leno). A question on a July 2004 Fox News/ Opinion Dynamics poll pitted Miller—whom some observers label a conservative—against another comedian with more of a reputation as a liberal, asking, "Who comes closer to representing your personal values: Comedian Whoopi Goldberg or comedian Dennis Miller?" The outcome was a virtual tie at 18 percent to 20 percent, with 4 percent saying "both," 34 percent volunteering "neither," and 24 percent saying that they were not sure.

Though many Americans like late night political comedians, the results from a December 2003/January 2004 Pew Research Center poll suggest that few would be willing to follow the lead of one such comedian. The survey asked, "If Jay Leno said he was supporting a presidential candidate, would you be more likely to vote for that candidate, less likely to vote for that candidate, or wouldn't it make any difference?" Only 3 percent said that they would be more likely to vote for the candidate; 84 percent said that it would not make a difference, and 10 percent said that they would be less likely to vote for the candidate. These answers are interesting in light of the controversy over Leno's introduction of Arnold Schwarzenegger at the California governor-elect's October 2003 victory celebration.[11] Some commentators, including Marty Kaplan of the University of Southern California's Annenberg School for Communication, saw Leno's appearance as an implicit endorsement: "What Leno's presence did is give legitimacy to the notion that it wasn't a partisan event, it wasn't a political event, it was somehow an American cultural event."[12] In contrast, representatives of The Tonight Show insisted that "Leno's appearance at the rally was out of 'friendship' and did not constitute a political endorsement."[13]

There are additional signs of a tendency on the part of poll respondents to not take The Tonight Show seriously. A Pew Research Center poll in February 1997 asked respondents whether they thought of it as "mainly being a news show or mainly being an entertainment show?"

An overwhelming majority (83 percent) said the latter, whereas a mere 1 percent said the former. A Pew poll that asked the same question in August 1989—during the Johnny Carson era—found similar percentages. As for *The Late Show*, an August 2000 Fox News/Opinion Dynamics poll presented the following choice: "Late night talk show host David Letterman has proposed a debate between George W. Bush and Al Gore on his show. Would you be more or less likely to watch a presidential debate if it were held on the Letterman show than if it were held using the traditional format?" Though 33 percent said that they would be more likely to watch a debate on *The Late Show*, 46 percent said that they would be less likely to do so (19 percent said that it would make no difference). Taken together, the results of these three polls suggest that many Americans do not see late night comedy shows as legitimate news sources or forums for public debate.

Learning from Late Night Comedy Shows

Other poll results, however, suggest that the public may use late night comedy shows as news sources nonetheless. An April/May 2004 Pew poll found that 46 percent of the respondents said that they liked it when news sources are "sometimes funny"; only 6 percent expressed dislike of humorous news sources. Moreover, substantial—though far from huge—percentages of Americans have told pollsters that they learn about presidential campaigns from late night comedy shows. The first such finding came from an April 1996 Pew poll that asked how often respondents "learn[ed] something about the presidential campaign or the candidates" from "late-night TV shows such as *David Letterman* and *Jay Leno*." Though most respondents said "never" or "hardly ever," 6 percent said "regularly" and 19 percent said "sometimes." A number of traditional news sources—including the *New York Times*, the *Washington Post*, *USA Today*, and the *Chicago Sun-Times*—ran stories about these findings, and Pew's subsequent polls on the subject have continued to receive extensive media coverage.

The next of these polls, conducted in February 2000, included the same question as before; this time, 9 percent said that they regularly learned from late night television shows, and 19 percent said that they did so sometimes. In addition, the poll included a question regarding whether respondents learned about the presidential campaign or the candidates from "comedy shows such as *Saturday Night*

Live and *Politically Incorrect.*" Here, the percentages were 6 percent and 19 percent, respectively. In a December 2003/January 2004 poll, Pew once again asked its question about learning from "late night TV shows such as *David Letterman* and *Jay Leno*," yielding results that were almost identical to the 2000 findings. When Pew repeated its question about political comedy shows, it substituted *The Daily Show* for the cancelled *Politically Incorrect*. In 2004, 8 percent said that they learned from such shows regularly, and 18 percent said that they did so sometimes.

The December 2003/January 2004 Pew poll, which took place during the Democratic presidential primary campaign, also included a new question: "Have you happened to see any of the Democratic candidates being interviewed or appearing as guests on news or entertainment programs?" Respondents who said yes were then asked whether they remembered the name(s) of the show(s) where they saw candidate appearances. Those who named late night comedy shows represented 4 percent of the entire sample and 10 percent of the respondents who said that they had seen a candidate appearance; *The Tonight Show*, *The Late Show*, *The Daily Show*, and *Saturday Night Live* were the most frequently cited late night comedy shows. Roughly as many respondents cited *The Daily Show*, a cable show, as cited each of the three broadcast network shows, a finding that may reflect its popularity with the Democratic contenders: of the nine major candidates, all but one appeared on Jon Stewart's show during the primary campaign (the one who did not, John Kerry, visited it that summer).[14]

Polling organizations also asked Americans how much they learned from late night comedy television when it came to two of the biggest political events in recent years: the deadlocked presidential election of 2000 and the terrorist attacks of September 11, 2001. The Florida recount saga provided a wealth of material to late night comedy shows—perhaps none more so than *The Daily Show*, which had labeled its 2000 presidential election coverage "Indecision 2000." In the episode from November 8, the day after Election Day, Stewart reflected on the outcome—or, rather, the lack thereof.

> This has been the craziest election any of us can remember. Calling this whole thing "Indecision 2000" was, at first, a bit of a light-hearted jab, perhaps an attempt at humor; we had no idea that people were going to run with that. We thought we were kidding, quite frankly, but indecision is exactly where we are right now.

In December 2000, Gallup asked how important "late-night talk shows such as *Jay Leno* or *David Letterman*" had been to survey respondents as sources of "information, news, and insight about the Florida recount controversy over the past several weeks." Of the interviewees, 6 percent said that such shows had been "extremely important" or "very important" sources of information; another 11 percent said that they had been "somewhat important."

The responses from late night comedy shows to the events of September 11, 2001, were much more somber. In the initial aftermath of the terrorist attacks, the shows stayed off the air. On September 17, 2001, the New York–based *Late Show* returned, with host Letterman making the following comments in his monologue.

> It's terribly sad here in New York City.... You can feel it. You can see it.... We're told that they were zealots fueled by religious fervor. Religious fervor. And if you live to be a thousand years old, will that make any sense to you? Will that make any goddamned sense?[15]

Bill Maher's comments on *Politically Incorrect* met with more controversy than did Letterman's; a week after the terrorist attacks, Maher said, "We have been the cowards lobbing cruise missiles from two thousand miles away. That's cowardly. Staying in the airplane when it hits the building, say what you want about it, it's not cowardly."[16] In response to Maher's remarks, White House Press Secretary Ari Fleischer stated, "There are reminders to all Americans that they need to watch what they say, watch what they do, and this is not the time for remarks like that."[17] A number of affiliates dropped the show; several months later, ABC cancelled *Politically Incorrect*.[18]

In broader terms, the terrorist attacks and their aftermath altered, at least temporarily, the tenor of late night political comedy. A content analysis conducted by the Center for the Media and Public Affairs found that from September 11 to December 31, 2001, Leno, Letterman, and O'Brien made fewer political jokes per show than they had from January 1 through September 10 of that year; what jokes they did make post-September 11 tended to target not domestic political figures, but Osama Bin Laden, the Taliban, and John Walker Lindh (known as the "American Taliban").[19] Furthermore, the guest lists for the shows included atypically high percentages of figures from the media, politics, and academia during the initial aftermath of terrorist attacks. During the midst of this period (in November to be specific), the Pew Research Center asked poll respondents how often they "learn[ed] something about terrorist attacks or the war on terrorism" from "late night TV shows such as *David Letterman* and *Jay Leno*." Here, 6 percent said that they did so regularly, and 11 percent said that they did so sometimes.

Who Says That They Learn from Late Night Comedy Shows?

In the Pew Research Center's April 1996, February 2000, and December 2003/January 2004 polls, young Americans were especially likely to say that they learned about presidential campaigns from these shows. Pew's report on the 1996 poll noted that 40 percent of those between the ages of eighteen and twenty-nine said that they regularly or sometimes learned about the campaign from late night shows such as David Letterman and Jay Leno, double the percentage among those fifty and older.[20] In 2000, the pattern was even more striking, with 47 percent of those under thirty saying that they learned from late night regularly or sometimes, compared to 18 percent of those fifty and older; in addition, 37 percent of those in the youngest age cohort said that they learned from comedy shows such as *Saturday Night Live* and *Politically Incorrect* regularly or sometimes, compared to 16 percent of those in the oldest cohort.[21]

In the December 2003/January 2004 poll, interviewees under the age of thirty cited comedy shows such as *Saturday Night Live* and *The Daily Show* as regular sources of campaign news almost as often (21 percent) as they cited newspapers or the evening network news (23 percent each).[22] Another 29 percent of those in this age group said that they sometimes learned from comedy shows, for a total of 50 percent (up 13 percentage points from 2000); among those fifty and older, the figure was less than a third of that. Once again, those under thirty were also particularly likely to say that they learned about the campaign from late night shows such as *Letterman* and *Leno*: 44 percent of them did so, more than double the percentage among those over fifty.

Do People Actually Learn Anything from
Late Night Comedy Shows?

Despite Pew's findings that many Americans—particularly younger ones—said that they learn about politics from late night comedy shows, some observers remain skeptical about the notion that people actually learn from these shows. "I read that, too, but I don't really believe it," *Daily Show* "correspondent" Stephen Colbert told one journalist.[23] He added that viewers "wouldn't enjoy *The Daily Show* if they were getting their news from us firsthand. They kind of have to know what's going on already to get the jokes." In broader terms, some scholars[24] have suggested that exposure to soft news sources can inform audience members, whereas others[25] have argued that preferences for soft news sources are largely unrelated to knowledge about politics.

The most obvious (but not necessarily the best) way to resolve the dispute would be to ask people whether they learned anything *new* from late night political comedy. Indeed, several polls have done just that. In its April/May 1992 poll, the Pew Research Center asked a follow-up to its questions about watching six different late night comedians or shows. Of those who said that they regularly or sometimes watched at least one of the six, 30 percent (or 21 percent of the full sample) also said that in doing so, they had "hear[d] things about the candidates or the presidential election campaign" that they had not heard previously. Two of the 1996 CBS News/*New York Times* polls included a similar question. In July, 27 percent said that by watching shows such as *Letterman*, *Leno*, and *O'Brien*, they had heard things about the campaign that they had not heard previously; in early October, 30 percent said so. The Pew Research Center's December 2003/January 2004 poll asked respondents who said that they regularly or sometimes learned from late night or comedy shows, "Do you ever learn things about the candidates or the presidential campaign on these shows that you haven't heard before?" Among the respondents who received this question, 40 percent (15 percent of the full sample) said yes; half of those under thirty said yes.[26]

Even these questions, however, rely on respondents' self-reports of whether they learned anything, and survey respondents may misperceive, misremember, or misrepresent what they have learned and where they have learned it. An alternative approach is to compare what respondents say about their use of late night comedy shows to how they perform on tests of factual knowledge about politics. The February 2000 and December 2003/January 2004 Pew Research Center polls included brief "pop quizzes" that allowed for such comparisons. In 2000, Pew found that respondents who said that they regularly learned about the campaign from late night television scored worse than average on political knowledge.[27] Four years later, Pew conducted a more sophisticated analysis that simultaneously took into account a range of other factors that could have been related to knowledge.

> Holding constant a person's education, interest, and use of other media sources, there is no evidence that people who say they learn about the campaigns from late night and comedy shows know any more about the candidates, and are at best only slightly more aware of major campaign events, than those who do not watch these programs.[28]

Judging by this evidence, Colbert's analysis would seem to be correct.

Then again, some analyses have suggested that the relationship between using late night comedy as a news source and political knowledge may be more complicated. National Annenberg Election Survey (NAES) polling conducted in July and September 2004 ascertained whether respondents watched "late-night comedy programs," and, if so, which of three programs—*The Late Show, The Tonight Show,* and *The Daily Show*—they watched most often. A comparison between respondents' answers and their scores on a knowledge test showed that *Daily Show* viewers knew more about the campaign than did *Late Show* or *Tonight Show* viewers. In the NAES report, Dannagal Goldthwaite Young also described another finding.

> *Daily Show* viewers have higher campaign knowledge than national news viewers and newspaper readers—even when education, party identification, following politics, watching cable news, receiving campaign information online, age, and gender are taken into consideration.[29]

Yet Young went on to note that the results could reflect more than one sort of causal relationship.

> *The Daily Show* assumes a fairly high level of political knowledge on the part of its audience—more so than *Leno* or *Letterman*. At the same time, because *The Daily Show* does deal with campaign events and issues, viewers might certainly pick up information while watching.[30]

Either way, one potential lesson may be that not all late night political comedy shows are equal when it comes to the knowledge level of their audiences.

Xiaoxia Cao's reexamination of the data from Pew's February 2000 and December 2003/January 2004 studies suggested that the relationship between using late night political comedy and knowledge about politics may depend on not just the type of show but also the age of the viewer.[31] After taking into account a wide range of other factors, she found that the relationship between self-reported learning from comedy shows such as *Saturday Night Live* and *The Daily Show* and political knowledge was stronger among younger respondents than among older respondents. In contrast, self-reported learning from late night talk shows such as *Letterman* and *Leno* was not related to knowledge in either age group. Cao accounted for the difference across age by speculating that the comedy show format is not only particularly appealing to younger viewers but also more effective at informing them than at informing older viewers; she accounted for the difference across shows, in turn, by arguing that the humor that appears on shows such as *Saturday Night Live* and *The Daily Show* is more complex and information-rich than is the humor on the late night talk shows.

Barry Hollander's analysis focused on the data from Pew's December 2003/January 2004 survey.[32] He concluded that watching late night shows such as *Letterman* and *Leno* was positively associated with recognition of campaign information but negatively associated with recall of campaign information (like Cao, he controlled for the effects of demographic variables). The latter relationship was stronger among older respondents than among younger respondents. Hollander also found that the younger viewers received "a modest benefit from viewing comedy programs in terms of both recall and recognition," whereas older viewers did not.[33]

Paul Brewer and Cao conducted another analysis that focused on the December 2003/January 2004 Pew data.[34] They found that respondents who reported seeing a candidate on a late night comedy show knew more about the presidential primary campaign than those who did not see a candidate on late night, even after controlling for numerous additional factors. The authors concluded that late night comedy shows might inform viewers by giving them opportunities to hear candidates speak at length rather than in brief sound bites.

An important point to consider is that all of these studies shared a key limitation: each relied exclusively on cross-sectional survey data (i.e., data from a single poll at a single point in time). Thus, none could fully isolate the effects of late night comedy use on knowledge from the effects of knowledge on late night comedy use.

Conclusion

Most Americans do not get the majority of their news from late night political comedy shows. The polls do say that many Americans watch such shows and hold favorable views of their hosts. At the same time, the polls capture several strands of skepticism about late night political comedy shows as primary news sources, forums for debate, and givers of endorsements. The polls also tell us that substantial percentages of the public—and even larger percentages of young people—have said that they learn about presidential campaigns and other key political events from such shows. On the other hand, the polls do not provide definitive answers regarding how much, if anything, the people who said that they learned from late night political comedy actually learned from it.

One certainty, however, is that pollsters should continue to ask Americans questions about late night political comedy. A particularly useful approach would be to conduct a panel study over the course of a campaign in which the same respondents completed multiple waves of a survey asking them what late night comedy shows they watched and how much they knew about politics. Such a study would allow for tests of how late night comedy shapes individual-level changes over time in knowledge. Another promising step might be to ask additional types of questions about late night comedy shows. In particular, pollsters could take the humor of late night political comedy shows more seriously by asking specific questions about what people find funny on such shows, as well as what questions about what ideas people bring to and take away from such humor.

Notes

1. Sharon Altaras, "Ignorance Isn't Funny; Becoming Informed Is No Laughing Matter," *Seattle Times*, August 15, 2004, sec. D.
2. Sean Smith, "Breaking News: ABC Had It Right," *Washington Post*, March 29, 2000, sec. A.

3. Matthew A. Baum, "Sex, Lies, and War: How Soft News Brings Foreign Policy to the Inattentive Public," *American Political Science Review* 96 (2002): 91–109; Matthew A. Baum, "Soft News and Political Knowledge: Evidence of Absence or Absence of Evidence?" *Political Communication* 20 (2003): 173–190; Matthew A. Baum, *Soft News Goes to War: Public Opinion and American Foreign Policy in a New Media Age* (Princeton, NJ: Princeton University Press, 2003); Matthew A. Baum, "Talking the Vote: Why Presidential Candidates Hit the Talk Show Circuit," *American Journal of Political Science* 49 (2005): 213–234. See also Paul R. Brewer and Xiaoxia Cao, "Candidate Appearances on Soft News Shows and Public Knowledge About Primary Campaigns," *Journal of Broadcasting & Electronic Media* 50 (2006): 18–35; Markus Prior, "Any Good News in Soft News? The Impact of Soft News Preference on Political Knowledge," *Political Communication* 20 (2003): 149–171.

4. Baum, *Soft News Goes to War*; Baum, "Talking the Vote."

5. Prior, "Any Good News in Soft News?"

6. David S. Niven, David, S. Robert Lichter, and Daniel Amundson, "The Political Content of Late Night Comedy," *Harvard International Journal of Press/Politics* 8 (2003): 118–133.

7. "Daily Show Viewers Knowledgeable About Presidential Campaign," *Annenberg Public Policy Center*, September 21, 2004.

8. Richard L. Berke and Kevin Sack, "The 2000 Campaign: The Debates; In Debate 2, Microscope Focuses on Gore," *New York Times*, October 11, 2000, sec. A.

9. Joe Urschel, "Late-Night Comics Having a Political Field Day," *USA Today*, July 28, 1992, sec. A.

10. Nevertheless, subsequent research has indicated that exposure to late night comedy can shape public opinion. See Jody Baumgartner and Jonathan S. Morris, "The Daily Show Effect: Candidate Evaluations, Efficacy, and the American Youth," *American Politics Research* 34 (2006): 341–367; Patricia Moy, Michael A. Xenos, and Verena K. Hess, "Priming Effects of Late-Night Comedy," *International Journal of Public Opinion Research* 18 (2005): 198–210.; Dannagal G. Young, "Late-night Comedy in Election 2000: Its Influence on Candidate Trait Ratings and the Moderating Effects of Political Knowledge and Partisanship," *Journal of Broadcasting & Electronic Media* 48 (2004): 1–22.

11. The same Pew Research Center poll found that respondents did not put much stock in Schwarzenegger's endorsement, either; for him, the figures were 6 percent, 77 percent, and 12 percent, respectively.

12. Sharon Waxman, "The Recall Show with Jay Leno," *Washington Post*, October 9, 2003, sec. C.

13. Marco della Cava, "Liberal Hollywood Takes a Wait-and-See Atti-
    tude," *USA Today*, October 13, 2003, sec. D.
14. The candidates who visited *The Daily Show* during the primary were
    Wesley Clark, Howard Dean, John Edwards, Dick Gephardt, Dennis
    Kucinich, Joe Lieberman, Carol Mosley-Braun, and Al Sharpton.
15. Eric Mink, "Dave from the Heart," *Daily News*, September 19, 2001.
16. Jeffrey P. Jones, *Entertaining Politics: New Political Television and
    Civic Culture* (Lanham, MD: Rowman & Littlefield, 2005), 3.
17. Ibid.
18. For further discussion, see ibid.
19. Center for Media and Public Affairs, "September 11th Joke Targets:
    'Can We Go and Do Shows Now?'" (Washington, DC: Center for
    Media and Public Affairs, 2002).
20. "TV News Viewership Declines: Fall Off Greater for Young Adults
    and Computer Users," *Pew Research Center for the People and the
    Press*, May 13, 1996.
21. "The Tough Job of Communicating with Voters," *Pew Research Cen-
    ter for the People and the Press*, February 5, 2000.
22. "Cable and Internet Loom Large in Fragmented Political News Uni-
    verse: Perceptions of Partisan Bias Seen as Growing, Especially by
    Democrats," *Pew Research Center for the People and the Press*, Janu-
    ary 11, 2004.
23. Steve Murray, "Comedy Phenomenon Deconstructs TV News,"
    Atlanta Constitution-Journal, October 3, 2004, sec. L.
24. See, e.g., Baum, "Soft News and Political Knowledge."
25. See, e.g., Prior, "Any Good News in Soft News?"
26. "Cable and Internet Loom Large in Fragmented Political News
    Universe."
27. "The Tough Job of Communicating with Voters."
28. "Cable and Internet Loom Large in Fragmented Political News Universe."
29. "Daily Show Viewers Knowledgeable About Presidential Campaign."
30. Ibid.
31. Xiaoxia Cao, "Political Comedy Shows and Young Americans' Knowl-
    edge About Primary Campaigns" (presented at the annual meeting of
    the American Political Science Association, Washington, DC, Sep-
    tember 1–4, 2005).
32. Barry A. Hollander, "Late-Night Learning: Do Entertainment Pro-
    grams Increase Campaign Knowledge for Young Viewers?" *Journal
    of Broadcasting & Electronic Media* 49 (2005): 402–415.
33. Ibid., 410.
34. Brewer and Cao, "Candidate Appearances on Soft News Shows and
    Public Knowledge About Primary Campaigns."

16

"It's Better Than Being Informed"
College-Aged Viewers of The Daily Show

Brandon Rottinghaus, Kenton Bird,
Travis Ridout, and Rebecca Self

In the 1992 presidential campaign, candidates began to turn away from the traditional television news media and toward the "new" news media in their quest to communicate with voters. Candidates found that they much preferred jovial banter with Larry King or David Letterman to answering the hard questions of the day from a network journalist. That trend has continued, and it is now *de rigueur* for presidential candidates to sit on Oprah's couch or humorously spar with Jon Stewart on *The Daily Show*. The normative implications of this development are still in dispute. Some observers see this shift from hard to soft news as damaging to the political process. Thomas Patterson, for instance, argues that the change has weakened people's interest in politics and the news, especially among young adults.[1] Others, however, see a silver lining in the shift to soft news, viewing it as a way to reconnect young people with politics. Under this view, young people may not sit down to read a daily newspaper, but they will watch *The Daily Show*, and in doing so, will unintentionally learn a lot about politics.

This chapter is an attempt to gain firsthand information about the role of soft news in politics from those who appear to use it most and the outlet they choose most often: young viewers (and non-viewers) of *The Daily Show*. We use focus groups to obtain detailed answers to questions concerning why students watch, what advantages they find in watching, and what effect this has on their perceptions of the media and politics. Through this research design, we are able to answer important theoretical questions concerning the role of infotainment in American politics. Although our results cannot be considered definitive or generalizable, we can address these important concerns and potentially initiate new research questions in ways that public opinion survey data cannot.

Humor and American Political Behavior

What evidence is there that young people learn from soft news or infotainment programs? Clearly, people do not turn on Jay Leno each night because they want to learn about the latest political developments; people watch soft news largely for its entertainment value.[2] The converse is also true: people who watch hard news do so because they want to be informed. Even though most people approach a program like *The Daily Show* wanting to be entertained rather than informed, might they still acquire some political knowledge from such programming? Multiple studies have attempted to answer this question, and almost all of them employ survey research in trying to identify learning effects.

Several survey-based studies have found evidence of learning effects for individuals watching soft news. For instance, attention to talk shows was positively associated with the ability of respondents to identify correctly which candidate in the 1992 presidential race supported several different policies.[3] Moreover, people who watched entertainment media knew more about the presidential primary candidates in 2000 than those who did not.[4] Consumption of entertainment-based programs and late night programs was also associated with better recognition of campaign events in the 2004 presidential primaries.[5] Broadening the scope beyond a campaign context, Matthew Baum found that people who were exposed to soft news programming paid more attention to certain international crises.[6] This was true even among those who were not attentive to international affairs. These studies lend support to the idea that soft news and entertainment news viewing can inform audiences, even when those audiences did not seek out "informative" news.

Yet others have questioned such findings. Markus Prior, for instance, pointed out that Baum's study measured only *attention to* certain events, not whether information about these political events was retained.[7] His own analysis discovered only one learning effect: use of soft news increased people's knowledge of a personal scandal involving Gary Condit, a member of Congress. Knowing such tabloid-style information is hardly impressive evidence that soft news is serving a vital role in informing the American electorate. Baum responded to Prior's work, however, pointing out that (1) people may learn in an online (as opposed to memory-based) fashion, updating their overall judgments even if they do not retain the component information, and (2) many of the factual questions that Prior's survey inquired about were events that had occurred months—in some instances over a year—in the past.[8] People may have acquired knowledge when it mattered (at the time of the event) and rationally forgotten it when it no longer mattered.

Notwithstanding Baum's arguments, there is some additional evidence for the "null findings" conclusion. For instance, attention to late night programs such as *The Late Show with David Letterman* or *The Tonight Show with Jay Leno* was unrelated to actual campaign knowledge.[9] Another study concluded that exposure to "new media," such as television talk shows, was only weakly, and highly inconsistently, related to voter learning about politics.[10] Other researchers have even discovered negative relationships between exposure to soft news or infotainment media and political knowledge. For example, increased attention to television was associated with less campaign knowledge,[11] talk show use predicted poorer placement of candidates on issue scales,[12] and exposure to late night television was negatively related to candidate recall in 2004.[13]

Taken as a whole, survey-based evidence gives very mixed support to the notion that talk show programs, soft news, and infotainment in general can fill the void in political knowledge among America's youth. Instead of adding one more finding to a literature that does not give a clear portrait of the effects of infotainment on the knowledge of young people, we decided to approach the question a different way: by speaking directly with young people whose news consumption habits have been continually linked to the soft news format.

Young Viewers and Media Use Patterns

Of particular interest to the study of effects of humor and infotainment on news viewers is the effect on younger viewers. In this section, we examine recent trends in the consumption of news by young viewers, especially those related to soft news. American teens, college students, and young adults in the twenty-first century have embraced new technology and the "new" media as a way of learning about politics and public issues. These citizens, sometimes referred to Generations X and Y, are increasingly turning to the Internet—and particularly to some second-generation features, such as Web portals and blogs, for news. There is also evidence that they are taking advantage of such technology as satellite broadcasts and digital-video recorders to view television programming on demand rather than on the networks' schedules.

Given developments in new media technologies, recent surveys of eighteen- to thirty-four-year-olds include little encouraging news for traditional print media. Newspapers were seen to "have no clear strengths and are the least preferred choice for local, national and international news."[14] This finding echoes other research that showed that fewer than one in five Americans ages eighteen to twenty-two read a daily newspaper—a rate one-quarter that of respondents age sixty-three to sixty-seven years.[15] Because newspaper readership by young people is often a reflection of family reading habits, research suggests a continued decline in the number of young people who acquire a habit of regularly reading a newspaper.[16] The conventional wisdom that newspaper readership would rise as the audience aged is no longer holding true. So where are young viewers turning when they want political news? According to a 2004 survey conducted for the Carnegie Corporation that looked at media use by Americans ages eighteen to thirty-four, the answer is television. More than 70 percent of this age group viewed local television news at least once a week, making it the most-used news source.[17]

Several researchers have attempted to evaluate the media's role in the perceived political disengagement by young Americans. Using data from the 2004 National Annenberg Risk Survey of Youth, Pasek et al. focused on a target population of fourteen- to twenty-two-year-old respondents.[18] The authors determined that the Internet was the most common form of media use, with nearly 60 percent of this age group reporting that they were online at least once a week. Surprisingly, a majority of these respondents also read a newspaper, watched national news on a network or cable channel, and listened to a radio news show, suggesting a fairly heavy media diet. This study found a positive correlation between political awareness and use of informational media, including Internet use, newspaper reading, and nightly television news or national cable news. However, heavy viewers of television scored less well on political awareness questions. Unfortunately, this study did not distinguish between news-based comedy programs such as *The Daily Show* and conventional entertainment television series.

Some research also suggests that young viewers (aged eighteen to twenty-nine) look to late night television comedy shows as a more credible source than traditional television news programs. A 2004 survey for the youth-engagement group Declare Yourself found that *The Daily Show*'s Jon Stewart was more trusted than two of the three major networks' anchors.[19] Asked whom they trusted to provide information about politics and politicians, one-quarter answered "none of them." NBC's Tom Brokaw finished first with 17 percent, followed by Comedy Central's Stewart at 16 percent. The late Peter Jennings (ABC) was third at 15 percent, followed by Dan Rather (CBS) at 10 percent. However, a subset of respondents who identified the Internet as their primary source of information ranked Stewart ahead of Brokaw in credibility, 23 percent to 18 percent.[20]

In furthering this discussion, Barry Hollander found that younger viewers tend to take away more information from such entertainment programs as *The Daily Show* than their older counterparts.[21] This research distinguished between recall and recognition of political knowledge, noting that

> Beyond moderate levels of viewing late-night programs, the improvement in recall disappears while the improvement in recognition increases. Or to put it another way, late-night television viewing increases what young people think they know about a political campaign but provides at best modest improvements to actual recall of events associated with the campaign.[22]

Further, David Mindich sought to measure the degree to which Americans under forty have disengaged from the news but also to determine why they have tuned out. He attributed the decline to four factors: complacency about the political system, declining trust of the traditional news media, loss of a sense of community, and the rise of suburbia. Mindich also analyzed the tension between information-based and entertainment-based media and his interviews showed that young people preferred such entertainment programs as *Survivor* to the political content of news networks such as CNN.[23] "If there is something that is making the lives of young people too busy to follow the news it is most likely television and other entertainment media," Mindich speculated.[24]

Focus Group Methodology

As noted, our primary data for this chapter come from focus groups conducted with several university-level students. Focus group research involves semi-structured conversations with a select group of individuals to gain information about their views and experiences of a topic.

Focus groups can help define research agendas and questions, especially in preliminary, exploratory, or initial stages of research and in situations where there is something to talk about, like segments from *The Daily Show* episodes in our case. More specifically, they can help researchers define subject areas in terms of participant-generated categories and conceptions. Focus groups may lead, therefore, to new terminology and models, unidentified connections between varied subjects, or unforeseen types of social interaction between participants. In the case of humor, developing interaction among participants, especially reactions to content, is important. Jenny Kitzinger argued that interaction delineates focus groups from group interviews because participants' worldviews show up in contrast and consensus.[25] And according to Luntz Research, "most pollsters know what voters think, but too few understand how voters feel. If understanding *why* is the objective, traditional telephone polling is simply not enough."[26] Because focus groups yield these particular types of information, they are often utilized in tandem with other methods, especially survey research, to add increased complexity, nuance, or depth to broader data sets.

The research team involved in this project conducted two semi-structured focus group meetings in early June 2005. Both groups consisted of University of Idaho students, the majority of whom majored or took classes in the Department of Journalism and Mass Media. Our interview guide led the students through several broad categories of information or interaction. First, we gathered basic demographic information about the students and asked about their familiarity with Jon Stewart and *The Daily Show*. Participants ranged from a Mormon father who had never seen the show to a self-selected female "fan" who watched daily on the Internet, heard about our focus group from a friend, and just showed up. Most students fell somewhere in between, having seen the show periodically depending largely on access to cable television.

Second, we asked students for general impressions and ideas about the show and how and why they watched the show. To provide focus and clarity for the groups, we then showed two fairly lengthy clips of opening segments of *The Daily Show* on two consecutive days. The first two segments featured an Amnesty International Report on Guantanamo Bay and a reenactment of CPR on a chicken. The second two segments featured reports on Tom DeLay indictment and the revealed identity of Watergate's "Deep Throat." The students discussed their reactions and ideas about the show with regard to those clips. Per our interview guide, each group concluded with discussion of how and with whom students watch and discuss *The Daily Show*.

How and Why Students Watch

To amplify our discussion in previous sections documenting the effect of humor on political dispositions and the sources of political news for young viewers, in this section we more closely examine several questions pertaining to college students' viewing of *The Daily Show*. We investigate two primary questions: (1) Why do these students watch *The Daily Show*? and (2) What are the advantages they articulate to watching *The Daily Show*, especially in relation to other news programs? Our selected cross-section of student focus groups at the University of Idaho is used to explore these questions with more detail. To maintain the anonymity of the students from the focus groups, we will refer to them only by gender and by class standing.

Laughing While Learning

To investigate our first question (why students watch), we directly posed questions to students inquiring about their purpose in tuning into *The Daily Show*. The most common reason provided to our focus group investigators, regardless of whether or not the student was a frequent watcher, was that the show was "funny" or "amusing." For example, an upper-division female student summarized this point in noting that, "I live on entertainment. If it's not entertaining, I'm gone. So, the fact that he's [Jon Stewart] entertaining makes the value go way up for me because I'll actually pay attention and retain it." Further, a female freshman argued that the humor cuts across party and ideology by noting, "It doesn't even matter like what party you're affiliated with. As long as it makes it funny, it's good."

Making the news relevant in a humorous was way often identified as a major benefit to watching *The Daily Show*, and helped retain the interest of the viewers. An upper-division female student argued

> You don't see a funny side of politics. You know, very rarely. It's just so cut and dry and that's why it's so boring. Like C-SPAN, I mean, you're not going to watch C-SPAN....and that's exactly what's going on....but you see Jon Stewart making fun of, like, the big political picture, and it's a lot easier to watch that to sit and watch these people debate things.

A male freshman quipped (after viewing a particular news segment), "I just think that younger generations appeal more to the comedic factor. It's just going to keep your interest more if you're going to laugh while you're learning stuff." Other students compared this humorous approach to other satire-based entertainment. For example, one upper-division male student equated *The Daily Show's* approach to news to that of late night comedian David Letterman and indicated

> I think he [Jon Stewart] just kinda added a little satire to it. So that you can take the same thing that you are tired of hearing about and think about it a little differently and kind of humorously. But at the same time he gives you the facts—but for every fact he gives you he gives you something kinda funny to think about it as well.

He ended by arguing that the humor news "frame" provided for a fresh perspective, indicating "For me, you get tired of hearing like the same story over and over and over again."

That idea that humor functions as a connector to political news complements previous findings. In practice, this has the effect of making students feel informed, or, as noted by an upper-class female student, "the jokes aren't as funny if you don't know what's going on." An underclass female student also noted, "I feel that it could work the other way too, though. You get your news from somewhere else and then you watch *The Daily Show*, and you're like *ah ha* that is funny." Of course, it is difficult to determine how much information is necessary to "get" the humor, but moderate exposure is likely sufficient.

Another effect of *The Daily Show* is that it allows for informal attention to news in a semi-serious way, especially in providing comic relief to students who often perceive news to be negative. An upper-division female noted, "I think it's because on the news you hear all the time...this person died...or 5 people died here and 5 people died here. And then you watch the show and you know there's going to be some comic relief out of what's going on right now." This concept was echoed by a female senior

> I just saw five minutes ago that 600 people died. It's hard to put it all together, as opposed to *The Daily Show*, they do it, but they do it with comedy. Even when he was making fun of how…this many people died in bombings…and now they're making progress [in Iraq]…and they've got it down to this many people are killed…they can still make light of a really sad situation. But in other channels you just realize how devastating those situations are.

The "seriousness" of news from other sources (and more generally in life) allows *The Daily Show* to offer an escape from reality. A female junior noted, "That's why people watch it. Everything is so serious. I've got a lot of things going on in my life. I deal with life and death situations every single day. I do watch regular network news, but if I didn't sit there and watch Jon Stewart poke fun at Donald Rumsfeld and Howard Dean and everybody else, it's…it makes my life easier, you know. Not everything has to be so serious all the time and that's what I think."

One often cited effect of humor on news consumption is that *The Daily Show* makes the news relevant and interesting to a group of people for whom political news is often uninteresting or arcane, thus potentially increasing news intake. One female senior noted

> I don't watch any other news source, I don't read the newspaper. I never have had the newspaper in our house, we never watch. I remember my teacher turning on the O.J. Simpson trial the last day and I didn't know who O.J. was. I was like in the third grade and I had no idea who he was. I mean, that's just kind of my background so my government teacher was the first person that introduced me to *The Daily Show* because she knew that I didn't pay attention at all. I would sit and watch it with her. He's [Jon Stewart] more likely to get my interest, so after I watch him, I'll go and look something up. Ok, what the hell was he talking about. I learn stuff and then I'm engaged. I'm ready to go find out other information. Regular news, I just tune it out because I get bored so quickly.

A junior female in the same focus group followed up this point and noted, "It's kind of like a lot of Comedy Central shows like *South Park*, the same thing. They address these issues that are everywhere in the news but present it in a way that younger people and people that aren't really hard core news followers can have an idea of what's going on." One student (an upper-class female) observed, "It's really pop culture news. They slide in everything that's going around in our culture right now, along with the news, as opposed to the other places that follow a certain structure. Other news channels stick to a main structure, but Jon Stewart does the news and slides in a lot of our pop culture along with it. So you get like all of it in this one show."

Easier to Understand Than CNN

Humor was not the only reason that students in our focus groups tuned into *The Daily Show*. Several students indicated that they watched because the news was presented in a more simple or easy-to-comprehend manner. This phenomenon seemed to be more prevalent in our focus groups with younger (underclass) students.[27] In particular, students with less knowledge of politics were confused by certain events, but on watching *The Daily Show* coverage of the same event, the event was made more clear and accessible. A female student noted, "It's like you're having a conversation with someone unlike CNN where it feels like you're being lectured to." Another female freshman argued, "Jon Stewart to me seems more personable like someone that you could talk to about stuff like he's like having a conversation with you about your beliefs. As weird as that would be, it's like, it's easier to understand rather than when you're watching CNN. It's some dude up there in a tie and jacket it's just like, blah blah blah."

A "Gateway" to Other News

Many students also indicated that *The Daily Show* served as a "gateway" to other kinds of news. Specifically, *entertainment* is the link between raising awareness of a news item and the desire for more information about that news item. For example, an upper-division male student noted, "It's like television has evolved from a news broadcast menu to be an entertainment medium. That's what it's there for. It's supposed to be on in the background to keep you kind of entertained or sit down and watch a movie or something that." Similarly, a lower-division female student again offered a link between political knowledge and infotainment, "Especially if you watch like CNN because he has a lot of CNN clips so, say you watch CNN and then you go to *The Daily Show* and you're like *ah* I saw that. I'm like, that's a different spin."

For some, however, the humor distracted them from the core facts of news. As much as humor attracts viewers, the humor also detracts from the credibility of *The Daily Show* news. One upper-division male student argued, "I was interested in finding out what's going on currently in the news, like, if I wanted to find out what was going on, I'd sit down and watch an hour of news and get it figured out and then go on. But, I don't really watch television for its comical value and stuff like that. So for me, I wouldn't sit down and turn that show on because I would be kind of distracted from the facts and cause I'd probably be rolling around on the ground laughing, but it would kind of take away from the actual factual information, for me at least." Comparing *The Daily Show* more to editorializing than news, a female freshman noted, "If I want to watch the news, I won't watch Jon Stewart. Usually I'll go to CNN, but I don't really watch him to get like news." Another underclass female noted, "It's hilarious, it was great but definitely I would never use it as a news source."

In some instances, *The Daily Show* served as a gateway to other news and as a resource to expand to additional sources of news. An underclassman female noted, "I think it's like a gateway to news, this show is. It'll introduce you to topics but then if you want to then, you know, get other details you didn't get here you can go read the paper." The effect also works the other way, where students might seek out *The Daily Show* for another perspective on news. Further, an upper-division female noted that, similar to *South Park*, "If nothing else, he [Jon Stewart] just kind of piques an awareness." In sharing the information with fellow students, one female upper-class student remarked, "So we get more when you read the papers, because I still watch the regular news, but I like Jon Stewart's version too. Just because I like to get both sides of it, really is what it is. You get bits and pieces of it and then you can read the whole story."

Depth of Coverage

Several participants also suggested that *The Daily Show* as a news source has more depth than other types of news outlets, especially traditional network news and cable news. This depth was argued to be constructed from the economic reality of the news media's

290 Brandon Rottinghaus, Kenton Bird, Travis Ridout, and Rebecca Self

creation of news, particularly in creating an appealing presentation to the news. Judging the quality of contemporary journalism in the United States, an upper-division male student noted, "He [Jon Stewart] does more of what I think U.S. news should be doing but when you watch the [network] nightly news or something like that it seems like they [*The Daily Show*] just spend a lot more time on whatever story they have."

Keeping viewers engaged may allow for *The Daily Show* to connect to a generation of students who are only sporadic news consumers (often, as noted above for eighteen- to twenty-four-year-olds, from multiple sources). An upper-division female argued, "One of the reasons Jon Stewart is so appealing is because the press is so busy trying to keep their ratings and not really offend anyone, and not have their bias show. Then you have someone like Jon Stewart who comes out and his comedy is funny, but he has a relentless agenda behind it." Following up on that point, an upper-class female student noted, "So, for *The Daily Show*'s little half hour, you get more in depth than you would have if you were just... you know... glancing at the television while I'm putting on my makeup and trying to listen to what Anderson Cooper had to say."

COMPARING AND CONTRASTING

Furthermore, the students in our focus groups argued that the news stories on the *Daily Show* are more willing to point out contradictions than news stories from other news sources, especially when politicians are caught changing their stories. One upper-division male student noted

> One thing that really stands out for me on the show was like, most regular news shows, they report what happened today, you know, or what's been going on for a couple of weeks. But, like, he'll [Jon Stewart] go back a long way, like, some of the things that are the most interesting to me are to see when he does a montage of what people have said, you know, through out their career. Like he did with Rumsfeld and that. But sometimes he'll go, like, five or six times. He'll say this person said this thing at this time... ok... ok... we've got some consistency going... then the last one will be... this person is totally saying something opposite of what they've always said.

Students are also more engaged when it comes to uncovering truth and cover-up in the media, in particular from a student who noted, "There's a lot of that [contrastive stories] where he goes back to what they have said [in] years prior to point out the hypocrisy of it." This tends to expose students to more kinds of media; from an upper-division male student:

> When Jon Stewart took over *The Daily Show*, he asked all of his writers to (inaudible) they wanted the comedy to be more politically based. He did it because he likes to point out the ridiculousness, as we said, of the politicians and media.

It is this phenomenon that distinguishes bias from pointing out hypocrisy; an upper-class male student noted, "He's just trying to say, look at all the hypocrisy here or, why are you so...it's just like if you said, well, I don't agree with what he's saying...then you'd probably say....ok, but this just helps you at least think about it from a different point of view." Another student (male, upper division) noted, "But then he does more research to find, like I've never seen other news places, where they will broadcast a press conference and then go back and show what the person said a year before."

In addition, our student focus group watchers argued *The Daily Show* brings up more stories that students had not seen on other news outlets. A lower-division female student noted, "I hadn't seen any of, like, the Tom DeLay stuff. I had heard about it but hadn't seen anything about it in the [Lewiston, Idaho] *Tribune*." Another student, after watching a segment on the Amnesty International report referring to Guantamano Bay camp as a "gulag," remarked, "If I had never seen it before, I wouldn't have necessarily thought that way." A lower-division student (in questioning another student's impression of the inadequacy of coverage) argues *The Daily Show* expands one's point of view: "You can turn to a different news station and you can watch what had happened, but if you hadn't seen it on *The Daily Show*, would you even have been aware that anything had happened?"

This depth was professed to allow students to engage the news with a more critical eye. A female uppper-class student noted, "At least some of it is bending the truth and exaggerating and taking it out of context but he's just making our generation more critical of the stories we hear in the news and not just taking them for face value." In addition, an upper-class male student noted, "I think it also gives you that when you do read the news, and you read something that makes you look at the news a different way. After you watch that show, to, like ... I know yesterday when I was reading the article (in the newspaper) about how they are saying that Jesus died of a blood clot. I know that it's just a matter of time and I wonder how many days until it's on *The Daily Show* (it will probably be on there tonight). So it makes you, not just in that respect, but when you see something that makes you more critical of the news I guess is what it does for me."

Conclusion and Discussion

Our focus group findings have given us a window into the benefits of watching humor-based news and the effect of that viewership on perceptions of the media and contemporary politics. We found that students can learn from *The Daily Show*, but the humor link is important in drawing them in and keeping their interest. *The Daily Show* (and other humor-based infotainment) has the potential to positively affect younger voters' attention to news and politics, possibly mitigating persistent "disaffection" found in younger voters. The humor "frame" appeared to appeal to students in part because of its blunt honesty—these soft news outlets (especially those using humor to discuss current events) exposed their "bias" to the viewer and were candid about demonstrating their journalistic point of view.

Furthermore, although we found that the humor was the biggest draw to *The Daily Show* for those students interviewed in our focus groups, this does not imply that there are not benefits of watching the "fake news" over "real news." The benefits listed by our focus group students include: seeing news from a different (and often more understandable) perspective, following up on the same stories for several months and exposing contradictions in public officials' statements, and providing in-depth coverage. Importantly, *The Daily Show* was also perceived as having the effect of being more intelligible and being presented in a more concise manner than other news formats. And, for whatever flaws people find with the content of the program, our focus group participants found that *The Daily Show* produced quality news without compromising depth or contrastive reporting. This development could have important implications for the future of news consumption habits by younger viewers.

Finally, that many in our focus groups indicated that *The Daily Show* serves as a "gateway" to news consumption is an important and potentially positive finding. If, as several of our focus group participants noted, watching news presented in a humorous manner leads younger viewers to seek out other "harder" sources of news, the impact of youth "disaffection" concerning American politics may be assuaged. This could foster a new (and unique) generation of news viewers and potentially arrest recent declining trends in the use of "traditional" news sources (especially newspapers). The preferences for more "entertaining" content may also engender alteration of content and style in the presentation of news.

Notes

1. Thomas E. Patterson, "Doing Well and Doing Good," John F. Kennedy School of Government, Harvard University, Faculty Research Working Papers Series, 2000.

2. Matthew A. Baum, "Sex, Lies, and War: How Soft News Brings Foreign Policy to the Inattentive Public," *American Political Science Review* 96 (2002): 91–109; Xiaoxia Cao, *Political Interest, Mass Media and Young Americans in the 2004 General Election* (PhD diss., University of Wisconsin-Milwaukee, 2005); Markus Prior, "Any Good News in Soft News? The Impact of Soft News Preference on Political Knowledge," *Political Communication* 20 (2003): 149–171.

3. Barry A. Hollander, "The New News and the 1992 Presidential Campaign: Perceived vs. Actual Political Knowledge," *Journalism and Mass Communication Quarterly* 42 (1995): 786–798.

4. Christopher A. Cooper and Mandi Bates, "I Learned It From Jay Leno: Entertainment Media in the 2000 Election" (unpublished manuscript, n.d.).

5. Barry A. Hollander, "Late-Night Learning: Do Entertainment Programs Increase Political Campaign Knowledge for Young Viewers?" *Journal of Broadcasting & Electronic Media* 49 (2005): 402–415.

6. Baum, "Sex, Lies, and War."

7. Prior, "Any Good News?"; Baum, "Sex, Lies, and War."

8. Matthew A. Baum, "Soft News and Political Knowledge: Evidence of Absence or Absence of Evidence?" *Political Communication* 20 (2003): 173–190.

9. Hollander, "The New News."

10. David H. Weaver. "What Voters Learn from Media," *Annals of the American Academy of Political and Social Science* 546 (1996) 34–47.

11. Hollander, "The New News and the 1992 Presidential Campaign."

12. Jack M. McLeod, Zhongshi Guo, Katie Daily, et al. "The Impact of Traditional and Nontraditional Media Forms in the 1992 Presidential Election," *Journalism and Mass Communication Quarterly* 73 (1996): 401–416.

13. Hollander, "Late Night Learning."

14. Wolfram Peiser, "Cohort Replacement and the Downward Trend in Newspaper Readership," *Newspaper Research Journal* 21 (2000): 11–22.

15. Ibid.

16. Ibid., 19.

17. Merrill Brown, "Abandoning the News," in *Journalism's Crisis of Confidence: A Challenge for the Next Generation*, Carnegie Corporation of New York. http://www.carnegie.org/pdf/journalism_crisis/journ_crisis_appendix_b-3.pdf.

18. J. Pasek et al., "America's Youth and Community Engagement: How Use of Mass Media Is Related to Civic Activity and Political Awareness in 14- to 22-Year-Olds," *Communication Research* 33 (2006): 115–135.

19. "The Emerging Electorate Survey: What Young Americans Say About the 2004 Election," *Luntz Research and Global Strategy Group*, November 2004. http://www.declareyourself.com/press/PDFs/report04/Emerging-ElectorateSurveyReport.pdf.

20. Ibid., 8.

21. Hollander, "Late-Night Learning."

22. Ibid., 411.

23. David T. Z. Mindich, *Tuned Out: Why Americans Under 50 Don't Follow the News* (New York: Oxford University Press, 2005).

24. Ibid., 65.

25. Jenny Kitzinger, "The Methodology of Focus Groups: The Importance of Interactions Between Research Participants," *Sociology of Health and Illness* 16 (1994): 103–21; Jenny Kitzinger, "Introducing Focus Groups," *British Medical Journal* 311 (1995): 299–303.

26. "The Emerging Electorate Survey."

27. Interestingly, and in keeping with other research findings, students in both groups indicated that older people introduced and/or talked to them about *The Daily Show*. At least two different students indicated that teachers showed *The Daily Show*—in two University of Idaho classes (history and political science) and in one high school setting. One student indicated that her mother watches and frequently discusses *The Daily Show* with her.

17

The Political Effects of Late Night Comedy and Talk Shows

Patricia Moy

With each passing presidential campaign, candidates have employed an increasingly wider range of media to reach the public.[1] In 1992, Bill Clinton sported a pair of sunglasses and played the saxophone on *The Arsenio Hall Show*. Two weeks later, he appeared in an MTV forum to answer questions posed by young adults in the audience. Ross Perot, while on *Larry King Live*, mentioned that he would run for president if volunteers in all fifty states would put him on the ballot.[2] Candidates' appearances in these media outlets allowed them not only to circumvent the journalist and the sound bite, but also to reach a different and potentially politically disengaged segment of the population. The "new news" or "nontraditional media" were clearly a novelty in the 1992 election campaign.[3] Or, as Diamond, McKay, and Silverman put it, "Pop goes politics."[4]

In 1996, however, the presence of these particular media receded. Diana Owen attributes this to the economic focus of such media, whose goals are ultimately entertainment and profit, not public service or bestowing attention on substantive political issues.[5] Moreover, she contends that the "decidedly anti-establishment" nature of these media deterred candidates from appearing in these media.[6] Instead, what appeared on the media landscape in the 1996 campaign was the Internet, with media organizations as well as candidates establishing their own Web sites.

It was not until the 2000 campaign that Americans saw a visible proliferation of media outlets for the candidates. In an unprecedented move, Steve Forbes announced his candidacy for presidency on the Internet. As Election Day drew closer (and passed), Al Gore and George W. Bush—aware that their presence on popular, nonnews shows could affect their standing with the public—vied to generate support through a series of orchestrated appearances.[7] Gore and Bush appeared on *Oprah*, *The Late Show with David Letterman*, *The Tonight Show with Jay Leno*, and *Saturday Night Live*; Gore's running mate Joe Lieberman even sang on *Late Night with Conan O'Brien*.[8] The 2000 election campaign saw *The Daily Show*, a comedy show in the guise of a news broadcast, rise to national prominence with its coverage of "Indecision 2000." In the 2004 election campaign, *Daily Show* host Jon Stewart interviewed Democratic presidential candidate John Kerry and vice presidential candidate John Edwards, with the latter satirically announcing his own candidacy for the presidency. *The Daily Show*'s presence at the Democratic and Republican National Conventions meant exposing viewers to another side of the political process as interviews were conducted with Governor Bill Richardson (D-NM), Senator Joe Biden (D-DE), and Senator John McCain (R-AZ).

The blurring of mediated news and entertainment has been accompanied by a concomitant rise in related studies. Following Diana Mutz's exhortation, scholars have begun to transcend traditional news-entertainment boundaries in studying political effects of the mass media.[9] Shifts in the media landscape have led scholars to hone in on nontraditional forms of news, often called "soft news" or "infotainment."[10] Indeed, researchers—including those represented in this volume—have examined, for example, how viewing late night comedy shows like *The Late Show with David Letterman* can influence knowledge and viewers' perceptions of the candidates, and how watching *Oprah* can influence certain forms of political behavior such as campaign participation and voting.[11]

This chapter takes a broader perspective to the study of such political effects. Using data from two national surveys, I empirically analyze claims that Americans are increasingly getting their campaign news from sources other than traditional news.[12] To what extent do these shifts in media use impact political knowledge and behavior, the mainstays of any democratic system? Moreover, given the results of these earlier, time-bound data sets, where should research in this area proceed?

Media, Political Knowledge, and Political Participation

It is almost a truism to speak of the crucial role the media play in democratic systems. Various theories dictate that a healthy democracy is predicated on being governed by the people, and preferably politically knowledgeable and active individuals.[13] As Gurevitch and Blumler note, one of the mandates of the media is to provide the populace with information it can use to make informed and meaningful decisions.[14] Despite discussions of what constitutes satisfactory levels of information and how citizens process that information, there is little debate that citizens use the media to learn about public affairs.[15] Similarly, much research has implicated media or media use as forces that enhance or impede various forms of political participation, either directly or indirectly.[16]

With respect to political knowledge, a large corpus of literature has documented the extent to which citizens learn from the media. Robinson and Levy's seminal work, *The Main Source*, shattered the longstanding myth that had arisen from decades of polls indicating that people used television as their main source of information.[17] Their study revealed that television may be the main source of information for those less educated, but, in fact, newspaper reading generated greater comprehension of political affairs than television news viewing. Robinson and Levy's ten-year update arrived at essentially the same conclusions, that "newspapers remain America's premier source of public affairs information."[18]

While *The Main Source* dealt with what is now considered traditional forms of news, newspapers, and television news, the contemporary media landscape of the twenty-first century is sufficiently different, thereby necessitating scrutiny of other sources of political news. This is particularly the case with political campaigns, where information suffuses into the public arena from all media sources.

Indeed, research conducted during presidential elections has examined the extent to which nontraditional news made a difference in the public's learning of political information. For example, Weaver and Drew investigated how much individuals learned from the media during the 1992 campaign, finding that nontraditional media had no bearing on knowledge of the campaign or likelihood of voting.[19] Chaffee, Zhao, and Leshner, on the other hand, concluded that interview/talk shows added to viewers' knowledge about the candidates.[20] In addressing the relationship between perceived and actual knowledge in the 1992 campaign, Hollander found that attention to MTV was negatively related to knowledge about the campaign, but attention to talk shows positively related to such knowledge.[21]

The 1996 campaign offered scholars yet another opportunity to investigate potential effects of these media. Some researchers discovered that use and attention to the Internet, late night talk shows, and MTV were unrelated to knowledge, while others found attention to television talk shows to be correlated with campaign interest.[22] More recent research conducted during the 2004 campaign indicates positive associations between consumption of television news, televised debates, and Internet news and voter learning.[23]

Interest and information alone, however, do not sustain a democracy. Citizens must also be active, and have adequate and equal opportunity to express their preferences and reasoning in a decision-making process.[24] However, the ideal of an active electorate has long fallen by the wayside, as political participation is not evenly distributed within or across societies.[25]

Studies of the linkages between media use and political participation generally involve either an implicit or explicit comparison of newspapers and television, whether they show three-quarters of the most politically apathetic relying most on television or voter turnout declining more sharply among those least reliant on newspapers.[26] More recently, McLeod et al. showed that reading about the campaign in newspapers was positively related to the likelihood of voting and other forms of conventional political participation at three different levels of control, while viewing campaign news on television was negatively related to these criterion variables.[27] The process by which media use is linked to political participation very well may be through cognitions.[28] According to this line of reasoning, mediated information will increase political knowledge, which in turn will increase levels of political participation.[29]

Operationalization and Methods

To explore the effects of these nontraditional media on political knowledge and participation, I analyze two data sets collected by Princeton Survey Research Associates on behalf of the Pew Research Center for the People and the Press. Fieldwork for these studies was conducted during the 2000 and 2004 election campaigns. In 2000, telephone interviews were conducted January 12–16, 2000 with a national probability sample of 1,091 adults at least eighteen years of age. For the latter, telephone interviews were conducted with 1,506 adults December 19, 2003 to January 4, 2004.

Political Knowledge.   My first criterion variable in 2000 was a summated index of three items that gauged respondents' knowledge about candidates in the campaign: the presidential candidate who was the governor of Texas at the time (74.3 percent correctly identified George W. Bush); the presidential candidate formerly the senator from New Jersey (Bill Bradley; 34 percent correct); and the name of the presidential candidate who had cosponsored a campaign finance reform bill in Congress (John McCain; 22 percent correct). The reliability coefficient for this index was Cronbach's alpha = .65. Appendix 1 includes the exact wording for all items included in our analyses. The knowledge index in 2004 was based on two items asking which candidate had served as an Army general (30.7 percent of respondents correctly identified Wesley Clark) and who had served as the majority leader in the House of Representatives (25.7 percent correctly identified Richard Gephardt). These two items were correlated strongly at $r = .55$ (Cronbach's alpha = .70).

Political Participation.   Studies of media use and political behavior during a campaign typically have as the criterion variable a measure of respondents' intention to vote in the upcoming election.[30] Although both 2000 and 2004 survey instruments did not include such a measure, respondents were asked their frequency of voting.

The 2000 questionnaire also contained a battery of political participation items asking respondents if they had ever expressed their opinions about politics and current events by contacting an elected official; contributing money to a candidate running for public office; joining an organization in support of a particular cause; attending a city or town council meeting in the community where s/he lived; and attending a political party meeting or function. Respondents then were asked if they had ever engaged in one of these behaviors in the last twelve months. A three-point item was derived for each act of political behavior, with zero reflecting never having engaged in one of these activities; 1 if the respondent had ever done so; and 2 if the respondent had done so in the last twelve months. These derived items were then summated to create a 0–15 scale of political participation (Cronbach's alpha = .72). The political participation index for 2004 was constructed in a manner similar to that used for the 2000 data, but was grounded in only four measures—the first three noted above and attending a campaign event (Cronbach's alpha = .65).

Media Use.   In 2000, respondents were asked the extent to which they learned about the campaign and candidates from various traditional news media (e.g., daily newspapers, network television news, local television news) and nontraditional sources of political information (including late night television shows like *The Tonight Show* and *The Late Show*, comedy shows including *Saturday Night Live* and *Politically Incorrect*, MTV, and the Web (Table 17.1). While these items do not directly gauge exposure or attention to media use, the extent to which one learns from a given media is in part a function of their attention to the medium.[31]

Although the same items were included for traditional hard news in 2004, the measures for nontraditional news differed somewhat. Not only did the exemplars from comedy shows include *Saturday Night Live* and *The Daily Show*, but also MTV had been dropped.

Demographics.   Six variables served as controls in our analyses: gender (52.9 percent female in 2000; 51.5 percent in 2004), age (M = 44.2 years, SD = 16.5 years in 2000; M = 45.6 years, SD = 17.5 years in 2004); education (median response of "some college" in 2004); income (median income category of $40,000 to under $50,000 in

TABLE 17.1.   Descriptive Statistics of Media Use Items

	2000		2004	
	Mean	(SD)	Mean	(SD)
Traditional News Sources				
Local TV news	3.08	(1.11)	3.02	(1.09)
Network news	2.95	(1.21)	2.85	(1.16)
Daily newspapers	2.85	(1.28)	2.65	(1.20)
Nontraditional Sources of Political News				
Late night TV (Letterman, Leno)	1.83	(1.13)	1.78	(1.09)
Internet	1.67	(1.19)	1.83	(1.21)
Comedy shows (*SNL, Politically Incorrect, The Daily Show*)	1.64	(1.07)	1.66	(1.10)
MTV	1.29	(.91)	—	—
N	1,091		1,506	

Entries for each item reflect means with standard deviations in parentheses. Due to variations in form, descriptive statistics for newspapers and comedy shows in 2000 are based on N = 556, and 1,587 for local television news in 2004.

2000; and $30,000 to under $40,000 in 2004); race (78.8 percent white); and political partisanship (42.6 percent Democrat and 42.4 percent Republican in 2000; 47.6 percent and 41.9 percent, respectively, in 2004).

Results

Use of Traditional and Nontraditional Sources of News About the Campaign. In both 2000 and 2004, respondents reported greater learning about the presidential campaign and candidates from traditional sources of news. Specifically, local television news was the source from which respondents reported learning the most, followed by network television news, and daily newspapers. Paired samples *t*-tests within each year indicated that all means differed significantly from the others at $p < .01$.

Among nontraditional sources of news, respondents in 2000 reported learning significantly more from late night television than the Internet, comedy shows, or MTV. Only learning from the Internet and learning from comedy shows did not differ significantly from each other. In 2004, however, the pattern of findings differed slightly with reported levels of learning from the Internet greater than late night television (at $p < .10$), both of which were statistically greater than learning from comedy shows.

Political Knowledge. As the hierarchical regression analyses in Table 17.2 reveal, political knowledge clearly is a function of one's sociodemographics, which accounted for a quarter to slightly over a third of the variance. In both years, males, older respondents, those with higher levels of education and income, and whites were significantly more likely to score higher on the political knowledge items. Republicans also were more likely to score higher, but only in 2000.

In addition, various aspects of traditional news media use were related to political knowledge both years: respondents who reported learning about the campaign from newspapers had higher levels of knowledge about the campaign, while those who reported learning from local television news manifested *lower* levels of actual knowledge. Analyses show that after controlling for both demographics and traditional media use, perceived learning from late night talk shows was negatively associated with knowledge (but only marginally so), and

TABLE 17.2.   Predicting Political Knowledge by Demographics, Partisanship, and Media Use

	2000	2004
Demographics		
Sex (female)	−.14[‡]	−.25[‡]
Age	.22[‡]	.25[‡]
Education	.38[‡]	.26[‡]
Income	.16[‡]	.17[‡]
Race (white)	.11[‡]	.11[‡]
Democrat	.05	.05
Republican	.07[†]	.05
R^2 (%)	35.5[‡]	27.4[‡]
Traditional News		
Newspapers	.11[‡]	.14[‡]
Network TV news	.07[*]	−.03
Local TV news	−.09[†]	−.09[‡]
Incremental R^2 (%)	1.6[‡]	2.5[‡]
Nontraditional News		
Late night talk shows	−.07[*]	−.10[*]
Internet	.07[*]	.14[‡]
Comedy shows	.09[†]	−.01
MTV	−.04	—
Incremental R^2 (%)	1.2[†]	2.3[‡]
Final R^2 (%)	38.4[‡]	32.2[‡]
Adjusted R^2 (%)	36.7[‡]	31.5[‡]

All coefficients are standardized upon-entry coefficients from hierarchical regression analyses.

[*]$p < .10$; [†]$p < .05$; [‡]$p < .01$.

use of (and presumably learning from) comedy shows was positively related to learning about candidates, but only in 2000. Reported learning from the Internet was related to actual knowledge both years.

Voting Frequency.   Like political knowledge, voting frequency was significantly related to demographic variables, though to a lesser degree (accounting for less than a quarter of the variance both years). Table 17.3 shows that age and education were predictors of voting frequency. However, in 2004, nonwhites and partisans also reported greater frequency of voting in the past.

Traditional news sources had a bearing on the extent to which one voted: reading newspapers (or at least reported learning from this medium) was positively related to voting in both years, but the only broadcast news to show any significant association in 2000 was network television news. For 2004, it was only local television news. With respect to the "new news," only Internet use/learning was positively related to frequency of voting, and that was only in 2004.

General Political Participation. The relationships between the antecedents noted in Table 17.3 and general political participation are similar to those for voting in some respects, but markedly different

TABLE 17.3. Predicting Political Participation by Demographics, Partisanship, and Media Use

	2000		2004	
	Frequency of Voting	Political Participation	Frequency of Voting	Political Participation
Demographics				
Sex (female)	.03	−.05	.02	−.05*
Age	.32‡	.15‡	.43‡	.23‡
Education	.26‡	.28‡	.13‡	.16‡
Income	.04	.21‡	.06†	.16‡
Race (white)	.06	.01	−.06†	.10‡
Democrat	.06	.05	.31‡	.13‡
Republican	.04	.04	.24‡	.11‡
R² (%)	21.0‡	20.9‡	23.7‡	15.2‡
Traditional News				
Newspapers	.12‡	.14‡	.11‡	.10‡
Network TV news	.10†	.09†	−.03	−.03
Local TV news	−.012	−.09†	.11‡	.01
Incremental R² (%)	.7‡	2.6‡	2.4‡	.9‡
Nontraditional News				
Late night talk shows	.05	.01	.03	−.03
Internet	.04	.17‡	.09‡	.18‡
Comedy shows	−.05	−.00	−.05*	.08‡
MTV	−.02	−.08†	—	—
Incremental R² (%)	.4	2.7‡	.7‡	2.8‡
Political Knowledge	.12‡	.09*	.17‡	.16‡
Incremental R² (%)	.9‡	.5*	1.9‡	1.7‡
R² (%)	25.0‡	26.6‡	28.8‡	20.6‡
Adjusted R² (%)	22.9‡	24.5‡	28.0‡	19.8‡

All coefficients are standardized upon-entry coefficients from hierarchical regression analyses.

*p < .10; †p < .05; ‡p < .01.

in others. Age, education, and income predicted participation in both surveys, but in 2004, higher levels of participation were found among whites and partisans as well.

If learning from the media reflects use of the media, then newspaper reading was strongly related to various forms of political behavior. Network TV news was positively related, and local TV news negatively, to participation in 2000. In 2004, these associations did not emerge from the data. Regarding nontraditional media, use of the Internet was positively related to participation in both surveys, and viewing/learning from comedy shows was positively related to such behaviors in 2004.

Political knowledge was significantly associated with voting frequency both years, but only with participation in 2004 (though positive, the coefficient in 2000 was only marginally significant).

Discussion

The goal of this chapter was to examine the extent to which nontraditional, infotainment-based sources of news contribute to Americans' sense of citizenship in light of social structure and use of "traditional" media. Overall, the analyses generated no surprises regarding the relationships between demographics and political knowledge and various forms of participation. Individuals' sociodemographic locations predict what they know, not an unexpected finding in light of previous research.[32] Although the differential impact of Democratic and Republican partisanship on knowledge in 2000 may come as a surprise, this finding may be attributed to the fact that the political knowledge scale comprised two items that asked respondents of Republican candidates and one that asked about a Democratic candidate. Similarly, results support the early socioeconomic model of participation.[33] That partisanship (regardless of direction) and race were additional predictors in 2004 of political activity may have been a function of the tenor of a campaign conducted in the midst of an ongoing war for which there was decreasing support.

Political knowledge and behavior, however, derive from factors other than demographics. This study is concerned with the effects of various media that have played an increasingly prominent role in American politics, as evidenced by campaigns 2000 and 2004. Simply put, the effects differ depending on the medium and the assumptions made.

If one assumes that reports of learning from a given medium are accurate and reflect use of that medium, then the findings presented herein echo one long-standing finding: newspaper use enhances citizenship by increasing levels of knowledge and political engagement. Under this assumption, the effects of watching network news would be mixed. Viewing would slightly enhance knowledge of political players in one year but not the other, and bolster levels of political participation only in 2000. Similarly mixed findings would emerge for local television news—depressing levels of knowledge in both years and participation, with the latter affected only in 2004.

With respect to the key media variables, assuming equity between use of a medium and learning from that medium would cast late night talk shows in an uncomplimentary light. These findings would then suggest that watching shows such as *The Tonight Show* or *The Late Show* serves as a deterrent to learning about candidates. However, from this perspective, the Internet and comedy shows such as *Saturday Night Live* and *Politically Incorrect* in 2000 would help promote knowledge gain. In the realm of political behavior, using the Internet would be similarly beneficial, and watching comedy shows would only mobilize audience members in one year. And watching MTV would have had a detrimental effect on political behavior.

If, on the other hand, one divorces reports of learning from a given medium from actual use of that medium, and interprets the media-related antecedent variables as merely perceived learning, then different conclusions emerge. Specifically, individuals who say they learned about the campaign from newspapers actually knew more about the campaign, but people who reported learning about the campaign from local television news knew significantly less about the candidates.

Despite outranking all other media as the source from which individuals learn about the campaign and candidates, local television news appears to be contributing least to knowledge about the campaign, at least as measured by these particular items. The data suggest that people's perceptions of learning from local television news are just that; they are unrelated to actual knowledge and negatively to political participation (in one year), though positively to voting frequency (also in only one data set). Perceptions of learning from network television news and newspapers, on the other hand, are more robust predictors; they contribute to one's knowledge, voting, and overall level of political participation (with network TV news making a difference only in 2000). Thus, of traditional news sources, newspapers once again have gained the status of favored child in studies of political learning.

Given the coefficients in Table 17.2, some perceptions of learning from nontraditional news sources may also be just perceptions. Reported learning from late night talk shows did not translate into knowledge, although perceived learning from the Web and comedy shows did correspond to higher levels of objective knowledge (with the latter only in 2000).

With respect to various forms of political behavior, perceived learning from nontraditional sources—if the measures were to be interpreted as only that—had some beneficial effects. People who learned about the campaign online were generally more likely to vote and be politically active during a campaign, and those who said they learned from a comedy show in 2004 also were more likely to be active.

Analysis of these data sets raises a number of very interesting points regarding the study of nontraditional news sources such as late night comedy. The first concerns the transmission of information and the measurement of knowledge gained from the consumption of such information. Doris Graber has long argued that information tests tend to privilege those pieces of information gained from print media, and has advocated for measures and closer study of the transmission and processing of audiovisual information.[34] The bulk of knowledge measures in campaign studies typically favor asking respondents who holds a particular office or how a given candidate stands on an issue. Thus incorporating items based on information gleaned from soft news could include questions related to politicians' personal lives or contextually based facts emerging from longer interviews.[35] After all, soft news information—viewed as "personally useful or merely entertaining"—can be used as the basis for political judgments.[36]

A second point of concern relates to the need to study the differential effects of these nontraditional sources of news. Although it is compelling for lay audiences to discuss and speculate on the effects of "late night talk shows" or "comedy shows," such discussions typically tend to treat each genre as a singular phenomenon. But parody-based *Saturday Night Live* is a different beast from *The Daily Show*, which is grounded in both political satire and live interviews. Similarly, to talk of "Web effects" would be to do injustice to the entire medium. But the search for differential effects should be based in the study of audience members as well. Considering how the media landscape has become increasingly fragmented, it is no surprise that different demographic groups have turned to sources that they feel have tailored toward them.[37] To study media effects on the consumers of these media would therefore be more appropriate, but to examine these effects in light of the larger media landscape would be most beneficial, even if this landscape shifts regularly.[38] Also, because political jokes succeed only when one understands the real-life context, it would be most inappropriate to conclude that politically apathetic citizens get the most out of politically oriented popular culture shows. In fact, audience members' levels of political sophistication can moderate the effects of viewing late night comedy shows (*Letterman* or *Leno*) and *Oprah* on various forms of political behavior.[39]

Finally, with the slow but certain infusion of infotainment and soft news content into our political lives, researchers need to concern themselves with the extent to which audience members can associate the sources from which they receive *any* type of information. If survey research is prone to issues of social desirability bias and recall, then scholars should seek to supplement their data with experimental or content-analytic methods, particular as they can help shed light on the effects of such content.

It is clear that the findings presented here and elsewhere support Delli Carpini and Williams's position that politics today "infotains" us.[40] With the distinction between news and entertainment holding increasingly less currency, future research should sustain efforts to explore the interaction of political news and entertainment values, production, and content, all of which can have great implications for democracy.

Appendix 1. Question Wording

Media Use Items.   Now I'd like to ask you about some specific ways in which you might be getting news about the presidential campaign. For each item that I read, please tell me how often, if ever, you LEARN SOMETHING about the PRESIDENTIAL CAMPAIGN or the CANDIDATES from this source.

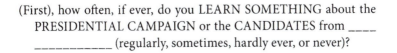

(First), how often, if ever, do you LEARN SOMETHING about the PRESIDENTIAL CAMPAIGN or the CANDIDATES from ____ _____ (regularly, sometimes, hardly ever, or never)?

Item asked of:

- MTV (2000 only)
- Late night TV shows such as *David Letterman* and *Jay Leno*; the Internet
- The local TV news about your viewing area
- The national nightly network news on CBS, ABC, and NBC
- Comedy shows such as *Saturday Night Live* and *Politically Incorrect* (2000 only)
- *The Daily Show* (2004 only)
- Your daily newspaper

Political Knowledge. Now I would like to ask you about some things that have been in the news. Not everyone will have heard about them. ...

Do you happen to know which of the presidential candidates is now governor of Texas? (2000)

Do you happen to know which of the presidential candidates was formerly a senator from New Jersey? (2000)

Do you happen to know which of the presidential candidates co-sponsored a campaign finance reform bill in Congress? (2000)

Do you happen to know which of the presidential candidates served as an Army general? (2004)

Do you happen to know which of the presidential candidates served as the majority leader in the House of Representatives? (2004)

Voting Frequency. How often would you say you vote—always, nearly always, part of the time, or never?

Political Participation. People express their opinions about politics and current events in a number of ways. I'm going to read a list of some of these ways. Have you EVER:

Contacted any elected official?

Contributed money to a candidate running for public office?

Joined an organization in support of a particular cause?

Attended a city or town council meeting in the community where you live? (2000 only)

Attended a political party meeting or function? (2000 only)

Attended a campaign event? (2004 only)

Thinking ONLY ABOUT THE LAST TWELVE MONTHS, that is since January of (1999/2003), have you... (items as above)?

Demographics
Sex: Ascertained by interviewer
Age: What is your age?
Education: What is the last grade or class that you completed in school?
Income: Last year, that is in (1999), what was your total family income from all sources, before taxes? Just stop me when I get to the right category:
Less than $10,000
$10,000 to under $20,000
$20,000 to under $30,000
$30,000 to under $40,000
$40,000 to under $50,000
$50,000 to under $75,000
$75,000 to under $100,000
$100,000 or more
Race: Are you, yourself of Hispanic origin or descent, such as Mexican, Puerto Rican, Cuban, or some other Spanish background? [IF YES] Are you white Hispanic, black Hispanic, or some other? [IF NO] What is your race? Are you white, black, Asian, or some other?

Political Partisanship.   In politics today, do you consider yourself a Republican, Democrat, or Independent?

[IF NOT A REPUBLICAN OR DEMOCRAT] As of today do you lean more to the Republican Party or more to the Democratic Party?

Notes

1. The author thanks Michael A. Xenos and Verena K. Hess for their contributions to projects and papers related to this chapter.
2. Philip Meyer, "The Media Reformation: Giving the Agenda Back to the People," in *The Elections of 1992*, ed. Michael Nelson (Washington, DC: Congressional Quarterly, 1993), 89–108.
3. Barry A. Hollander, "The 'New News' and the 1992 Presidential Campaign: Perceived vs. Actual Political Knowledge," *Journalism & Mass Communication Quarterly* 72 (1995): 786–798; Jack M. McLeod,

Zhongshi Guo, Katie Daily, et al., "The Impact of Traditional and Nontraditional Forms of Mass Media in the 1992 Presidential Election," *Journalism & Mass Communication Quarterly* 73 (1996): 401–416.

4. Edwin Diamond, Martha McKay, and Robert Silverman, "Pop Goes Politics: New Media, Interactive Formats, and the 1992 Presidential Campaign," *American Behavioral Scientist* 37 (1993): 257–261.

5. Diana Owen. "The Press' Performance," In *Toward the Millennium: The Elections of 1996*, ed. Larry J. Sabato (Needham Heights, MA: Allyn & Bacon, 1997).

6. Ibid., 219.

7. Frank Bruni, "The Election: Putting Out More Flags," *New York Times*, December 3, 2000, section 4, 3.

8. Caryn James, "The 2000 Campaign: The Talk Show Front—Critic's Notebook; Blurring Distinctions While Chasing Laughs," *New York Times*, September 22, 2000, A19.

9. Diana C. Mutz, "The Future of Political Communication Research," *Political Communication* 18 (2001): 231–236.

10. John Zaller, "A New Standard of News Quality: Burglar Alarms for the Monitorial Citizen," *Political Communication* 20 (2003): 109–130; Michael X. Delli Carpini and Bruce A. Williams, "Let Us Infotain You: Politics in the New Media Environment," in *Mediated Politics: Communication in the Future of Democracy*, eds. W. Lance Bennett and Robert M. Entman (New York: Cambridge University Press, 2001), 160–181.

11. Dannagal G. Young, "Late-night Comedy in Election 2000: Its Influence on Candidate Trait Ratings and the Moderating Effects of Political Knowledge and Partisanship," *Journal of Broadcasting & Electronic Media* 48 (2004): 1–22; Jody Baumgartner and Jonathon S. Morris, "The Daily Show Effect: Candidate Evaluations, Efficacy, and American Youth," *American Politics Research* 34 (2006): 341–367; Patricia Moy, Michael A. Xenos, and Verena K. Hess, "Communication and Citizenship: Mapping the Political Effects of Infotainment," *Mass Communication & Society* 8 (2005): 111–131; Matthew A. Baum and Angela S. Jamison, "The Oprah Effect: How Soft News Helps Inattentive Citizens Vote Consistently," *The Journal of Politics* 68 (2006): 946–959.

12. "The Tough Job of Communicating with Voters," *The Pew Research Center for the People and the Press*, February 5, 2000. http://people-press.org/reports/display.php3?PageID=242.

13. Orit Ichilov, *Political Socialization, Citizenship Education, and Democracy* (New York: Teachers College Press, 1990); Robert A. Dahl, *Democracy and Its Critics* (New Haven, CT: Yale University Press, 1989).

14. Michael Gurevitch and Jay G. Blumler, "Political Communication Systems and Democratic Values," in *Democracy and the Mass Media*, ed. Judith Lichtenberg (Cambridge, UK: Cambridge University Press, 1990), 269–289.

15. See, for example, Michael X. Delli Carpini and Scott Keeter, *What Americans Know about Politics and Why It Matters* (New Haven, CT: Yale University Press, 1996); Doris A. Graber, *Processing Politics: Learning from Television in the Internet Age* (Chicago: University of Chicago Press, 2001); Gerald M. Kosicki and Jack M. McLeod, "Learning from Political News: Effects of Media Images and Information-processing Strategies," in *Mass Communication and Political Information Processing*, ed. S. Kraus (Hillsdale, NJ: Lawrence Erlbaum Associates, 1990), 69–83; "TV Remains Dominant News and Product Information Source, New Poll Reveals," *Roper Organization*, May 28, 1997. http://www.roper.com.

16. See, for example, Sidney Verba, Kay L. Schlozman, and Henry E. Brady, *Voice and Equality: Civic Voluntarism in American Politics* (Cambridge, MA: Harvard University Press, 1995); Russell W. Neuman, *The Paradox of Mass Politics: Knowledge and Opinion in the American Electorate* (Cambridge, MA: Harvard University Press, 1986); Robert D. Putnam, "Bowling Alone: America's Declining Social Capital," *Journal of Democracy* 6 (1995): 65–78.

17. John P. Robinson and Mark R. Levy, *The Main Source: Learning from Television News* (Beverly Hills, CA: Sage, 1986).

18. John P. Robinson and Mark R. Levy, "News Media Use and the Informed Public: A 1990s Update," *Journal of Communication* 46 (1996): 129–135.

19. David Weaver and Dan Drew, "Voter Learning in the 1992 Presidential Election: Did the 'Nontraditional' Media and Debates Matter?" *Journalism Quarterly* 72 (1995): 7–17.

20. Stephen H. Chaffee, Xinshu Zhao, and Glenn Leshner, "Political Knowledge and the Campaign Media of 1992," *Communication Research* 21 (1994): 305–324.

21. Hollander, "The 'New News' and the 1992 Presidential Campaign."

22. Thomas J. Johnson, Mahmoud A. M. Braima, and Jayanthi Sothirajah, "Doing the Traditional Media Sidestep: Comparing the Effects of the Internet and Other Nontraditional Media with Traditional Media in the 1996 Presidential Campaign," *Journalism & Mass Communication Quarterly* 76 (1999): 99–123; Dan Drew and David Weaver, "Voter Learning in the 1996 Presidential Election: Did the Media Matter?" *Journalism & Mass Communication Quarterly* 75 (1998): 292–301.

23. Dan Drew and David Weaver, "Voter Learning in the 2004 Presidential Election: Did the Media Matter?" *Journalism & Mass Communication Quarterly* 83 (2006): 25–42.
24. Dahl, *Democracy and Its Critics*.
25. Samuel H. Barnes and Max K. Kaase, *Political Action: Mass Participation in Five Western Democracies* (Beverly Hills, CA: Sage, 1979); Verba et al., *Voice and Equality*.
26. Stephen E. Bennett, *Apathy in America 1960–1984: Causes & Consequences of Citizen Political Indifference* (Dobbs Ferry, NY: Transnational Publishers, 1986); Stephen D. Shaffer, "A Multivariate Explanation of Decreasing Turnout in Presidential Elections, 1960–1976," *American Journal of Political Science* 25 (1981): 68–95.
27. McLeod et al., "The Impact of Traditional and Nontraditional Forms of Mass Media."
28. J. David Kennamer. "How Media Use During Campaign Affects the Intent to Vote," *Journalism Quarterly* 64 (1987): 291–300.
29. See also Gurevitch and Blumler, "Political Communication Systems and Democratic Values."
30. Dan Drew and David Weaver, "Voter Learning in the 1996 Presidential Election"; Johnson et al., "Doing the Traditional Media Sidestep"; McLeod et al., "The Impact of Traditional and Nontraditional Forms of Mass Media"; Weaver and Drew, "Voter Learning in the 1992 Presidential Election."
31. Steven H. Chaffee and Joan Schleuder, "Measurement and Effects of Attention to Media News," *Human Communication Research* 13 (1986): 76–107.
32. See, for example, Delli Carpini and Keeter, *What Americans Know About Politics and Why It Matters*.
33. Lester W. Milbrath, *Political Participation* (Chicago: Rand McNally, 1965); Sidney Verba and Norman H. Nie, *Participation in America: Political Democracy and Social Equality* (New York: Harper & Row, 1972).
34. Doris A. Graber, "Why Voters Fail Information Tests: Can the Hurdles be Overcome?" *Political Communication* 11 (1994): 331–346; Doris A. Graber, "Say It with Pictures," *The Annals of the American Academy of Political and Social Science* 546 (1996): 86–96.
35. Joanna Weiss, "Late-night's Not a Laugher for Candidates," *Boston Globe*, November 23, 2003, C1; e.g., why George W. Bush referred to *New York Times* reporter Adam Clymer by an expletive; Patricia Moy, Michael A. Xenos, and Verena K. "Hess Priming Effects of Late-night Comedy," *International Journal of Public Opinion Research* 18 (2006): 198–210.
36. Zaller "A New Standard of News Quality," 129; Sam L. Popkin, *The Reasoning Voter: Communication and Persuasion in Presidential Elections* (Chicago: University of Chicago Press, 1991).

37. As in the case of young adults and late night talk shows; "The Tough Job of Communicating with Voters."
38. See, for example, Nojin Kwak, Xiaoru Wang, and Lauren Guggenheim, "Laughing All the Way: The Relationship between Television Entertainment Talk Show Viewing and Political Engagement among Young Adults" (paper presented at the annual meeting of the Association for Education in Journalism and Mass Communication, Toronto, Canada, August 2004).
39. Moy et al., "Communication and Citizenship."
40. Delli Carpini and Williams, "Let Us Infotain You."

18

The Daily Show and Attitudes toward the News Media

Jonathan S. Morris and Jody C Baumgartner

Now commonly referred to as the "fourth branch" of the United States government, the news media have become an increasingly high-profile participant in the political process. Although the media are the primary window through which the public looks to observe the issues and events of the political world, the media are a recognized political entity themselves.[1] This recognition opens the institution up for criticism similar to that directed at Congress, the executive branch, or the courts. Thus, just as Congress and the president are often blamed for societal ills, blame often falls on the media as well.[2]

While political leaders and institutions have always been subject to parody, modern-day humorists and satirists are increasingly turning their attention toward the mass media. Similarly to Congress or the president, the media are lampooned most intensely when major gaffes occur, such as the Jason Blair plagiarism scandal at the *New York Times*, or the "Rathergate" debacle at CBS in 2004 when *60 Minutes* used falsified documents to investigate George W. Bush's service in the National Guard during the Vietnam War. On television there are several examples of humorists ridiculing the personalities and practices of the mass media on a regular basis. Since the turn of the century, one of the most visible lampooners of the media has been *The Daily Show* with Jon Stewart, which gained notoriety by consistently mocking mainstream journalism's approach to covering politics in America. Not only does *The Daily Show* directly criticize the media's missteps through humor, but the program is also framed as a "fake news" show that satirically highlights the modern news media's self-aggrandizing, commercialism, and tendency to over-editorialize its coverage. These forms of critical humor, we contend, resonate with viewers as public trust in the media continues to plummet in America.

This chapter will demonstrate that, although *The Daily Show* is well known for lambasting political leaders and institutions, it is particularly critical of the mass media. We will first discuss the relationship between the media and the public. Then, using examples from *The Daily Show*, we will illustrate the various methods through which this popular "fake news" program and its host, Jon Stewart, ridicule the media. Finally, we will use experimental and survey evidence to demonstrate that exposure to *The Daily Show* negatively impacts trust and support for the mass media among its primary audience—young adults.

Public Perceptions of the News Media

Overall, the public does not think very highly of the news media. According to survey data from the Pew Research Center for the People and the Press, over half of the American public (53 percent) say they often do not trust what news organizations are saying.[3] In addition, over two-thirds (69 percent) report seeing a fair or great amount of political bias in news coverage, while only 7 percent see no bias at all.[4] Figure 18.1 demonstrates the clear trend in how the public's support for the media has eroded since the 1970s.[5] The percentage of Americans displaying confidence in the press has declined, while the percentage of those displaying cynicism toward the institution has

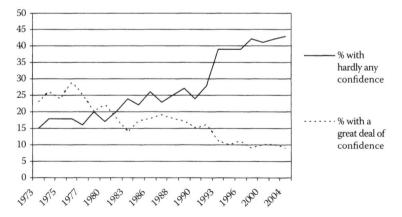

Figure 18.1.   Public support for the press.

increased. In 1976, 26 percent of the American public had "a great deal of confidence" in the press. By 2004, this percentage of support had dropped to 9 percent. By the same token, only 18 percent of the population had "hardly any confidence" in the press in 1976. In 2004, this number had increased to 43 percent.[6]

Why has confidence in the media declined so sharply? Certainly, the media are not the only institution to see their public support decline in recent decades. Support for government and other public institutions have steadily declined as well, and overall trust in these institutions has dropped off significantly.[7] Some observers have pointed to event-driven causes of this declining support and trust, such as Vietnam, Watergate, the Monica Lewinsky scandal, or the more recent intelligence failures surrounding the U.S.–led invasion of Iraq. The media too have had their fair share of embarrassing high-profile events that damaged their credibility. During the 2000 presidential election, the majority of the television news stations offering election-night coverage prematurely announced a winner before the evidence was clear.[8] In 2004, CBS News ran a feature story on *60 Minutes* that chronicled the service record of President Bush in the National Guard during the Vietnam War. This story, which was highly critical of Bush's service to the National Guard, relied on forged documents that eventually discredited the story and irreversibly damaged the reputation CBS News anchor, Dan Rather.

While event-driven explanations can offer contextual nuance to the continuing decline in public support for political institutions (like the media), they only go so far. In 1975, a more encompassing theory was posited by Michael Robinson, who argued that the televised medium was to blame.[9] Specifically, Robinson articulated the concept of "videomalaise," which contends that negative news coverage of political issues and events drives increases in cynicism among the viewing audience. Following the turbulence of Vietnam and Watergate, the media appeared to take a much more cynical approach to the political world.[10] This negative outlook, combined with increased market competition on television and beyond, compelled political journalists to add more controversy to their coverage in order to attract a larger audience.[11] This tactic has taken the form of highlighting personality clashes,[12] scandals,[13] partisan rivalry,[14] and covering politics as a strategic game between self-obsessed political actors.[15] In short, news coverage is sensationalized.[16] When the media highlights a sensationalized picture of politics, public approval for the featured actors and institutions tends to drop. The visual medium of television tends to exacerbate this reaction by appealing to the negative emotions of the viewers more than text-based media, such as newspapers.[17]

In the context of videomalaise, the media's cynical approach to politics appears to have generated a backlash from the public. That is, not only does support for government institutions decline, but support for the media drops as well. In this regard, efforts among journalists to create a more entertaining product appear self-defeating.[18] While sensationalized coverage may draw better ratings than dry policy-based news, the public often responds coldly to the media for acting irresponsibly or unfairly.[19] The public finds the media's stories on personal impropriety too invasive and/or politically irrelevant compared with more important policy issues.[20] For example, the public soured on the media for obsessing on the Monica Lewinsky scandal as well as the extramarital affairs of otherwise obscure congressmen such as Robert Packwood in the 1990s and Gary Condit in 2001. Other reports of financial malfeasance or government corruption are often viewed as unsubstantiated hearsay from self-absorbed journalists attempting to gain notoriety, rather than objective whistle-blowing.

The public is also critical of the media's increasing tendency to blend news with entertainment, otherwise known as *infotainment*.[21] An increasing number of news sources are competing for smaller pieces of the ratings pie. The result is increased market competition in a fragmented media environment.[22] Attempts to attract viewers by "livening up" the news with entertainment are becoming more transparent, and responses from potential viewers can be quite negative.[23]

Another factor associated with hostile attitudes toward the media is the growing tendency of "attacking the messenger" in the news.[24] Elected officials, pundits, and writers (especially those on the right) have become extremely critical of the news media since the 1970s. This anti-media sentiment has been voiced with increased frequency in recent years. The most common criticism along these lines is that the media have a "liberal bias."[25] However, others have argued that the media have become a timid institution that is more interested in profit and notoriety than acting as a public watchdog.[26] The media do not often tackle questionable policy decisions, since they are seen as having limited allure to potential viewers. The result is that significant government policies, such as the War on Terror and Gulf War II, are not sufficiently analyzed by the media.[27]

Jon Stewart, *The Daily Show,* and the News Media

The host of *The Daily Show,* Jon Stewart, appears to subscribe to several of the above criticisms of the media. On several occasions Stewart has articulated his frustration with the mainstream media's approach to covering the Bush administration. His frustration is primarily that the Washington press corps is too self-interested to risk upsetting the administration. In a 2003 interview, Stewart told Bill Moyers

> You know what's great? Watch a Bush press conference, and then turn on Tony Blair and Parliament, where he literally has to sit in front of his most vociferous critics.... Contrast that with a press conference that Bush had on the eve of war. [Imitating Bush] "Uh, okay, the next question is Jim. Is there a Jim here? Yeah, you got the next one.... That is not the agreed upon question. We're gonna move on. Ralph, you got something?" It's an incredibly managed theatrical farce. And it's incredible to me that people [in the press] are playing along with it. And they say that they're playing along with it because they're afraid of losing access. You don't have any access. There's nothing to lose.

When discussing political biases of television news reporters and journalists, Stewart points much of his criticism at the Fox News Channel and its perceived rightward bias and closeness to the Bush administration. For example, Stewart once sarcastically claimed in an interview, "I enjoy watching Fox News and I think every country should have their own Al Jazeera." Also, when former Fox News anchor and talk radio host Tony Snow was hired in 2006 to become Bush's press secretary, Stewart quipped, "In other words, the White House is considering paying a Fox News reporter to tell the public what they want the public to hear. I hope he's up to the job."

This negative perception of Fox News's association with the Bush administration can also be seen from Stewart's comments on *The Daily Show* following Vice President Dick Cheney's 2006 hunting accident in which he mistakenly shot seventy-eight-year-old Harry Whittington.

> A mere five days after shooting a man in the face, Vice President Dick Cheney broke his silence about the incident by submitting to a no-holds-barred grilling at a public press conference. I'm just kidding.... Actually, he sat down with Brit Hume on Fox News for not so much a grilling— more of a teat suckle.

Not too long after that event, news leaked from the administration that hotels in which the vice president stayed were instructed by advance teams to tune all televisions to Fox News before Cheney arrived in the room. In reaction to this news, Stewart told viewers that

> Here's the detail I found most interesting: all the television sets must be tuned to Fox News. Wow! Because god forbid he walks into a hotel room, and the TV is on another channel, and he finds out what a sh---y job he's been doing.

Because Cheney is one of Stewart's favorite targets, he added a further dig on the controversial vice president by noting, "There was one other detail on the bottom of the [hotel instructions]; it was handwritten and somewhat cryptic. He also requests a rifle, some ammo, and an old man's face."

Stewart, however, is not only critical of the Fox News Channel. He also finds a great deal of fault with twenty-four-hour cable news networks in general. For instance, in a 2003 interview with Howard Kurtz of CNN's *Reliable Sources*, Stewart took the cable news industry to task for overusing the terms "breaking news" or "news alert" to grab the attention of viewers.

> *Stewart:* But yeah, you know, the 24-hour news cycle is the visual medium, so if they've got pictures of immigrants jumping off of a boat into the water, I guess that beats a [political] stump speech.
>
> *Kurtz:* Breaking news.
>
> *Stewart:* Yes, exactly, breaking news. Although, quite frankly, you guys broke it. I mean, let's face facts. I mean, breaking news—the words breaking news I don't even think can be used any more.
>
> *Kurtz:* They've been overused?
>
> *Stewart:* Well, during the [Washington, DC] sniper thing, they just left it up there. They just literally left up the "breaking news" graphic.

Stewart often runs a skit that ridicules television news' efforts to fill airtime when there is nothing that can even remotely act as "breaking news" or "news alerts." This segment is called "Slow News Day" and features clips from television news shows covering people and events that hardly qualify as "news." Examples include (1) Al Roker's *Today Show* interview with the cast members of the 1980s sitcom *The Facts of Life*; (2) members of the Fox News morning show, *Fox and Friends*, spending three hours of their broadcast attempting to pressure actor Hugh Grant into an interview; or (3) a detailed discussion on Fox News regarding the shape and evolution of Geraldo Rivera's mustache.

At the outset of the Gulf War in 2003, Stewart reminded his viewers on *The Daily Show* that his intent was to make people laugh, and not to provide serious commentary. However, he also added a jab on the rest of television news, which says a great deal regarding how he views the credibility of his cable news competitors.

> But we are at war, and we here at *The Daily Show* will do our best to keep you informed of any late-breaking…*humor* we can find. Of course, our show is obviously at a disadvantage compared to the many news sources that we're competing with…at a disadvantage in several respects. For one thing, we are fake. They are not. So in terms of credibility we are, well, oddly enough, actually about even. We're about even.

In a number of instances, Stewart has pointed out cable news' penchant for filling airtime with overly heated arguments that have little relevance to public policy or civic discourse. This criticism is mostly pointed at high-octane political talk shows, such as *Hardball with Chris Matthews*, *Hannity and Colmes*, or *The O'Reilly Factor*. To mock the common tendency of these programs to regress into partisan yelling matches with little public value, *The Daily Show* has a recurring parody titled "Great Moments in Punditry." This skit features small children reading the transcripts from particularly contentious and uncivil moments from these political talk shows, which highlight the absurdity and childishness of the programs.

Arguably, Stewart's most poignant moment in criticizing the media, however, did not occur on *The Daily Show*. Instead, it occurred on October 15, 2004, when Stewart appeared as a guest on the program *Crossfire*, a political debate show that had run on CNN since 1982. During the interview, Stewart vehemently chastised the shows hosts, Tucker Carlson and Paul Begala, for irresponsibly (and badly) covering politics.

> *Stewart:* And I made a special effort to come on the show today, because I have privately, amongst my friends and also in occasional newspapers and television shows, mentioned this show as being bad. I wanted to—I felt that that wasn't fair and I should come here and tell you that I don't—it's not so much that it's bad, as it's hurting America. But I wanted to come here today and say…. Stop, stop, stop, stop hurting America. And come work for us, because we, as the people.
>
> *Carlson:* How do you pay?

Stewart: Not well. But you can sleep at night.... See, the thing is, we need your help. Right now, you're helping the politicians and the corporations. And we're left out there to mow our lawns.

Begala: By beating up on them? You just said we're too rough on them when they make mistakes.

Stewart: No, no, no, you're not too rough on them. You're part of their strategies. You are partisan, what do you call it…hacks.

Begala: Let me get this straight. If the indictment is—and I have seen you say this—that *Crossfire* reduces everything, as I said in the intro, to left, right, black, white. Well, it's because, see, we're a debate show.

Stewart: No, no, no, no, that would be great. I would love to see a debate show. To do a debate would be great. But that's like saying pro wrestling is a show about athletic competition.... You have a responsibility to the public discourse, and you fail miserably.

Carlson: Wait. I thought you were going to be funny. Come on. Be funny.

Stewart: No. No. I'm not going to be your monkey.

Stewart's brutal exchange with the *Crossfire* hosts gained significant attention, and soon thereafter clips from the interview were circulating on the Internet. Clearly, Stewart's criticism of *Crossfire* resonated with much of the public, as countless bloggers, media critics, and (ironically) pundits began to echo his point about political debate programs. A few months later, the program was taken off the air. In discussing the cancellation, the president of CNN, Jonathan Klein, said that, "I agree wholeheartedly with Jon Stewart's overall premise [about political debate shows]."[28]

The preceding discussion illustrates how Stewart overtly criticizes the news media's coverage of politics. These examples, however, do not do *The Daily Show*'s parody of the media complete justice. Beyond obvious jokes at the expense of news journalists, *The Daily Show* is an ongoing satire of the news—even when it is mocking a different institution or individual. From start to finish, the program is a nonstop parody of the television news media, complete with a news anchor at a desk and superimposed graphic images to his upper-right side. Furthermore, almost every broadcast of *The Daily Show* features an off-studio special report from a farcically over-dramatic and self-indulgent "correspondent," who consistently acts aloof or grossly unaware. While these skits frequently get laughs at the expense of others (usually everyday people or politicians), the media lampoon is ever present.

The Effects of *The Daily Show*'s Coverage of the Media

What effect, if any, does this ridicule of the news media have on viewers? As we have discussed, there is already a preexisting notion among the public that the media are not competent or trustworthy, and it is entirely possible that viewers of *The Daily Show* simply laugh at the program's spoofs. Most likely, the program's cynical approach to the media—and politics in general—appeals primarily to individuals who are themselves cynical. That is, those individuals afflicted with videomalaise are more likely to enjoy a program that mocks the media more than individuals who do not have videomalaise. However, *The Daily Show*'s youthful audience is not entirely comprised of individuals with preexisting videomalaise. Young viewers, who have less concrete political ideas then their older counterparts, are particularly attracted to *The Daily Show* and more likely to learn from it.[29] Thus, it may be possible that *The Daily Show* actually drives videomalaise instead of simply capitalizing on it.

In order to examine the relationship between viewing *The Daily Show* and attitudes toward the media, we present evidence from a controlled laboratory experiment in which subjects were exposed to campaign coverage of politics via *The Daily Show* or standard broadcast television news (*CBS Evening News*). We also examine survey data from the Pew Research Center.

Experiment participants were selected on a voluntary basis from introductory-level courses in political science at a medium-sized public university. The first group (n = 245) viewed a short video clip of selected coverage of the two major presidential candidates and their campaigns on *The Daily Show*. The clip featured a compilation of several short segments on each candidate, which lasted just over eight minutes. The second group (n = 198) viewed a video clip of similar length and focus. However, the content of this condition was segments from election coverage on *CBS Evening News*. Like *The Daily Show* clip, this clip was composed of segments that focused equally on both candidates. However, unlike *The Daily Show* clip, the CBS clip contained no humor. The tone was serious and reflected what would be considered mainstream television campaign coverage. Because the intent of this analysis is to examine the effects of exposure to *The Daily Show* on young adults, the use of the *CBS Evening News* clip provides a baseline of comparison between humorous and traditional television news. The third condition of the experiment contained no video stimulus. This group (n = 289) served as the control.[30] Subjects who watched *The Daily Show* or the CBS clip filled out a posttest questionnaire immediately afterward. Control group subjects completed the same questionnaire, but watched no news clip.

The focus of the clips from *The Daily Show* and *CBS Evening News* were not on the news media. Instead the coverage focused exclusively on the 2004 presidential candidates and their campaigns. No overt criticism of the news media was made in the clips. Only *The Daily Show's* subtle parody of the media was present, as it always is in their programming. Nevertheless, Table 18.1 shows that exposure to the clips from *The Daily Show* had a significant negative effect on multiple measures of trust and approval for the news media, even when controlling for various attitudinal and demographic variables. According to estimates from the posttest questionnaire, exposure to *The Daily Show* was significantly linked to increased cynicism toward the news media. Specifically, subjects exposed to *The Daily Show* were significantly more likely to agree that the media care more about profit then providing legitimate news, and they were less likely to agree that they trust the news media to cover political events fairly and accurately. The last column of Table 18.1 also shows that exposure to *The Daily Show* also significantly decreased the subjects' overall ratings of the news media in covering politics.

Table 18.1 also shows, however, that exposure to the program did not significantly increase the subject's chance of agreeing that the news media have a liberal bias. While recent media critics of Jon Stewart argue that his show is unduly harsh on the Bush administration and overly soft on the Democratic opposition, our findings do not demonstrate any effect of exposure on this account. This is, of course, not surprising given the shortness of the experimental news clips.

Coefficients from the logit estimates displayed in Table 18.1 cannot be directly interpreted to demonstrate the magnitude of the effect of the independent variable (in this case, exposure to the video clips). Therefore, estimates from Table 18.1 have been converted into predicted probabilities that are displayed in Table 18.2 while holding the control variables at their mean values. As can be seen, while the effects of exposure to *The Daily Show* are not overwhelming, they

TABLE 18.1. Experimental Results: Exposure to *The Daily Show* and Attitudes toward the Media

	Media Care More about Profit Than Providing Legitimate News	Trust Media to Cover Political Events Fairly and Accurately	News Media Have a Liberal Bias	Overall Rating of News Media's Performance in Covering Politics
	(1 = strongly disagree; 2 = disagree; 3 = neither agree nor disagree; 4 = agree; 5 = strongly agree)			(1=poor; 2=only fair; 3=good; 4=excellent)
Daily Show[a]	.36 (.17)*	-.43 (.17)†	.09 (.17)	-.30 (.18)*
CBS Evening News[b]	.03 (.18)	-.18 (.17)	-.03 (.18)	.01 (.18)
White[c]	-.00 (.21)	.19 (.20)	.01 (.20)	-.02 (.22)
Male[d]	.59 (.15)†	-.03 (.14)	.23 (.15)	-.47 (.15)†
Party ID[e]	.10 (.07)	-.20 (.07)†	.58 (.08)†	-.21 (.07)†
Party intensity[f]	-.06 (.11)	.18 (.11)*	.18 (.11)	.15 (.12)
Constant 1	-3.12	-1.95	-.89	-2.65
Constant 2	-1.23	-.24	.39	-.82
Constant 3	-.37	.41	2.41	2.36
Constant 4	1.62	2.40	4.11	—
LR^2	26.74†	14.78*	89.73†	24.80
N	671	674	673	669

All entries are ordered logit coefficients with standard errors in parentheses.

[a]*1=Exposed to The Daily Show; 0=Exposed to CBS News or control group.*
[b]*1=Exposed to CBS News; 0=Exposed to The Daily Show or control group.*
[c]*White=1; Nonwhite=0*
[d]*Male=0; Female=0*
[e]*1=Strong Democrat; 2=Democrat; 3=neither Democrat nor Republican; 4=Republican; 5=Strong Republican.*
[f]*1=Neither Democrat nor Republican; 2=Democrat or Republican; 3=Strong Democrat or strong Republican.*
**p* < .05; †*p* < .01 (one-tailed).*

TABLE 18.2.   Predicted Probabilities by Experimental Exposure

	Probability of agreeing that news media care more about profit than providing legitimate news	Probability of agreeing that they trust media to cover politics fairly and accurately	Rating news media's performance in covering politics in America good or excellent
Daily Show	.77	.27	.48
CBS Evening News	.70	.32	.56
Control Group	.70	.36	.55

Predicted probabilities are based on the models presented in Table 18.1, with all other independent variables set at their mean. Probabilities were generated in STATA 9.2 using CLARIFY.

are not marginal, especially considering that party identification and partisan intensity are held constant. It is also noticeable that the differences between the *CBS Evening News* condition and the control group are, in fact, marginal. These probabilities demonstrate that the effect of the experimental stimuli was not only statistically significant, but also substantively significant.

The limitation of controlled experimental analysis is that the environment in which the stimuli are administered is not always an accurate depiction of the "real world." To preserve internal validity, experimental environments are highly controlled. The negative side effect of this control, however, is a lack of generalizability (i.e., external validity) of the experimental findings. In addition, subjects used in experimental analyses are often unrepresentative of the overall population, which also may threaten generalizability. To address this shortcoming, we examine survey data obtained from the Pew Research Center with the goal of replicating our experimental findings among a more generalizable population. Specifically, we analyze data collected from the 2004 Biennial Media Consumption Survey, which contain several indicators of media exposure as well as attitudes toward the news media. The survey was conducted in 2004 and administered to a nationally representative sample of 3,000 adults from April 19 to May 12. The margin of error for the entire sample is ±2 percentage points. However, because the Pew survey breaks up the questionnaire into two separate forms with unique and overlapping variables, we are only able to use the responses from Form 1, which constitutes roughly half of the original sample (n = 1,493). Thus, the margin of error for our sample is ±3 percentage points.

To accurately measure attitudes toward the media, we employ two items from the survey. The first item asks respondents to agree or disagree with the statement that "People who decide what to put on TV news or in the newspapers are out of touch with people like me" (1 = completely disagree; 2 = mostly disagree; 3 = mostly agree; 4 = completely agree). The second item asks respondents to agree or disagree with the statement that "I often don't trust what news organizations are saying" (1 = completely disagree; 2 = mostly disagree; 3 = mostly agree; 4 = completely agree). Because these items are closely related and measure the same concept of support for the news media (alpha = .58), we combined the measures into an additive index where higher scores translate into higher levels of cynicism toward the media.

The independent variable of interest is exposure to *The Daily Show*. Specifically, respondents were asked how often they watch the program (1 = never; 2 = hardly ever; 3 = sometimes; 4 = regularly). We also statistically control for exposure to other sources of news, such as late night talk shows such as *Leno* or *Letterman*, daily newspapers, network news, or cable news. All of these items are also measured on a scale of 1 to 4 (1 = never; 2 = hardly ever; 3 = sometimes; 4 = regularly). Finally, we include demographic and socioeconomic control variables as well.

As the results in Table 18.3 demonstrate, the relationship between exposure to *The Daily Show* and cynicism toward the media appear to be conditional. On the full sample of respondents, there is no relationship. And, it is also important to note that the relationship between exposure to other late night talk shows, such as *Leno* or *Letterman*, is *negatively* associated with cynicism toward the news media. At first glance, the null findings on the full sample of adults might appear to contradict our experimental findings. However, as the second and third set of estimates in Table 18.3 illustrate, cynicism effects do appear in younger adults (age eighteen to thirty), while among adults over the age of thirty, exposure to *The Daily Show* is unrelated to cynicism.

This age differentiation is substantively significant. While our findings show that the cynicism effects of *The Daily Show* are limited to only young adults, it is this section of the population that watches the program the most frequently. According to the survey data we analyzed, almost one in three adults (32 percent) age eighteen to

TABLE 18.3.   News Cynicism by Media Exposure (Pew Data)

Variable	Full Sample	18–30 years old	>31 years old
The Daily Show	−.01 (.05)	.21 (.09)*	−.00 (.07)
Leno/Letterman	−.16 (.04)†	−.09 (.08)	−.15 (.05)†
Daily newspaper	.02 (.09)	.25 (.18)	−.11 (.11)
Network news	−.12 (.04)†	−.06 (.08)	−.16 (.04)†
Cable news	−.02 (.04)	−.08 (.09)	.00 (.05)
White[a]	.23 (.12)	.07 (.22)	.15 (.14)
Male[b]	.13 (.09)*	.05 (.19)	.15 (.10)
Education	−.04 (.03)	−.06 (.06)	−.03 (.03)
Income	.00 (.02)	.03 (.04)	−.02 (.03)
Party ID[c]	−.00 (.03)	−.00 (.06)	−.01 (.03)
Ideology[d]	−.19 (.03)†	−.13 (.10)	−.15 (.06)†
Constant	6.27 (.27)†	5.16 (.56)*	6.58 (.30)
Adjusted R^2	.04	.01	.04
N	1,154	233	921

All entries are regression coefficients with standard errors in parentheses.
[a]*1 = White; 0 = Nonwhite*
[b]*1 = Male; 0 = Female*
[c]*1 = Democrat; 2 = Democratic leaner; 3 = Independent/no preference/other;*
4 = Republican leaner; 5 = Republican.
[d]*1 = Very conservative; 2 = Conservative; 3 = Moderate/don't know; 4 = Liberal;*
5 = Very liberal.
$*p < .05$; $†p < .01$ (one-tailed).

thirty watch *The Daily Show* at least sometimes, compared with only 11 percent of those over the age of thirty. Thus, the effect is greatest on those who are most apt to watch the program.

Conclusion

The credibility of the news media has eroded dramatically over the past several decades, well before Jon Stewart went on the air. Of course, public support for virtually all political institutions has slid during this same time period, but there is cause for concern regarding the mass public's contempt for the media. The media are the primary intermediary institution through which citizens witness and experience the world of politics. As cynicism toward the media continues to increase, unhealthy distrust for all aspects of politics is sure to continue.

While Jon Stewart's program plays a very small role in driving overall attitudes toward the news media in America, there is no denying that he and his program are gaining attention and influence in America. For many young adults, Jon Stewart is the most trusted name in *news*. As his criticism of mainstream news gains greater attention, more and more young adults may begin questioning the legitimacy of the mass media. This may, in turn, limit the media's ability to serve as a watchdog of elected officials.

As we mentioned earlier in this chapter, *The Daily Show* is no longer the only one of its kind. A spin-off of *The Daily Show*, titled *The Colbert Report*, has become immensely popular and was nominated for an Emmy award in 2006. *Colbert* appears to be even more critical of the media than Stewart, constantly satirizing high-profile news personalities such as Bill O'Reilly and Geraldo Rivera. Ironically, Fox News is also reportedly working on its own late night comedy-based program, which will no doubt be highly critical of the mainstream press as well. While the proliferation of these satire-based programs grows, the mainstream media will continue to be an easy target, and public opinion may respond.

Notes

1. Timothy E. Cook, *Governing with the News* (Chicago: University of Chicago Press, 1998); Bartholomew H. Sparrow, *Uncertain Guardians* (Baltimore, MD: Johns Hopkins University Press, 1999).

2. Kenneth Dautrich and Thomas H. Hartley, *How the News Media Fail American Voters* (New York: Columbia University Press, 1999); James Fallows, *Breaking the News* (New York: Vintage Books, 1996); Tom Fenton, *Bad News* (New York: Regan Books, 2005).

3. "News Audiences Increasingly Politicized: Online News Audience Larger, More Diverse," *The Pew Research Center for the People and the Press*, June 8, 2004. http://people-press.org/reports/display.php3?ReportID=215.

4. "Cable and Internet Loom Large in Fragmented Political News Universe: Perceptions of Partisan Bias Seen as Growing, Especially by Democrats," *The Pew Research Center for the People and the Press*, January 11, 2004. http://people-press.org/reports/display.php3?ReportID=200.

5. Seymour M. Lipset and William Schneider, *The Confidence Gap* (New York: Free Press, 1983); Robert D. Putnam, *Bowling Alone* (New York: Simon & Schuster, 2000).

6. These data were taken from the cumulative data file of the General Social Survey, 1972–2004.

7. Marc J. Hetherington, *Why Trust Matters* (Princeton, NJ: Princeton University Press, 2005). Also see Lipset and Schneider, *The Confidence Gap*; and Putnam, *Bowling Alone.*

8. Stephen J. Farnsworth and S. Robert Lichter, *The Nightly News Nightmare* (Lanham, MD: Rowman & Littlefield, 2003).

9. Michael J. Robinson, "American Political Legitimacy in an Era of Electronic Journalism: Reflections on the Evening New," in *Television as a Social Force: New Approaches to TV Criticism*, eds. Douglass Cater and Richard Adler (New York: Praeger, 1975).

10. Stephen E. Bennett et al., "Video Malaise Revisited: Public Trust in the Media and Government," *Harvard International Journal of Press/Politics* 4 (1999): 8–23; Thomas E. Patterson, *Out of Order* (New York: Vintage, 1994).

11. James Fallows, *Breaking the News* (New York: Vintage, 1996).

12. Diana C. Mutz and Byron Reeves, "The New Videomalaise: Effects of Televised Incivility on Political Trust," *American Political Science Review* 99 (2005): 1–15.

13. Larry J. Sabato, *Feeding Frenzy* (New York: Free Press, 1993). Larry J. Sabato, Mark Stencel, and S. Robert Lichter, *Peepshow: Media and Politics in an Age of Scandal* (Lanham, MD: Rowman & Littlefield, 2000).

14. Mark J. Rozell, *In Contempt of Congress: Postwar Press Coverage on Capitol Hill* (New York: Praeger, 1996).

15. Joseph N. Cappella and Kathleen H. Jamies, *Spiral of Cynicism* (New York: Oxford University Press, 1997); Patterson, *Out of Order.*

16. Richard L. Fox and Robert W. Van Sickel, *Tabloid Justice* (Boulder, CO: Lynne Rienner, 2001).

17. John R. Hibbing and Elizabeth Thiess-Morse, "The Media's Role in Public Negativity Toward Congress: Distinguishing Emotional Reactions and Cognitive Evaluations," *American Journal of Political Science* 42 (1998) 475–498; Mutz and Reeves, "The New Videomalaise."

18. Jonathan S. Morris, "The Effects of Dramatized Political News on Public Opinion," *The American Review of Politics* 25 (2004): 321–343.

19. Stephen E. Bennett, Staci L. Rhine, and Richard S. Flickinger, "Assessing Americans' Opinions About the News Media's Fairness in 1996 and 1998," *Political Communication* 18 (2001): 163–182.

20. Andrew Kohut and Robert C. Toth, "The Central Conundrum: How Can People Like What They Distrust?" *Harvard International Journal of Press/Politics* 3 (1998): 110–117; Norman J. Ornstein and Michael J. Robinson, "Why Press Credibility Is Going Down," *Washington Journalism Review* (1990); Bennett et al., "Assessing Americans' Opinions."

21. Ornstein and Robinson, "Why Press Credibility Is Going Down."

22. James T. Hamilton, *All the News That's Fit to Sell* (Princeton, NJ: Princeton University Press, 2004); Darrell M. West, *The Rise and Fall of the Media Establishment* (Boston: Bedford, 2001).

23. Fallows, *Breaking the News*; Morris, "The Effects of Dramatized Political News"; Mutz and Reeves, "The New Videomalaise."

24. Craig Crawford, *Attack the Messenger: How Politicians Turn You Against the Media* (Lanham, MD: Rowman & Littlefield, 2006); David Brock, *The Republican Noise Machine* (New York: Crown, 2004).

25. Bernard Goldberg, *Bias: A CBS Insider Exposes How the Media Distort the News* (Washington, DC: Regnery, 2002); L. Brent Bozell, *Weapons of Mass Distortion: The Coming Meltdown of the Liberal Media* (New York: Crown, 2004); Ann Coulter, *Slander: Liberal Lies About the American Right* (New York: Crown, 2002).

26. Eric Alterman, *What Liberal Media?: The Truth About Bias and the News* (New York: Basic Books, 2003).

27. Tom Fenton, *Bad News: The Decline of Reporting, the Business of News, and the Danger to Us All* (New York: ReganBooks, 2005).

28. Bill Carter, "CNN Will Cancel 'Crossfire' and Cut Ties with Commentator," *New York Times*, January 6, 2005.

29. Dannagal G. Young and Russell M. Tisinger, "Dispelling Late-Night Myths: News Consumption Among Late-Night Comedy Viewers and the Predictors of Exposure to Various Late Night Shows," *Harvard International Journal of Press/Politics* 11 (2006): 113–134.

30. The experiment was a posttest-only control group design. Donald T. Campbell and Julian C. Stanley, *Experimental and Quasi-Experimental Designs for Research* (Chicago: Rand McNally, 1963).

19

Conclusion
Why Political Humor Is Serious Business

Doris Graber

Political humor is funny—but it isn't, really, when one takes a close look. Political humor has always been serious business because it can be used to mask the sting of political criticism by making it seem lighthearted, even when that isn't the intention. Like Teflon coating, the veneer of humor shields the jester from becoming the proverbial victimized messenger killed for carrying an unwanted message. Yet the message still conveys its assessment to audience members who see through its protective covering.

When humor highlights information unlikely to be conveyed in unvarnished form—for whatever reasons—it often aids and abets an essential function in governance. It alerts inattentive publics to the foibles, inanities, and failures of their political leaders in a way that delights audiences and motivates some members to action. When this potent political tool is shunned, as routinely happens during major political crises, a vital part of the American system of checks and balances is lost. The 2001 terrorist strike against the United States is an example. Most criticism of the government, humorous and other-wise, was suspended. Although the suspension was short-lived in the light of 20/20 hindsight, it was harmful and greatly regretted.

I learned early in life that there was far more to humor than simply doing something that provoked laughter. The fact that humor has serious aspects became clear to me after my young sister and I rigged up the garden hose one evening so that our dad would get a surprise soaking when he stepped into the backyard. The trick worked flaw-lessly, and she and I thought it was hilariously funny. But my usually fun-loving Dad, soaked to the skin in his pricy business attire, was not amused. He yelled at us and sent us off to bed without supper.

I learned four things from that failed attempt to be a comedian: first, and most importantly, people don't agree about what is or isn't funny; second, there are strong social taboos about who is a suitable target for humor, with parents often on that taboo list; third, a physical or verbal assault, however many laughs it produces, may cause material damage as well as psychological pain that leads to anger and other negative reactions. Lastly, because humorous stories arouse emotions that sharpen information retention, they tend to be often repeated. Repetition then makes them even more memorable.

These pearls of wisdom came to mind as I read the essays about political humor in all its various incarnations in *Laughing Matters: Humor and American Politics in the Media Age*. Yes, laughing has always mattered in politics. The essays in this book demonstrate that it may matter even more now than in earlier times. There are several reasons. Thanks to modern means of communication, access to new technologies is easy and costs very little. Political messages reach many more people than ever before. The author of Chapter 8 reports that the JibJab Web site received 10.4 million unique visitors in July 2004 to view its "This Land" cartoon. By comparison, the Web sites of presidential candidates Bush and Kerry each received 1.5 million visitors in the same month. Even at their peak, in October 2004, the Kerry site attracted only 3.7 million viewers, while 3.2 million viewers turned to the Bush site.

Moreover, important and politically alert audiences are often attracted to humorous messages and claim to learn from them. When survey respondents were asked about learning information regarding the 2004 presidential election from humor offerings presented by *Saturday Night Live* or Jon Stewart's *The Daily Show*, 26 percent of the viewers said that they had gained political insights from the show. The figure for young adults stood at 50 percent.

People often discount the significance of humor because decoding it can be tough for average citizens. Many humorous messages require sophistication to understand. That explains why many people who watch and enjoy these shows are also more politically sophisticated than the average person. The *Daily Show* audience seems to be the smartest of all. But, humor-coated messages also often miss their mark because they do not resonate with audience members. Major reasons are that they either require more political background knowledge than viewers possess or that they do not conform to viewers' sense of what is or is not funny. Political cartoons can be especially difficult to decode, even when they use well-known symbols like the Statue of Liberty as an emblem of freedom or Pinocchio's nose to signify lying. In fact, research shows that much of the audience routinely misconstrues the cartoonists' meanings.[1]

Humor, Humor Everywhere

It is amazing how pervasive political humor is in American popular culture. *Laughing Matters* makes that important fact amply clear. The format of the humorous message does not seem to matter much when it comes to successfully performing the traditional functions of political humor. Political humor formats include news broadcasts styled as "infotainment" in which regular news is presented with touches of humor. They also encompass political cartoons in the print media, on television, and on the Internet. Regardless of the venue, these messages elicit chuckles and laughs by employing exaggeration, ridicule, and sarcasm.

Political humor also includes the monologues on late night comedy shows like Jay Leno's *Tonight Show* and David Letterman's *Late Show* or the more extensive mocking of politics and politicians on *The Daily Show* and *The Colbert Report*. Other formats are the humorous ditties and impersonations by stand-up comedians and political impersonators like Mark Russell and Steve Bridges or the comedy segments featured on *Saturday Night Live*.

Then there is the rich menu of entertainment television. A good example is *The Simpsons* cartoon serial, created by Matt Groening and examined by authors in this book and even separate book-length treatments.[2] *The Simpsons* has been popular now for more than fifteen years and many of its characters have become iconic figures in popular culture. People refer to them in conversations and their names are sprinkled liberally throughout news stories and editorials. The show proves that political humor can be timeless when it spoofs common human situations that arise perennially with only a change in the identity of the characters.

Comic strips are another very popular genre for political humor. Garry Trudeau's *Doonesbury* is a good example. For thirty years its cartoon characters have inspired controversy over major political issues. There has also been much discussion of humorous films such as Charlie Chaplin's skits about Hitler or Michael Moore's 2004 documentary,

Fahrenheit 9/11, which satirizes politics during the George W. Bush administration.

The Political Effects of Humor

In this concluding chapter I have chosen to focus primarily on one of the two main themes in *Laughing Matters*—the impact of humor on political life in the United States. I emphasize political effects because many average citizens, along with large numbers of social scientists, still believe that humor is politically unimportant. How can something that makes you laugh be taken seriously, they ask, as they brush off humorous messages as lighthearted fluff. Their widely shared assumption is that comedy is an inappropriate and ineffectual format for conveying serious political messages. That assumption has become shaky in a climate when news is increasingly pervaded by entertainment and entertainment is pervaded by serious debates, albeit conducted with a smiling face. *Laughing Matters* tells the story.

The idea that serious learning is incompatible with humor has had disastrous consequences. It has encouraged dull, ponderous, fact-overloaded presentations of political information in all types of mass media, as well as in classrooms and public lectures. Use of such user-hostile formats ignores the fact that learning is stimulated when audiences become involved and aroused. The types of prose considered scholarly enough to please academic purists tend to bore general audiences who then tune out. By contrast, the language of humor thrives in the marketplace of ideas while the language of academia falters.

The disdain for humor is akin to the prejudice that turned people away from studying emotions in the past and that has perpetuated the myth that serious rational thinking and emotional arousal are incompatible. Fortunately, as *Laughing Matters* demonstrates, social scientists are now abandoning these legacies of Descartes and other seventeenth- and eighteenth-century philosophers who considered arousing messages as antithetical to rational thinking.

What People Learn from Humor

What kinds of political information are viewers of humor-laden messages learning? Are they steeping themselves in cynicism, misinformation, or loading their brains with trivia and cheap jokes? Or are they learning important facts about the game of politics, its players, or sociopolitical issues like global warming or the shortcomings of public schools? When *Saturday Night Live* actors parody presidential debates or inaugural addresses, do viewers gain fresh insights into the pivotal issues of the campaign or do they learn to view politics as little more than silly verbal sparring? The answer to these questions is "all of the above." Learning ranges from counterproductive impressions of political life to important facts and insights.

The extent and nature of learning vary and depend heavily on the thrust of the questions through which researchers try to probe knowledge. Factual learning is sparse, but gaining insights and refreshing memories are fairly common, judging from my research and the research presented and discussed in *Laughing Matters*.[3] It is also worth mentioning that humorous stories rarely call attention to situations that were previously unknown and totally ignored by mass media. That means that humorous stories are more likely to enhance and deepen what people already know, rather than contribute totally new knowledge.

What inferences do people draw from the political information presented to them in a humorous mode? Many assertions have been made about that issue in this book and elsewhere, but the jury is still out. We simply do not know enough about audience members' processing of humorous messages. It will require a lot of intensive research to find solid answers, and they are apt to be very diverse for various types of audiences.

However, a limited number of specific humor effects have been tested, albeit with contradictory outcomes. For instance, some researchers claim that there is no evidence that humor affects viewers' assessment of candidates. The presumed explanation is that humor is not taken seriously because people believe that it is an intentionally distorted representation of a particular situation. Other researchers disagree and contend that humorous stories make viewers judge political candidates more on personality traits rather than issues, benefiting the Clinton and Bush candidate types. Still other researchers are content with raising important questions like "How do presidential debates satirized on *Saturday Night Live* affect elections?"

Injecting humor into discussions about election campaigns may also tell people that politicians have a sense of humor. This may make them seem more down-to-earth and more likable.[4] Politicians certainly believe that. That is why in recent elections candidates for high office, including the presidency, have appeared in humorous skits on nationally syndicated entertainment shows. Bill Clinton, George W. Bush, and other presidential hopefuls have made appearances on humorous shows a routine part of election campaigns. However, there are also claims to the contrary, arguing that humorous depictions harm candidates. For example, several chapters in *Laughing Matters* report the widely believed assertion that President Ford's clumsiness in *Saturday Night Live* skits contributed to his loss of the 1976 election. Similarly, satirical reports about Senator Hillary Clinton may diminish her chances for becoming a viable contender for the presidency.

Some scholars claim that humor is democratizing because it pulls leaders off their pedestals and reveals them as ordinary citizens. That might be true, but skits may also transform them into laughable stereotypes who deserve little or no respect. Obviously, many governments take humor seriously. Making fun of the political leader in an authoritarian society is generally cause for formal punishment, including the death penalty in some countries. The crime of *lèse majesté*—offense against the dignity of the sovereign or the state, dates back to Roman times. It was often considered an act of treason that did severe harm to the state by undermining the government's authority, and it was punished accordingly.

The function—and consequences—of political humor is different in democracies. Humor is appreciated and thrives because it is deemed an important tool for calling attention to delicate political issues. The legendary cartoons of Thomas Nast that led to the downfall of New York's Tweed gang and Herbert Block's cartoons that diminished the policies of president Richard Nixon are often cited as examples of cartoon offensives with desirable outcomes. There are many other examples where humorous messages probably contributed to political outcomes, but proving such causal links is always tricky in complex political situations, where a multiplicity of factors interact in manifold ways.

Childhood Lessons Revisited

Pondering why it is so difficult to assess the effects of political humor brings me back to the lessons I learned about joking in my childhood. Now I understand why people do not agree about what is or is not funny. The chief reason is the fact that humor is the end product of complex interactions, rather than a tangible object or status. It is generated by the interaction of a particular message stimulus presented in a humor-congenial environment and the attitudinal matrix that individual viewers bring to the message and its environment. Unfortunately most researchers of the effects of political humor have focused only on variations in message stimuli, ignoring variations in the environment, and in a receiver's attitudinal/informational matrix. Many of the essays in this book are happy exceptions to this general rule.

When it comes to joking about a complex topic like politics, as mentioned earlier, understanding often requires more prior knowledge and sophistication than the average American is able to command. For instance, the vast majority of *Simpsons* viewers apparently do not catch the satire—sarcasm, irony, double entendre—of the show, just like the vast majority of *All in the Family* viewers did not see the humor in redneck Archie Bunker's prejudiced commentaries. Political hyperbole all too often falls on deaf ears!

It is easy to forget how diverse populations are, even in a single community in a single country, like the United States. Cultural and attitudinal diversity means that people differ in their views about who and what are appropriate targets for humor. Which authority figures may be the butt of jokes? May a Danish newspaper satirize the Prophet Mohammed when doing so is likely to be offensive to Muslims worldwide? The serious and worldwide repercussions of the Danish incident underline the potentially profound consequences of political humor. They also raise important questions about the scope of press freedom and government censorship when it comes to satire, irony, and sarcasm, as well as with issues of press sensitivity and press responsibility.

Which situations, and which of their components, are appropriate for tongue-in-cheek treatment? Disagreements about these matters can lead to serious political controversies. Is it hilarious or poor taste to have a musical comedy about the Enron debacle, which sent dozens of high-level corporate officials to prison and caused the financial ruin of thousands who lost their jobs and savings? Should political humor be limited to trivial aspects of a situation? Should it make fun of the human foibles of various actors but stay away from serious issues of policy and performance? Or is a focus on the heart of issues a required target for the serious political humorist, bent on improving political life? These are hot-potato issues for jesters who want to speak truth to power. As has been the custom since the Middle Ages, it may still require a professional comic to deliver the most potent humor-coated barbs successfully.

The impact of humor is diminished if its shelf life is short. Unfortunately, most research has failed to test how lasting humor effects are. A major difficulty in testing the effects of humorous stories, including their longevity, is the fact that effects that show up in the laboratory may not be detectable in real-life situations where multiple stimuli abound and people are likely to be cross-pressured and distracted.

There is solid evidence that many funny stories become staples of collective memory. When they are repeated over and over again, memories are refreshed and the humorous story lingers. A good example is the publicity generated about former president Gerald Ford when he died in 2006. Old clips from *Saturday Night Live* mocking him for clumsiness saturated the airwaves. Were the effects of these clips the same in 2006 as they had been thirty years earlier during the 1976 presidential campaign? We do not know.

What about the wounds inflicted by humorous assaults? Again, we are doomed to deal with puzzling variability. The contributors to this book claim that they affect or do not affect election outcomes in various ways. They argue that humor plays a role in cynicism about politics and that it encourages or discourages participation. They see it as a sign of political health or political malaise. And they are probably right—all of them. A stimulus that is experienced in diverse ways, depending on the receivers and the circumstances, is bound to produce diverse outcomes.

My final childhood lesson relates to memorability. In an age when information overload is an ever-present danger, people are geared toward ignoring messages or discarding them quickly from short-term memory. We don't want to remember any more than what is absolutely necessary, because the supply of information tendered to us exceeds human memorization capabilities. Still, besides remembering what is essential (like information needed to perform our daily tasks), we also tend to remember things that make good stories to retell others, especially if the stories are funny. People young and old intuitively know that humor and laughing are good for mind and body. As French philosopher Voltaire noted some three hundred years ago: "The art of medicine consists of keeping the patient amused while nature heals the disease."

Most people like humor because its components—incongruity, surprise, absurdity, and the like—generate laughing, which is a pleasant sensation. They commit humorous stories to memory to rekindle this pleasant reaction in themselves and others. That makes such stories elements in people's repertoire of criteria on which they draw when forming political opinions and making decisions. When people retell humorous stories, they become part of the process of message diffusion through which oft-repeated tales spread rapidly and widely throughout society.[5]

In fact, the most prevalent and most significant contribution of political humor may not be what information audiences learn from it or what inferences they draw or even what political consequences ensue. Rather, the most significant effect of humorous messages may be that they spur attention to politics and encourage some citizens to become links in the far-reaching chains of political message dissemination.

As with most humor effects, ambiguity prevails even here. What is often true is also often untrue. If humor is so memorable, why do some of us, myself included, have such a tough time recalling the funny stories we recently heard? There was that good one with which I intended to conclude this chapter. What was it? Sadly, for the world of me, I don't remember. It has escaped me beyond retrieval, at least until I hear it again!

Notes

1. J. P. Trostle, ed. *Attack of the Political Cartoonists: Insights and Assaults from Today's Editorial Pages* (Madison, WI: Dork Storm Press, 2004).

2. For example, Steven Keslowitz, *The Simpsons and Society* (Tucson, AZ: Hands Off Books, 2004); Chris Turner, *Planet Simpson* (Cambridge, MA: Da Capo Press, 2004).

3. Doris Graber, Kevin Navratil, and Gregory Holyk, "How Television Dramas Raise Citizens' Civic IQ," presented at the Annual Meeting of the American Political Science Association, Philadelphia, PA, September 2006.

4. Baum, Matthew A. "Talking the Vote. Why Presidential Candidates Hit the Talk Show Circuit," *American Journal of Political Science* 49 (2005): 213–234.

5. Everett Rogers, *Diffusion of Innovations* (New York: Free Press: 2003).

Editors

Dr. Jody C Baumgartner received his PhD from Miami University in 1998 and is an assistant professor of political science at East Carolina University. He has authored or coauthored books on presidential campaigns, presidential impeachment, and the vice presidency, and over twenty book chapters and articles on various subjects. His latest interest is the effects of various forms of humor on political attitudes and behavior.

Dr. Jonathan S. Morris received his PhD from Purdue University in 2002 and is an assistant professor of political science at East Carolina University. His research focus is on political communication and public opinion. Dr. Morris has published several articles on cable news and American politics.

Contributors

AMUNDSON, DANIEL Daniel Amundson is the research director of the Center for Media and Public Affairs.

BAYM, GEOFFREY Geoffrey Baym received his PhD in communication from the University of Utah in 2001 and is an assistant professor of media studies at the University of North Carolina–Greensboro. His research interests lie in the evolving styles and standards of news media and American political discourse. Recent scholarly articles include a solo-authored exploration of *The Daily Show* published in *Political Communication,* and a coauthored survey of the field of communication philosophy in the *Journal of Communication.* He also has published solo-authored articles on various aspects of television news in *Journalism, Rhetoric and Public Affairs, Journal of Communication Inquiry,* and the *Western Journal of Communication.*

BIRD, KENTON Kenton Bird is an associate professor of journalism and director of the School of Journalism and Mass Media at the University of Idaho. He holds a bachelor's degree in journalism from the University of Idaho, a master's degree in journalism history from University College, Cardiff Wales, and a PhD in American studies from Washington State University. In 1989, he was a congressional fellow of the American Political Science Association, working as a congressional staff member in Washington, DC. His research interests include political reporting, media history, civic journalism, and the relationship between public opinion and public policy.

BREWER, PAUL Paul R. Brewer received his PhD from the University of North Carolina–Chapel Hill in 1999 and is an associate professor of journalism and mass communication at the University of Wisconsin–Milwaukee. His research interests include public opinion and political communication. He has authored or coauthored articles in such journals as the *American Journal of Political Science,* the *Canadian Journal of Political Science,* the *Harvard International Journal of Press/Politics,* the *Journal of Broadcasting & Electronic Media,* the *Journal of Politics, Political Behavior,*

Political Communication, Political Psychology, Public Opinion Quarterly, and *Social Science Quarterly.*

CAO, XIAOXIA Xiaoxia Cao received her master's degree in mass communication from the University of Wisconsin–Milwaukee and is a doctoral student at the Annenberg School for Communication at the University of Pennsylvania, Philadelphia. Her research interests include the psychological aspects of political communication and the effects of entertainment-oriented media on political knowledge, public opinion, and voting behavior. She is the coauthor of "Candidate Appearances on Soft News Shows and Public Knowledge about Primary Campaigns" in the *Journal of Broadcasting & Electronic Media*. She also presented a paper titled "Political Comedy Shows and Knowledge about Primary Campaigns among Young Americans" at the 2005 annual meeting of the American Political Science Association.

CAUFIELD, RACHEL Rachel Paine Caufield received her PhD from The George Washington University in 2001. She is currently an assistant professor at Drake University in Des Moines, Iowa, where she teaches the courses the American Political System, Congress and the Legislative Process, the American Presidency, Judicial Politics, the Senior Seminar in Law, Politics, and Society, and an honors course entitled Modern Political Satire. Her current research interests include judicial selection, interbranch relationships (particularly Supreme Court–Congress interaction), and satire as a form of political discourse. She is the author of "In the Wake of White: How States are Responding to Republican Party of Minnesota v. White and How Judicial Elections are Changing," published in the *Akron Law Review* in spring 2005; and has authored a chapter for a new book on judicial elections, published by NYU Press in summer 2006. She is also working on a new book manuscript that explores the importance of political satire in shaping political discourse. In 2000–2001, she was a Research Fellow at The Brookings Institution in Washington, DC; and she currently serves as the Research and Program Consultant to the Hunter Center for Judicial Selection at The American Judicature Society in Des Moines.

COMPTON, JOSH Josh Compton (PhD, University of Oklahoma) is department chair and assistant professor of communication at Southwest Baptist University. His research interests include resistance to influence, political communication, and mass media. His research has appeared in *Communication Yearbook, Human Communication Research*, and *The Forensic, Communication Quarterly,*

Health Communication, and *STAM Journal*. He and a coauthor have a chapter in a book examining rhetoric of Pope John Paul II.

FRALEY, TODD   Todd Fraley, PhD, is an assistant professor at the School of Communication at East Carolina University, where he researches media and popular culture.

FRANCIA, PETER L.   Peter Francia is an assistant professor in the department of political science at East Carolina University. He received his PhD in 2000 from the Department of Government and Politics at the University of Maryland, College Park. His teaching areas include the presidency, Congress, and American social and protest movements. His research interests include campaign finance, elections, and the role of interest groups and political parties in American politics. He is the author of the Columbia University Press book, *The Future of Organized Labor in American Politics*. He is a coauthor of the 2003 Columbia University Press book, *The Financiers of Congressional Elections: Investors, Ideologues, and Intimates*. His work also has appeared in *Social Science Quarterly*, *American Politics Research*, and *State Politics & Policy Quarterly*.

GRABER, DORIS A.   Doris A. Graber is a professor of political science at the University of Illinois at Chicago and a faculty associate in the Department of Communication and in the Institute of Government and Public Affairs. She received her PhD from Columbia University in New York, and has taught at Northwestern University, the University of Chicago, and the Kennedy School at Harvard University. She is the author of numerous articles and books dealing with political communication including *Processing the News: How People Tame the Information Tide* (1993), *Mass Media and American Politics*, 6th ed. (2002), the award-winning *Processing Politics, Learning from Television in the Internet Age* (2001), and *The Power of Communication: Managing Information in Public Organizations* (2003). She has served as a vice president of the American Political Science Association and as president of the Midwest Political Science Association, the Midwest Association for Public Opinion Research, and the International Society of Political Psychology. She serves on many editorial boards and is founding editor of *Political Communication*, and book review editor of *Political Psychology*.

GUEHLSTORF, NICHOLAS   Nicholas P. Guehlstorf is an assistant professor in the Department of Political Science and Environmental Sciences Program at Southern Illinois University–Edwardsville. Guehlstorf's research focuses on the integration of democratic values into environmental policy and considers the theoretical problems with citizen involvement, economic consideration, and scientific information in decision making. His most recent publications include the book *The Political Theories of Risk Analysis* (Springer, 2004) and the article "The Role of Culture in Risk Regulations: A Comparative Study of Genetically Modified Corn in the United States of America and European Union" in *Environmental Science and Policy* (2005; with Lars K. Hallstrom).

HALLSTROM, LARS Lars K. Hallstrom is an associate professor of political science and Canada Research Chair in Public Policy at St. Francis Xavier University (StFX) in Nova Scotia, Canada. A specialist in comparative public policy and environmental policy and politics, he has also published in the fields of international relations theory, American participatory politics, pedagogy and technology, and gender politics. Select recent publications include "Risk, Culture, and the Regulation of Genetically Engineered Corn in the USA and European Union" with N. Guehlstorf in *Environmental Science and Policy*; "Gendering Governance? Civility and the Gender Gap in Poland" in *Canadian-American Slavic Studies*; "Eurocratising Enlargement? EU Elites and NGO Participation in European Environmental Policy" in *Environmental Politics*; and "Environmental Movements in East Central Europe: Between Technocracy and the 'Third Way'" in *The Politics of Global Arrogance and the Role of Emancipatory Movements* (J. Leatherman & J. Webber, eds.). In 2005 Dr. Hallstrom started the Canadian Foundation for Innovation–funded StFX Public Policy and Governance Research Centre, a dedicated facility for both quantitative and qualitative policy-relevant research and researchers.

HENDREN, ABBY Abby Gail Hendren is a doctoral candidate at the College of Journalism and Communications at the University of Florida. She is exploring political communication in both research and course work. Her research interests include media coverage of women political candidates and leaders, the impact of media on young voters, and individual-level influences on media content. She earned her master's degree in mass communication with an emphasis in political science from Oklahoma State University in 2004. Abby earned her bachelor's degree from Texas Christian University in public relations and advertising with a minor in political science.

KAID, LYNDA LEE Lynda Lee Kaid is a professor of telecommunication in the College of Journalism and Communications at the University of Florida. She previously was a George Lynn Cross Research Professor at the University of Oklahoma, where she also served as the director of the Political Communication Center and supervised the Political Commercial Archive. Her research specialties include political advertising and news coverage of political events. A Fulbright Scholar, she has also done work on political television in several Western European countries. She is the author/editor of more than twenty books, including *The Handbook of Political Communication Research*, *The Millennium Election*, *Political Television in Evolving European Democracies*, *Civic Dialogue in the 1996 Presidential Campaign*, *Videostyle in Presidential Campaigns*, *The Electronic Election*, *New Perspectives on Political Advertising*, *Mediated Politics in Two Cultures*, *Political Advertising in Western Democracies*, and *Political Campaign Communication: A Bibliography and Guide to the Literature*. She has written over one hundred journal articles and book chapters and over one hundred convention papers on various aspects of political communication. She has received over $1 million in external grant funds for her research efforts, including support from the U.S. Department of Commerce, the U.S. Department of Education, the National Endowment for the Humanities, and the National Science Foundation. Dr. Kaid is a former president of the Political Communication Divisions of the International Communication Association and the National Communication Association, and has served in leadership roles in the American Political Science Association.

LANDREVILLE, KRISTEN   Kristen Landreville is a graduate student at the College of Journalism and Communications at University of Florida. She earned her bachelor's degree in journalism and online media from the University of Florida in 2004. Her research interests include political and campaign communication, international communication, and environmental communication. She has contributed a coauthored chapter on late night talk shows and the 2003 Iraq war in the book *Global Media go to War*. She has also coauthored an article on hyperlinking and blogging in the 2004 U.S. presidential election for *Journalism Studies*. Additionally, she has an article on political advertising and effects on young voters in the 2004 presidential election in *American Behaviorial Scientist*.

LICHTER, S. ROBERT   Robert Lichter received a PhD from Harvard University. He is president of the Center for Media and Public Affairs and has authored or coauthored numerous books, including *The Nightly News Nightmare* (Rowman & Littlefield).

LINDBERG, TIM   Tim Lindberg is a 2006 graduate of the University of Minnesota–Morris with degrees in political science and history. He begins graduate school in political science in fall 2007.

MARTIN, JUSTIN   Justin Martin is a Roy H. Park Fellow and PhD student at the University of North Carolina–Chapel Hill. He has

published various articles and book chapters in the areas of political communication, religion in mass media, and mass media in
the Arab world. As a Fulbright Scholar, Martin spent the 2005–6
academic year in Jordan researching Middle Eastern newspapers.
He holds degrees from High Point University and the University
of Florida.

MOY, PATRICIA   Patricia Moy received her PhD from the University of
Wisconsin. She is the Christy Cressey Professor of Communication
at the University of Washington. Her research focuses on public
opinion and political communication in democratic systems; she
studies how communication shapes public opinion, citizens' trust
in government, and political behavior. Moy's scholarship has been
published in refereed journals including *Communication Research*,
*International Journal for Public Opinion Research, Journal of Applied
Social Psychology, Journal of Communication*, and *Political Communication*. In her book *With Malice Toward All? The Media and Public Confidence in Democratic Institutions* (coauthored with Michael
Pfau), she examines media depictions of key democratic institutions and the effects of such portrayals on citizens' knowledge of
and trust in these institutions. Moy sits on the executive council of
the American Association for Public Opinion Research. She currently serves as associate editor for *Public Opinion Quarterly*, and
is the vice-chair of the International Communication Association's
Political Communication Division.

NILSEN, DON L. F. & ALLEEN PACE   Don and Alleen Nilsen are both
professors of English at Arizona State University. Don received his
PhD from the University of Michigan, while Alleen received hers
from the University of Iowa. Together they wrote the *Encyclope-
dia of 20th-Century American Humor* published by Oryx Press
(Greenwood) in 2000. It was chosen by the American Library
Association as one of 20 Outstanding Academic Books 2000 and
by *Choice* magazine in 2001 as a highly recommended reference
book. They are founding members of the International Society for
Humor Studies. Don is now the historian of ISHS; he was executive secretary from 1986 to 2004. Alleen edited the organization's
newsletter from 1994 to 2003. They have both written extensively
on humor and language. Don was most recently quoted in the
October 2005 issue of *Psychology Today* in an article on humor
and gender. On July 24, 2005, they were both quoted by Richard
Lederer in the *New York Times*; and in July Don was quoted in a
full-page article in the *New York Times* under the headline, "The
Joke Is Dead." Alleen is coauthor of *Literature for Today's Young
Adults* (Longman), now in its seventh edition. Since 1980 it has

been the leading textbook used in young adult literature classes in departments of English, schools of library science, and colleges of education. Together Don and Alleen coauthored *Language Play* (Newbury House). Alleen more recently edited *Living Language* (Allyn & Bacon), a textbook for introduction to language classes.

NIVEN, DAVID S. David Niven received a PhD from Ohio State University and is an associate professor of political science at Ohio University. Niven's work on media and politics has earned research grants from the American Political Science Association and the Shorenstein Center on Press, Politics, and Public Policy at Harvard University. He has been published in numerous journals including *Polity*, *Social Science Quarterly*, *Journalism and Mass Communication Quarterly*, *Harvard International Journal of Press/Politics*, *Political Communication*, and *Women and Politics*. Niven is the author of *Tilt? The Search for Media Bias* (Praeger) and coauthor of *Racialized Coverage of Congress: The News in Black and White* (Praeger).

O'LOUGHLIN, PAULA L. Paula L. O'Loughlin is a an associate professor of political science at the University of Minnesota–Morris. Her field is political psychology and she has previously published work on media, human rights, and women and politics.

POSTELNICU, MONICA Monica Postelnicu is an assistant professor at the Manship School of Mass Communication at Louisiana State University. Her research focuses on the effects of new media and new communication technologies on political life and public affairs. She investigates online candidate communication during campaigns, alternative sources of political information, and online youth mobilization efforts.

RIDOUT, TRAVIS Travis N. Ridout is an assistant professor of political science at Washington State University. He earned his PhD in 2003 at the University of Wisconsin–Madison and specializes in the study of campaigns, political participation, and the mass media. Ridout has published work on political advertising and its effects in the *Annual Review of Political Science* and *Political Behavior*, and is working on a book manuscript on that topic. He also has published an article on voter turnout and a book chapter about presidential primary front-loading.

ROTTINGHAUS, BRANDON Brandon Rottinghaus is an assistant professor of political science and director of the Bureau of Public Affairs Research at the University of Houston. He holds a master's degree and a PhD in political science (with emphasis in political communication) from Northwestern University (2005). His research interests include the public presidency, presidential leadership, the media, public opinion, and executive–legislative relations. His work on these subjects has appeared in *Political Science Quarterly, American Politics Research, Presidential Studies Quarterly,* and *Congress and the Presidency.*

SELF, REBECCA Rebecca Self is on the faculty at Franklin College in Lugano, Switzerland. She earned a bachelor's degree in international communication from Hampshire College, Amherst, Massachusetts, and master's and doctoral degrees in media studies from the University of Colorado. She previously taught at the University of Colorado and the University of Idaho. Self's research interests include the influence of the Walt Disney Corp. and its characters and theme parks on American culture.

SHEAGLEY, GEOFF Geoff Sheagley is a recent graduate of the University of Minnesota–Morris. He plans on entering graduate school in fall 2007.

SHOUSE, ERIC Eric Shouse, PhD, is an assistant professor in the School of Communication at East Carolina University, where he researches media and popular culture.

VOTH, BEN Ben Voth is an associate professor of communication at Miami University–Ohio. He received his doctorate in communication from the University of Kansas in 1994. He has published articles on American public address, including an article on the role of humor in the presidential election of 2000. He is also the director of Miami University's speech and debate program, which won the national title in rhetorical criticism three years in a row (2001–3) and qualified teams to the elimination rounds of the national debate tournament in 2003 and 2004. He has published regularly in *Argumentation and Advocacy,* the top journal of the American Forensics Association.

YOUNG, DANNAGAL GOLDTHWAITE Dannagal Goldthwaite Young is an assistant professor at the University of Delaware. She received her doctorate from the University of Pennsylvania in 2007. Her research interests include political satire and its effects on public opinion, parody and satire as modes of political communication, nontraditional sources of political information and their cognitive implications, and, more generally, the intersection of entertainment and information. She is the recipient of numerous honors and awards for research and teaching. Young has published articles in the *Journal of Broadcasting and Electronic Media* ("Late Night Comedy in Election 2000: Its Influence on Candidate Trait Ratings and the Moderating Effects of Political Knowledge and Partisanship," 2004), *The Communication Review* ("Sacrifice, Consumption, and the American Way of Life: Advertising and Domestic Propaganda during World War II," 2004), as well as a book chapter ("The

Power of Numbers: Examining Subpopulations with the NAES")
in *Capturing Campaign Dynamics*. She has also authored several
National Annenberg Election Survey press reports and numerous
nonacademic publications and press coverage articles.

Index